STEVEN RAICHLEN'S
HEALTHY
LATIN COOKING

200 SIZZLING RECIPES FROM
MEXICO · CUBA · CARIBBEAN · BRAZIL
AND BEYOND

BY STEVEN RAICHLEN

FOREWORD BY CRISTINA SARALEGUI

INTRODUCTION BY HANNIA CAMPOS, PH.D.
HARVARD SCHOOL OF PUBLIC HEALTH

RODALE

To Jake
who opened a restaurant
and
To Betsy and Marc
who got married!

Cover and Interior Photographer: Beatriz DaCosta
Interior Illustrator: Randy South
Front Cover Recipe: Argentinian Mixed Grill (page 283)

Library of Congress Cataloging-in-Publication Data

Raichlen, Steven.
    [Healthy Latin Cooking]
    Steven Raichlen's healthy Latin cooking : 200 sizzling recipes from México, Cuba, Caribbean, Brazil, and beyond / by Steven Raichlen ; foreword by Cristina Saralegui ; introduction by Hannia Campos.
        p.   cm.
    Includes index.
    ISBN 0–87596–497–4 hardcover
    ISBN 0–87596–498–2 paperback
    1. Cookery, Latin American.   2. Low-fat diet—Recipes.   I. Title.   II. Healthy Latin cooking.
TX716.A1R42   1998
641.5'638—dc21   98–22947

Distributed to the book trade by St. Martin's Press

    4   6   8   10   9   7   5   3   hardcover
            8   10   9   7   paperback

In all Rodale cookbooks, our mission is to provide delicious and nutritious recipes Our recipes also meet the standards of the Rodale Test Kitchen for dependability, ease, practicality, and, most of all, great taste. To give us your comments, call (800) 848-4735.

ACKNOWLEDGMENTS

Writing this book has been a lot of fun, but it wasn't all sipping margaritas and munching tostones. Many have worked long and hard to produce the book that you hold in your hands. My sincere thanks to:

My wife, Barbara, for her love and support of this and all of my projects.

Stepson and awesome Chef Jake, the JADA staff, and Roger Thrailkill, who helped with recipe testing. Good luck with the new restaurant!

Rodale cookbook editor David Joachim, for his skillful editing, support, and musical input.

Elida Proenza, friend and recipe tester extraordinaire.

Cristina Saralegui, for writing the foreword and for her good works for the Latino community in Miami and elsewhere.

Hannia Campos, Ph.D., for her thoughtful, well-researched introduction.

Angelika Scherp, for her graceful translation of the book into Spanish.

Beatriz DaCosta, for gracing the book with her stunning photographs.

Selene Yeager, for her work on the Latin Super Food boxes.

Donna Morton de Souza, for the nutritional analyses.

Kim Werner, for her indefatigable copyediting.

Oldways Preservation and Exchange Trust, for permission to use the Healthy Traditional Latin American Diet Pyramid.

Efraín Vega, founder of Yuca restaurant in Miami and one of the most innovative restaurateurs in the United States; Yuca manager, Billy Bean, and chef Luis Contreras.

Douglas Rodríguez, formerly of Yuca and now chef-owner of Patria in New York City and the father of Nuevo Latino cuisine.

Maricel Presilla, food historian and author.

Pat Corpora, Peter Igoe, and Debora T. Yost of Rodale Books, who came up with the idea for this book and asked me to write it.

Anne Egan, managing editor of Rodale cookbooks.

Abel Delgado, who edited the Spanish edition of the book.

All my other friends at Rodale: Tania Attanasio, JoAnn Brader, Kathy D. Everleth, Jennifer L. Kaas, Sandra Salera Lloyd, Dennis Lockard, Susan Massey, Pat Mast, Jen Miller, Tom Ney, Cindy Ratzlaff, Melinda B. Rizzo, Jean Rogers, Donna G. Rossi, Sharon Sanders, Darlene Schneck, Debra Sfetsios, Patrick T. Smith, and Nancy Zelko.

CONTENTS

FOREWORD

BY CRISTINA SARALEGUI, JOURNALIST AND HOST OF *EL SHOW DE CRISTINA*

As I mention in my autobiography, *Cristina! My Life as a Blonde*, ever since I can remember, I have seen myself as an adventurer. I am always exploring new things for the sake of personal growth. In the 1970s, I brought this concept to the Spanish-language *Cosmopolitan* magazine. As *Cosmo*'s editor, I redefined the Cosmo Girl as a self-reliant woman who is capable of achieving her own goals.

This concept carries over to my talk show, where we delve into a variety of topics every day. Unlike many talk-show hosts, I prefer to use *El Show de Cristina* as a forum where people are educated as well as entertained, and most important, where new ideas are explored.

When Steven Raichlen approached me with this healthy Latin cookbook, the explorer and educator in me was immediately intrigued. After all, "healthy Latin cooking" seems like an oxymoron. We Hispanics deep-fry so many dishes in gallons of oil that it seems impossible to make them healthy and tasty at the same time. And we certainly need these dishes to be healthy. Millions of Hispanics have health problems related to our delicious but deadly high-fat delicacies.

Well, I'm glad to say that Steven has done it. With a few easy twists, he has managed to keep the flavor in our traditional dishes like *arroz con pollo, flan,* and *mole* while making them heart- (and waist-) healthy at the same time. All of his cooking secrets are explained in full.

Try a bite of Steven Raichlen's *lechón asado* or lean, mean *maduros*. You'll find that these dishes taste great, but more important, they're an investment in your health and that of your family.

In Spanish, the word *health* is *salud.* That is the word we use to say "cheers" when somebody takes a drink. When somebody takes a bite to eat, instead of *bon appétit*, we say *buen provecho*. The interesting thing is that *provecho* also means "benefit." So explore this book and reap its many benefits. *Salud—¡y buen provecho!*

Cristina

INTRODUCTION

THE LATIN AMERICAN DIET PYRAMID: A HEALTHY FOUNDATION

There are 29 million Latinos living in the United States. If you count Puerto Rico, the number jumps to nearly 33 million. Latinos are one of the fastest growing populations in the United States. Experts say that Latinos may soon be the second largest ethnic group in America.

And here's the best news: Most Latin Americans will live long lives. Estimates by the Centers for Disease Control and Prevention predict that Latin American men will live to age 74, while Latin American women will live to age 79. That's an increase of more than 40 years since the early 1900s. But will those extra years be healthy and happy? Here's how to make sure that they are.

THE BUILDING OF THE PYRAMID

Scientists have discovered that the things you do (or don't do) today have a huge impact on your health tomorrow. And there's a lot that you can do today to ensure a high quality of life as you age.

Much of it comes down to what you eat day to day and how physically active you are.

To develop specific tips for Latinos, top scientists and food experts spent years studying Latino dietary and lifestyle habits in both the United States and Latin America. These groundbreaking studies were organized by Oldways Preservation and Exchange Trust, a non-profit food-history and nutrition-education group, and the prestigious Harvard School of Public Health. The efforts of these organizations and countless other food and health professionals helped build a simple set of dietary and lifestyle recommendations: the Healthy Traditional Latin American Diet Pyramid.

You may have seen diet pyramids before. The first diet pyramid was introduced in 1992 by the U.S. Department of Agriculture (USDA). Unfortunately, the nutrition advice in the USDA pyramid had little to do with the traditions and diets of Latinos. For example, traditional Latin foods like beans and nuts do not raise the "bad" LDL cholesterol in your blood. In fact, these foods can help protect against chronic diseases. However, the USDA pyramid lumped beans and nuts together with meat and eggs, which actually have the potential to increase the "bad" cholesterol in your blood and raise the risk of chronic disease.

The Latin American diet pyramid sets the record straight. It shows that traditional Latin foods can be quite healthy. It explains what to eat on a daily basis to help prevent disease. Plus, the pyramid teaches you about a good-for-you lifestyle, making it easier to achieve your health goals. Eat and live according to the pyramid, and you'll be in a better position to boost your health, increase your energy, and lift your mood. Like the stone pyramids of ancient America's largest and most impressive city, Teoti- huacán (tay-o-tee-WAH-cahn), northeast of present-day Mexico City, the Latin American diet pyramid is your foundation for a long and healthy life.

VIVA VARIETY

There are three major levels to the Latin American diet pyramid. For each level, we explain the food recommendations and give some background on why they're so important. As you read, refer to the illustration on page 4 to see each of the three levels.

In all three levels, a strong emphasis is placed on variety. It seems that the ancients had it right after all. The traditional diet of ancient Latin America included an extraordinary variety of foods—mostly fruits, vegetables, legumes, and grains. Today, leading health organizations like the American Heart Association, the American Cancer Society, the National Cancer Institute, and the USDA agree that the healthiest diets are indeed based on balance and variety. A wide array of foods ensures that you'll get the most nutrients. The Latin American diet pyramid reflects this emphasis. Be sure to explore the magnificent spectrum of foods in all three sec-

THE HEALTHY TRADITIONAL
LATIN AMERICAN DIET PYRAMID

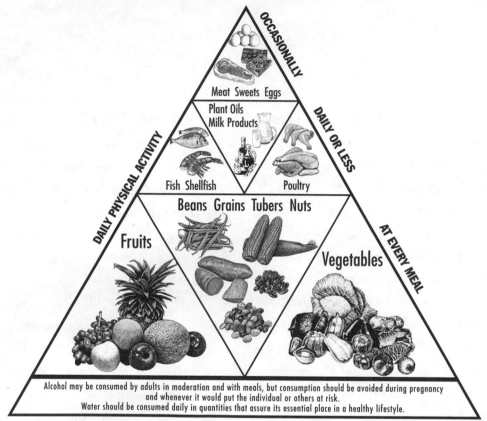

OCCASIONALLY

Meat Sweets Eggs

DAILY OR LESS

DAILY PHYSICAL ACTIVITY

Plant Oils
Milk Products

Fish Shellfish

Poultry

Beans Grains Tubers Nuts

Fruits

Vegetables

AT EVERY MEAL

Alcohol may be consumed by adults in moderation and with meals, but consumption should be avoided during pregnancy
and whenever it would put the individual or others at risk.
Water should be consumed daily in quantities that assure its essential place in a healthy lifestyle.

tions of the pyramid. When you shop and cook, strive to include some foods that are new to you and look for foods with contrasting colors, flavors, and textures.

AT EVERY MEAL: PLANT FOODS

Plant foods are the foundation of a healthy Latin American diet. These foods are at the base of the pyramid to indicate that they are the building blocks, just like the real building blocks used to make the pyramids of ancient Teotihuacán. Legumes, grains, tubers, nuts, fruits, and vegetables should be included at every meal and can be eaten in large amounts.

Legumes are some of the healthiest foods in this level of the pyramid. These include peas, lentils, and a staggering number of beans, such as black beans, red beans, white beans, pinto beans, and even lima beans. Legumes are a great source of protein. Unlike most protein-based foods (meats and dairy products, for instance) legumes come with almost no fat. Research shows that legumes also lower "bad" LDL cholesterol and triglycerides in your blood. Plus, they help stabilize blood sugar—good news for people with diabetes. Beans are tops for vitamins, too. One cup of cooked beans provides half the recommended daily amount of folate, a nutrient recommended for pregnant women to help prevent birth defects. Lentils are even better. They provide 90 percent of the recommended amount of folate. Legumes are also high in fiber which, according to studies, can help prevent heart disease and certain cancers such as colon cancer.

Corn, quinoa, amaranth, and rice have long been staple grains in Latin American cooking. These are excellent sources of complex carbohydrates, which help give you long-lasting energy. Grains don't slouch on vitamins, either. They're full of nutrients like folate, magnesium, and vitamin E. According to researchers, grains can even help protect against heart disease—when they are prepared the old-fashioned way. That is, when they are unrefined or used as "whole grains." Unfortunately, most people today eat refined white rice and white flour, which have had many of the beneficial nutrients removed. To get more vitamins and minerals in your diet, look for whole grains like corn (including corn tortillas), quinoa, brown rice, and whole-wheat flour tortillas.

You might think that nuts are off-limits in a healthy diet because of their high fat content. But research shows that that's not true. "One thing that has become clear is that not all dietary fats are the same when it comes to increasing risk for heart disease," says Frank Sacks, M.D., associate professor of medicine and nutrition at Harvard University and chair of the planning committee for the Latin American diet pyramid. "Nuts are an excellent source of healthy unsaturated fat that can actually help lower the cholesterol in your blood," he says. Nuts are also cholesterol-free and a good source of protein and fiber. One ounce of peanuts contains 7 grams of protein, only 2 grams of saturated fat, and 2 grams of fiber. The 17 grams of unsaturated fats in peanuts may seem high, but remember that this type of fat can be good for you. According to Dr. Sacks, unsaturated fats are not a predictor of increased body weight. Inactivity is.

The star foods at the base of the pyramid are fruits and vegetables. These foods are generally excellent sources of fiber, carotenes, vitamin C, and other beneficial phytochemicals (plant chemicals). Some key *verduras* (cooked vegetables traditionally used in stews and soups) in the Latin diet include yuca, sweet potatoes, pumpkin, and plantains. Diets high in fruits and vegetables may be especially important for Latinos to protect against the cancers that they experience more of—stomach and cervical cancer. One Latin food that's bursting with healthy fruits and vegetables is salsa—so eat more of it, especially cooked salsas like *Salsa ranchera* (Ranch-Style Tomato Salsa, page 296). Studies show that lycopene, a type of carotene found in cooked tomatoes, can help protect against cancer. Experts also recommend avoiding commercially available fried vegetables like fried potatoes (*papas fritas*) and fried plantains (*mariquitas*). These foods often contain a type of fat called trans-fatty acids, which can be hard on your heart and arteries because they tend to raise blood cholesterol levels. Instead, prepare foods at home with unsaturated oils like canola oil, olive oil, and corn oil. Or use alternative cooking methods like the "bake-frying" method used for many of the recipes in this book.

Here's more good news about traditional Latin foods. Avocados are now considered one of the healthy ingredients in the Latin American diet. As with nuts, studies show that avocados are high in heart-healthy monounsaturated fat. This is the same type of fat that makes olives and olive oil such a beneficial part of the Mediterranean diet. Plus, three slices (about ¼ cup) of avocado contain only 60 calories. That's almost half the calories in 2 tablespoons of cream cheese and a third the calories in 2 tablespoons of butter. To avoid the unwanted calories and saturated fat in butter and cream cheese, try luscious, creamy mashed avocados as a spread. Mashed avocados also make delicious accompaniments to tortilla, rice, soup, and bean dishes.

GO BACK TO YOUR ROOTS

The practice of eating *verduras*—and fresh fruits—on a daily basis is an important component of the traditional diet in Latin America. For instance, fruits like bananas make great snacks and are easy to carry around. But fewer Latinos are eating fruits and vegetables these days. What happened to the mango? Where are the chiles, corn, yuca, and plantains? "Not in the contemporary

Latin American diet," says John P. Foreyt, Ph.D., director of the Behavioral Medicine Research Center at Baylor College of Medicine in Houston and a member of the planning committee for the Latin American diet pyramid. "The traditional Latin American diet has been largely replaced by unhealthy North American foods," he says.

As Latinos have become acculturated in the United States, they have begun to adopt North American foods and eating habits. Hamburgers and soft drinks have become more common snacks than burritos and guavas. Many modern Latinos now consider traditional foods like beans to be "low-class." Meat is often preferred over grains, fruits, and vegetables because it is seen as the privilege of the wealthy and successful. As a result, the health profile of Latinos has begun to more closely match that of non-Latino Americans. According to the American Cancer Society, the leading cancer sites for Latinos are the same as those for non-Latinos: prostate, breast, lung, colon, and rectum.

The new dietary patterns of Latinos may also be leading to lower intakes of important nutrients. A study from the Centers for Disease Control and Prevention and the Illinois Cancer Council of Chicago showed that a large number of Latinas living in Chicago are not getting the recommended daily allowance (RDA) of several vitamins and minerals. About one-quarter of the women in the study reported getting less than 66 percent of the recommended amounts of vitamin A, vitamin C, and B vitamins like thiamin, niacin, and riboflavin. About half reported taking in less than 66 percent of the RDA for calcium, zinc, and folate. And more than 80 percent took in less than 66 percent of the RDA for iron, an important nutrient for women. Fiber was another lacking nutrient. Only 32 percent of Latinas took in more than 20 grams of fiber each day. Most nutritionists recommend getting 25 to 35 grams of fiber a day. These results don't include nutrients from nutritional supplements, but only 25 percent of women in the study took nutritional supplements.

For all these reasons, the Latin American diet pyramid emphasizes traditional Latin foods. Studies show that the customary foods of the region, like beans, grains, fruits, and vegetables, are the basis of a healthy diet. "The traditional Latin diet and lifestyle probably helped protect Latinos against most cancers," says Anna Giuliano, Ph.D., director of the Minority Cancer Prevention and Control Program and assistant professor at the Arizona Cancer Center in Tucson. "However, traditional patterns are changing and cancer incidence is increasing among Latinos," she says. What's her advice? "Eating more fruits and vegetables can help prevent these cancers," she says. And she is not alone. According to the National Cancer Institute, dietary change can help prevent 35 percent of most major cancers.

The next time you sit down to eat, think about what's on your plate. Is there some grain? Some bean? Some fruit or vegetable? Learn from the ancient Latin Americans and strive to include these traditional Latin foods at every meal. They do a body good.

DAILY OR LESS: SEAFOOD, POULTRY, MILK PRODUCTS, AND PLANT OILS

Foods like fish, poultry, and dairy products are mainstays on the Latin table. Traditional Latin stews are teeming with fish and shellfish. Paella is topped with a colorful variety of seafood and chicken. And many Latin desserts include some type of dairy product, as in *Arroz con leche* ("rice with milk," or rice pudding; see page 322).

All of these foods are important sources of protein. Fish and chicken are particularly good sources of lean protein because they don't include a lot of saturated fat. Protein is a key nutrient for adults. Proteins are integral structural components of body tissue, and they perform important roles as enzymes, hormones, and antibodies. They also aid in blood clotting and energy production. On average, women need between 50 and 80 grams of protein a day, while men need between 60 and 90 grams.

However, these foods are not the only source of proteins. According to the USDA Dietary Guidelines for Americans, if you eat a variety of vegetables, grains, and beans, you will ensure an adequate amount of protein in your diet. For this reason, experts recommend that you eat seafood, poultry, and dairy products daily or less. Quite simply, these foods are not as healthy for you as those at the base of the pyramid. They generally contain more saturated fat, cholesterol, and sodium. So eat fish, chicken, turkey, and milk products in slightly smaller amounts than those foods at the base of the pyramid. This is the natural proportion in many traditional Latin American dishes, such as *Arroz con pollo* (Chicken with Rice, page 244), where the chicken (pollo) is

THE GOOD FAT IN SEAFOOD

Fish and shellfish abound in Latin American cooking. Sole, flounder, snapper, shrimp, scallops, mussels, clams—even squid and octopus—are regularly found on Latin American dinner tables. Many types of seafood contain a special type of fat called omega-3 fatty acids. According to nutrition experts, omega-3's can help lower blood cholesterol, prevent hypertension (high blood pressure), reduce risk of stroke, and help prevent heart disease. A study at the University of Washington in Seattle found that eating 5.5 grams of omega-3 fatty acids a week (about 3 ounces of seafood) can cut your heart attack risk in half. A good supply of omega-3's may also reduce the risk of breast cancer. Plus, most seafood is very low in saturated fat. The next time you're planning a meal, think fish. It's smart for your heart.

shredded or cubed and added to a flavorful mixture of rice and vegetables.

When choosing milk products, look for those that are naturally low in saturated fat, like buttermilk and yogurt. Opt for cheeses made with some skim milk, like part-skim Cheddar and Monterey Jack. Fortunately, *queso blanco* a popular Latin cheese—is one of the lowest in saturated fat. What about ice cream? You don't need to eliminate it entirely. But nutritionists recommend saving higher-fat dairy foods like ice cream for special celebrations. Or choose lower saturated fat alternatives like low-fat frozen yogurt.

Cooking fats are included in this middle level of the pyramid. And that

brings us to one of the most controversial foods in Latin American cooking: lard. The cooking of the original Amerindians did not include lard. However, after the conquistadores brought it from Spain, rendered pork fat became an essential flavor ingredient in Latin dishes. Mexican refried beans just don't taste right without it. Of course, lard is not among the healthiest cooking fats because it's derived from animal sources that include significant amounts of cholesterol and saturated fat. But there are ways to use small amounts of lard for flavor. Many of the recipes in this book use just a bit of lard mixed with healthier fats like canola oil, olive oil, or corn oil. By mixing lard with

THE SKINNY ON SALT AND HIGH BLOOD PRESSURE

Salt contains one of the most misunderstood nutrients in your diet. Believe it or not, sodium is necessary for important body functions. Its chief job is to help maintain your body's balance of fluids. However, diets that contain too much salt may lead to high blood pressure and osteoporosis. So should everyone limit their salt intake? Not necessarily. Not all people respond to high-salt diets in the same way. If you have normal blood pressure, there's a good chance that you are not salt-sensitive. Even if you have high blood pressure, you may not be salt-sensitive. The fact is, there are bigger risk factors for high blood pressure than too much salt in your diet. Inactivity, excess body fat, and stress are better predictors of hypertension than salt.

Of course, that doesn't mean that it's okay to pile on the salty chips and snack-foods. Nutritionists still recommend that most folks limit salt intake to about 1 teaspoon of salt per day (2,400 milligrams of sodium). To help keep your salt consumption at healthy levels, avoid eating too many salty snacks and canned foods. Look for low-sodium varieties of canned vegetables. To reduce the sodium in canned beans, rinse them well before using.

plant oils, you can keep the familiar flavor of your favorite foods like refried beans while also enjoying the health benefits of a diet that's low in saturated fat and higher in heart-smart monounsaturated fats.

Whenever possible, choose liquid fats like canola oil and olive oil over solid fats like lard and vegetable shortening. And only use as much as you need. For instance, go easy on the cooking oil when making *sofrito* (sautéed vegetables). Nonstick pans are a great help here. The surface of these pans helps prevent food from sticking so that you don't have to use as much oil.

OCCASIONALLY: MEATS, SWEETS, AND EGGS

The top of the Latin diet pyramid shows foods that are best eaten occasionally—or less than once a week. These foods include beef, pork, eggs, and sweets. That doesn't mean cutting them out altogether, but it does mean putting the emphasis on the other two levels of the pyramid.

Foods at the top of the pyramid tend to be high in saturated fat. And according to statistics, Latinos tend to overeat saturated fat. How much? Studies show that Mexican-American women derive 12 percent of their energy from fat. Mexican-Americans and younger Cuban-Americans (ages 20 through 39) eat the highest amount of saturated fat. Puerto Ricans and older Cubans (ages 40 through 74) eat the lowest.

The biggest problem with eating saturated fat is that it could increase your risk of heart disease by raising the "bad" LDL cholesterol in your blood. Half of the Latinos living in the United States have high cholesterol levels (over 200 milligrams per deciliter), according to the American Heart Association. This puts many Latinos at risk for developing heart disease, the leading cause of death among Latinos.

THE LATIN AMERICAN SWEET TOOTH

Half of the top level of the Latin diet pyramid shows foods that are high in saturated fat. The other half consists of foods that are high in sugar. Sugar plantations were a big part of the New World economy after Christopher Columbus brought sugarcane to the region. "As a result, Latin Americans developed a taste for sugar, sweets, and desserts. Today, Latinos tend to gravitate toward sweet snack foods and sugary sodas. Cola is now a major source of calories among Latinos," says Dr. Foreyt.

Experts recommend eating sweets and desserts only occasionally. These foods are made with large amounts of refined white sugar, brown sugar, raw sugar, maple syrup, or honey. Nutritionally speaking, sweets and sodas are made up of mostly simple sugars, or simple carbohydrates. Unlike the beneficial complex carbohydrates in grains, the simple carbohydrates in sugar provide only empty calories and little or no nutritional value to your body. And those extra calories can turn into body fat if they're not worked off through physical activity.

What's more, this extra weight in your body can increase the sugar in your blood and lead to diabetes. One in every four Latinos has diabetes, and Latinos are two to four times more likely to have this disease than any other ethnic group. Is diabetes dangerous? You bet. It is the fourth leading cause of death among Latin American women and the ninth leading cause of death among Latin American men. Diabetes can also lead to health complications like blindness, kidney disease, nerve disease, amputations, heart disease, and stroke. One study shows that diabetes even increased the risk of tuberculosis among middle-aged Latinos living in California. Unfortunately, only about half of the people with the disease are aware that they have it. That's why the American Diabetes Association refers to diabetes as the silent killer. Next time you want something sweet, reach for a piece of fruit.

PUTTING THE PYRAMID INTO PRACTICE

Now you've seen all the recommendations of the Latin American diet pyramid, from the foundation to the top. Here's a summary in a slightly different form. Numerous studies show that the healthiest diets for Latinos look like this:

✦ High in beans like lentils, black beans, red kidney beans, and pinto beans

✦ High in fruits like mangoes, bananas, and papayas

✦ High in vegetables like cacti, tomatoes, cassava, sweet potatoes, and avocados

✦ High in whole grains like corn, quinoa, whole-wheat tortillas, and brown rice

✦ High in fish, seafood, poultry, and nuts

✦ Include monounsaturated fat oils like canola and olive oil

✦ Include polyunsaturated fat oils like corn oil

✦ Low in refined grains like white rice, white flour, and the products made from them

✦ Low in red meats like beef and pork

✦ Low in full-fat dairy products like whole milk, sour cream, ice cream, and cheese

✦ Low in hydrogenated fats (which contain harmful trans-fatty acids) from products like margarine, cookies, French fries, and chips

✦ Low in sweets, eggs, and sugary sodas

You can put this healthy diet to work for you and your family today. Instead of buying sugary sodas, try unsweetened iced tea or sparkling water. Or look to traditional Latin drinks like *limonada* (lemonade), and *tamarindo* (tamarind drink). Some of the best-tasting and most nutritious drinks in the world come from Latin America. *Horchatas* (coolers) and *batidos* (milkshakes) get their sweetness and flavor from vitamin-rich fruits instead of from sugar. You'll find recipes for many of these drinks in this book.

Use meats and eggs in smaller amounts in your cooking. Think of them as supplements to the more nutritious foods like beans, grains, fruits, and vegetables. Or try the slimmed-down versions of your favorite meat and egg dishes throughout this book. Lower-fat versions of dishes like *parillada* (grilled meats) and *huevos rancheros* (Mexican ranch eggs) can be enjoyed a little more often.

Try replacing the meat in your favorite recipes with turkey or chicken. In most ground beef recipes, you can replace about half of the beef with lean ground turkey breast without much flavor difference. Throughout the rest of this book, you'll find plenty more ways to enjoy your favorite foods with less saturated fat and more flavor.

THE FINAL PIECE OF THE PUZZLE

A healthy diet goes a long way toward solving the mystery of lifelong health and vitality. A healthy lifestyle is the final piece of the puzzle.

You may have noticed that the Latin pyramid includes more than just dietary recommendations. This is the first diet pyramid to include important lifestyle tips. When experts gathered to study the traditional Latin American diet, they found that people in ancient Latin America enjoyed a relatively healthy lifestyle, too. Men and women were quite active, didn't smoke, and drank lots of water (because water was one of the only readily available beverages around).

Today, however, the Latino lifestyle has changed right along with the Latino diet. The Behavioral Risk Factor Surveillance Study found that 6 in every 10 modern Latinos are not physically active. Research from California State University, Los Angeles, shows that Latinos are reducing their physical activity and watching more TV.

You might guess that this inactivity leads to extra body weight. You're right. According to the comprehensive National Health and Nutrition Examination

Survey, almost half of Mexican-Americans and a third of Cuban and Puerto Rican men and women were found to be overweight (or obese). That means that they carry around 20 percent more body weight than is optimal for good health.

After cigarette smoking, excess body weight is the greatest cause of disease in most populations that have risen above poverty, according to Walter Willett, M.D., Dr.PH, chair of the department of nutrition at the Harvard School of Public Health. Excess body fat accounts for the large majority of adult-onset diabetes and a large proportion of hypertension (high blood pressure), coronary heart disease, stroke and cancers of the breast, colon, and endometrium. Everyone interested in health should pay close attention to preventing excess weight gain, particular after age 20, says Dr. Willett.

That's why the Latin pyramid recommends daily physical activity for all Latinos. Should you run out and buy exercise equipment and work out for hours and hours each day? Not necessarily. According to the Center for Health Promotion at the Harvard School of Public Health, 30 minutes of moderate physical activity three times a week is enough to strengthen your heart and keep you

healthy. Physical activity may also help protect you from breast cancer, diabetes, and high cholesterol, experts say. Researchers from Colorado State University in Fort Collins showed that Mexican-American women who exercise can significantly increase the "good" HDL cholesterol and reduce the "bad" triglycerides in their blood.

Another bonus of physical activity is stable blood pressure. According to the American Heart Association, 2 out of every 10 U.S. Latinos or Latinas have high blood pressure. Americans of Puerto Rican, Cuban, and Mexican heritage are more likely to have high blood pressure than non-Latinos. By increasing your physical activity just a little bit each day, you can help lower your blood pressure or reduce your risk of developing high blood pressure.

Best of all, increased physical activity helps you lose weight and feel great. And that can lower your risk of several different diseases.

Practically any daily activity that increases your breathing and results in some sweat can be considered moderate physical activity. Experts at the American Heart Association say that moderate physical activity includes dancing, walking, climbing stairs, gardening, yard work, and active housework.

This means that you don't have to yank on a pair of sweats and run 10 miles or lift weights for two hours to be in shape. Why not take advantage of Latin America's rich musical heritage and dance your way into shape? With salsa, merengue, cumbia, Latin pop and rock, samba, and tango, there's plenty of music to keep you moving—and in shape, too. Even if you decide that your two left feet rule out dancing, the important thing is to find a fun physical activity that will be easy to make a regular part of your life.

You may not realize it, but drinking water can also help you stay healthy. The Latin American pyramid recommends drinking about eight 8-ounce glasses of water a day. Water keeps your body hydrated and helps you feel full so that you don't overeat. Instead of reaching for soda when you're thirsty, grab a tall glass of refreshing, ice-cold water.

Because alcohol is a popular part of Latin culture, the Latin American pyramid makes some recommendations here as well. Some research shows that alcohol in moderation can help reduce the risk of heart disease and diabetes. Experts say that alcohol can be considered part of a healthy diet if consumed in moderation. But, alcohol is a double-edged sword. The positive effects of this substance can disappear very quickly if you drink too much. Researchers at the Harvard School of Public Health found that more than two drinks per day combined with an inadequate intake of folate (found in beans, fruits, and vegetables) can double your risk of colon cancer. The Latin American pyramid emphasizes that if you do drink alcohol, do it in a moderate and responsible manner. That means limiting alcohol to no more than two drinks per day. (A drink is defined as 4 ounces of wine, one shot of liquor, or 12 ounces of beer.) If you're a pregnant woman, health officials recommend avoiding alcohol altogether.

The best thing about the Latin American diet pyramid is that it combines the truths of age-old wisdom with the most up-to-date scientific information. So take a tip from the ancestors in ancient Latin America. Eat healthy foods, stay active, and enjoy life in a responsible way. Think *Sol, canto, y comidas de espanto*! ("Sun, singing, and wonderful meals"). Follow the path of the pyramid, and good health will meet you along the way.

—*Hannia Campos, Ph.D.*
Harvard School of Public Health

A CULINARY TOUR OF LATIN AMERICA

Latin America is a food-lover's paradise. Few cuisines in the world boast such explosive flavors, ethnic diversity, culinary sophistication, and potential health benefits as that of the vast and varied region that stretches from the Río Grande in the north of México to the Tierra Del Fuego at the southernmost tip of South America.

This book is a celebration of Latin American cooking. From the fiery salsas and satisfying tortilla dishes of México to the soulful stews of the Spanish-speaking Caribbean, from the robust grilled meats of Argentina to the exquisite fish soups of Chile, the variety and range of Latin American foods have something for every palate.

For a long time, Latin food has gotten a bad rap among health-minded eaters—largely on account of a few well-known dishes that aren't particularly healthy. You know the culprits: deep-fried burritos and *chicharrones* (pork rinds), cheese-smothered enchiladas, ever-present red meats, and plenty of sugary desserts. In the following chapters, we'll look more closely at some of these nutritional offenders and show you how to slash the fat, sugar, sodium, and other unhealthy elements in traditional recipes while keeping the bold flavors.

But for the moment, let's focus on the positive elements in the cuisines of Latin America. Few regions in the world have a richer, more varied, more healthy set of raw materials.

A BIT OF GEOGRAPHY

The region known as Latin America is home to around a half billion people (just about twice the population of the United States), spread across 22 countries stretching 7,000 miles from the southern border of the United States to the icy shores of Cape Horn, Argentina. The region includes dozens of different climatic, topographic, and geological zones, ranging from snow-capped mountains to tropical rain forests, from grassy plains (the Pampas) to palm-fringed Caribbean beaches, and from cactus-studded deserts to plantation-covered highlands.

Depending on where you live in Latin America, you might eat grains and potatoes grown a mile above sea level or fruits and coconuts cultivated at the ocean's edge. Your fish might come from the Atlantic Ocean, Pacific Ocean, the Gulf of México, or the Caribbean Sea. It might even come from several of these bodies of water if you happen to live in México, Guatemala, Honduras, Nicaragua, Costa Rica, Panamá, or Colombia.

Spanish is the official language in 21 of the 22 countries in Latin America—the legacy of the Spanish explorers, conquistadores, colonists, and holy men who settled the region in the centuries following the arrival of Christopher Columbus in 1492. Portuguese is the official language of Latin America's largest and most populous country, Brazil. Actually, hundreds of other languages are spoken in Latin America, ranging from indigenous tongues, like Nahuatl in México and Guarani in Paraguay, to recent imports like Italian and German, spoken respectively in Argentina and Brazil.

Latin American cooking reflects this cultural diversity. There's as much difference between Mexican, Cuban, and Brazilian cooking as there is between Italian, French, and German cooking. Yet most North Americans tend to lump Latino cuisines together—possibly because of exposure only to food from the three largest Latino subgroups in the United States: Mexican, Puerto Rican, and Cuban.

CULINARY COMMON GROUND

Of course, there are similarities among the cuisines of Latin America. Latin ingredients, equipment, and methods have unique culinary characteristics, thanks to the common raw materials and the shared cultural and religious heritage of the Spanish and Portuguese settlers.

All Latin American countries use prodigious amounts of onions, garlic, and bell peppers—the ingredients of the ubiquitous *sofrito* (vegetable sauté). Like French mirepoix, sofrito consists of onions, garlic, a variety of bell peppers, and sometimes tomatoes sautéed until soft in olive oil or lard. Sofrito is the foundation for literally thousands of Latino dishes.

All Latin American countries also make extensive use of the four primary foods of the New World: corn, beans, squash, and chiles. Virtually every country has a version of the tamale (cornmeal dough wrapped and cooked in a corn husk or other vegetable leaf). In Venezuela, they're called *hallacas*, and they're flavored with annatto oil and cooked in a banana leaf. Bolivia's *humitas* use a combination of fresh and dried corn, which is steamed in a corn husk. Nicaragua is home to the king-size tamale, known as *nacatamal*—a jumbo packet of cornmeal, rice, meat, vegetables, and herbs cooked in a plantain leaf.

Beans are common currency in Latin America. *Frijoles refritos* (mashed refried black beans) are enjoyed in México. *Cazuelitos* (Little Pots of Red Beans with Sour Cream, page 79) are savored in Nicaragua. And Argentinians love their *Ensalada de porotos* (South American Bean Salad, page 118). Beans are one of the healthiest Latin American ingredients. They're an excellent source of protein, plus cancer-fighting soluble fiber and antioxidants.

Indigenous peoples of Latin America had an uncanny sense of nutri-

tion. The combination of beans and grains forms a complete protein providing all nine of the essential amino acids that the body needs. And this form of protein is extremely low in fat compared with most other forms of protein (meat, poultry, and dairy products, for instance). The Latin American food repertory abounds with these bean-grain combinations, from Cuba's whimsically named *moros y cristianos* ("Moors and Christians," literally, black beans and rice) to México's bean-and-tortilla burritos to the *baleadas* (tortillas stuffed with kidney beans) of El Salvador and Honduras.

Winter squashes are the third healthy mainstay of the Latin American diet. And every part of the vegetable is used, from the flowers (an ingredient in Mexican soups and quesadillas) to the whole squash, which is often used as an edible cooked vessel, as in Argentina's *carbonada criolla*, a stew cooked and served in hollowed-out squash. Orange-fleshed squashes are a valuable source of beta-carotene and vitamin A, nutrients that have been shown to fight everything from heart disease to cancer.

But if there's one defining ingredient in the cuisines of Latin America, it's those fiery members of the Capsicum family, better known as the chiles. Chiles were one of the first exports from the New World to the Old. Within a century of their "discovery" by Columbus, they had circumnavigated the globe and been carried to lands as far flung as India, China, Hungary, and West Africa, where their sharp bite was embraced with gusto.

Chiles are used throughout every country in Latin America, but in very different ways. For México, they are the very lifeblood of the cuisine. In Argentina and Uruguay, hot-pepper flakes are added to the ubiquitous table sauce, *chimichurri*. Puerto Ricans and Cubans wouldn't dream of cooking without mild red and green bell peppers and *ajíes dulces*, but they generally don't go in for the fiery flavors of México and Central America. Peruvians, on the other hand, like their food hot and spicy, using plenty of *ají amarillo* (yellow chiles).

Chiles are the key flavor ingredient in one of México's greatest gifts to the world of healthy eating: salsa. Bursting with flavor and free of fat, these piquant vegetable mixtures are used to spice up everything from Yucatán *pebil* (pit-roasted meats) to Tex-Mex fajitas. What you may not realize is that the love of salsa-like condiments continues down the continent, from Central America throughout South America. Costa Rica's *Encurtido* (Pickled Onion Relish, page 313) is a sort of salsa; so is Puerto Rico's *ají-li-mójili* (cilantro and pepper "pesto"), as is Guatamala's *chirmol* (tomato salsa) and Chile's *pebre* (parsley-garlic "pesto"). Throughout the Americas, cooks use salsa-like condiments for adding explosive flavors without fat.

Despite these common threads, there has been relatively little culinary cross-pollination among the regions of Latin America. That's starting to change in North America, where a new generation of Latino chefs has been scouring the motherland for inspiration to create their Nuevo Latino cuisine. In each country, they find that cooks do things just a little differently.

THE MYSTIQUE OF MÉXICO

Of Latin America's many cuisines, México's is perhaps the best known to North Americans. It's also the region's most distinctive and complex. The reason for this sophistication is simple: When the Spanish conquered the New World in the 1500s, México possessed the most highly evolved indigenous culture on the continent. The Spanish discovered huge cities with elaborate architecture, advanced communication and transportation systems, and a colorful and complex cuisine. Today, there are more than 150 different types of tortillas in México, more than 80 types of tamales, more than a dozen types of corn-based drinks, and more than 120 ways to prepare corn on the cob.

Mexicans use dozens of herbs and spices and more than 50 different types of fresh and dried chiles to build layer upon layer of flavor. There are hundreds of different salsas alone, ranging from the familiar *pico de gallo* ("rooster's beak" salsa) and *ranchera* (lime-scented cooked tomato sauce) to the exotic *x'nipec* (pronounced "schnee-PECK"), an incendiary habanero chile salsa that has remained virtually unchanged since the days of the ancient Mayans. As for the *moles* (gravies) of central México, some contain more than 25 ingredients and traditionally require a full day—if not two—of cooking. There's a lot more to Mexican cooking than the simple Tex-Mex fare that defines the subject for many North Americans.

THE SOUL OF THE SPANISH CARIBBEAN

The Spanish-speaking Caribbean has its own set of distinct flavors, determined again by the region's history.

Cuba, Puerto Rico, and the Dominican Republic were the first lands colonized by the Spanish. At that time, the indigenous cooking was relatively simple. For this reason, Spanish-Caribbean cooking remains closest to that of Spain.

The Spanish would certainly recognize the sofrito that forms the foundation of Cuban, Dominican, and Puerto Rican cooking. They'd also recognize the contrast of sweet and salty flavors (thanks to the addition of raisins, prunes, capers, and olives) that characterize so many of the dishes on these islands. Many of the dominant seasonings in the region's cooking—cumin, oregano, cinnamon, and anise—come from Spain (or from the Arab world, via Spain), as do the delightful sharpness of fresh orange and lime juice and the ancient Mediterranean flavors of wine and olive oil. The *asopaos* (soupy stews) of Puerto Rico and the Dominican Republic and the *arroz con pollos* (chicken and rices) of all three islands are direct descendants of Spanish paella.

That's not to say that the Spanish-speaking Caribbean wasn't also influenced by indigenous cooking. Consider a dish like *Ajiaco* (Spanish-Caribbean Beef and Vegetable Stew, page 110), a soulful stew chock-full of native vegetables like yuca, malanga, calabaza, and corn. The earthy-flavored, rust-colored spice known as annatto often stands in for the more expensive Spanish saffron in many dishes. Culantro, known as *recao* in Puerto Rico, (an indigenous herb that tastes similar to cilantro) joins bay leaf and parsley as staples among Spanish-Caribbean herbs. Tropical fruits, such as papayas and soursops, have become popular fruits for jams, jellies, and ice creams.

Spanish-Caribbean cooking remains some of the mildest Latino cooking in terms of its heat levels (with the exception of some Dominican dishes). It's ideal for people who are put off by México's chile hellfires. If you have a sweet tooth, you'll find plenty of desserts here, too. The Spanish-speaking Caribbean was home to some of the New World's first sugar plantations. Since the arrival of sugar, the region's variety of desserts has become quite extensive.

CENTRAL AMERICA— A CULTURAL CROSSROADS

Central America reflects the characteristics of both Mexican and Spanish-Caribbean cooking, but it has a personality all its own. As in México, tortillas are the staff of life, but they're thicker in Guatemala and Nicaragua. In El Salvador, tortillas come stuffed with beans, meat, and cheese (see the recipe for *Pupusas salvadoreñas*, or Salvadoran Stuffed Tortillas, on page 206). I like to think of these stuffed tortillas as Salvadoran Pop-Tarts. In Central America, the salsas of México come in the form of pickles and slaws, like Costa Rica's *Encurtido* (Pickled Onion Relish, page 313) and Central America's *Ensalada de repollo* (Central American Slaw, page 116). These condiments are served with grilled meats and boiled vegetable dishes like Nicaragua's *Vigorón* (Yuca, Slaw, and Pork Cracklings, page 140).

Seafood figures prominently on Central America's culinary landscape, especially in countries like Panamá and Costa Rica. These countries border on two major bodies of water: the Atlantic and Pacific Oceans.

Central America is also quite fertile on land. Much of the world's bananas and plantains ripen on its volcanic slopes. Plantains are a major staple in this part of Latin America. They're served in a variety of forms, from *Maduros* (Grilled Ripe Plantains, page 144) to Panamá's and Colombia's *Patacones* (fried, mashed, refried plantains, or Plantain "Surf-boards," page 143).

NORTHERN SOUTH AMERICA—WHERE THE MOUNTAINS MEET THE SEA

Northern South America, especially the Andean Mountain nations of Ecuador, Bolivia, and Perú, bring us some of the most exciting and exotic food in Latin America. Potatoes and the highly nutritious grain quinoa originated in the region and still play a major role in the cuisine. Perú alone boasts more than 100 different potato varieties, including a blue potato that has become the darling of trendy chefs in North America and an unusual, naturally freeze-dried potato that is frozen and dried by the wind and icy temperatures of the Andean plateaus.

Perú has some of the most distinctive and spicy food in South America. The preferred seasoning is *ají amarillo*, a fiery yellow chile that puts bite into everything from *caucau* (Peruvian Seafood Stew, page 240) to *pinchos* (kabobs) to *papa a la huancaina* (spicy, cheesy potato salad). The large Japanese community in Perú has had something of an Asian effect on Peruvian cooking. Indeed, one of the most celebrated chefs in

North America, Nobu Matsuhisa, is of Japanese ancestry and grew up in the country's capital, Lima.

The cuisines of Colombia and Venezuela display more of a Spanish influence. Consider such Spanish-style local specialties as *Sancocho* (meat and vegetable stew, page 290) and *Mariscada* (Seafood Stew, in the style of Spanish *zarzuela*, page 235). But make no mistake: There are plenty of indigenous Indian-inspired dishes here, too. Venezuela's *hallacas* (annatto-flavored corn tamales wrapped and cooked in plantain leaves) are wildly popular to this day. Another indigenous dish is the *arepas* (cornmeal cakes) eaten in both Venezuela and Colombia. Made with a special precooked cornmeal, arepas are reminiscent of Italian polenta. The basic recipe contains only cornmeal and water, but some cooks make more lavish versions that include cheese or meat.

The coastal regions have played an equally important role in shaping the cuisines of northern South America. The coastlines of Colombia and Venezuela form the southern boundary of the Caribbean Basin. Fish, shrimp, and coconut milk figure prominently in the cooking of these countries. Colombia, Ecuador, and Perú account for nearly half of South America's Pacific coastline. Appropriately, Ecuador was the birthplace of what is arguably the most famous fish dish in South America: *ceviche*. (Although, Peruvians lay claim the dish's parentage, too.) Ceviche is a simple mixture of thinly sliced fresh seafood pickled in a marinade of lime juice or sour orange juice, onions, garlic, salt, and sometimes chiles. The acids in the citrus make the fish tender and white, as though it has been cooked over heat. Today, ceviche is made with myriad different types of fish and shellfish and is also enjoyed throughout México, Central America, and as far south as Chile.

SOUTHERN SOUTH AMERICA—A BEEF-LOVER'S BACKYARD

The fifth gastronomic region in Latin America is southern South America, comprised of the nations of Chile, Paraguay, Uruguay, and Argentina. We're in beef country now. Argentinians consume as much as 2 pounds of beef per person per day. Uruguayans eat beef at an average of 11 to 13 meals a week. Beef production is centered in the Pampas, the vast grasslands stretching from the outskirts of Buenos Aires to Asunción, Paraguay, and Río Grande do Sul, Brazil.

In the early twentieth century, the beef trade made Argentina the wealthiest nation in both North and South America.

For the most part, beef is eaten simply in southern South America: grilled on vertical spikes in front of a campfire (*asado*) or cooked over wood on a grill (*parrilla*). The accompaniments are equally simple: a robust tomato-onion-pepper relish known as salsa criolla and a pesto-like parsley-garlic-vinegar sauce called *chimichurri* (Chileans enjoy a similar sauce called *pebre*). Paraguay's national soup, *So'o-Iosopy*, is built around finely ground beef. Sometimes thin cuts of meat and poultry are stuffed with vegetables, then rolled and grilled, as in Uruguay's colorful *Pamplona de pollo* (Stuffed Chicken Breasts, page 245) and Argentina's well-named *matambre* (literally, "hunger-killer"). And sometimes, but not often enough for my taste, the relentless onslaught of meat is broken up with grilled vegetables, such as eggplant, peppers, and mushrooms.

Don't get me wrong. There's more to the region's gastronomy than just beef. Consider *sopa paraguaya*, a Paraguayan cornbread that resembles North American corn pudding. Chileans take the dish one step further in their popular *pastel de choclo*, a rib-sticking casserole of corn, chicken, beef, sofrito, olives, raisins, and hard-cooked eggs served in the pot in which it was cooked. Chile is also one of the world's great havens for fish-lovers. The country boasts 2,600 miles of Pacific coastline and an extraordinary variety of seafood. *Locos* (Chilean abalone) plays an important role in the country's cuisine, as does *Caldillo* (Chilean Fish Stew, page 232), a chowderlike soup made with a prized Pacific seafood called *congrio* (conger eel).

THE SAVORY SAMBAS OF BRAZIL

Our last stop on this brief tour of the cuisines of Latin America is Brazil. The largest country in Latin America boasts a very different style of cooking due to its colonization by Portugal, not Spain.

Brazil's cuisine is as diverse as its 156 million inhabitants. The Portuguese brought a lasting taste for olives, onions, garlic, shellfish, and *bacalao* (salt cod). The Indians of Brazil's rain forests taught the Europeans how to enjoy a host of tropical fruits and vegetables, from *mandioca* (cassava root) to *cajú* (green cashews). Africans added okra, yams, peanuts, dried shrimp, and palm oil to the Brazilian melting pot—not to men-

tion an extreme fondness for fiery malagueta chile peppers. These foods were introduced when African slaves were brought to the New World to work the sugar plantations. The African influence can be seen Brazil's *Moqueca de peixe* (Brazilian Seafood Stew, page 238), a sort of *Bahian* (northern Brazilian) bouillabaisse flavored with garlic, cilantro, and coconut milk.

Brazil's national dish, *feijoada* (black bean stew), is perhaps the most lavish bean dish in Latin America. It contains more than a dozen different cuts of pork and other meats. Brazilians love beans and serve them at almost every meal in dozens of delectable dishes. Given the local fondness for palm oil, bacon, and other saturated fats, it might be stretching things a bit to call Brazilian cooking health food. Nonetheless, menus abound with corn, wheat, rice, and other grain dishes, plus a dazzling array of tropical fruits.

WHAT'S IN A NAME?

Latin America's incredible ethnic and gastronomic diversity has led to an almost Tower of Babel–esque confusion of nomenclature.

Depending on where you are in Latin America, the same name can refer to extremely different dishes. In México and Central America, *tortilla* refers to a cornmeal flat bread, while in the Spanish-speaking Caribbean, it describes a Spanish-style omelet chock-full of onions and potatoes. In México, *enchilada* means a dish of rolled corn tortillas filled with cheese or chicken, while in Honduras, it describes a sort of open-faced sandwich made from a crisply fried tortilla topped with stewed shredded chicken. And when Cubans, Dominicans, or Puerto Ricans speak of *enchilado*, they have in mind a spicy seafood stew.

But equally confusing is the fact that there are many different names in Latin America for the same foods or dishes. Meat pies are called *empanadas* in Cuba and Chile, *pastelitos* in Nicaragua, and *salteñas* in Bolivia. Red beans and rice are called *congrí* in eastern Cuba, *gallo pinto* in Costa Rica, and "rice and beans" in coastal Guatamala (an echo, perhaps, of the English heritage of neighboring Belize). *Frijoles* is the generic term for beans in many parts of Latin America, but Puerto Ricans call them

habichuelas. The pumpkinlike squash known as *calabaza* in México and the Spanish-speaking Caribbean is called *huicoy* in Guatamala, *abóbora* in Brazil, and *ahuyuma* and *zapallo* in southern South America.

In translating this book, we have chosen the terms most widely used by Hispanic communities living in the United States and included common alternatives whenever possible. The glossary on page 50 also defines ingredients and lists alternate names.

HEALTH AND HISTORY OF LATIN AMERICAN COOKING

Juárez is a Mexican border city that's literally a stone's throw from El Paso, Texas. To get to Juárez from El Paso, you need only walk across a bridge that takes you over the Río Grande. The crossing lasts about 10 minutes and it transports you from one country to another, one culture to another, and one cuisine to another. When I took the walk, it revealed some of the key health issues in Latin American cooking.

My first stop in Juárez was the central food market (my first stop in any city). As a cook, I was struck by the incredible wealth of raw materials, especially the quality and variety of fruits and vegetables. There were crimson mountains of slender red *chiles de árbol*, silolike stacks of *nopales* (cactus paddles), and bins brimming with *naranjas agrias* (sour oranges) and tiny, tangy, yellowgreen Mexican limes. From woven baskets rose the fragrant aromas of herbs such as *epazote* and *hoja santa* ("holy" leaf with a taste similar to licorice). Tables sagged under mounds of soft, juicy, shockingly red tomatoes that had been

grown and harvested for their flavor, not—as is usually the case in the United States—for their ability to be shipped from coast to coast without spoiling.

It was, in short, a produce-lover's dream—an eye-popping display of luscious fruits and vegetables that would be the envy of any health-minded cook in North America.

As I came to the edge of the market, I found myself on the opposite end of the health spectrum—a street lined with fry shops. One stall after another was filled with greasy piles of *chicharrones* (fried pork rinds). The air (and soon my shirt) was thick with the smell of rendered pork fat. I made my way past mounds of pork and chicken cracklings, deep-fried meats, and tubs of solid lard.

Fresh produce and fried pork rinds, luscious vegetables and fat-laden meats, exquisitely fragrant fruits and pools of saturated animal fat—herein lies the paradox of Latin American cooking. It starts with raw materials that are the very foundation of a healthy diet. Then, it makes extensive use of animal fats and deep-fat frying.

BACK IN THE DAYS . . .

A bit of regional history helps explain the enigma of Latino cooking. The Americas are believed to have been settled by Asiatic nomads who walked across the Bering Strait as early as 38,000 B.C. At the time, a land bridge joined Asia and Alaska. Some 9,000 years ago, according to food historian Reay Tannahill in her book *Food in History*, cave dwellers in the Tamaulipas Mountains of México began to domesticate two essential foods of the pre-Colombian Americas: squash and chile peppers. By 3000 B.C., the peoples of Perú succeeded in domesticating the potato.

In time, great civilizations arose throughout the region. In central México, the Aztecs flourished; Central America was home to the Mayans; and in western South America, the Incas ruled. Each civilization built impressive cities and produced agricultural and technological achievements that rivaled any in Europe. By the time the Spanish arrived, the Americas offered an astonishing assortment of ingredients and sophisticated and complex cuisines.

Ponder for a moment how many of the world's primary foods originated in the Americas. Potatoes, corn, squash, avocados, chayotes, sweet potatoes, jícama, yuca, malanga, and cactus—to name just a few vegetables. Tomatoes, tomatillos, pineapples, papayas, guavas, cherimoyas, passion fruit, cashews, walnuts, brazil nuts, and peanuts—to name a few fruits and nuts.

Chile peppers were also native to the Americas, as were seasonings like allspice and annatto. Even turkey was a New World food (the people of México domesticated it). So was the arrowroot used to thicken the gravy. As for sweets, the entire world's dessert repertory would be severely impoverished without two ingredients that originated in Latin America: vanilla and chocolate. Food historians suggest that the native peoples of the Americas had a much more interesting, diverse, and healthy selection of foods available in their markets in the fifteenth century than Europeans did in theirs.

Hundreds of dishes popular in Latin America today originated with the Aztecs, Mayans, and Incas—from the salsas, *moles*, and tortilla dishes beloved by Mexicans to the ajiacos (meat and vegetable stews) and barbecued meats enjoyed in the Spanish-speaking Caribbean. The English word *barbecue* originated on the island of Hispaniola from the Arawak Indian term *barbacoa*, which refers to the cooking technique of spicing and smoke-drying meat on lattices of green wood built over a fire. The Incas invented the grain puddings and potato soups now prized by Peruvians and Bolivians. The toasted manioc flour enjoyed by modern Brazilians, Uruguayans, and Argentinians (who sprinkle it over grilled meats) originated with native Indians of the Amazon. Tamales and their cousins *nacatamales*, *pasteles*, *hallacas*, and *humitas* were popular throughout the region. These variations on a theme of a corn-based dough cooked in a corn husk or banana leaf seem to have sprung up simultaneously all over the continent.

NUTRITIONAL WISDOM OF THE ANCIENTS

The most striking fact is that the pre-Columbian diet was intuitively healthy. The main ingredients were vegetables, fruits, and grains. Meats and seafood were used more as condiments than as principle dishes. Fats were virtually unknown, as flavor came mostly from nutrient-rich chile peppers and indigenous seasonings such as annatto, allspice, *epazote*, and *hoja santa*. In the absence of sugar (which came later with Christopher Columbus), sweets were kept to a minimum. As for coffee, distilled alcohol, and other stimulants, they simply didn't exist.

Native Latin Americans also had very advanced cooking methods. Corn was traditionally soaked in limewater (an alkaline medium) making niacin, an important vitamin found in corn, available to the body. This preparation method protected Latin Americans from devastating maladies like pellagra, a disease discovered later in Spain and associated with corn consumption. For years, scientists did not understand why pellagra was not common in México and Central America, where corn is eaten nearly every day. By preparing their corn in limewater and making niacin available, Latin Americans protected themselves from the disease.

Many foods native to the region were also nutritional gold mines. Quinoa, the ancient grain of the Incas, contains 3 times as much protein as wild rice and 30 times as much phosphorus as bananas. A ½-cup serving of the Aztec grain amaranth boasts a whopping 28 percent of the Daily Value (DV) for protein, while wheat provides only 21 percent. Amaranth also contains more of the essential amino acids lysine and methionine than barley. Amaranth was used by the Aztecs for traditional religious ceremonies, so Hernando Cortés and his followers outlawed its cultivation in an effort to stop human sacrifices. In so doing, this nutritious grain was virtually eliminated from the Latin American diet for centuries.

Beans were another super food in the Aztec nutritional arsenal. Many of the world's most popular beans, such as black beans, kidney beans, pinto beans, and lima beans (named for the capital of Perú) originated in the Americas. Beans are one of the best sources of protein. A ½-cup serving of cooked beans contains about 15 percent of the DV (depending on the variety) and little of the artery-clogging saturated fat found in animal proteins. Beans are loaded with fiber, most of which is cholesterol-lowering, blood sugar–controlling soluble fiber, and kidney beans especially are associated with a lower risk of heart disease,

stroke, and colon cancer. Plus, they're rich in folate and the antioxidants that are known as polyphenolics, which in test-tube studies worked better than vitamin C in keeping fat in the blood from oxidizing—the first step in the formation of artery-clogging sludge, thereby reducing heart disease risk.

Winter squash are rich in vitamin A and beta-carotene, which may help protect you from cancer. Chiles are loaded with vitamin C, which may do everything from protect gums and skin and reduce the risk of heart disease to ward off colds and lower cancer risk, according to researchers.

Many of these foods are now recommended throughout the world as the basis of a healthy diet geared toward life-long vitality. It seems that pre-Colombian cooks anticipated modern nutrition researchers by centuries. Even today, in rural parts of Latin America, many people eat a traditional diet based on these nutritious beans, grains, and vegetables—with just a sparing use of meat.

OLD WORLD MEETS NEW WORLD

The arrival of the Spanish in the New World revolutionized the region's indigenous cuisines and put the "Latin"

(continued on page 32)

LATIN AMERICAN FOOD TIME LINE

38,000 B.C.

Asiatic nomads are believed to have crossed the Bering Strait and settle the Americas.

6000 B.C.

Maíz (corn) is cultivated in the Tehucan Valley in México and beans are grown in Perú.

1492

Christopher Columbus "discovers" the Americas. He also discovers foods there unknown in the Old World, including corn, sweet potatoes, chile peppers, allspice, and pineapples. The arrival of the Europeans in turn revolutionizes New World food over the next few decades, as they bring livestock (cattle, sheep, pigs, chickens, and horses), wine, oil, rice, and spices, plus new technologies such as metal cookware, baking, deep-fat frying, and the art of distillation.

1501

Spanish settlers at Santo Domingo bring the first African slaves to Hispaniola, an island in the West Indies. The slave trade begins. By the 1700s, 7 million Africans are enslaved in the Americas. Africans introduce their own foods to the New World, including okra, palm oil, and yams.

7000 B.C.

Cave dwellers in México's Tamaulipas Mountains begin to domesticate two essential foods of the pre-Colombian Americas: squash and chile peppers.

3000 B.C.

The potato is domesticated in Perú.

1493

Sugarcane brought from the Canary Islands is planted by Columbus at Santo Domingo, capital city of the Dominican Republic. The stage is set for the plantation economy and slavery in the Caribbean and Brazil, not to mention the Latin American passion for sweet desserts.

1502

Columbus drinks *xocoatl* (chocoatl) aboard his ship in the Gulf of Honduras. This drink is made from pounded cocoa beans and spices. It is the precursor to modern-day hot chocolate. Columbus is unimpressed but takes some home with him anyway.

1519–1521

Hernando Cortés begins the conquest of México. Europeans get their first glimpse of Mexican foods such as tortillas, *moles*, salsas, and turkey.

1816

Argentina declares independence from Spain. México does the same in 1821. Brazil declares independence from Portugal one year later. The cuisines of these regions start to diverge from that of the motherland.

1930

According to one legend, the margarita is invented by Doña Bertha, owner of Bertita's Bar in Taxco, México. Around the same time period, other bartenders on both sides of the Río Grande lay claim to the drink's invention.

1991

For the first time in history, salsa sales surpass ketchup in U.S. supermarkets. The Latinization of the American diet goes into full swing.

1529

A Spanish missionary reports that the Aztecs put chile peppers on everything they eat, including chocolate.

1912

Pharmacologist Wilbur Scoville devises the first system for measuring the relative "heat" of a chile pepper, ranging from 0 to 300,000 Scoville Units. The jalapeño pepper measures a modest 2,500 to 5,000 Scoville units. The incendiary habanero chile tips the scales at 250,000 to 450,000 Scoville units.

1973

Mexican-born Ninfa Laurenza popularizes fajitas in North America at her Ninfa's Restaurant in Houston. The Tex-Mex food boom is born.

1996

Oldways Preservation and Exchange Trust and the Harvard School of Public Health develop the Healthy Traditional Latin American Diet Pyramid (see page 4). This pyramid emphasizes the healthy traditional foods of Latin America and offers diet and lifestyle recommendations to help Latin Americans live healthier lives.

in Latin American cooking. The Spanish brought some good and some controversial changes to the region's traditional food ways.

First, the good news. The Spanish introduced a host of Old World ingredients to the Americas. Meats like beef, lamb, pork, goat, and chicken were new to this part of the globe. Dairy products, like milk, cream, sour cream, and cheese had never been used in the region. Citrus fruits like oranges and limes (which are now essential in Mexican and Spanish-Caribbean cocktails and marinades) were hitherto unknown. Grains like wheat flour for making bread and pastries, and even rice, were new. Seasonings like cumin and oregano (now cornerstones of Spanish-Caribbean cooking), saffron, cinnamon, cloves, nutmeg, and anise brought diverse flavors to the New World table.

Sugar, in the form of sugarcane, arrived in 1493 in what is now the Dominican Republic. Without it, there may never have been a Latino dessert like flan. Other key imports included beverages like coffee and brandy.

The Portuguese were also active in the transcontinental trade, bringing a wide variety of Old World, African, and Asian foods to the Americas. Portuguese slavers and supply ships introduced two fruits that would become mainstays in the Latin diet: bananas and mangoes. Millions of slaves were brought from Africa to work the sugarcane plantations that soon stretched from Havana in Cuba to Bahia in East Brazil. And with them came palm oil, yams, and okra.

Equally influential were the new kitchen technologies introduced by Europeans. The oven (invaluable for baking breads and desserts), metal pots and pans, and techniques for sautéing, deep-frying, and rendering pork fat changed the face of Latin American cooking. Europeans also brought several new manufacturing technologies that had a profound impact on New World economies and nutrition: the oil and grape press, the wine barrel, the lambic or still, and the sugar mill.

So what's the bad news? You just read about it. It turns out that much of what the Europeans introduced to Latin America eventually created an unhealthy diet for the region's inhabitants. Meats, lard, butter, cream, cheese, sugar, and alcohol would in time lead to increased risk of obesity, heart disease, some types of cancer, and diabetes. The adoption of deep-fat frying as one of the preferred cooking methods also had a harmful effect.

The traditional Latin American diet

has yet another outside influence with mixed health consequences: North America. As Latin American countries like México and Brazil have become more industrialized and affluent, they have begun to take on the poor eating and lifestyle habits of their North American neighbors. Consumption of plant-based foods and vigorous physical activity have decreased, while consumption of red meats, fast food, high-fat snack foods, and tobacco products have risen dramatically.

"In our studies, carbonated beverages are the number one source of calories for Mexican Americans living in southern Texas," reports Rebecca Reeves, R.D., doctor of public health and chief dietitian at the Baylor College of Medicine Nutrition Research Clinic in Houston. The next most popular foods among Mexican Americans are beans, flour tortillas (which replaced corn tortillas), and beef. "Beans," says Dr. Reeves, "are a healthy component of the diet, but they are cooked with excessive amounts of fat."

To witness this unhealthy progression, you need only look at traditional Latino dishes that have crossed the border into North America. Consider that Tex-Mex favorite, tacos. South of the border, the taco (or *taquito*, as it's more commonly known) consists of a fresh, soft corn tortilla garnished with a few shreds of grilled meat, heaping spoonfuls of shredded cabbage, diced onion, radish, and other fresh vegetables, explosively flavorful and utterly fat-free salsas, and perhaps a smidgen of full-flavored cheese. The traditional dish consists primarily of grains (tortillas) and vegetables, with a tiny portion of meat and cheese used for flavoring. Take a look at the traditional Mexican *taquito* when it becomes the Americanized taco that we know at U.S. fast-food emporiums. It looks nothing like the original. The tortilla is deep-fried to make a crisp shell that stays closed. The lean grilled meat becomes fat-drenched ground beef. The chopped vegetables give way to watery iceburg lettuce. And the light sprinkle of sharp-tasting cheese becomes a gluey carpet of bland-tasting processed cheese product. It's an ignominious and unhealthy end for one of México's healthiest street foods.

TRADITIONAL FLAVOR WITH A FRACTION OF THE FAT

The traditional Latin American diet has certainly changed with the times. It began as one of the world's healthiest, emphasizing grains, vegetables, and fruits. But today, much Latino cooking can pose a threat to your health. The key to healthy Latin cooking is getting the best of both worlds—the Old and the New. That means combining the traditional healthy Latin diet with the familiar flavors of contemporary Latin home cooking.

For instance, plantains are a traditional favorite, particularly in the Spanish-speaking Caribbean and Central America. Using contemporary cooking methods, they're often deep-fried to make *Tostones* (Twice-Cooked Plantains, page 142), *Maduros* (Grilled Ripe Plantains, page 144), and *Patacones* (Plantain "Surfboards," page 143). To get the familiar flavors of these dishes with less fat, I use a method called bake-frying. The food is simply brushed with oil and baked at a high temperature to replicate the process of deep-frying. The fat savings are tremendous. (See page 41 for more on bake-frying.) I use the bake-frying method for healthy versions of dishes as diverse as Mexican *Chiles rellenos con elote* (Chiles Rellenos with Corn, page 146) and Panamanian *Carimañolas* (Stuffed Yuca Fritters, page 87).

Meat is another favorite ingredient of the Latin palate. Think about the profligate consumption of meat in Uruguay and Argentina, where as much as 2 pounds of beef is consumed per person per day. To make healthier versions of familiar meat dishes, I harken back to the traditional Latin American diet, using lean cuts of meat and using them more sparingly. For a richly flavored *Parillada argentina completa* (Argentinian Mixed Grill, page 283) without all the fat, I use a little less meat and incorporate more vegetables into the meal. Or check out the robust *Ropa vieja* (Braised Skirt Steak, page 260) or *Carne guisada estilo salvadoreño* (Salvadoran Beef Stew, page 262). These dishes have all the traditional flavor with a lot less fat.

Sugary drinks and desserts are popular from one end of Latin America to the other. Most add loads of empty calories to your diet with no nutritional return. Again, I looked back to the traditional Latin American diet for answers. It offered up plenty of classic fruit-based drinks made without excess sugar, like *Agua de horchata* (Cinnamon-Almond Cooler, page 349) and a variety of *batidos*, the original fruit smoothies (see the recipes beginning on page 348).

Some traditional drinks even include health-boosting grains like oats and corn, and they taste terrific. Other drinks, like *Chocolate mexicano* (Mexican Hot Chocolate, page 344) needed only a few small changes to make them healthier. Desserts were a little trickier, but with minor adjustments, I found that you can enjoy healthful versions of treats like *Flan* (page 316) and *Tres leches nicaragüense* (Nicaraguan Three Milks Cake, page 328) without missing the fat for a second.

By merging traditional Latin American dishes with contemporary methods for healthy cooking, you can indulge to your heart's content in great-tasting Latin food. Many of the cuisine's classic dishes are already healthy and bursting with fresh flavors. For the others, it's only a matter of making a few minor changes in ingredients and cooking methods. The payoff is tremendous. Over time, a change here and a change there can lead to reduced risk of disease, more energy, increased vitality, and a greater joy of eating.

A NOTE ON RECIPES

Each recipe in this book contains a "Before" and "After" nutritional analysis under the heading "Nutrition Snapshot." The "Before" analyses were calculated using a typical version of the recipe. The "After" analyses were calculated using the ingredients and methods listed in the recipe that follows the analysis. In many cases, the traditional recipe is naturally healthy, as in salsas. In these cases, no change to the recipe was made, and the "Before" and "After" analyses are identical. In all cases, "optional" ingredients are not included in the analysis. Salt is included in the analysis only when specific amounts of salt are listed in the recipe. When alternatives are given in the ingredient list, the analysis is based only on the first ingredient. Recipes with the "Pronto!" logo can be prepared in 30 minutes or less.

SECRETS OF HEALTHY LATIN COOKING

It doesn't take much to make tra-ditional Latin food healthier. In fact, many of the customary ingredients are naturally healthy. A few new ingredi-ents, some new cookware and tech-niques, and a subtle shift in the way you think about recipes, meals, and menu planning can be enough to enact the transformation to a healthy diet for you and your family.

THINK FLAVOR, NOT FAT

Intense flavors, not fats, create the real richness of healthy, satisfying Latin food. Call on the wide spectrum of sea-sonings in Latin cooking to boost fla-vors without adding fat. Look to robust flavorings like chiles. They range from medium-hot, grassy-tasting jalapeños to cool and smoky dried chiles pasillas. Condiments such as vinegar and soy sauce might add that needed bit of zip in your favorite recipe. Or use souring agents such as tamarind and sour or-ange juice to lend a flavor counterpoint to the sweet ingredients in a recipe. Don't forget herbs and spices. Fresh or dried, they can elevate a dish from the flavor doldrums without a speck of fat. Herbs like cilantro and oregano and spices like cumin and anise are key fla-voring ingredients in countless Latin dishes. Fresh herbs are best, especially when it comes to cilantro and parsley. The dried varieties of these herbs aren't nearly as flavorful.

If you have a recipe that calls for a lot of fat and only a little of these intensely flavored ingredients, reverse the propor-tion. Use more robust seasonings and aro-matics to keep the flavor while skipping the fat. Here are some other ways to make your Latin cooking healthier.

Choose fats that have flavor. I don't advocate eliminating fat completely. In-stead, I recommend using less. One or two tablespoons of oil or lard are usually enough to sauté vegetables, make salad dressings and marinades, and baste grilled foods. But it's important to choose a fat that gives you flavor. The two main fats used in this book are olive oil and, believe it or not, lard. Both of these ingre-dients have some nutritional bonuses and both are very high in flavor.

Mix lard with oil. Lard is the traditional cooking fat of much of Latin America, especially México and the Spanish-speaking Caribbean. It's prized not only for its affordability and convenience but also for its rich flavor. Dishes as diverse as Puerto Rican *pasteles* (meat pies) and Mexican refried beans simply don't taste right unless they contain this essential Latin ingredient.

On the down side, lard is fairly high in saturated fat, which has the potential to raise blood cholesterol and put you at risk for heart disease. It's also somewhat low in the more heart-healthy monounsaturated fat. To take advantage of lard's incredible flavor without putting yourself at risk for disease, use a combination of lard and oil in your cooking. This combination works wonders in low-fat versions of dishes like refried beans. But remember that fat is fat, no matter what it's source. Try not to use more than 1 teaspoon of lard per person in any given dish.

Place the fat where you can taste it. Throughout the recipes in this book, you'll see that fats like olive oil are brushed onto tortillas or drizzled over salads just before serving. The surface application of fat guarantees that the first thing that your tongue will taste is the olive oil or lard. That first impression is the most important. Food brushed with fat can taste as though it has fat throughout it. Yet it will be healthier because the fat is only on the surface.

Take stock. Chicken and vegetable stocks are instrumental in reducing the fat but keeping the flavor in Latin cooking. In the *Tamales mexicanos* (Mexican Tamales, page 170) and the *Nacatamales* (Nicaraguan Tamales, page 174), you'll find stock added to the *masa* (cornmeal dough) with only a minimal amount of the traditional lard. Stock retains the familiar texture of the cornmeal dough without all the fat of lard. You can substitute stock for some or all of the oil in salad dressings, for the cream in soups and casseroles, and for the lard or oil in a variety of cornmeal dishes.

Stock has so much flavor, you won't miss the fat—especially if you use homemade stocks like the ones beginning on page 360. If you don't have time to make stock from scratch, use canned. Be sure to buy a variety with less sodium and fat than conventional types. If you buy a low-sodium variety that's not low in fat, here's how to defat the broth at home. Put the whole can the refrigerator. When you open the can, the fat will have congealed on top. Simply scrape it off, and you're good to go.

Eat less meat. Many Latinos enjoy eating meat. And there's nothing wrong with that. But experts say that eating too much can lead to a host of health woes, including heart disease and colon cancer. One of the keys to good health is eating less meat and using leaner cuts. Consider the numbers: 5 ounces of lean pork tenderloin contains only 5.6 grams of fat, 1.9 grams of saturated fat, and 75 milligrams of cholesterol. The same amount of fatty pork shoulder tips the scales at 31 grams of fat, 11.4 grams of saturated fat, and 90 milligrams of cholesterol. On average, the meat recipes in this book give you a 4- to 6-ounce serving of a lean cut of meat. When properly flavored and combined with grains and vegetables, this amount provides satisfaction aplenty—minus the ill health consequences.

Use meat as a condiment. Another strategy for healthier eating is increasing the proportion of grains and vegetables to meats. Mexicans do this instinctively when they eat *taquitos* (soft tacos), fresh tortillas that are garnished with shredded cabbage, diced tomatoes, salsa, and just a small amount of highly flavored meat. Try this strategy in your favorite soups and stews. The 4 ounces of beef per person in the *Carne guisada estilo salvadoreño* (Salvadoran Beef Stew, page 262) is a moderate amount compared with that of the original dish. And the new version is still loaded with flavor. The only major difference is an increase in the proportion of vegetables to meat and the addition of more seasonings.

Try turkey instead of beef. Many cooks find that they can substitute turkey for beef in their favorite ground beef dishes. You can replace up to half of the ground beef in *picadillo* and other chopped beef dishes with lean ground turkey breast without much change in the flavor. If you're used to eating mostly red meats, make this change gradually. At first, try replacing just one-quarter of the beef with ground turkey breast. Once your taste buds have time to adjust, slowly move up to using half beef and half turkey. Soon you may find that you like the dish with all turkey. And by then, you will have saved dozens of fat grams.

Skin your chicken. Chicken is one of the most popular, tasty, and economical foods in Latin America. Most of the fat in chicken is concentrated in the skin. The second-highest source of fat is the dark meat. If you want to trim the fat in a chicken dish, use the leanest cut: skinless chicken breasts. Chicken breasts may be more expensive, but they pay off big time in fat savings. And if you buy the boneless variety, they're easier to use. Even if you use chicken legs or whole chickens, you can still benefit from some fat savings. Simply remove the skin and visible fat before eating.

Trade in whole eggs for whites. Most of the fat and cholesterol in an egg resides in the yolk. Egg whites are almost pure protein. So are egg substitutes, which consist chiefly of pasteurized egg whites with a little food coloring. Use egg whites or egg substitutes for making healthier Mexican egg breakfasts like *Huevos rancheros modernos* (Huevos Rancheros, page 186) and *Chilaquiles* (Tortilla, Egg, and Green Salsa Casserole, page 204). To fire up the flavor, add chiles and extra spices. For egg-based

desserts like *Flan* (page 316), use egg whites or a combination of whole eggs and egg whites.

GET SWEET ON SUGAR ALTERNATIVES

Fats aren't the only nutritional culprits in Latino cooking. Sugar is a Latin obsession. Latin desserts tend to be very sweet by North American standards. And to satisfy the Latin sweet tooth, soft-drink bottlers often add more sugar to the beverages made for the Latin American market.

According to health experts, high sugar consumption can lead to tooth decay, diabetes, increased triglyceride levels (which raises your risk of heart attack), and unwanted weight gain. Throughout this book, I've reduced the amount of sugar in traditional desserts without sacrificing flavor. In many cases, you can cut the sugar in a traditional recipe by up to 30 percent with no perceptible flavor loss. Here are some other ways to cut your sugar intake while keeping the sweetness.

Look for healthier sweeteners. One way to make desserts more healthy is to use alternative sweeteners, like honey, molasses, or one of the Latin American brown sugars such as *piloncillo*. These ingredients are less refined than white sugar, so they contain trace elements of healthy vitamins and minerals. One tablespoon of molasses contains 585 milligrams of potassium and 3.2 milligrams of iron. Plus, these sweeteners have more flavor. Sugar is merely sweet, while honey, molasses, and *piloncillo* have a distinctive earthy caramel or malt flavor in addition to the sweetness. That extra flavor allows you to use less.

Sweeten with spices and extracts. To enrich the taste of desserts without extra sugar, look to spices, flavorings, and extracts. Use whole vanilla beans and cinnamon sticks; the peel (oil-rich outer rind) of oranges, limes, and lemons; and perfumed flavorings like orange flower water and real vanilla extract. These ingredients are particularly good for pumping up the flavor of desserts made with dairy products, like puddings and custards. Try them in sauces and syrups, too.

Flavor up with fruit. Many Latin American desserts use mango, pineapple, papaya, soursop, mamey, or other fruits for sweet flavor. The natural fructose in these foods is gentler on your body because it is more gradually digested than the sucrose in white sugar. In your favorite recipes that use fruit, try increasing the amount of fruit and decreasing the amount of sugar. That will make your desserts healthier without eliminating the sweetness.

GO EASY ON THE SALT

According to official health organizations such as the American Heart Association, a diet high in sodium may increase risk of high blood pressure. But that risk is mostly for salt-sensitive individuals, not everyone. If you're in doubt about how much salt you can handle, ask your doctor.

Everyone's tolerance for salt differs, so many of the recipes in this book direct you to season with salt "to taste." In these recipes, I usually use only a pinch or two. Use as much or as little as you feel comfortable with. And if you're trying to cut back on salt intake, here are a couple of ways to do it.

Break out the seasonings. Instead of relying on salt for flavor, look to herbs, spices, and condiments. Chiles are fantastic flavor boosters. Flavored vinegars, such as the *Vinagre de piña* (Pineapple Vinegar, page 379) can perk up a dish at the last minute. And fresh herbs like cilantro and parsley are loaded with bright, clean tastes. If a recipe needs a shot of flavor, don't hold back the spices and seasonings.

Rinse your beans. Canned beans are a great time-saver, shaving as much as 2 hours off cooking time. But most brands of canned beans are loaded with sodium. When buying canned beans, look for low-sodium varieties. Drain the beans in a colander and rinse with cold water. Thoroughly rinsing any canned beans can slash the sodium levels by up to 50 percent.

DITCH THE HIGH-FAT ROUTINE

We've been focusing mostly on ingredients, but cooking methods have a lot to do with healthy cooking, too, particularly when it comes to fats. Break out of old cooking habits by trying a few new tricks. Here are some of my favorite ways to make healthy versions of traditional dishes.

Try frying in the oven. Deep-fat frying is one of the most popular cooking methods in traditional Latin cooking. It's also one of the greatest sources of fat. How do you keep that mouth-watering golden brown color and cracklingly crisp crust without the excess fat? "Fry" your foods in the oven. One of my favorite techniques is something I call bake-frying.

It dramatically lowers the fat in fried foods. What's more, it's cheaper and cleaner than deep-frying.

From fritters and *empanadas* to *tostones* and plantain chips, countless Latino favorites can be bake-fried instead of deep-fried. Here's the basic method: Preheat the oven to 400°F. Place the food on a nonstick baking sheet and lightly spray or brush the food with oil. (You don't even need oil with some items, like tortilla chips.) Bake the food until crisp and golden brown, turning once to ensure even cooking.

You can use this method for breaded meats and seafood, too. Dust the food with flour, dip it in beaten egg whites, and dredge it in bread crumbs, shaking off the excess. Then place the food on a nonstick baking sheet, lightly coat the food with oil, and bake until crisp and brown. The high heat of the oven and a small amount of oil mimic the effects of deep-fat frying. You get a satisfyingly crunchy crust without all the artery-clogging fat.

Fire up your grill. Grilling is a superb way to create intense flavors with little or no fat. The high heat of the grill imparts a delicious flame-broiled taste. If you cook over charcoal or wood, the food also picks up a haunting smoky aroma. This culinary truth isn't lost on the *asadors* (grill masters) of Argentina and Uruguay, who raise the act of grilling to the level of art. Many Latin dishes that are traditionally pan-fried or deep-fried taste wonderful when grilled. To get a taste of what I mean, try the Cuban grilled *Masitas de puerco* (Spiced Pork Bites, page 285) or Colombia's *Bistec a la criolla* (Creole Steak, page 261).

Send up smoke signals. The best fuel for grilling is wood. Latin American grill masters from Juarez to Buenos Aires grill their meats over wood to intensify the flavor. Charcoal briquettes are more readily available in North America. But here's an easy way to achieve the robust smoky flavor of wood-grilled food using your charcoal grill. Head for your nearest hardware store, cookware shop, or gourmet shop and buy a bag of aromatic wood chips. For northern Mexican–style grilling, buy mesquite chips; for Argentinian-style grilling, use oak. Soak the chips in cold water to cover for 1 hour, then drain well. Toss the chips on the coals before you add the food. You'll need about 2 cups of wood chips to grill meat for 4 servings.

Roast your way to aroma. To boost the flavor of vegetables and nuts, roast

them in a dry skillet before cooking. Mexicans routinely do this with onions, garlic, tomatoes, and chiles that are destined for rich-tasting moles and salsas. The vegetables are roasted in a flat cast-iron griddle (called a comal) until the skins are black and blistered. This stove-top technique imparts a delicious charred flavor to the vegetables, caramelizing their natural sugars.

Pan-roasting is another great way to bring out the flavor of nuts, seeds (like pumpkin seeds), and bread crumbs. Roast the nuts, seeds, or crumbs in a dry skillet over medium heat, shaking the pan often, until fragrant and lightly browned. Then, use as little as half as much as the recipe calls for. By roasting these foods, you boost their flavors so that you don't need to use as much.

Sauté in a nonstick skillet. The advent of nonstick cookware revolutionized healthy cooking. With a nonstick skillet, you can sauté vegetables for a *sofrito* (sauté) or *guiso* (stew) and use only a fraction of the fat that you'd need for stainless steel or cast-iron skillets. The slick surface of nonstick cookware helps keep the food from sticking, so you only need a small amount of cooking fat (1 tablespoon for 4 servings will generally do it). When baking food on a nonstick baking sheet, coat the food (instead of the pan) with oil for the best results.

Make magic with marinades. Marinating is one of the most important no-fuss secrets to boosting the flavor of foods without fat. Cubans regularly marinate meats and seafoods in adobo, a tangy marinade including cumin, garlic, and sour orange juice. Similar mixtures are found in Puerto Rico, the Dominican Republic, and Central America. In Brazil, cooks would be lost without their *tempeiro*, a combination of garlic, lime juice, hot peppers, and bell peppers. Marinades can intensify the flavors in almost any meat, chicken, or fish dish. The traditional mari-

nades of Latin America include lemon juice or lime juice, garlic, and cumin (see the recipe for *ceviche* on page 90). Mexicans often add guajillo or chipotle chiles, while Peruvians add *ají amarillo* chiles.

Once you start experimenting with these healthy ingredients and techniques, they'll soon become second nature in your cooking. Best of all, you and your family will get to enjoy all the tasty fruits of your labors. And you'll be cooking your way down the path to a healthy Latin diet.

GUIDE TO LOW-FAT FOODS

Healthy Latin cooking is surprisingly similar to traditional Latin cooking. In fact, a healthy diet can be as easy as making a few small changes to your shopping list. Simple switches to lower-fat alternatives can dramatically reduce the fat in your cooking without sacrificing flavor. Here's a guide to the key ingredients that can help you make a sound investment in health. Keep these on hand for fantastic meals.

DIP INTO LOW-FAT DAIRY PRODUCTS

Milk products like cream, sour cream, and cream cheese present one of the greatest challenges for the healthy Latin cook. These ingredients are used in everything from savory appetizers to dulcet desserts. Fortunately, today's supermarkets are teeming with a wide array of lower-fat options.

Milk and cream. As a rule, we use skim milk in my family. The fat savings are considerable: 1 cup of skim milk has only 90 calories, 0.4 grams of fat, and 4 milligrams of cholesterol. The same amount of whole milk has 150 calories, 8 grams of fat (5 of them saturated), and 33 milligrams of cholesterol. Switching to skim is an easy way to start reducing the fat in your diet and cooking today. If you're used to whole milk, try 2 percent low-fat milk at first. Once you're comfortable with that, switch to 1 percent. You'll find that low-fat milks, including skim milk, work well in most Latin foods, particularly desserts. Sweets like *natillas* (puddings) and flans can retain the rich flavors of the original with the addition of just a few flavor boosters. To make up for the lost richness of whole milk, add vanilla, cinnamon, or grated lemon or orange peel before cooking.

One of the most popular desserts in Latin America is *Dulce de leche* (Milk Caramel, page 324), a sort of liquid fudge or caramel sauce made by boiling down milk and sugar. To make an easy, low-fat version, I use sweetened condensed skim milk and boil it down right in the can.

Evaporated skimmed milk. Before the advent of refrigeration, evaporated milk was a popular shelf-stable dairy product in Central America and the Spanish-speaking Caribbean. In fact, it still is. And here's the best part: A simple switch from evaporated milk to evaporated skimmed milk can save you 70 calories, 10 grams of fat, and 33 milligrams of cholesterol per ½ cup. Because it's used mostly in baked desserts with other ingredients, any flavor difference is hardly perceptible.

Sweetened condensed milk. This thick, sweet dairy product has become a cornerstone of Latin baking. It's essential for making rich, silky flans, luscious *dulce de leche*, and creamy drinks like Puerto Rican *coquito*, a type of eggnog made with coconut milk. Try using sweetened condensed skim milk. It has less fat, calories, and cholesterol than regular sweetened condensed milk and is available in most supermarkets. Sweetened condensed skim milk can also be used to replace some or all of the high-fat coconut milk in desserts like *Tembleque* (Shivering Coconut Pudding, page 323) and *Tres leches nicaragüense* (Nicaraguan Three Milks Cake, page 328).

Sour cream. A wide variety of Mexican dishes are garnished with a dollop of thick and rich sour cream. Hondurans and other Central Americans use a sour cream–like product called *Mantequilla hondureña* (Honduran "Butter," page 209)

to accompany tortilla dishes like *Baleada* (Bean Tortilla, page 208). To reduce the fat in these recipes, I call for nonfat or low-fat sour cream. Using these lower-fat products can add up to considerable fat savings. A quarter-cup of regular sour cream contains 123 calories, 12 grams of fat (8 of them saturated), and 26 milligrams of cholesterol. The same amount of nonfat sour cream has only 34 calories and virtually no fat, saturated fat, or cholesterol. Because the quality of low-fat sour creams varies from brand to brand, be sure to shop around for the brand that you like best. There are good ones out there.

Cheeses. Latin America is home to some of the world's finest cheeses, from Central America's *queso blanco* to Argentina's *provoleta*. Nothing can rival the rich flavor and creamy texture of cheese. However, many varieties of cheese are loaded with saturated fat and cholesterol.

As you probably know, many low-fat and nonfat cheeses are available at your local supermarket. I find the texture and flavor of these cheeses to be troublesome, at best. It may surprise you, but I recommend buying the strongest, sharpest, most richly flavored traditional cheese that you can find. Then use just a little bit. My refrigerator is never short on good cheeses like *queso blanco* (if unavailable, substitute sharp Cheddar, Parmesan, or Greek feta), *queso oaxaqueño* (if unavailable, substitute Romano cheese), sharp cheddar cheese, aged gouda, Parmesan, and Romano. Because these cheeses have such strong flavors, a little goes a long way. For example, 1 tablespoon of grated queso blanco is enough to give most people the rich cheesy flavor that they seek. And that amount contains only 52 calories, 4 grams of fat, 3 grams of saturated fat, and 13 milligrams of cholesterol. In fact, Mexican cooks often use less than 1 tablespoon of queso blanco to garnish a dish.

To maximize the flavor of cheese, be sure to place it where you can taste it right off the bat: sprinkled on top of a dish or individual serving. That way, the first thing that you taste is cheese, which creates the impression that cheese is found throughout the dish.

Cream cheese. I'm about to contradict myself here. The one exception to my philosophy of using a little of a full-flavored, full-fat-cheese is cream cheese.

Low-fat cream cheese has a reasonably good texture and piquant flavor similar to the original product. I use it for making a great-tasting low-fat guava cheesecake that has half the calories and a quarter the fat of a typical *Torta cremosa de queso y guayaba* (Guava Cheesecake, page 327). Low-fat cream cheese tastes a lot better than nonfat cream cheese, but the latter will work for the recipes in this book if you need to severely restrict your fat intake.

FAT FACTS

Switching to low-fat ingredients goes a long way toward building a healthier diet. But cooking fats are also a big piece of the puzzle. Here's a look at the best fats for healthy Latin cooking.

Lard. Rendered pork fat (lard) is absolutely essential to authentic Mexican cooking. And while it may seem like the world's unhealthiest fat, it turns out that lard is actually better for you than butter.

Consider the facts. Lard contains about half the cholesterol and a third of the saturated fat of butter. Teaspoon for teaspoon, it contains less total fat than olive oil or canola oil. That's because it contains more water.

So, should you do all your cooking in lard? Well, not so fast. Lard may contain less total fat than olive oil and canola oil, but it contains more harmful saturated fat and less beneficial monounsaturated fat. Here's the best compromise: Use a combination of both lard and canola oil in your cooking. If a traditional recipe calls for lard, use half lard and half canola oil. Lard provides the signature flavor of Latin cooking, while canola oil contributes heart-healthy monounsaturated fat (and less total fat than if you used all canola oil).

The best-tasting lard is freshly rendered pork fat from a neighborhood *carnicería*, or butcher. It will be soupy at room temperature and loaded with flavor. Commercial lard, sold in 1-pound blocks, is available at Hispanic markets and many supermarkets, although it's becoming harder and harder to find this ingredient in non-Latino neighborhoods.

Olive oil and canola oil. These are the two main types of oil that are called for in this book. The first is a full-flavored, fruity oil made from pressed olives. The second is a clear, flavorless oil made from rapeseed.

Olive oil offers the health-minded cook two great benefits. First, it has a wonderful flavor that manages to be nutty, fruity, and aromatic all at the same time. Olive oil is also the highest in monounsaturated fats, which, according to nutritionists, can help increase the beneficial "good" HDL cholesterol and reduce the "bad" LDL cholesterol in your blood, thereby lowering your risk of heart disease.

There's certainly a powerful historical precedent for using olive oil in Latin American cooking. Olive oil was probably the first oil brought to the Americas by the Spanish and the first oil used for cooking in the New World. Plus, some of the best-tasting olive oils come from Spain. Even if it has been replaced by cheaper vegetable oils in contemporary Latin America, olive oil still adds an authentic Spanish accent to countless dishes.

Olive oil comes in two main grades: extra-virgin and pure. Extra-virgin is the most richly flavored, pressed from the choicest olives and containing the least amount of acidity (less than 1 percent). Extra-virgin olive oil is available in any supermarket. Pure olive oil is a highly refined oil that, for reasons of excess acidity or a poor flavor, can't be sold in its natural state. After refining, the oil has between 1 and 1.5 percent acidity.

Often, the manufacturers add a little extra virgin oil to bolster the flavor. Compared with extra-virgin oil, regular olive oil may seem bland, but it's considerably less expensive and useful for dishes where the olive flavor is not critical. When recipes in this book call for extra-virgin olive oil, the oil is being used for its intense flavor. When a recipe calls for olive oil, the oil is needed only for cooking, so you can use a less expensive variety.

Use canola oil when you want a fat that has no distinctive flavor. I often use canola oil for doughs and sometimes for sautéing. Canola oil allows the natural flavors of the foods being cooked to come through more clearly.

Spray oil. Fat is one of the single biggest health problems in the traditional Latin diet. Many recipes in this book call for spray oil or nonstick spray, which is available in cans at any supermarket. Look for either canola oil spray or olive oil spray. The advantage of spray oil is simple: It enables you to apply a microscopically thin layer of oil to plantain chips, breaded chicken breasts, and other foods that can then be bake-fried in the oven. This thin layer of oil enables the foods to develop a crisp crust without drenching them in fat. Spray oil has another advantage: It's amazingly quick and easy to use, saving you time in the kitchen.

CLEVER ALTERNATIVES

Dairy products and cooking oils present the best opportunities to reduce fat in the Latin American diet. But there's no reason to stop there. Keep the flavor that you love without piling on the pounds by using these clever alternatives, too.

Canadian bacon. This is a cured, smoked bacon made from lean pork loin instead of fatty pork belly. Use Canadian bacon to add the rich smoky flavor of regular bacon, with only a fraction of the fat. It makes a great alternative to fatty cuts of pork in dishes like *Sopa de frijoles negros a lo cubano* (Cuban Black Bean Soup, page 102) and Spanish-Caribbean *Mofongo* (Garlicky Plantain Puree, page 74).

Coconut milk. This ingredient is often used to make Brazilian, Colombian, and Honduran soups and desserts. It's a rich creamlike liquid that's extracted from the flesh of freshly grated coconut. Unfortunately, it's also high in fat. A quarter-cup of coconut milk contains 138 calories, 14 grams of fat, and 13 grams of saturated fat.

Here are two alternatives. The first is low-fat coconut milk (sometimes labeled "light" coconut milk in grocery stores). Look for this product in Asian and Hispanic markets, gourmet shops, and the international aisle of large supermarkets.

The second alternative is to combine regular or light coconut milk with coconut water (the cloudy liquid found in the center of a coconut). Coconut water contains virtually no fat, but it's rich in coconut flavor. By using this combination in the popular drink *Coquito* (Coconut Eggnog, page 352), the fat content drops a whopping 87 percent.

Wonton and egg roll wrappers. I once made a startling discovery. I tried making *empanadas* and *pastelitos* using commercial wonton wrappers instead of the traditional pastry dough. The results were fan-

tastic. These thin sheets of noodlelike dough contain a fraction of the fat found in the traditional lard- or shortening-based pastry. Using wonton wrappers slashes fat and calories in significant amounts. A typical serving of pork empanadas made with traditional pastry contains about 420 calories, 28 grams of fat, 5 grams of saturated fat, and 56 milligrams of cholesterol. Made with wonton wrappers, the same amount of *Pastelillos de cerdo a lo puertorriqueño* (Pork Empanadas, page 80) comes down to just 201 calories, 5.2 grams of fat, only 1.6 grams of saturated fat, and just 32 milligrams of cholesterol.

There's another advantage to using egg roll and wonton wrappers: The dough is already made and rolled out, so you can assemble the empanadas in minutes. Look for these thin sheets of ready-made dough in the produce section of most supermarkets and at Asian markets. You can also use egg roll wrappers cut into quarters.

GLOSSARY OF INGREDIENTS AND EQUIPMENT

Some Latin American ingredients and equipment may be new to you. Some may be like old friends. Here's a brief profile of the key players so you can get to know them better.

Amaranth (amaranto). This is a tiny, round, light brown seed native to Central America. The seed comes from a bush with brilliantly colored leaves. The foot-long seed head can contain up to 500,000 seeds, each the size of a grain of sand. Tiny amaranth is a nutritional gold mine: a good source of high-quality protein with five times as much iron and three times as much fiber as whole wheat. A 3½-ounce serving has more calcium than an 8-ounce glass of milk. Look for it in health food stores and Hispanic markets. To pop amaranth, place 1 tablespoon of seeds in a large, deep, dry pot over medium-high heat. Shake the pot to keep the seeds moving. They will pop in seconds like popcorn. Or, see the source list on page 66 for where to find prepopped amaranth.

Anise; anise seed (anís). A tiny brown seed with a sweet licorice-like flavor, anise is used in Mexican moles and Latin American pastries and desserts. The seed comes from an annual plant in the parsley family. For the most flavor, crush anise seeds before using.

Annatto (achiote). This hard, rectangular, rust-colored seed has a tangy, earthy, almost iodine-like flavor. Native to Central America and the Caribbean, it's used widely in these regions and in México (especially in the Yucatán). Annatto is often sold in paste form in these regions, but the paste is harder to come by in the United States (see page 66 for some sources). Most recipes in this book use the seeds, which are available in Hispanic markets and most North American supermarkets. There are several ways to prepare annatto seeds. You can grind them to a powder in a spice mill; soak them in orange juice or water until soft, then crumble; or fry them in oil or lard to make a fragrant, orange-colored cooking fat (see the *Aceite de achiote*, or Annatto Oil, recipe on page 380). A pinch of annatto paste can be substituted in recipes calling for annatto seed. A spoonful of paprika will add the same color, but not the same taste.

Apple banana (plátano manzano).
A short, stubby banana with a pleasant
tartness reminiscent of apples, the
apple banana is about 4 to 6 inches
long and 1 to 1½ inches wide. Let ripen
at room temperature until the skin
splits and becomes dark or spotted and
the fruit is squeezably soft. It's available
in large supermarkets and Hispanic
markets.

**Banana leaves; plantain leaves
(hojas de plátano).** These are large,
shiny green leaves used as wrappers for
making *Nacatamales* (Nicaraguan
Tamales, page 174), and other tamale-
like dishes. They're also used for pit-
roasting in the Yucatán (see *Pollo pibil*,
or Roasted Spiced Chicken, page 248).
The leaves impart a nutty, aromatic
flavor when used as a cooking wrapper.
Available fresh in some Hispanic communities, they are more often found
frozen at Hispanic and Asian markets. If
unavailable, you can use heavy-duty foil
for wrapping, though you'll lose the aromatic flavor.

Bean masher (aplastadora). A
wooden pestle similar to a potato masher,
this is used for mashing beans and is
available at Mexican markets.

**Boniato (batata; camote; Latin
American sweet potatoes).** These hard,
red-skinned, white-fleshed tubers have a
flavor akin to roasted chestnuts. They
are rich in vitamins A and C and include
some protein. Boniatos are much less
sweet than North American sweet potatoes. Although most Americans have
never heard of them, boniatos are the
world's sixth largest food crop. They are
widely available at Hispanic markets and
some large supermarkets. Look for firm
boniatos free of crumbling ends or tiny
wormholes. Prepare boniatos any way
that you would prepare potatoes or
sweet potatoes, especially by baking,
boiling, steaming, and sautéing. Peeled
boniatos should be rubbed with cut
lemon or kept in water to prevent discoloring. Serve boniatos immediately after
cooking, as they become starchy if they
stand for too long.

**Calabaza (huicoy; abóbora;
ahuyuma; zapallo).** A round, hard-
shelled, thick-fleshed winter squash, calabaza is similar in texture and flavor to

butternut squash, but denser and richer. It's used throughout Latin America.

Carne seca (tasajo). This is dried salted beef, a key ingredient in Latin American meat and vegetable stews (*ajiacos*).

Chayote (huisquil; guisquil). Chayote is a tropical squash from a trailing vine related to the cucumber. Native to México, it was cultivated by the Aztecs. Today, it is popular throughout the Caribbean and Brazil. Chayote is shaped like an avocado and can weigh anywhere from 6 ounces to 2 pounds. Depending on the species, the peel can be tan, brown, or green, smooth-skinned or furrowed, and even covered with Velcro-like prickles. Chayote has a delicate flavor similar to cooked cucumber. The first step in cooking chayotes is to boil or steam them whole until tender. If using only the flesh of the squash, peel with a vegetable peeler prior to cooking and cook for 30 to 40 minutes, or until soft. If the chayote will be stuffed, leave the skin on during cooking.

Cherimoya. Native to the highlands of South America, this large, green, dimpled, heart-shaped fruit is deliciousness incarnate. The ivory-colored flesh has a slightly grainy texture, like a pear, with a creamy consistency and complex flavor hinting at mango, pineapple, and custard. It's used in South American drinks and fruit salads.

Chicharrones. These are crispy fried pork rinds. Not a particularly healthy ingredient, but an undeniable favorite, especially in the Spanish-speaking Caribbean and Central America. For a low-fat alternative, cut lean ham steak into cubes and bake in a hot oven until crisp, then blot with paper towels.

Cilantro (fresh coriander leaf). The explosively pungent leaves of the coriander plant, cilantro is an indispensible ingredient for salsa and is widely used throughout the Spanish-speaking Caribbean and Central and South America. When dried, cilantro loses most of its flavor. Fortunately, fresh cilantro is available at most supermarkets. Some people hate cilantro. If you perceive a soapy flavor in the herb, you may be mildly allergic to it.

Cinnamon sticks (ramitas o rajas de canela). Cinnamon sticks are the dried bark of a tropical evergreen tree. There are two types—Ceylon and cassia—but most packages don't specify which type you're getting. Whole cinnamon sticks have a more intense and pleasing flavor than ground cinnamon. Small bottles of cinnamon sticks can be somewhat expensive at supermarkets. To save money, buy whole sticks in bulk at health food stores or Hispanic or Indian markets.

Coconut milk (leche de coco). This creamy white liquid extracted from freshly grated coconut has a consistency similar to half-and-half. Coconut milk is used like a dairy product in the Caribbean, Central America, and Brazil. Unfortunately, it is high in saturated fat, but light versions are available. Look for light coconut milk in the international aisle of large supermarkets or at gourmet shops and Asian markets. One way to get a great coconut-milk flavor without all the fat is to combine coconut water (see the description below) with a small amount of regular or light coconut milk.

Coconut water (agua de coco). This is the cloudy liquid inside a coconut. When you buy a coconut, shake it; you should be able to hear the water slosh around inside. If you don't, the coconut is probably past its prime. To extract the coconut water, use a screwdriver to poke out the "eyes" at the stem end of the coconut. (A few gentle taps with a hammer or rolling pin will do it.) Invert the coconut over a measuring cup with a mesh strainer between the nut and the cup. A typical coconut yields ½ to ¾ cup water.

Comal. A low-sided, cast-iron skillet, the comal is used in México for dry-roasting tomatoes, onions, garlic, chile peppers, and tortillas. Dry-roasting imparts a rich charred flavor. If you don't have a comal, use a cast-iron skillet or nonstick frying pan.

Culantro (recao). This Caribbean herb has thumb-shaped dark green leaves with jagged edges. The flavor is similar to cilantro, but with a whiff of celery and parsley. It's available in Hispanic markets. If you can't find it, substitute one sprig of cilantro for every culantro leaf.

Cumin (comino). One of the defining flavors of Latin cooking, this small, sickle-shaped seed has a musky, earthy flavor. The ground form is usually used in Latin America. Ground cumin is available in spice aisles everywhere.

Epazote. A strongly aromatic and somewhat bitter-tasting herb, it's peculiar aroma lives up to one of its English names: pigweed. It is also known as wormseed, lamb's quarters, goosefoot, and Jerusalem oak. There's something clean, woodsy, and almost antiseptic about its flavor. The herb is used throughout México and Central America. Mexicans claim it reduces the tendency of beans to produce flatulence. Epazote is sold fresh and dried at Mexican and

(continued on page 59)

HOT, HOT, HOT: A GUIDE TO CHILE PEPPERS

Of all the gifts that the New World bestowed on the Old, none had a wider impact than chile peppers. Within a century of its "discovery" by Columbus, the chile pepper had literally circumnavigated the globe and been introduced to regions as diverse as China, India, Thailand, Africa, and Hungary. Everywhere it went, the chile was enthusiastically embraced.

Yet nowhere did the use of chiles become more widespread and sophisticated than in the motherland, the Americas. At least one member of the chile pepper family is enjoyed in every country in Latin America—from Perú's *ají amarillo* to Brazil's fiery *malagueta*. México is best known for chile eating. And rightly so. Mexican cooks use an extraordinary variety of fresh and dried chile peppers to create a whole spectrum of gustatory effects.

Many types of chile peppers are used throughout the recipes in this book. Most varieties can be found at your local supermarket or at Hispanic markets. When appropriate, I have suggested substitutions, but for authentic flavor, try to find the chiles specifically called for. If you have trouble tracking down a chile, see the sources on page 66 for door-to-door delivery.

FRESH CHILES (CHILES FRESCOS)

Anaheim (California; California green; chile verde). This slender, dark green chile is 6 to 8 inches long, 1 to 1½ inches wide. It's mild to moderately hot, with a grassy flavor akin to bell peppers. The relatively large size of the anaheim makes it ideal for stuffing. It is sometimes used to make canned mild green chile peppers. When allowed to ripen, the anaheim is known as a California red.

Habanero. The world's hottest chile, the habanero is 50 times hotter than a jalapeño. The size and shape are more or less that of a walnut. Habaneros have a smooth green, yellow, orange, or red skin and a tongue-blistering bite that may make you feel like you've just bitten into a high-voltage cable. Behind the fierce bite is a complex flavor that is both floral and smoky. No wonder habaneros are popular throughout México (especially the Yucatán), Central America, and the Spanish-speaking Caribbean.

The Scotch bonnet chile is often mistaken for the habanero. Although similar to the habanero, the Scotch bonnet is usually yellow in color and slightly more bonnet-shaped than walnut-shaped.

Jalapeño. The most widely available chile pepper, the jalapeño is bullet-shaped, dark green, 2 to 3 inches long, and ½ to 1 inch wide. It has a sharp, peppery sting that is experienced chiefly in the back of the mouth and throat. Older jalapeños have striated skin and are usually hotter. When smoke-dried, the jalapeño is known as a chipotle chile (see the description on page 56). Jalapeños also come pickled in salt and vinegar. The pickling juice adds a pleasant tartness that offsets the fire of the chiles. Pickled jalapeños are available in the international aisle of most supermarkets. They can be stored in the refrigerator for up to three months.

Poblano. A large (4 inches long, 2½ inches wide), dark green, tapered chile commonly used for stuffing, the poblano looks somewhat like an elongated green bell pepper with collapsed sides. The flavor also hints at bell pepper, but is hotter and more aromatic. If unavailable, use green bell peppers, adding a little minced jalapeño for heat. When dried, the poblano is known as an ancho chile (see the description on page 56).

Rocotillo. The rocotillo chile looks like a miniature pattypan squash. Orange, yellow, or pale green, it's no larger than the tip of your thumb. Like the habanero chile, the rocotillo is highly fragrant and aromatic. Unlike the habanero, the rocotillo isn't the least bit hot. It's a key ingredient in Spanish-Caribbean cooking. If unavailable, Puerto Rico's *ají dulce* or Cuba's *cachucha* make good substitutes. If you can't find those, substitute 2 tablespoons of chopped red bell pepper for every 6 rocotillos called for.

Serrano. A small, bright red or green, torpedo-shaped chile similar in flavor to a jalapeño, the serrano chile is a bit longer and more slender than the jalapeño. For cooking, the two are interchangeable.

(continued)

DRIED CHILES (CHILES SECOS)

Ají amarillo. The name literally means "yellow chile." This golden yellow stinger is about 3 to 4 inches long and just ½ to ¾ inches wide. Ají amarillo is the premier chile in Perú, where it's used to flavor everything from *caucau* (seafood stew) to *papa a la huancaina* (potato salad). Fiery and fruity, it comes in three basic forms: dried, powdered, and in a paste. The three forms can be used interchangeably. Look for ají amarillo in markets catering to a Peruvian clientele. Or substitute cayenne or hot paprika mixed with a pinch of turmeric for color.

Ají mirasol. Similar to ají amarillo, but larger, darker, and milder, the flavor is fruity and medium-hot. It's used in México to make yellow mole and in the Spanish-speaking Caribbean to make sauces.

Ancho. This is a dried poblano chile. Large (3 to 4 inches long and 2 to 3 inches wide), flat, reddish-black in color, and wrinkled like a prune, the ancho has a complex, earthy-fruity flavor with hints of coffee, tobacco, and dried fruit. It's relatively mild in terms of heat, but very flavorful. It's essential for Mexican mole sauces.

Cascabel. Literally, "sleighbell chile," this is a small, reddish-brown, cherry-shaped chile with loose seeds that rattle when shaken. It's hot and slightly sweet with woodsy overtones, and it's used mostly in salsas.

Chipotle. One of the most interesting chiles in the Mexican arsenal, the chipotle is a smoke-dried jalapeño. The flavor is a complex mixture of fire and smoke (the smoking process seems to intensify the heat). The best varieties are the *chipotles grandes*—tan-brown, leathery, striated chiles that are 3 to 5 inches in length. *Moras rojas* are smaller (about 2 inches long), sweeter, and less expensive. Chipotles are sold in two basic forms: dried and canned. The latter come in a spicy tomato sauce called *adobo*. I like canned chipotles because you also get the flavor dividend of the sauce. Canned chipotles can be refrigerated in their adobo sauce in an airtight container for up to six months.

De árbol. The name translates as "chile from the tree." A small, bright red chile in the cayenne family, it's as slender as a green bean and red hot. It's popular in the north of México.

Guajillo. A long (4 to 6 inches), slender, smooth-skinned, reddish-brown chile with a sweet, mild flavor, the guajillo is one of the most common chiles in México. It's a veritable workhorse used in countless soups, moles, salsas, and spice pastes. It's fairly mild by Mexican heat standards with an earthy sweetness like that of paprika.

Hontaka. A small, thin, wrinkled red chile originally from Japan and widely used in Peruvian cooking, the hontaka is fiery hot. If unavailable, use crushed red-pepper flakes.

Malagueta. Brazil's premier chile, the malagueta is a tiny, ridged red or green chile usually sold dried, but sometimes pickled. It's used to add fire to Brazilian table sauces.

Mulato. Literally, "half-breed." Related to the ancho, the mulato is a type of dried poblano chile. It's about 3 to 4 inches long and shaped like an elongated triangle. It has heavily wrinkled, shiny, dark brown to jet-black skin. The flavor is earthy, rich, and smoky, with hints of tobacco and chocolate. The heat is gentle, especially if the seeds are removed. The chile mulato is a key ingredient in Mexican *Mole poblano* (Turkey in Chile-Chocolate Sauce, page 222).

New Mexico red. These are also called *chiles de raja* ("wreath chiles"), as they are often tied into wreaths. These elongated, shiny, smooth-skinned, mild-flavored chiles are usually ground to make New Mexican chili powder. You can also find them whole for making sauces. In certain parts of Texas, this chile is known as *chiles colorados*.

Pasilla. Named for the raisin (*pasa* in Spanish) on account of its wrinkled, dark, black skin, the pasilla is moderately hot to very hot. The taste is both sweet and slightly bitter, with suggestions of licorice and raisins. If unavailable, substitute anchos or mulatos.

Piquín. Piquín is a very tiny, red chile with a fiery bite. Ground cayenne pepper makes a good substitute.

(continued)

CHILE TIPS

✦ Most of the heat in a chile pepper resides in the seeds and ribs. If you like a milder chile flavor, remove the ribs and seeds. It's a good idea to wear plastic or rubber gloves when handling chiles, especially if you have sensitive skin. Or try this trick: Prepare the chiles by using two utensils at once. A comfortable knife and a grapefruit spoon work well. Slice the chile lengthwise with the knife. Then, hold the chile down with the flat side of the knife and use the spoon to scrape out the ribs and seeds. Now switch focus and hold the chile with the spoon while slicing or chopping with the knife. Using this method, you need never touch the cut chiles with your hands.

✦ To add mild heat to simmering dishes, cut a few slits in a whole fresh chile and add it to the dish while cooking. Remove and discard the chile before serving.

✦ To use a dried chile, remove the stem, tear open the chile, and discard the seeds. Soak the chile in warm water to cover for 20 minutes, or until soft and pliable. Chop or use as directed. To intensify the flavor, toast the chile in a dry skillet or under the broiler before soaking.

✦ Chili powder (intended for seasoning the popular stew) is made with ground dried chiles and sometimes seasonings such as oregano, cumin, and salt. To get the most forthright flavor for the recipes in this book, use pure chili powder made solely from ground chiles. Pure chili powder is available in the spice aisle or international section of most supermarkets. If you can't find it, see the sources on page 66.

✦ Supermarkets sometimes refer to chile peppers as hot peppers or chiles. While the spellings may vary, these terms all refer to the same botanical family of Capsicum peppers.

Hispanic markets and grows wild in parks and abandoned lots all over the United States. There is no substitute.

Guascas. This distinctively flavored, aromatic Colombian herb is used in *Ajiaco colombiano* (Colombian Chicken and Vegetable Stew, page 112). The herb is rarely seen in North America. Many Colombians residing in the United States use canned asparagus as a substitute.

Guava. A small green or yellow egg-shaped tropical fruit, when ripe, it exudes a slightly musky, intensely perfumed aroma suggestive of peaches, lemons, and honey. The only problem with this otherwise perfect tropical fruit is that it's filled with tiny rock-hard seeds, making it virtually impossible to eat out of hand. To solve the problem, guava is usually served cooked, often in jam form or seeded and poached (see the recipes on pages 336 and 338). Guava also comes in paste form—a thick, ruby-colored marmalade-like jelly used in many Latino desserts. The best brands are sold in flat cans in the canned fruit section of the supermarket.

Jícama (pronounced HEE-kama). This is a crisp, tan-skinned, white-fleshed, turnip-shaped root in the bean family. The flesh of jícama is much beloved in México, where it's often eaten raw with a sprinkle of salt, lime juice, and chili powder. The flavor has been described as a cross between an apple and a potato.

Lard (manteca). Lard is rendered pork fat. Hardly a fashionable ingredient in North America, but an important flavoring and traditional fat in Latin cooking—especially in the Spanish-speaking Caribbean and Central America. See "Fat Facts" on page 46 for a discussion of lard's surprising health profile.

Malanga (yautía). This elongated root looks like a gnarled, brown-skinned carrot. The flesh can be pink, yellow, or cream-colored. The flavor is suggestive of potatoes and beans. Firm-fleshed malanga tastes best boiled, steamed, and stewed. It's traditionally served with salty meats and spicy sausages and in stews, like *sancocho*. Its somewhat musty flavor may take some getting used to for Anglos, but Latinos love it.

Mamey (mamey sapote). Beloved by Cubans, mamey looks like an elongated coconut. Its rough brown skin encases bright orange flesh. Mamey is ripe when squeezably soft. The flavor lies somewhere between melon and sweet potato, with a hint of marzipan. Cut it in half lengthwise and eat it with a spoon. Or puree and mix with eggs and sweetened condensed milk to make *Flan* (page 316).

Mango. "The peach of the tropics" is how it's described in Miami. The mango's yellow to orange flesh has an intensely fragrant and refreshing flavor suggestive of peach and pineapple. Mangoes are enjoyed throughout Latin America. Mexicans love to snack on green mangoes sprinkled with salt and chili powder. A ripe mango will be soft to the touch and very fragrant. Some varieties remain green, even when ripe. If you have sensitive skin, wear plastic gloves when handling mangos. Some people are allergic to the sap.

Mariquita cutter. This slotted board with a supersharp blade is used for cutting plantains, yucas, and other root vegetables into thin strips for baking and frying.

Masa. A thick paste of ground cooked corn, you may be able to find plastic bags of freshly ground masa in Hispanic markets. If not, it's easy to make your own by mixing *masa harina* (a type of cornmeal made from dried cooked corn) with water. *Masarepa* (also called arepa flour) is a fine white cornmeal used for making *Arepas* (Cornmeal Flatcakes, page 179) and *Hallacas venezolanas* (Venezuelan Mushroom Tamales,

page 176). Look for masa harina and masarepa in Hispanic markets and the international aisle of large supermarkets.

Metate (piedra). This flat, volcanic grind stone with a stone pestle is used in México and Central America for grinding nuts, seeds, and vegetables.

Molcajete (tejolote). This is a Mexican volcanic stone mortar and pestle that is used for pureeing vegetables for salsas and moles. You can use a blender or a food processor instead, but Mexicans insist that the flavor won't be quite as robust.

Molinillo. This intricately carved wooden beater is used for making drinks like *Chocolate mexicano* (Mexican Hot Chocolate, page 344) and *Pinolillo* (Chocolate Cornmeal Milkshake, page 345). The molinillo is twirled upright between the palms of the hands until the drink is light and frothy.

Nopalitos. The fleshy paddles of a young prickly pear cactus, these taste somewhat like cooked green beans. If you have a Mexican market in your area, look for tender, small- to medium-size paddles that are 6 to 8 inches long and weigh about 6 ounces each. You can also find canned nopalitos in Hispanic markets, specialty shops, and the international aisle of some large supermarkets. If you can't find nopalitos, cooked green beans make an interesting substitute.

Papaya (lechosa; fruta bomba). I love the Cuban name of this tropical fruit: *fruta bomba* (literally, "bomb fruit," on account of its grenadelike shape and shrapnel-like seeds). Papaya is found throughout the tropics, where it can grow to the size of a football, if not beyond. In its green state, it is sometimes used as a vegetable. Ripe papaya has a sweet, musky flavor that can be brought into focus with a squeeze of lime juice. Let papayas ripen at room temperature until soft and yielding. Cut the fruit in half lengthwise, scoop out the seeds, and eat with a spoon. Or puree papaya with ice and sweetened condensed milk to make a *batido* (Latino milkshake). See the *batido* recipes beginning on page 348.

Parrilla. This cast-iron grid or grate is used for grilling throughout Latin America, especially in Argentina and Uruguay.

Passion fruit (granadilla, parcha, maracuyá). This round, lime-size fruit has bright orange, highly perfumed, bracingly tart flesh. The leathery skin can be red, brown, purple, or green. The flesh is riddled with tiny crunchy black seeds, which are edible, although not to everyone's liking. For this reason, the pulp is usually strained and enjoyed in juice form. Passion fruit is too tart to eat straight, but is excellent in sauces and cocktails.

Piloncillo (panela; rapadura). Mexican *piloncillo*—pressed, unrefined dark brown sugar—usually comes molded in pyramid-shaped chunks. It's used for making desserts and syrups. It's harder than North American dark brown sugar, but the latter can be used as a substitute. To use *piloncillo*, grate it on a hand grater before measuring.

Plantain (plátano). Banana-scented and banana-shaped, the plantain (accent on the first syllable) is inedible in its raw state. But boil, bake, or roast a plantain, and you're ready to taste one of the most popular foods in Latin America. Plantains are eaten at every stage of ripeness, from youthful green to yellow to black. When green (*verde*), a plantain tastes bland and starchy, like a potato, having little flavor or sweetness. But green plantains can be thinly sliced and bake-fried like potato chips (see *Mariquitas*, or Plantain Chips, on page 71), or boiled and mashed to make a popular Puerto Rican snack (see *Mofongo*, or Garlicky Plaintain Puree, on page 74). When semi-ripe with yellow and black skin (*pintón*), the plantain becomes sweeter, like a commonplace banana, while retaining a pleasant acidity. Even at its most sweet and ripe with black skin (*maduro*), the plantain holds its shape, which makes it useful for cooking. Maduros, literally, "ripe ones," are so popular fried or baked in Latin America that the dish simply goes by the name *Maduros* (Grilled Ripe Plantains, page 144). Plantains are a good source of potassium and vitamin C. They're also a traditional Latin folk remedy for ulcers.

Pressure cooker (olla de presión; olla exprés). Used widely in Latin America for cooking beans and stews, a pressure cooker slashes cooking time by as much as 75 percent. Modern pressure cookers have numerous safety features that make them easier and safer than conventional old-style jiggle-top models.

Pumpkin seeds (pepitas). The hulled green seeds of pumpkin or squash, these are used throughout México and Central America to make *Pollo en mole verde de pepitas* (Chicken in Green Pumpkin Seed Sauce, page 251) and other dishes. In Guatamala, the ground seeds are called *pepitoria*.

Queso blanco (queso fresco). This salty, sharp white cheese has a firm texture that you might say makes your teeth squeak. Depending upon the recipe, substitutes vary from feta cheese to Parmesan to sharp Cheddar.

Quinoa. A tiny, round, ivory-colored grain, quinoa is native to the Andes Mountains. When cooked, it swells to four times its size and looks like a tiny disk with a C-shaped "tail" in it (the seed sprout). Cooked quinoa has a delicate, earthy, nutty flavor and a soft, somewhat crunchy consistency a little reminiscent of caviar. Before cooking, be sure to rinse quinoa in a strainer until the water runs clear. Rinsing removes its somewhat bitter, grassy-tasting coating, which is believed to be a natural insect repellent. Some quinoa comes prerinsed, but it's better to play it safe. Quinoa is incredibly nutritious. It has more protein than any other grain and is high in calcium and potassium. Best of all it cooks in half the time of regular rice and it's easy to digest. Quinoa is available at health food stores and in the international or grain aisles of large supermarkets.

Sapodilla (sapote). A round or egg-shaped fruit with a thin, dusky brown skin and off-white flesh, sapodilla tastes like a pear soaked in maple syrup. It's enjoyed throughout the Spanish-speaking Caribbean and Central America. Let the fruit ripen at room temperature until squeezably soft. Cut it in half and eat it with a spoon.

Sofrito. The cornerstone of countless Latino dishes, including soups, stews, rices, beans, and tamales, sofrito is a richly flavored sauté that usually includes onions, garlic, and bell peppers. Depending on the country, rocotillo peppers, tomatoes, scallions, bacon, culantro, cilantro, and even curry powder may be added.

Sour orange (naranja agria). Sour orange is a member of the citrus family that looks like an orange (although much less uniform in appearance), but tastes like a lime. It is used widely in Spanish-Caribbean and Central American cooking. If unavailable, substitute fresh lime juice with a little fresh orange juice in a ratio of 3 to 1.

Star anise (anís estrellado). A star-shaped spice from Southeast Asia with a smoky, licorice-like flavor, star anise is used to flavor syrups and desserts in Spanish-Caribbean cooking. Although similar in flavor, star anise and anise seed (see page 50) are botanically different. Star anise comes from a small evergreen tree in the magnolia family, while anise seed comes from an annual plant in the parsley family.

Star fruit (carambola). Star fruit is an elongated, yellow, deeply ribbed fruit that forms a five-pointed star when sliced crosswise. The succulent, crunchy flesh combines the tartness of citrus with the sweetness of grape. Found in the Spanish Caribbean and México, it's also available in many North American supermarkets.

Sugar apple (anona). An oval fruit covered with light green knobby protuberances, the sugar apple is filled with a gooey, sweet, custardlike pulp. Let the fruit ripen until it looks rotten, then cut it in half and eat it with a spoon.

Tamarind (tamarindo). Tamarind is a long, curved, brown tropical seed pod with a fruity sweet-sour pulp. (Imagine the flavor of prune puree mixed with lime juice and a whiff of wood smoke.) Tamarind is popular in México and the Spanish-speaking Caribbean, where it's used to flavor sauces, candies, and drinks. If you live in a city with a large Hispanic, Asian, or Indian population, you may be able to find fresh tamarind pods (look for pods with cracked tan-brown skins) or blocks of peeled tamarind pulp with the seeds. The easiest form to use is tamarind water or tamarind puree (*pulpa de tamarindo*), a seedless puree made by blending tamarind pulp and water. Hispanic, Asian, and Indian markets and some supermarkets sell tamarind puree on the shelf or in the freezer section. To make your own at home, see the recipe for *Pulpa de tamarindo* (Tamarind Puree) on page 381.

Taro (dasheen). This is a large, barrel-shaped tuber with concentric ring-like markings and a shaggy, barklike skin. The flesh may be white, cream-colored, or even lavender and turns purplish or gray when cooked. The flavor is similar to a potato, with overtones of artichoke and chestnut. Taro is popular in the Spanish-speaking Caribbean and northern South America, where it's an essential ingredient in such meat and vegetable stews as *ajiaco* and *sancocho*. The best methods for cooking taro are steaming, boiling, and stewing. Like many Latin American root vegetables, taro becomes starchy and heavy as it sits. It's best when served the moment it's cooked.

Tomatillo (tomate verde; miltomate; fresadilla; husk tomato). A small, round, pale green fruit with a papery husk belonging to the ground cherry family, tomatillos have a pleasantly tart but fruity flavor reminiscent of green tomatoes. The defining ingredient in México's *salsa verde* (green salsa), tomatillos are used throughout Central America. They're available fresh at Hispanic markets and at an increasing number of North American supermarkets. To use, peel off the papery husk. It's natural for the skin of the fruit to feel sticky. In a pinch, canned tomatillos can be substituted.

Tortilla press. This is a hinged wooden or metal press with two flat plates between which a ball of masa is flattened into a tortilla. A variety of inexpensive models are available at Mexican markets and cookware shops.

Tostón press (tostonera). This small, hinged wooden press is used for flattening fried or boiled plantain pieces into *Tostones* (Twice-Cooked Plantains, page 142). It's available at Spanish-Caribbean and Central American markets.

Valencia-style rice (arroz valenciana; arroz tipo valencia). A short, starchy grain similar to Italian Arborio rice, valencia-style rice is used for making *Paella* (Paella, page 166), *Asopao de mariscos* (Seafood Soupy Rice, page 161) and *Arroz con pollo* (Chicken with Rice, page 244). Arborio rice can be used as a substitute (albeit more expensive). Valencia-style rice is available in Hispanic markets and in the rice section or international aisle of large supermarkets.

Vanilla bean (vaina de vainilla). The long, slender seed pods of an orchid native to Central America, whole vanilla beans provide a richer flavor than vanilla extract. Vanilla bean pods are filled with innumerable dustlike, fragrant black seeds. Cut the bean in half lengthwise and infuse it in warm milk or sugar syrup to flavor desserts. Or bury a split vanilla bean in a canister of granulated or confectioners' sugar for a few days to make vanilla sugar.

Yams (ñames). Yams are the largest root in the vegetable kingdom. Native to Africa, the yam was brought to the New World by African slaves, who called it *igname*. Most of what passes for yam in the United States is actually sweet potato. There's no mistaking the real yam: It's color is white, ivory, or pale yellow. When freshly sliced, it exudes a sticky juice. The flavor recalls potato with a faint hint of chestnut. And yams are never sweet. Yams can be boiled, sautéed, steamed, or baked, yet they are much drier than American sweet potatoes. Yams can grow up to 6 feet in length and weigh up to 600 pounds. Given their size, they are usually sold in pieces. Store yams in a cool, dry place. Yams are rich in zinc, potassium, and folic acid.

Yuca (manioc). So popular is this starchy tuber among Latin Americans, there's a restaurant in Miami named Yuca. Picture a slender, elongated root vegetable with tapered ends, ranging from 4 inches to well over 2 feet in length. The skin is a sort of smooth, brownish bark; the flesh is as white as bone; the flavor is bland, but exquisitely buttery. You may be more familiar with it than you think. Yuca is the root used to make tapioca. Yuca is also made into flour, which is used in a variety of Caribbean and Brazilian dishes. Boiled *Yuca con mojo* (Yuca with Garlic-Lime Sauce, page 139) is one of Cuba's national dishes. There's almost no end to the uses for yuca. To prepare the root, cut it crosswise into 2-inch rounds and pare off the barklike skin and pink layer underneath. Remove the fibrous cord in the center either before or after cooking. Like other Latin American root vegetables, yuca should be served at once; it becomes starchy and heavy when it sits for too long.

THE LATIN MARKETPLACE

Most of the ingredients used in this book are available at supermarkets. Others can be found in Hispanic markets. If you have trouble finding anything, here are my favorite retail and mail-order sources across the United States. Asterisks indicate stores that offer shipping or mail-order services.

CALIFORNIA

*Catalina's Market
1070 Northwestern Avenue
Los Angeles, CA 90029
Mexican, Central American, and South American foods. Also carries tortilla presses.

*Frieda's
4465 Corporate Center Drive
Los Alamitos, CA 90720
Web site: http://www.friedas.com
Hispanic produce, chiles, corn husks, banana leaves, posole, and much more.

*Melissa's/World Variety Produce
P.O. Box 21127
Los Angeles, CA 90021
Web site: http://www.melissas.com
Fresh and dried Latin American produce, chiles, grains, avocado leaves, and more. Free catalog.

*Mo Hotta Mo Betta
P.O. Box 4136
San Luis Obispo, CA 93403
Web site: http://www.mohotta.com
Mexican spices, masa harina, chile peppers, annatto seeds, hot sauces, and tortilla presses.

COLORADO

*Tamale Factory
4841 Barnes Road
Colorado Springs, CO 80917
A retail store and mail-order company that sells mild and hot tamales.

FLORIDA

Los Gauchitos
4315 NW 7th Street, #2125
Miami, FL 33126
Argentinian and Uruguayan products.

ILLINOIS

*Garden Row Foods
9150 West Grand Avenue
Franklin Park, IL 60131
Web site: http://www.xnet.com/~hotfoods
Dried chiles, canned chipotles, and hot sauces.

*Nu-World Amaranth
P.O. Box 2202
Naperville, IL 60567
Variety of amaranth products.

KANSAS

*Calido Chile Traders
5360 Merriam Drive
Merriam, KS 66203
Retail and mail-order store for hot sauces, salsas, snacks, drink mixes, condiments, and seasonings.

MASSACHUSETTS

International Market
365 Somerville Avenue
Somerville, MA 02143
Brazilian foods.

Star Markets Company
625 Mt. Auburn Street
Cambridge, MA 02138
Web site: http://wharvest.com
Wide variety of Hispanic produce such as malanga (yautía), batata, yuca, chayote squash, sugarcane, plantains, Honduran pineapples, and an assortment of hot peppers.

MISSOURI

*Tropicana Market
5001 Lindenwood Street
St. Louis, MO 63109
Mexican, Central American, South American, and Spanish-Caribbean foods, including annatto seeds. Also carries tortilla presses.

NEW MEXICO

*Coyote Cafe General Store
132 West Water Street
Santa Fe, NM 87501
Web site:
http://www.interart.net/food/coyote.cafe/
default.html
Chile peppers, masa harina, Mexican chocolate, spices, herbs, dried beans, and hot sauces.

*Leona's Foods
P.O. Box 579
Chimayo, NM 87522
Web site: http://www.leonasfoods.com
Tortillas, tamales, chile peppers, and other Southwestern ingredients.

NEW YORK

*Dean and DeLuca
Catalog Department
560 Broadway
New York, NY 10012
Web site: http://www.dean-deluca.com
Chile peppers, pozole, dried beans, avocado leaves, pumpkin seeds, annatto seeds, Mexican chocolate, masa harina, and spices.

PUERTO RICO

*Isla
P.O. Box 9112
San Juan, Puerto Rico 00908-0112
Web site: http://www.latino.com/isla/
Mail-order source for traditional Puerto Rican seasonings, coffee, and hot sauces.

TEXAS

*El Paso Chile Company
909 Texas Avenue
El Paso, TX 79901
Chile peppers, nopalitos, salsas, dips, spices, tortilla presses, and other Southwestern products.

APPETIZERS AND SNACKS
Entremeses

Mexicans call them botanas. Nicaraguans call them antojitos. Whatever you call them, some of the world's best appetizers come from Latin America.

Many Latin appetizers are naturally healthy, offering loads of flavor with little or no fat. Consider the Mexican Shrimp Cocktail (page 83), Yucatán Bean and Pumpkin Seed Appetizer (page 78), and Peruvian-Style Ceviche (page 90). Of course, many others are nutritional land mines filled with fatty cuts of meat or deep-fried in oceans of oil.

You can still enjoy these starters by using a few simple healthy cooking techniques. Instead of deep-frying, I use a technique called bake-frying. It enables you to cook fritters and chips in the oven until they're cracklingly crisp. Try this method to make healthier Tortilla Chips (page 70), Plantain Chips (page 71), and Salt Cod Fritters (page 89). You can also bake-fry a variety of turnovers, like Pork Empanadas (page 80) and Bolivian Meat Pies (page 85). To cut the fat and fuss of traditional empanada dough, I use wonton wrappers instead. Now, empanadas can take less time, have less fat, and taste just as lip-smackingly good as the original.

RECIPES

TORTILLA CHIPS

Totopos   *México*

Nutrition Snapshot	Before	After
Per serving (6 chips)		
Calories	133	56
Total Fat g.	9.1	0.6
Saturated Fat g.	3.4	0.1
Cholesterol mg.	8	0

Who says tortilla chips have to be unhealthy? In this recipe, the chips are crisped by baking them in a hot oven instead of frying them in lard. For an offbeat twist, use blue corn tortillas.

6   yellow or blue corn tortillas (6" in
     diameter), cut into 6 wedges each
     Salt (optional)

Preheat the oven to 350°F.

Arrange the tortillas in a single layer on 2 nonstick baking sheets. Coat the chips with nonstick spray. Sprinkle lightly with salt (if using).

Bake for 10 minutes, or until crisp. Transfer to a rack to cool.

Makes 6 servings (36 chips)

¡Fiesta!
Mexican Cinco de Mayo Feast

The fifth of May is a popular Mexican holiday observed by Mexican communities in Latin America and the United States. This day commemorates the defeat of French troops at the Battle of Puebla in 1862. Here's a Mexican fiesta with all the trimmings and a lot less fat.

Spiced Tomato Juice (*Sangrita*, **page 357**)

Tortilla Chips (*Totopos*, **page 70**)

Guacamole (*Guacamole*, **page 75**)

Tomato, Onion, and Jalapeño Salsa (*Pico de gallo*, **page 296**)

Mexican Steamed Mussels (*Caldo de mejillones*, **page 233**)

Beef Fajitas (*Fajitas de res*, **page 214**)

Cinnamon-Sugar Crisps (*Buñuelos*, **page 333**)

PLANTAIN CHIPS

Mariquitas

Cuba
Nicaragua

Nutrition Snapshot	Before	After
Per serving (6 chips)		
Calories	228	139
Total Fat g.	13.8	3.7
Saturated Fat g.	51	0.6
Cholesterol mg.	0	0

Plantain chips are enjoyed throughout the Spanish-speaking Caribbean. In Miami, they're sold as a snack on street corners. Traditionally, the chips are deep-fried. But you can achieve the same potato-chip crispness by baking with only a small amount of oil. I like to slice the plantains lengthwise for a long, wavy chip that looks great stood upright in salsas and mashed vegetables. You can also slice them on the diagonal to make oval chips. The easiest way to slice plantains is on a mandoline or plantain slicer (available at Hispanic markets). If you don't have a mandoline, thinly slice the plantains with a vegetable peeler or sharp knife.

2   **green plantains, peeled (see tip) and thinly sliced**

1   **tablespoon olive oil or nonstick spray**

Salt (optional)

Preheat the oven to 350°F. Coat a nonstick baking sheet with nonstick spray.

Arrange the plantains in a single layer on the prepared baking sheet. Brush the tops of the slices with oil or generously coat with nonstick spray. Season with salt (if using).

Bake for 10 minutes, or until golden brown and crisp. Transfer to a rack to cool.

Makes 4 servings (24 chips)

Cooking Tip

✦ To peel a green plantain, cut off the ends and make 3 or 4 slits down the length of the plantain, cutting just through the skin. Place the plantain in a medium bowl and cover with warm water. Let soak for 10 minutes, or until the skin is softened. Run your thumb under the slits to ease the skin off the plantain.

LATIN SUPER FOOD: PLANTAINS

Latin Americans use plantains much like North Americans use potatoes. These banana-like fruits are made into starchy side dishes to complement steaks and chicken. Or they're fried up for snacks like Twice-Cooked Plantains (page 142) and Plantain "Surfboards" (page 143). They also have bunches of disease-fighting nutrients inside every peel.

Like bananas, plantains are chock-full of potassium. One cup of the cooked fruit delivers more than 700 milligrams or 20 percent of the Daily Value (DV) for potassium. More than 30 studies have shown that taking potassium supplements can help lower blood pressure. After researchers analyzed these studies, they agreed that a diet low in potassium can be a culprit behind high blood pressure, and that increasing your daily dose of potassium can help bring high blood pressure levels back down to normal. Plus, that same cup of plantain gives you almost 50 milligrams of magnesium, another nutrient that helps keep blood pressure in check, particularly for people who are sensitive to sodium.

Does the burning pain of an ulcer have you clutching your stomach? Reach for a plantain. Long recommended as a folk remedy for ulcers, unripe plantains contain compounds that help thicken the layer of protective mucous membrane in the stomach, which can help prevent as well as heal existing ulcers, according to experts.

Plantains serve up respectable amounts of the immunity-boosting nutrients vitamin A, vitamin C, and vitamin B_6, too. You can get about 28 percent of the DV for vitamins A and C and 18 percent of the DV for vitamin B_6 in each cupful of cooked plantain you eat.

Known as cooking bananas, plantains are commonplace in Latin American and Caribbean kitchens. But they're rather rare in North American homes. To get more of this heart-smart fruit on your plate, just boil or bake plantains like you would potatoes. Or try some Latin favorites like Grilled Ripe Plantains (page 144), Garlicky Plantain Puree (page 74), and Plantain Soup (page 99).

PLANTAIN SPIDERS

Arañitas de
plátano

Puerto Rico

Nutrition Snapshot	Before	After
Per serving (6 pieces)		
Calories	237	147
Total Fat g.	13.9	3.8
Saturated Fat g.	1.9	0.6
Cholesterol mg.	0	0

I've always loved the name of this Puerto Rican appetizer: Arañita *literally means "little spider." With some imagination, the slender shreds of plantain do, indeed, look like spider legs. Traditionally, the shredded plantains are deep-fried. In this low-fat version, they're bake-fried with just a touch of oil. To bolster the flavor (after all, fried food does taste a bit richer), I add extra garlic and ginger. Serve these with Cilantro-Pepper Sauce (page 311).*

2   large green plantains, peeled (see page 386)

6   cloves garlic, thinly sliced and cut into thin slivers

1   piece fresh ginger (1" long), peeled, thinly sliced, and cut into thin slivers

Salt and ground black pepper

1   tablespoon olive oil or nonstick spray

Preheat the oven to 400°F. Coat a nonstick baking sheet with nonstick spray.

Grate each plantain on the coarse side of a hand grater or in a food processor fitted with a grating disk. Transfer to a medium bowl. Add the garlic and ginger. Season with salt and pepper. Toss to mix.

Using 2 spoons or your fingertips, loosely shape the mixture into 1" balls. Flatten slightly. (Don't pack the plantain shreds too tightly. They should look spindly and lacy.) Arrange the flattened balls on the prepared baking sheet. Brush the balls with the oil or generously coat with nonstick spray.

Bake for 12 minutes, or until golden brown and crisp. Transfer to a platter and season with more salt and pepper, if desired.

Makes 4 servings (24 pieces)

GARLICKY PLANTAIN PUREE

Mofongo   *Puerto Rico*

Nutrition Snapshot	Before	After
Per serving		
Calories	486	192
Total Fat g.	24.6	6.2
Saturated Fat g.	9.1	1
Cholesterol mg.	60	4

Plantain puree is a staple in the Spanish-speaking Caribbean. Depending on how it's prepared, it can be called mofongo, mangú, or fufú. The traditional version is deep-fried in lard, then mashed with chicharrones (fried pork rinds). To lower the fat, I simmer the plantains in chicken stock. The smoky pork flavor comes from lean Canadian bacon instead of high-fat chicharrones.

2	green plantains, peeled and cut into ½"-thick slices (see page 386)
2	cups Chicken Stock (page 360) or fat-free reduced-sodium chicken broth
1½	tablespoons olive oil
1	small onion, finely chopped
3–4	cloves garlic, minced
1	ounce (1 slice) Canadian bacon, cut into thin slivers
	Salt and ground black pepper
2	tablespoons finely chopped chives or scallion greens

In a large saucepan over medium heat, combine the plantains and stock or broth. Simmer for 10 minutes, or until the plantains are very tender. Drain in a strainer, reserving the cooking liquid. Leave the plantains in the strainer.

Heat the oil in the saucepan. Add the onions, garlic, and bacon. Cook for 4 minutes, or until the onions are just beginning to brown. Stir in the plantains and mash with a pestle or the back of a wooden spoon. Add the reserved stock as necessary to obtain a thick, creamy puree. Season with salt and pepper.

Transfer to a serving bowl. Sprinkle with the chives or scallion greens.

Makes 4 servings

Cooking Tip

✦ For this recipe, I sometimes like to use a pintón, a half-ripe plantain with yellow skin that has a hint of banana-like sweetness, but really tastes more starchy than sweet. (See page 61 for a complete discussion of plantains.)

Variation

Vegetarian Garlicky Plantain Puree: Substitute vegetable stock for the chicken stock and omit the Canadian bacon. Add a few drops of liquid smoke and 1 tablespoon lightly toasted pine nuts. To toast the nuts, place them in a dry nonstick skillet and cook, shaking the pan often, for 3 to 5 minutes, or until golden and fragrant.

GUACAMOLE

Guacamole

México

Nutrition Snapshot	Before	After
Per serving (¹/₄ cup)		
Calories	100	61
Total Fat g.	8	4
Saturated Fat g.	0	0.8
Cholesterol mg.	0	0

It's hard to imagine a Mexican meal without guacamole. Alas, avocados are high in fat. So I lightened the traditional recipe by replacing some of the avocados with tomatillos (Mexican green tomatoes). Serve the guacamole with Tortilla Chips (page 70) or thin slices of jícama. For a spicier guacamole, use 2 chile peppers and leave in the seeds.

4	tomatillos (8 ounces total), peeled and rinsed
¼	medium onion, coarsely chopped
¼	cup coarsely chopped fresh cilantro
1–2	jalapeño chile peppers, seeded (wear plastic gloves when handling)

1	clove garlic
2	small avocados (12 ounces total), peeled and pitted
1	tomato, chopped
1	tablespoon lime juice
	Salt and ground black pepper

In a food processor or blender, combine the tomatillos, onions, cilantro, chile peppers, and garlic. Puree until smooth. Add the avocados; puree.

Transfer to a medium serving bowl. Stir in the tomatoes and lime juice. Season with salt and black pepper.

Makes 10 servings (2½ cups)

Cooking Tips

✦ Guacamole is best when eaten within a few hours of preparation.

✦ To make guacamole the old-fashioned way, mash the avocado with a fork in a medium serving bowl. Stir in the other ingredients and mix until well-combined.

✦ For a guacamole that's even lower in fat, use Florida avocados. They contain about 30 percent less fat than Haas avocados.

LATIN SUPER FOOD: AVOCADOS

Domesticated in México for thousands of years, avocados are an integral part of Latin American meals. Often they're made into sauce, but sometimes they take center stage stuffed with shrimp or chicken as a main course. In the past, most nutritionists recommended limiting or avoiding this high-calorie, high-fat fruit. Now, research suggests that avocados deserve a prominent place on the healthy Latin menu.

It's true that just half an avocado can set you back more than 150 calories and 15 grams of fat. But most of that fat is monounsaturated—the kind that is actually good for your heart. In a small study done in México, researchers compared the effects of a regular low-fat diet with the effects of a low-fat diet that included avocado, on both healthy people and people with high cholesterol levels. They found that both groups had an improvement in cholesterol levels. Better yet, those with high cholesterol who also ate avocados experienced significant drops in dangerous LDL (bad) cholesterol and triglycerides (blood fats that can contribute to heart disease) and an increase in healthy HDL (good) cholesterol. These findings are consistent with other studies that show that increased consumption of monounsaturated fats helps keep your cholesterol levels in check.

Avocados are also filled with fiber—10 grams in each fruit, which is almost half of what experts say we need each day. Fiber not only lowers cholesterol, helping to prevent high blood pressure and heart disease, but it also reduces the risk for certain cancers, particularly colon cancer.

And vitamins? Avocados are full of them. Inside their shells, avocados contain loads of potassium, an important nutrient for keeping blood pressure at healthy levels. The creamy green fruit also provides respectable amounts of antioxidant vitamin C, immunity-building vitamin A and copper, memory-retaining vitamin B_6, red blood cell–boosting iron, heart-healthy magnesium, and hard-to-find pantothenic acid, which helps your body convert food into energy.

To get more of the good green stuff on your plate, serve your next meal with Guacamole (page 75) or Venezualan Avocado Sauce (page 308).

JALAPEÑO POPPERS

Ratitos

Tex-Mex

Nutrition Snapshot	Before	After
Per popper		
Calories	135	34
Total Fat g.	11.3	1.4
Saturated Fat g.	1.9	0.3
Cholesterol mg.	4	1

These nibblers are hot! To lighten up traditional poppers, I stuff the chiles with scallion-flavored cream cheese, then bake-fry them. Have a beverage on hand to put out the fire. Milk-based drinks work best.

24	large jalapeño chile peppers	3	tablespoons chopped fresh cilantro
½	cup low-fat or nonfat cream cheese, at room temperature	3	egg whites
¼	cup grated sharp Cheddar cheese	2	tablespoons skim milk
½	cup cooked or frozen and thawed corn kernels	1	cup unbleached or all-purpose flour
4	scallions, trimmed and finely chopped	½	teaspoon salt
		½	teaspoon ground black pepper

Preheat a comal (a griddle for cooking tortillas) over high heat. Or preheat a gas or electric burner to high. Working in batches, place the chile peppers in the comal or directly on top of the burner. Roast, turning occasionally, for 2 minutes, or until most of the skin is blistered and blackened. Transfer to a plate. When cool enough to handle, scrape off the blackened skin (wear plastic gloves when handling) with a paring knife. Discard the skin.

Cut a slit running the length of each chile pepper in the outwardly curving side of the pepper. Gently pinch the ends together to open the slit. Using the tip of the paring knife and a small spoon, scrape out and discard the seeds and membranes.

Preheat the oven to 400°F. Coat a nonstick baking sheet with nonstick spray.

Using a spoon, vigorously beat the cream cheese in a medium bowl until creamy. Stir in the Cheddar, corn, scallions, and cilantro. Place about 2 teaspoons of the cheese mixture in each pepper and pinch the slit closed.

In a shallow bowl, lightly beat together the egg whites and milk.

In another shallow bowl, whisk together the flour, salt, and black pepper. Dip each pepper first in the flour mixture, shaking off the excess, then in the egg-white mixture, then again in the flour mixture. Arrange on the prepared baking sheet. Coat the tops of the peppers with nonstick spray.

Bake the peppers for 20 minutes, or until crisp and golden brown.

Makes 24

YUCATÁN BEAN AND PUMPKIN SEED APPETIZER

Ybez

México

Nutrition Snapshot	Before	After
Per serving (5 tablespoons)		
Calories	92	92
Total Fat g.	0.3	0.3
Saturated Fat g.	0.1	0.1
Cholesterol mg.	5	5

■ *discovered this unusual botana (bar snack) at the central food market in Mérida in the Yucatán, México. The pumpkin seeds add an offbeat flavor and, when combined with the beans, give you a nutritionally complete source of protein. There are two traditional ways to serve ybez (ee-BEZ): with chips as a dip or on lettuce leaves as a salad. The tomato isn't strictly traditional, but I like its color and flavor.*

¼ cup hulled pumpkin seeds (pepitas)	¼ white onion, finely chopped
1 can (15½ ounces) white beans, rinsed and drained	¼ cup finely chopped cilantro
1 tomato, finely chopped	3–4 tablespoons lime juice
	Salt and ground black pepper

Toast the pumpkin seeds in a small skillet over medium heat, shaking the pan often, for 3 minutes, or until lightly browned. Transfer to a bowl to cool. Coarsely chop in a food processor or with a sharp knife.

In a medium serving bowl, combine the pumpkin seeds, beans, tomatoes, onions, cilantro, and 3 tablespoons of the lime juice. Season with salt and pepper. Toss to combine. Season with more salt and lime juice, if desired.

Makes 8 servings (2½ cups)

Cooking Tip

✦ For extra richness, add 1 tablespoon extra-virgin olive oil along with the lime juice. The oil will increase the fat content to 2 grams per serving.

Pronto!

LITTLE POTS OF RED BEANS WITH SOUR CREAM

Cazuelito de
frijoles

Nicaragua

Nutrition Snapshot	Before	After
Per serving		
Calories	340	140
Total Fat g.	24	3.8
Saturated Fat g.	11.8	0.5
Cholesterol mg.	37	0

Cazuelito is a popular Nicaraguan antojito, or appetizer. The dish takes its name from the tiny earthenware pot in which it is traditionally baked. To reduce the fat and calories, I cut back on the oil used for frying the beans and replace the regular sour cream with nonfat sour cream.

1	tablespoon olive oil or lard
1	small onion, finely chopped
1	jalapeño chile pepper, seeded and minced (wear plastic gloves when handling)
1	clove garlic, minced
1	can (15½ ounces) small red kidney beans, rinsed and drained

½	cup Chicken Stock (page 360) or fat-free reduced-sodium chicken broth
3	tablespoons chopped fresh cilantro
	Salt and ground black pepper
1	cup nonfat sour cream
4	sprigs fresh cilantro

Preheat the oven to 400°F.

Heat the oil or lard in a large nonstick skillet over medium heat. Add the onions, chile peppers, and garlic. Cook, stirring often, for 5 minutes, or until the onions are lightly browned. Increase the heat to high. Add the beans, stock or broth, and chopped cilantro. Cook for 5 minutes, or until the beans have absorbed the liquid. Season with salt and black pepper.

Spoon the beans into 4 small earthenware crocks, ramekins, or custard cups. Spoon the sour cream on top. Bake for 5 minutes, or until the sour cream is thoroughly heated. Garnish each with a sprig of cilantro.

Makes 4 servings

Cooking Tip

✦ Some nonfat sour creams are better than others. Taste a few brands to find your favorite.

Regional Variation

Mexican Little Pots of Red Beans with Sour Cream: Add 1 ounce Canadian bacon along with the onions. Use 2 jalapeño chile peppers instead of 1.

PORK EMPANADAS

Pastelillos de
cerdo a lo
puertorriqueño

Puerto Rico

Nutrition Snapshot	Before	After
Per serving (4½ pieces)		
Calories	420	201
Total Fat g.	27.5	5.2
Saturated Fat g.	5.2	1.6
Cholesterol mg.	56	32

Empanadas *(meat pies) are enjoyed throughout Latin America—from México to Argentina. The crust is usually made with lard or shortening, and then the little pies are deep-fried. To cut back on fat, I use wonton wrappers, which can be baked with only a small amount of oil. Best of all, wonton wrappers are quicker and easier to use than traditional empanada dough. Look for them in the produce section of any supermarket. This pork filling is from Puerto Rico. Because "empanada" refers to a breaded food, in Puerto Rico the Spanish name for this dish is pastelillos.*

8	ounces boneless lean pork loin, trimmed of all visible fat and cut into ½" cubes
½	small onion, finely chopped
½	red bell pepper, finely chopped
½	tomato, seeded and chopped
2	tablespoons raisins
4	pimiento-stuffed green olives, coarsely chopped
1	tablespoon chopped fresh cilantro or flat-leaf parsley
1	clove garlic, minced
1	tablespoon tomato paste
¼	cup Chicken Stock (page 360), fat-free reduced-sodium chicken broth, or water
½–¾	teaspoon ground cumin
	Salt and ground black pepper
1–2	tablespoons unseasoned dry bread crumbs (optional)
36	(3") wonton wrappers or round Chinese ravioli wrappers
1	egg white, lightly beaten

In a large saucepan over medium heat, combine the pork, onions, bell peppers, tomatoes, raisins, olives, cilantro or parsley, garlic, and tomato paste. Add the stock, broth, or water. Add ½ teaspoon of the cumin. Season with salt and black pepper. Simmer, stirring often, for 5 minutes, or until the pork is no longer pink.

Transfer the mixture to a food processor and coarsely grind. The mixture should be fairly dry; if it is too runny, add the bread crumbs. The filling should be highly seasoned; sprinkle with more cumin, salt, and black pepper, if desired. Transfer to a bowl and refrigerate the filling until cold.

Preheat the oven to 400°F. Coat a nonstick baking sheet with nonstick spray.

Arrange a few wonton wrappers on a work surface. Lightly brush the edge of each wrapper with egg white. (The egg white helps make a tight seal.) Place a tablespoon of filling in the center and fold the wrapper in half to make a triangular pastry, or a half moon–shaped pastry if using round wrappers. Crimp the edges with a fork. Place the finished empanadas on the prepared baking sheet while you make the rest.

Coat the tops of the empanadas with nonstick spray. Bake, turning occasionally, for 6 to 8 minutes, or until crisp and golden brown.

Makes 8 servings (36 pieces)

Variation

Lenten Empanadas: During Lent, replace the pork filling with 2 cups of the Salt Cod a la Vizcaína (page 231). Finely chop and drain the excess juices from the salt cod before using.

GUAVA AND CHEESE EMPANADAS

Empanadas de
guayaba y queso

Cuba

Nutrition Snapshot	Before	After
Per serving (4½ pieces)		
Calories	548	161
Total Fat g.	41.4	0.6
Saturated Fat g.	9.8	0.1
Cholesterol mg.	42	4

Fruit and cheese filling makes these empanadas a popular breakfast item and snack in the Spanish-speaking Caribbean. Light cream cheese keeps the fat content very low. Guava paste is a thick, ruby-colored, marmalade-like jelly used in many Latino desserts. The best brands are sold in flat cans in the canned fruit section of the supermarket. Or check the international section.

36	(3") wonton wrappers or round Chinese ravioli wrappers	4	ounces guava paste, cut into 36 small pieces
1	egg white, lightly beaten	4	ounces low-fat cream cheese, cut into 36 small pieces

Preheat the oven to 400°F. Coat a nonstick baking sheet with nonstick spray.

Arrange a few wonton wrappers on a work surface. Lightly brush the edge of each wrapper with egg white. (The egg white helps make a tight seal.) Place 1 piece of guava paste and 1 piece of cream cheese in the center and fold the wrapper in half to make a triangular pastry, or a half moon–shaped pastry if using round wrappers. Crimp the edges with a fork. Place the finished empanadas on the prepared baking sheet while you make the rest.

Coat the tops of the empanadas with nonstick spray. Bake, turning occasionally, for 6 to 8 minutes, or until crisp and golden brown.

Makes 8 servings (36 pieces)

BEEF AND POTATO EMPANADAS

Empanadas de
res y papas

Argentina

Nutrition Snapshot	Before	After
Per serving (4 1/2 pieces)		
Calories	616	197
Total Fat g.	48.1	2.6
Saturated Fat g.	10.6	1.0
Cholesterol mg.	70	25

These spicy beef pies are served as a complimentary appetizer at Argentinian steak houses. To reduce the fat and cholesterol, I replaced some of the beef with potatoes.

8	ounces beef sirloin, trimmed of all visible fat and cut into 1/2" cubes
1	small potato, peeled and finely chopped
1/2	small onion, finely chopped
1	clove garlic, minced
1	cup Chicken Stock (page 360) or fat-free reduced-sodium chicken broth
2	tablespoons chopped fresh flat-leaf parsley

1/4–1/2	teaspoon ground cumin
1/4–1/2	teaspoon ground allspice
	Ground black pepper
	Pinch of ground cloves
	Salt
1–2	tablespoons unseasoned dry bread crumbs (optional)
36	(3") wonton wrappers or round Chinese ravioli wrappers
1	egg white, lightly beaten

In a large saucepan over medium heat, combine the beef, potatoes, onions, garlic, stock or broth, parsley, 1/4 teaspoon of the cumin, 1/4 teaspoon of the allspice, 1/4 teaspoon pepper, the cloves, and salt. Simmer, stirring often, for 10 minutes, or until the beef is tender and the potatoes are soft. Pour off any remaining stock. Transfer the mixture to a food processor and coarsely grind. The mixture should be fairly dry; if it is too runny, add the bread crumbs. The filling should be highly seasoned; sprinkle with more cumin, allspice, pepper, and salt, if desired. Transfer to a bowl and refrigerate the filling until cold.

Preheat the oven to 400°F. Coat a nonstick baking sheet with nonstick spray.

Arrange a few wonton wrappers on a work surface. Lightly brush the edge of each wrapper with egg white. (The egg white helps make a tight seal.) Place a heaping teaspoon of filling in the center and fold the wrapper in half to make a triangular pastry, or a half moon–shaped pastry if using round wrappers. Crimp the edges with a fork. Place the finished empanadas on the prepared baking sheet while you make the rest.

Coat the tops of the empanadas with nonstick spray. Bake, turning occasionally, for 6 to 8 minutes, or until crisp and golden brown.

Makes 8 servings (36 pieces)

MEXICAN SHRIMP COCKTAIL

Cóctel de camarones   *México*

Nutrition Snapshot	Before	After
Per serving		
Calories	278	128
Total Fat g.	1.8	0.8
Saturated Fat g.	0.7	0.3
Cholesterol mg.	342	142

In North America, the emphasis of shrimp cocktail is on the shrimp—with the sauce as something of an afterthought. In México, the sauce is the main attraction—with the tiny shrimp (a dozen could fit in a soup spoon) used only as a flavoring. And there's a surprise ingredient: orange soda.

1	cup low-sodium or regular ketchup
⅔	cup orange soda or orange juice
2–2½	tablespoons lime juice
2	tablespoons dry white wine or nonalcoholic white wine
2	teaspoons Worcestershire sauce
1	teaspoon Maggi seasoning (see tip) or Worcestershire sauce

1	teaspoon hot-pepper sauce
	Salt and ground black pepper
3	cups cooked, peeled, and deveined shrimp (preferably baby shrimp); see tip
6	leaves baby or center romaine lettuce

In a large bowl, whisk together the ketchup, soda or orange juice, 2 tablespoons of the lime juice, the wine, Worcestershire sauce, Maggi seasoning or Worcestershire sauce, and hot-pepper sauce. Season with salt and black pepper. Taste and add more lime juice or salt, if desired. Stir in the shrimp. Cover and marinate in the refrigerator for 5 minutes or up to 24 hours before serving.

Divide the shrimp mixture among 6 sundae or martini glasses. Garnish each with an upright lettuce leaf.

Makes 6 servings

Cooking Tips

✦ Maggi seasoning is a flavorful gravy base with a rich caramel-like taste. It is available in the spice aisle of most supermarkets.

✦ To cook baby shrimp, bring a large pot of water to a boil. Add the shrimp and cook for 2 minutes, or until firm and pink.

NICARAGUAN MEAT PIES

Pastelitos
nicaragüense

Nicaragua

Nutrition Snapshot	Before	After
Per serving (4 pieces)		
Calories	448	225
Total Fat g.	27.8	9.3
Saturated Fat g.	5.4	2.1
Cholesterol mg.	18	16

Meat pies are obligatory finger fare at any Nicaraguan special occasion. North Americans may find the dusting of sugar on the pastries a curious touch. Believe me, the contrast of sweet and salty is quite pleasant. It's similar to serving sugar-based barbecue sauce with spareribs.

DOUGH

2	cups unbleached flour
⅓	cup margarine
½	teaspoon salt
½–⅔	cup ice water

FILLING

6	ounces boneless lean pork loin, trimmed of all visible fat and cut into ½" cubes
½	tomato, seeded and finely chopped
½	small onion, finely chopped
½	green bell pepper, finely chopped
½	rib celery, finely chopped
4	pitted green olives, coarsely chopped
2	tablespoons dried currants
1	clove garlic, minced
1	tablespoon tomato paste
½	cup water
2	tablespoons unseasoned dry bread crumbs (optional)
	Salt and ground black pepper
1	egg white, lightly beaten
¼	cup sugar

To make the dough: In a large bowl or food processor fitted with a metal blade, combine the flour, margarine, and salt. Stir or process for 2 minutes, or until the mixture feels crumbly, like sand. Add ½ cup of the water and stir or process for 1 to 2 minutes, or until the dough comes together. The dough should be soft and pliable; add more water, if needed. Wrap the dough in plastic and refrigerate for 2 hours.

To make the filling: In a large saucepan over medium heat, combine the pork, tomatoes, onions, bell peppers, celery, olives, currants, garlic, tomato paste, and water. Simmer for 10 minutes, or until the pork is tender. Pour off any excess liquid. Transfer the mixture to a food processor or blender and coarsely grind. The mixture should be fairly dry; if it is too runny, add the bread crumbs. Season with salt and black pepper.

Preheat the oven to 400°F. Coat a nonstick baking sheet with nonstick spray.

On a floured surface, roll out the dough as thinly as possible. Using a cookie cutter, cut the dough into 2" circles. Fold and roll the scraps to use all the dough. Place a small spoonful of filling in the center of half of the dough circles. Brush the edges of the dough with water. Place the remaining circles on top. Crimp the edges shut with a fork. Arrange on the prepared baking sheet. Whisk together the egg white and a pinch of salt. Lightly brush over the top of each pastry and sprinkle with the sugar. Bake for 20 minutes, or until golden brown.

Makes 10 servings (40 pieces)

Cooking Tip

✦ To save time and reduce the fat even further, use 80 round wonton wrappers in place of the traditional dough. For each pastelito, brush the edge of a wrapper with egg white. (The egg white helps make a tight seal.) Place a heaping teaspoon of filling in the center and top with a second wrapper. Crimp the edges with a fork to seal.

BOLIVIAN MEAT PIES

Salteñas
bolivianas

Bolivia

Nutrition Snapshot	Before	After
Per piece		
Calories	141	99
Total Fat g.	7.4	2.3
Saturated Fat g.	2.5	0.4
Cholesterol mg.	19	6

O*f all the variations on empanadas (meat pies and pastries), Bolivia's salteñas are my favorite. These luscious pastries make a great snack, hors d'oeuvre, or meal in themselves. I like to use a yeast dough because it has a lot less fat than the traditional short pastry made with lard.*

DOUGH

1   package (¼ ounce) active dry yeast

1   tablespoon sugar

3   tablespoons warm water (105° to 115°F)

½–¾   cup warm skim milk (105° to 115°F)

3   tablespoons olive oil

1   egg white

1¼   teaspoons salt

2¾   cups unbleached or all-purpose flour

FILLING

½   medium onion, finely chopped

¼   green bell pepper, finely chopped

2   cloves garlic, minced

1   small tomato, peeled and chopped (see page 383)

1   medium potato, peeled and cubed

6   ounces boneless, skinless chicken breast, cubed

¼   cup raisins

3   pimiento-stuffed green olives, chopped

1   tablespoon drained capers

1   cup Chicken Stock (page 360) or fat-free reduced-sodium chicken broth

  Salt and ground black pepper

¼   cup cooked or frozen and thawed peas

2   tablespoons liquid egg substitute or 1 egg white

To make the dough: In a small bowl, combine the yeast, sugar, and water. Let stand for 5 minutes, or until foamy.

Transfer the yeast mixture to a food processor. Add ½ cup of the milk, the oil, egg white, salt, and flour. Process with on/off turns for 3 minutes, or until the dough is soft and pliable; add more milk, if needed. (Alternatively, combine the ingredients in a large bowl. Mix together with your fingers. Turn onto a lightly floured work surface and knead for 8 minutes, or until smooth.)

Coat a large bowl with nonstick spray. Transfer the dough to the bowl and cover with plastic wrap. Let rise for 1 hour, or until doubled in bulk. Punch down the dough and refrigerate for 1 hour.

To make the filling: In a large saucepan, combine the onions, bell peppers, garlic, tomatoes, potatoes, chicken, raisins, olives, capers, and stock or broth. Season with salt and black pepper. Simmer over medium heat for 10 to 15 minutes, or until the chicken is no longer pink in the center, the potatoes are soft, and most of the stock has been absorbed. Season with additional salt and black pepper, if desired. Let the filling cool to room temperature, cover, and refrigerate until cold.

To assemble and bake: Preheat the oven to 350°F. Coat a nonstick baking sheet with nonstick spray.

Cut the dough in half. Roll out each half on a lightly floured work surface to a thickness of ⅛". Using a small bowl or ramekin as a guide, cut out circles of dough that are 4" in diameter. Reroll the scraps and continue making circles until all the dough is used. You should have 24 circles.

Lightly brush the outside edge of a dough circle with water. Place a heaping tablespoon of filling in the center. Fold the dough circle in half to make a half moon–shaped turnover. Pleat the edges with your fingers or crimp with a fork. Repeat to use all the dough and filling.

Arrange on the prepared baking sheet. In a cup, beat together the egg substitute or egg white and a pinch of salt. Lightly brush on top of the turnovers. Bake for 20 minutes, or until golden brown.

Makes 24

Variations

Lenten Fish Pies: During Lent, replace the chicken with 6 ounces soaked, cooked salt cod or 6 ounces crabmeat.

Bolivian Vegetable Pies: Replace the chicken with ¾ cup cooked or canned chickpeas, rinsed and drained.

STUFFED YUCA FRITTERS

Carimañolas   *Panamá*

Nutrition Snapshot	Before	After
Per serving (2 fritters)		
Calories	608	418
Total Fat g.	26.3	4
Saturated Fat g.	4.9	0.6
Cholesterol mg.	24	24

These zeppelin-shaped fritters turn up whenever Panamanians gather for a meal and good times. The "dough" is actually boiled mashed yuca filled with a sort of beef hash. To slash the fat, I make the hash (or picadillo) with lean ground turkey and bake-fry the fritters in the oven.

FILLING

1	tablespoon canola oil
½	medium onion, finely chopped
¼	green bell pepper, finely chopped
1	clove garlic, minced
8	ounces lean ground turkey breast, crumbled
1	culantro leaf or cilantro sprig, finely chopped
¼	teaspoon ground cumin
¼	teaspoon curry powder
	Ground black pepper
2	teaspoons tomato paste
2	tablespoons water
	Salt

CRUST

14	cups cold water
	Salt
2½	pounds yuca, cut crosswise into 2" pieces and peeled (see tip on page 88)
	Ground black pepper
1	cup unbleached flour
¾	cup liquid egg substitute or 6 egg whites, lightly beaten
1	cup lightly toasted unseasoned dry bread crumbs

To make the filling: Heat the oil in a small nonstick skillet over medium heat. Add the onions, bell peppers, and garlic. Cook, stirring occasionally, for 4 minutes, or until the onions are soft but not brown. Add the turkey, culantro or cilantro, cumin, curry powder, and ¼ teaspoon black pepper. Cook, chopping and stirring with a wooden spoon, for 2 minutes. Stir in the tomato paste and 2 tablespoons water. Cook for 6 minutes, or until the turkey is cooked and all the liquid has evaporated. (The mixture should be quite dry.) The mixture should be highly seasoned; add salt and more black pepper, if desired. Remove the pan from the heat and let cool to room temperature. Transfer to a bowl, cover, and refrigerate until ready to use.

To make the crust: Pour 12 cups of the water into a large pot. Lightly salt the water and bring to a boil over high heat. Add the yuca to the pot and cook for 10 minutes. Add 1 cup of the remaining water. Return to a boil and cook for 5 minutes. Add the remaining 1 cup water and return to a boil. Cook for 5 minutes, or until the yuca is very soft. (The additions of cold water help tenderize the yuca.)

(continued)

Drain, reserving ½ cup of the cooking liquid. When cool enough to handle, scrape out and discard any fibers with a fork. Place the yuca in a medium bowl. Using a potato masher or pestle, mash the yuca to a smooth paste. If the yuca is too dry to mash, add some of the reserved cooking liquid. Season with salt and pepper. Let cool to room temperature, cover, and refrigerate for at least 6 hours and up to 24 hours.

To assemble and bake: Divide the yuca into 16 even pieces and roll each into a ball. With your thumb, make a depression in the center of each ball. Add 1 tablespoon of the filling. Pinch the top of each ball closed with your fingers. Gently roll the balls into an elongated oval shape between the palms of your hands. Continue to use all the yuca and filling.

Preheat the oven to 400°F. Coat a nonstick baking sheet with nonstick spray.

Place the flour, egg substitute or egg whites, and bread crumbs in 3 separate shallow bowls. Dip each fritter in the flour, then in the egg, then in the bread crumbs. Shake off the excess bread crumbs.

Arrange the fritters on the prepared baking sheet. Coat the tops with nonstick spray. Bake for 20 minutes, or until crisp and golden brown.

Makes 16

Cooking Tip

✦ To peel the yuca, stand the pieces on a cutting board, cut side down. Cut off the peel with a paring knife using downward strokes.

Variations

Cuban Stuffed Yuca Fritters: Replace the filling with 1 cup Turkey Picadillo (page 257).

Stuffed Boniatos: Substitute mashed boniatos (Caribbean sweet potatoes) for the yuca.

Stuffed Plantains: Substitute mashed semi-ripe plantains (pintones) for the yuca. Peel the plantain before boiling.

SALT COD FRITTERS

Bacalaítos

Various countries

Nutrition Snapshot	Before	After
Per serving (4 fritters)		
Calories	553	379
Total Fat g.	23.5	4.7
Saturated Fat g.	3.5	0.9
Cholesterol mg.	186	150

These spicy salt cod fritters are traditionally deep-fried, but great-tasting fritters can be bake-fried. To keep the mixture moist, I add potatoes. Start this recipe the day before so that you have plenty of time to soak the salt cod. Spanish-Caribbean Salsa (page 305) makes a tasty dip.

1	**pound skinless salt cod**
1	**pound baking potatoes, peeled and cut into 1" cubes**
1	**small onion, minced**
2	**cloves garlic, minced**
1	**habanero or 1–3 jalapeño chile peppers, minced (optional); wear plastic gloves when handling**
2	**tablespoons finely chopped fresh flat-leaf parsley**

1	**egg**
1	**egg white or 3 tablespoons liquid egg substitute**
¼	**teaspoon ground black pepper**
	Pinch of salt (optional)
3	**tablespoons + 1 cup fine unseasoned dry bread crumbs**

Place the cod in a medium bowl. Cover with cold water. Let soak in the refrigerator for 24 hours; change the water twice while soaking and rinse off the cod each time you change the water.

Place the cod in a large saucepan and cover with cold water. Bring to a boil over high heat. Drain and rinse with cold water. Return the cod to the pan and cover with cold water. Bring to a boil again, drain, and rinse. Return the cod to the pan and cover again with cold water. Bring to a boil, reduce the heat to medium, and simmer for 10 minutes, or until tender. Drain and rinse with cold water. Blot dry with paper towels. Pick through the fish and remove any bones. Process the cod in a food processor or blender for 1 minute, or until very finely chopped.

Place the potatoes in a large saucepan and cover with cold water. Bring to a boil over high heat. Reduce the heat to medium and simmer for 10 minutes, or until tender. Drain well. Return the potatoes to the pan. Cook and stir over medium heat for 1 minute, or until the water has evaporated. Remove the pan from the heat. Mash the potatoes in the pan with a potato masher or pass through a food mill.

Add the cod to the potatoes and stir to combine. Add the onions, garlic, chile peppers (if using), and parsley. Stir to combine. Beat in the egg and egg white or egg substitute. Season with the black pepper and salt (if using). Let cool, cover, and refrigerate for 2 hours, or until chilled. The mixture should be soft but not

(continued)

wet; if it looks too wet, stir in 2 to 3 tablespoons of the bread crumbs.

Preheat the oven to 400°F. Coat a nonstick baking sheet with nonstick spray.

Place 1 cup of the bread crumbs in a shallow bowl. Pinch off 1" balls of the cod mixture and flatten them into 2" patties. Dip each patty in the bread crumbs and shake off the excess. Arrange the patties on the prepared baking sheet. Coat the tops with nonstick spray.

Bake, turning once, for 15 to 20 minutes, or until crisp and golden brown. Transfer to a serving platter.

Makes 12 servings (48 fritters)

PERUVIAN-STYLE CEVICHE

Ceviche a lo peruano

Various countries

Nutrition Snapshot	Before	After
Per serving		
Calories	164	164
Total Fat g.	1.7	1.7
Saturated Fat g.	0.4	0.4
Cholesterol mg.	41	41

Ceviche (seh-VEE-cheh) is made by marinating seafood in a piquant mixture of lime juice and seasonings, then serving it cold. Traditionally, ceviche is served uncooked, but not exactly raw. The acid (citrus juice) in the marinade makes the seafood tender and white, as if it has been cooked. Note that the recipe below calls for the fish to be cooked before marinating. That is because the quality of fish varies widely. Cooking the fish is the best way to ensure food safety. This dish can be made with a staggering variety of fish and shellfish, from flounder to octopus. Sweet potatoes and corn are the traditional Peruvian accompaniments.

1½	pounds fresh gray sole, flounder, snapper, or other delicate white fish, cut into ½" pieces
1	red onion, thinly sliced and broken into rings
2	hontaka chile peppers (see page 57), crumbled (wear plastic gloves when handling), or 1 to 2 teaspoons red-pepper flakes
1	clove garlic, minced
¼	cup chopped fresh flat-leaf parsley
½	cup lime juice
½	cup lemon juice
	Salt
	Ground black pepper
1	large sweet potato, peeled and cut into 6 equal pieces
3	quarts water
1	large ear corn, shucked and cut into 6 equal pieces
6	leaves Boston lettuce

Preheat the grill or broiler.

Coat the fish with nonstick spray and grill on a grill tray or broil 4" from the heat for 2 to 3 minutes per side, or until cooked through and the fish flakes easily when tested with a fork. Transfer the fish to a large glass or stainless steel bowl and let cool. Stir in most of the onions (reserve a few rings for garnish), the chile peppers or red-pepper flakes, garlic, parsley, lime juice, lemon juice, 1 teaspoon salt, and ½ teaspoon black pepper. Cover and marinate in the refrigerator for 30 minutes to 1 hour.

Meanwhile, in a large pot over high heat, combine the sweet potatoes and water. Bring to a boil and boil for 5 minutes. Add the corn and cook for 5 minutes more, or until the potatoes and corn are tender. Drain and rinse. Refrigerate until chilled.

Season the ceviche with more salt and black pepper, if desired. To serve, arrange the lettuce on 6 plates. Using a slotted spoon, mound the ceviche in the center. Garnish each plate with a slice of sweet potato, some of the corn, and a few reserved onion rings.

Makes 6 servings

Regional Variation

Colombian Ceviche: Replace the soul, flounder, or snapper with 1½ pounds sea bass. Reduce the amount of red onions to ½ a red onion. Add ½ cup chopped green bell peppers, 1 seeded and minced jalapeño chile pepper, 2 tablespoons white vinegar, and 2 tablespoons lemon juice.

SOUPS AND STEWS
Sopas y guisos

Most Latinos eat soup at least once a day—more often than many Anglos. Latino soups are dazzling in their diversity, ranging from Spanish-Caribbean Beef and Vegetable Stew (page 110) to México's fiery Smoky Chicken-Tomato Soup (page 106). For hot weather, cold soups like Gazpacho (page 94) and Chilled Yuca Soup (page 95) are a refreshing rescue. And on cold winter evenings, nothing takes the chill off like White Bean and Collard Green Soup (page 101).

Relying on fresh vegetables, seafood, and only small amounts of meat, the majority of Latino soups are naturally low in fat. Some soups are made with butter and cream. To update these to today's health standards, I use evaporated skimmed milk instead of cream, which creates a rich, luscious texture without all the fat. Even pureed beans can create a rich consistency with no added fat, as in Mexican Pinto Bean Soup (page 103).

Latino cuisine has so many wonderful seafood stews that I put them in a separate chapter. For seafood stews, see the fish and shellfish recipes beginning on page 226. Only the seafood soups are included here.

RECIPES

GAZPACHO

Gazpacho

Spain

Nutrition Snapshot	Before	After
Per serving		
Calories	247	83
Total Fat g.	21	2.4
Saturated Fat g.	2.8	0.3
Cholesterol mg.	0	0

This icy vegetable soup from Andalucía is one of Spain's national treasures. Enormous quantities are sipped not only in Spain but also in Latin America. To make a low-fat version, I replaced some of the olive oil with vegetable stock. The traditional olive-oil flavor comes from drizzling extra-virgin oil on top of the soup, so it's the first thing you taste.

6	large, very ripe tomatoes, cored	2–2¼	cups Vegetable Stock (page 361) or defatted reduced-sodium vegetable broth
2	cucumbers, peeled and seeded	4–6	tablespoons red-wine vinegar
1	red bell pepper, quartered	2	slices country-style white bread, crusts removed, chopped
1	green bell pepper, quartered		Salt and ground black pepper
1	medium red onion, quartered	3	tablespoons finely chopped fresh flat-leaf parsley
4	scallions, trimmed	1–2	tablespoons extra-virgin olive oil
2	cloves garlic		

Seed and finely chop 1 of the tomatoes; set aside in a small serving bowl. Quarter the remaining 5 tomatoes. Finely chop 1 cucumber; set aside in a small serving bowl. Finely chop 1 quarter of each of the bell peppers; set aside in a small serving bowl. Finely chop 1 onion quarter; set aside in a small serving bowl. Finely chop the scallions; set the scallion greens aside in a small serving bowl.

In a blender, combine the scallion whites, remaining onions, garlic, 2 cups of the stock or broth, 4 tablespoons of the vinegar, the bread, and the remaining tomatoes, cucumbers, and bell peppers. Puree until smooth. The gazpacho should be thick but pourable; add a little more stock or broth, if needed. Season with salt and black pepper.

Transfer the gazpacho to a large bowl. Stir in the parsley. Cover and refrigerate for at least 30 minutes for the flavors to develop.

Just before serving, season with more salt, black pepper, and vinegar, if desired; the gazpacho should be highly seasoned. Ladle into serving bowls and sprinkle a little oil on top. Set the bowls of chopped vegetables on the table with spoons. Let each diner garnish the gazpacho with the chopped tomatoes, cucumbers, bell peppers, scallion greens, and onions.

Makes 8 servings

CHILLED YUCA SOUP

Yucassoise   *United States*

Nutrition Snapshot	Before	After
Per serving		
Calories	476	264
Total Fat g.	33.1	3.9
Saturated Fat g.	18.8	0.6
Cholesterol mg.	109	1

One of the hallmarks of Nuevo Latino cooking is its playfulness. Another is its freedom to borrow ingredients and cooking methods from cuisines around the world. Put them together and you get this refreshing soup—a Latino take-off on France's famous vichyssoise (potato-leek soup). Yucassoise was once a specialty at Yuca restaurant in Miami. To slash the fat in the original version, I replace the heavy cream with evaporated skimmed milk and nonfat sour cream. The flavor is as fantastic as ever.

1½   tablespoons olive oil

3   leeks, trimmed, washed, and finely chopped

5   scallions, whites finely chopped and greens thinly sliced

2   cloves garlic, minced

1   pound yuca, peeled, cored, and cut into 3" × ½" strips

3½–4   cups Chicken Stock (page 360) or fat-free reduced-sodium chicken broth

1   cup evaporated skimmed milk

1   bay leaf

1   cup nonfat sour cream

Salt and ground white or black pepper

3   tablespoons snipped fresh chives

Heat the oil in a large heavy saucepan over medium heat. Add the leeks, scallion whites, and garlic. Cook, stirring often, for 5 minutes, or until the vegetables are soft but not brown. Add the yuca, 3½ cups of the stock or broth, the evaporated milk, and bay leaf. Loosely cover the pan and cook for 15 minutes, or until the yuca is tender when tested with a fork. Stir in the sour cream and cook for 5 minutes, or until the yuca is very soft. Season with salt and pepper. Remove and discard the bay leaf.

Transfer the soup to a blender and puree. Strain into a serving bowl and let cool to room temperature. Cover and refrigerate for 4 hours, or until cold. The soup should be the consistency of heavy cream; if it is too thick, add a little more stock. Taste and add more salt and pepper, if desired. Stir in 1½ tablespoons of the chives. Ladle the soup into bowls and garnish each with some of the remaining chives and reserved scallion greens.

Makes 6 servings

CILANTRO SOUP

Sopa de cilantro   *México*

Nutrition Snapshot	Before	After
Per serving		
Calories	442	167
Total Fat g.	31.4	5.3
Saturated Fat g.	11.9	0.1
Cholesterol mg.	68	13

Here's an unusual soup for people who like cilantro. Even if you don't think you like cilantro, try the soup because the herb's distinctive flavor is utterly transformed by simmering. This recipe was inspired by one of Mexico City's most fashionable restaurants, La Valentina.

1	large or 2 small poblano chile peppers
2	bunches fresh cilantro, stemmed
1	medium onion, coarsely chopped
2	cloves garlic, minced
4½	cups Chicken Stock (page 360), fat-free reduced-sodium chicken broth, or water

	Salt and ground black pepper
1	corn tortilla (6" diameter), thinly slivered
2	tablespoons nonfat sour cream
2	tablespoons coarsely grated queso fresco or Romano cheese

Preheat a gas burner, electric burner, or broiler to high. Place the chile pepper(s) directly on top of the burner or under the broiler. Roast, turning occasionally, for 6 to 8 minutes, or until charred and blackened on all sides. Transfer to a paper bag. When cool enough to handle, scrape off as much of the skin (wear plastic gloves when handling) as possible with a paring knife. Don't worry about a few charred pieces of skin; they'll add a nice smoky flavor. Split the chile pepper(s) and remove and discard the seeds.

In a blender or food processor, combine the chile peppers, cilantro, onions, and garlic; puree until smooth. Transfer to a large saucepan. Pour in the stock, broth, or water. Simmer over medium-high heat for 5 to 8 minutes. The soup should be highly seasoned; sprinkle with salt and black pepper. Reduce the heat to low and keep warm.

Meanwhile, preheat the oven to 400°F.

Arrange the tortilla slivers on a nonstick baking sheet. Bake for 3 minutes, or until lightly toasted. Transfer to a plate to cool.

Ladle the soup into bowls. Spoon 1½ teaspoons of the sour cream in the center of each. Divide the tortilla strips among the bowls and sprinkle each with 1½ teaspoons of the cheese.

Makes 4 servings

CUCUMBER SOUP

Sopa de pepino   *Guatemala*

Nutrition Snapshot	Before	After
Per serving		
Calories	271	113
Total Fat g.	23.6	3.7
Saturated Fat g.	11.2	0.5
Cholesterol mg.	61	0

If you're used to using cucumbers for salad, this delicate soup from Guatemala will come as a revelation. To scale back the fat, I enrich the soup with nonfat sour cream instead of heavy cream. The flavor bonus is a delightfully sour tang that complements the mildness of the cucumber.

1	tablespoon extra-virgin olive oil
1	medium onion, finely chopped
1	yellow or green bell pepper, finely chopped
2	cloves garlic, minced
2	tablespoons chopped fresh flat-leaf parsley
2	cucumbers, peeled and cut into ½" pieces

3	cups Chicken Stock (page 360) or fat-free reduced-sodium chicken broth
¾	cup nonfat sour cream
	Salt and ground black pepper
2	tablespoons snipped fresh chives

Heat the oil in a large saucepan over medium heat. Add the onions, bell peppers, garlic, and parsley. Cook for 4 minutes, or until the onions are soft but not brown. Add the cucumbers and cook for 1 minute. Add the stock or broth and sour cream. Increase the heat to high and bring to a boil. Reduce the heat to medium and simmer for 5 minutes, or until the cucumbers are very soft. Transfer the soup to a blender and puree. Season with salt and black pepper.

To serve, ladle the soup into serving bowls. Sprinkle with the chives.

Makes 4 servings

MEXICAN CORN SOUP

Sopa de elote   *México*

Nutrition Snapshot	Before	After
Per serving		
Calories	647	356
Total Fat g.	36.6	4.1
Saturated Fat g.	15.6	0.6
Cholesterol mg.	82	0

Here's México's version of corn chowder. Unlike North American corn chowder, it's free of cream and butter, so it's naturally low in fat. I've jazzed up the soup with roasted poblano chiles and onions.

1	poblano chile pepper or green bell pepper
1	medium onion, quartered
2	cloves garlic
2	cups fresh or frozen and thawed corn kernels (see tip)
6	sprigs fresh or dried epazote
1	bay leaf

4	cups Chicken Stock (page 360) or fat-free reduced-sodium chicken broth
3	tablespoons chopped fresh cilantro
	Salt and ground black pepper
1–2	tablespoons pure chili powder
1	lime, cut into 4 wedges

Preheat the broiler.

Place a comal (a griddle for cooking tortillas) or a large heavy skillet over medium-high heat. Add the chile pepper or bell pepper, onions, and garlic. Roast, turning occasionally, until nicely browned. The garlic will take 3 to 4 minutes; the pepper and onions will take 6 to 8 minutes. Transfer to a plate to cool. Scrape as much skin off the chile pepper (wear plastic gloves when handling) or bell pepper as possible. Finely chop the pepper, onions, and garlic.

In a large saucepan over medium heat, combine the peppers, onions, garlic, corn, 2 sprigs of the epazote, the bay leaf, and stock or broth. Bring to a simmer. Reduce the heat to medium-low and gently simmer for 8 to 10 minutes, or until the corn is soft. Remove and discard the bay leaf. Puree the soup in a blender; return it to the pan. Stir in the cilantro and cook for 1 minute. Season with salt and black pepper.

Ladle the soup into serving bowls and garnish each with a sprig or sprinkling of epazote and a sprinkling of chili powder. Serve each with a lime wedge for squeezing into the soup.

Makes 4 servings

Cooking Tip

✦ To cut the kernels from fresh corn, lay the cobs on a cutting board. Cut off large strips of kernels with broad sweeps of a large knife.

PLANTAIN SOUP

Sopa de plátano

Cuba
Puerto Rico

Nutrition Snapshot	Before	After
Per serving		
Calories	269	195
Total Fat g.	12.9	4.4
Saturated Fat g.	6.1	0.7
Cholesterol mg.	24	0.2

Green plantains are a classic stomach-soother in Latin American cooking. My Cuban friends make a batch of this healing soup whenever someone in the family has a stomachache.

1	tablespoon extra-virgin olive oil	2	green plantains, peeled (see tip), quartered lengthwise, and thinly sliced
1	small onion, finely chopped		
1	carrot, finely chopped	1	small bunch cilantro, stemmed and finely chopped
1	rib celery, finely chopped		
2	cloves garlic, minced	½–1	teaspoon ground cumin
4–4¼	cups Chicken Stock (page 360) or fat-free reduced-sodium chicken broth	1	bay leaf
			Salt and ground black pepper

Heat the oil in a large heavy saucepan over medium heat. Add the onions, carrots, celery, and garlic. Cook, uncovered, for 3 to 4 minutes, or until the onions are soft but not brown. Add 4 cups of the stock or broth and bring to a boil over high heat. Add the plantains, most of the cilantro (reserve a few tablespoons for garnish), ½ teaspoon of the cumin, and the bay leaf. Season with salt and pepper. Return to a boil. Reduce the heat to medium-low and simmer, uncovered, for 40 to 50 minutes, or until the plantains are very tender.

Remove and discard the bay leaf. Transfer half of the soup to a blender; puree until smooth. Return to the pan. If the soup is too thick, add a little more stock. Season with more salt and cumin, if desired. Sprinkle the reserved cilantro on top.

Makes 4 servings

Cooking Tip

✦ To peel a green plantain, cut off the ends and make 3 or 4 slits down the length of the plantain, cutting just through the skin. Place the plantain in a medium bowl and cover with warm water. Let soak for 10 minutes, or until the skin is softened. Run your thumb under the slits to ease the skin off the plantain.

MUSHROOM AND SQUASH-BLOSSOM SOUP

Sopa de hongos
y flor de calabaza

México

Nutrition Snapshot	Before	After
Per serving		
Calories	309	205
Total Fat g.	17.8	4.1
Saturated Fat g.	8.5	0.7
Cholesterol mg.	38	3

Oscar Rodríguez, of La Valentina restaurant, is one of the most gifted chefs in Mexico City. His genius lies in combining commonplace ingredients in unexpected ways. Consider the following soup, which features squash blossoms and mushrooms. The only change that I've made is to use evaporated skimmed milk instead of regular evaporated milk. I also add a small amount of flour to compensate for the thinness of the fat-free milk.

1 tablespoon lard or olive oil

1 medium onion, finely chopped

2 cloves garlic

1 pound mushrooms, thinly sliced

16 squash or pumpkin blossoms, thinly sliced crosswise

1 tablespoon all-purpose flour

1 can (14 ounces) evaporated skimmed milk

3½ cups Chicken Stock (page 360) or fat-free reduced-sodium chicken broth

Salt and ground black pepper

¼ cup chopped fresh flat-leaf parsley

Heat the lard or oil in a large saucepan over medium heat. Add the onions and garlic. Cook for 4 minutes, or until the onions are soft but not brown. Add the mushrooms; cook, stirring often, for 6 minutes, or until the mushrooms are tender and most of the mushroom liquid has evaporated. Add the squash or pumpkin blossoms; cook for 3 minutes, or until wilted. Stir in the flour; cook for 2 minutes. Stir in the evaporated milk. Increase the heat to high and bring to a boil. Stir in the stock or broth and return to a boil. Reduce the heat to medium-low. Simmer for 5 to 8 minutes, or until richly flavored and the vegetables are soft. Season with salt and pepper.

Just before serving, stir in the parsley. Simmer for 1 minute more.

Makes 4 servings

Variation

Mushroom and Squash Soup: Replace the squash or pumpkin blossoms with 1 cup finely chopped pumpkin or butternut squash. Simmer the soup for 10 to 15 minutes after adding the stock or broth, or until the squash is soft.

Pronto!

WHITE BEAN AND COLLARD GREEN SOUP

Caldo gallego

Various countries

Nutrition Snapshot	Before	After
Per serving		
Calories	420	219
Total Fat g.	22.6	4.6
Saturated Fat g.	8.2	0.7
Cholesterol mg.	69	4

Caldo gallego literally means "Galician broth." Galicia is a province in the northwest region of Spain. When Galicians emigrated (mostly to Cuba), they brought this classic bean-and-green soup with them. The traditional recipe calls for loads of salt pork and chorizo (a type of spicy Latin American sausage). This updated version gets the same meaty flavor with lean serrano (dry-cured) ham. To speed up the prep time, I make the soup with canned beans.

1   tablespoon extra-virgin olive oil

1   medium onion, finely chopped

1   ounce serrano ham or prosciutto, cut into ¼" pieces

2   cloves garlic, minced

4   cups Chicken Stock (page 360) or fat-free reduced-sodium chicken broth

1   medium potato, peeled and cut into ½" pieces

1   can (19 ounces) white beans, rinsed and drained

1   bay leaf

8   ounces fresh or frozen and thawed collard greens or kale

    Salt and ground black pepper

Heat the oil in a large saucepan over medium heat. Add the onions, ham or prosciutto, and garlic. Cook for 5 minutes, or until the onions are soft but not brown. Add the stock or broth, potatoes, beans, and bay leaf. Simmer for 5 minutes, or until the potatoes are almost tender.

Cut the stems off of the collard green leaves or kale and discard. Roll up the leaves and slice crosswise into ½" slivers. Add to the soup. Simmer for 5 minutes, or until the greens and potatoes are tender. With the back of a wooden spoon, mash about one-quarter of the beans and potatoes against the side of the pan to thicken the soup. Simmer for 1 minute. Season with salt and pepper. Remove and discard the bay leaf.

Makes 4 servings

Variation

Vegetarian White Bean and Collard Green Soup: Use vegetable stock instead of chicken stock. Omit the ham (or replace it with tofu sausage, which can be found in the freezer case at many supermarkets) and add a few drops of liquid smoke.

CUBAN BLACK BEAN SOUP

Sopa de frijoles
negros a lo cubano

Cuba

Nutrition Snapshot	Before	After
Per serving		
Calories	424	275
Total Fat g.	18.3	5
Saturated Fat g.	6.4	0.9
Cholesterol mg.	27	4

When it comes to comfort foods, black bean soup is in a class by itself. The Cuban version is particularly soulful, relying on a robust sofrito (sauté of aromatic vegetables) to flavor the beans. To create a rich and creamy texture (with no added fat), a portion of the beans are pureed. To cut back on the saturated fat, I use Canadian bacon instead of regular bacon and olive oil instead of bacon fat. Cachucha chile peppers are a very mild, tiny pepper from Cuba. If unavailable, use rocotillos (see page 55), ají dulce, or red bell peppers.

1	pound dried black beans, sorted and rinsed
9	cups water
6	cachucha chile peppers or ½ green bell pepper, cored and seeded
6	cloves garlic
2	medium onions
1	bay leaf
1	whole clove
2	tablespoons extra-virgin olive oil
1	green bell pepper, finely chopped
2	ribs celery, finely chopped
2	ounces Canadian bacon, thinly slivered
½	cup dry white wine or nonalcoholic white wine
1–1½	tablespoons red-wine vinegar
1	teaspoon ground cumin
1	teaspoon dried oregano
	Salt and ground black pepper
¼	cup nonfat sour cream
¼	cup finely chopped scallion greens

Combine the beans and water in a large heavy pot and let soak overnight in the refrigerator. (This step can be omitted if you use a pressure cooker.)

The next day, add the chile peppers or bell-pepper half and 2 cloves of the garlic to the beans. Halve 1 of the onions. Pin the bay leaf to 1 of the onion halves with a clove; add it to the beans along with the other onion half. Bring to a boil over high heat. Reduce the heat to low, cover loosely, and simmer, stirring occasionally, for 1 hour, or until the beans are tender. (The beans and vegetables can also be cooked in a pressure cooker. Pressure-cook soaked beans for 7 minutes and unsoaked beans for 15 minutes, or until tender.)

Heat the oil in a large nonstick skillet over medium heat. Finely chop the remaining onion. Mince the remaining 4 cloves garlic. Add the onions and garlic to the skillet along with the chopped bell peppers, celery, and bacon. Cook for 4 minutes, or until the vegetables are soft but not brown.

Stir the vegetables into the beans. Add the wine, vinegar, cumin, and oregano. Season with salt and black pepper. Cover and reduce the heat to medium-low. Gently simmer for 10 minutes, or until the beans are very soft.

Remove and discard the bay leaf, halved onions, and whole garlic cloves. Using a slotted spoon, transfer 2 cups of the beans to a bowl and mash with the back of a wooden spoon or puree in a food processor or blender. Stir back into the soup. Season with additional salt, black pepper, and vinegar, if desired.

Ladle the soup into serving bowls and top each with a dollop of sour cream and a sprinkling of scallion greens.

Makes 8 servings

Regional Variation

Guatemalan Black Bean Soup: Omit the cachucha chile peppers or bell-pepper half when cooking the beans. Omit the chopped bell pepper and celery when making the sofrito (vegetable sauté). Substitute dry sherry for the white wine and omit the vinegar, cumin, and oregano.

PINTO BEAN SOUP

Sopa tarasca   *México*

Nutrition Snapshot	Before	After
Per serving		
Calories	314	189
Total Fat g.	16.9	3.1
Saturated Fat g.	4.1	0.4
Cholesterol mg.	12	0

Central México is home to this rich bean soup. Charring the onions, tomatoes, and chiles creates so much flavor that you don't need a lot of fat. The preferred chile is the pasilla, a dried chile pepper that's wrinkled like a raisin. If unavailable, use dried ancho chiles or 2 tablespoons pure chili powder.

3	tomatoes, stem ends removed
1	onion, quartered
3	cloves garlic
1	jalapeño chile pepper, seeded (wear plastic gloves when handling)
2	pasilla or ancho chile peppers (wear plastic gloves when handling)
3–3¼	cups warm Chicken Stock (page 360) or fat-free reduced-sodium chicken broth

3	tablespoons finely chopped fresh cilantro
1½	tablespoons lard or olive oil
3	cups cooked or rinsed and drained canned pinto beans
	Salt and ground black pepper
1	corn tortilla (6" diameter), cut into thin strips
3	tablespoons nonfat sour cream
1	tablespoon chopped fresh chives or scallion greens

Preheat the broiler.

In a roasting pan, combine the tomatoes, onions, garlic, and jalapeño chile pepper. Broil, turning occasionally, for 3 minutes per side, or until nicely browned. Transfer to a blender.

Tear the pasilla or ancho chile peppers open (wear plastic gloves when handling) and discard the seeds. Broil the pasilla or ancho chile peppers for 10 seconds per side, or until lightly toasted. (Be careful; they burn easily.) Transfer to a small bowl and add 1 cup of the stock or broth. Let soak for 15 minutes, or until soft. Transfer the chile peppers to the blender; reserve the stock. Add the cilantro and puree until smooth.

Heat the lard or oil in a large deep saucepan over medium heat. Add the puree. Cook and stir for 5 minutes, or until thick. Stir in the beans and 2 cups of the remaining stock. Season with salt and black pepper. Simmer for 8 minutes. Transfer the soup to the blender and puree. Return it to the pan. If the soup is too thick, add a little more stock. Season with more salt, if desired.

Meanwhile, preheat the oven to 400°F.

Spread the tortilla strips on a baking sheet. Bake for 3 minutes, or until crisp.

Ladle the soup into serving bowls. Top each with 1½ teaspoons of the sour cream. Sprinkle with the tortilla strips and the chives or scallion greens.

Makes 6 servings

Cooking Tip

✦ For a fanciful touch, whisk the sour cream until creamy and put it in a squirt bottle (a restaurant-style plastic ketchup bottle works well). Squirt decorative zigzags or squiggles of sour cream over the soup.

Pronto!

YUCATÁN CHICKEN-LIME SOUP

Sopa de lima   *México*

Nutrition Snapshot	Before	After
Per serving		
Calories	612	389
Total Fat g.	37.9	10.5
Saturated Fat g.	8.6	2.3
Cholesterol mg.	136	118

This is about the best chicken soup that I've ever tasted. Plus, it's good for you. Lime juice is loaded with immune-boosting vitamin C. Chile peppers blast open stuffed sinuses. And garlic acts as an antibiotic. I can't think of a better remedy for a cold or a rainy day.

4   corn tortillas (6" diameter), cut into thin strips

1   large tomato, halved crosswise and seeded

1   tablespoon olive oil

1   medium onion, finely chopped

8   cloves garlic, minced

2–8   serrano chile peppers, thinly sliced (wear plastic gloves when handling)

4   cups Chicken Stock (page 360) or fat-free reduced-sodium chicken broth

1½   cups shredded cooked chicken breast

1   bay leaf

4–6   tablespoons lime juice

¼   cup chopped fresh cilantro

Salt and ground black pepper

Preheat the oven to 400°F.

Arrange the tortilla strips on a baking sheet. Bake for 3 minutes, or until lightly toasted. Transfer to a plate to cool.

Working over a small bowl, grate each tomato half on the coarse side of a hand grater. Discard the skin.

Heat the oil in a large saucepan over medium heat. Add the onions, garlic, and chile peppers. Cook for 4 minutes, or until the onions are soft but not brown. Stir in the tomatoes, stock or broth, chicken, and bay leaf. Simmer for 5 minutes. Stir in 4 tablespoons of the lime juice and the cilantro. Season with salt and black pepper. Remove and discard the bay leaf. Taste and add more lime juice, if desired. Ladle into serving bowls and sprinkle each with some of the tortilla strips.

Makes 4 servings

Cooking Tip

✦ If you have an asbestos tongue, add the full amount of serrano chile peppers.

SMOKY CHICKEN-TOMATO SOUP

Caldo tlalpeño *México*

Nutrition Snapshot	Before	After
Per serving		
Calories	572	238
Total Fat g.	31	6.5
Saturated Fat g.	9.5	1.3
Cholesterol mg.	205	64

This soup takes the edge off a cold winter night. Chipotles (smoked jalapeño chile peppers) give the broth plenty of smoke and fire—just the way they like it in Tlalpan, México, where the dish originated. I use boneless, skinless chicken breasts to trim the fat.

2–4	dried or canned chipotle chile peppers	1	can (15 ounces) chickpeas, rinsed and drained
2	tomatoes	6	cups Chicken Stock (page 360) or fat-free reduced-sodium chicken broth
1	tablespoon lard or olive oil		
1	onion, finely chopped	2	sprigs epazote
2	cloves garlic, minced		Salt and ground black pepper
6	scallions, finely chopped		
1	pound boneless, skinless chicken breasts, cut into ½" pieces		

If using dried chile peppers, stem and tear in half (wear plastic gloves when handling). Remove and discard the seeds. Place in a small bowl and cover with warm water. Let soak for 30 minutes, or until soft. Drain well. If using canned chile peppers, use them as is.

Heat a comal (a griddle for cooking tortillas) or large nonstick skillet over medium-high heat. Add the tomatoes and roast, turning occasionally, for 8 minutes, or until the skins are charred and blistered. Transfer to a plate to cool. Scrape off the burnt skin with a paring knife and core the tomatoes. Transfer to a blender. Add the chile peppers; puree until smooth.

Heat the lard or oil in a large saucepan over medium heat. Add the onions, garlic, and most of the scallions (reserve 3 tablespoons of the scallion greens to sprinkle on top). Cook, stirring often, for 5 minutes, or until lightly browned. Increase the heat to high. Add the tomato mixture. Cook, stirring often, for 5 minutes, or until thick and fragrant. Stir in the chicken, chickpeas, stock or broth, and epazote. Season with salt and black pepper. Reduce the heat to medium and simmer for 20 minutes, or until the chicken is no longer pink and the broth is richly flavored. Season with more salt and black pepper, if desired.

Ladle the soup into serving bowls and sprinkle with the reserved scallion greens.

Makes 6 servings

SHRIMP SOUP

Chupe de
camarones

Ecuador

Nutrition Snapshot	Before	After
Per serving		
Calories	611	481
Total Fat g.	23.1	7.3
Saturated Fat g.	12.5	2.7
Cholesterol mg.	230	182

This soulful soup is Ecuador's version of chowder. If you can get shrimp with the heads on, they'll enrich the flavor of the broth. If not, supermarket shrimp with the shells taste almost as good.

4   cups Fish Stock (page 362) or bottled clam juice

1   pound shrimp (1½ pounds if heads are on), peeled and deveined (shells reserved); see tip

1   tablespoon butter

1   onion, minced

1   clove garlic, minced

3   tablespoons chopped fresh flat-leaf parsley

2   potatoes, peeled and cut into ½" pieces

4   lasagna noodles, broken into 2" pieces

2   ears corn, shucked and cut crosswise into 1" rounds

1   can (14 ounces) evaporated skimmed milk

    Salt and ground black pepper

1   lime, cut into 4 wedges

In a medium pot, combine the stock or clam juice and reserved shrimp shells; simmer for 15 minutes.

Meanwhile, melt the butter in a large heavy pot over medium heat. Add the onions, garlic, and 2 tablespoons of the parsley. Cook for 4 minutes, or until the vegetables are soft but not brown.

Strain the stock into the pot with the vegetables, increase the heat to high, and bring to a boil. Add the potatoes, noodles, corn, evaporated milk, and shrimp. Reduce the heat to medium and simmer for 10 minutes, or until the potatoes and noodles are soft. Season with salt and pepper.

Ladle the soup into serving bowls and sprinkle with the remaining 1 tablespoon parsley. Serve each with a lime wedge for squeezing into the soup.

Makes 4 servings

Cooking Tips

✦ If using shrimp with the heads on, buy 1½ pounds. Remove the heads with a sharp knife and add to the stock along with the reserved shrimp shells. The heads will be strained out with the other solids when you strain the stock into the pot with the vegetables.

✦ The corn in this soup is meant to be nibbled off the cob.

HONDURAN FISH SOUP

Sopa de hombre   *Honduras*

Nutrition Snapshot	Before	After
Per serving		
Calories	704	331
Total Fat g.	41.7	7.6
Saturated Fat g.	27.3	1.3
Cholesterol mg.	291	180

Hondurans *consider this seafood soup a no-fail remedy for a hangover. Hence the name sopa de hombre, or "man's soup" (I suppose Honduran women generally show more restraint when it comes to alcohol). The traditional soup is made with copious amounts of coconut milk, which is high in saturated fat. To make a healthier soup, I use coconut water (the clear liquid inside a coconut) with a small amount of light coconut milk (see page 53) for texture and flavor. Feel free to vary the seafood based on what's available in your area and what's freshest at the time of purchase. This recipe was inspired by Copeland Marks, author of the fascinating Central American cookbook,* False Tongues and Sunday Bread.

4	ripe (brown) coconuts
1	tablespoon canola oil
1	onion, finely chopped
1	red bell pepper, finely chopped
2	cloves garlic, minced
½–1	teaspoon red-pepper flakes
2	tomatoes, peeled (see page 383), seeded, and finely chopped
½	cup finely chopped fresh flat-leaf parsley
¼	cup tomato paste
1	cup light coconut milk
5	cups Fish Stock (page 362) or 4 cups bottled clam juice + 1 cup water

1	bay leaf
1	green plantain, peeled (see page 386) and chopped
4	live blue crabs, halved (see tip)
16	small clams or mussels, scrubbed and beards removed
1	pound shrimp, peeled and deveined
2	pounds sea bass, cod, or haddock fillets, cut into 1" pieces
½	cup fresh bread crumbs, toasted (see tip)
	Salt and ground black pepper

Punch the eyes out of the coconuts with a screwdriver. Drain the coconuts into a measuring cup and set aside. You should have about 2 cups coconut water. If desired, save the coconut shells for serving Coconut Eggnog (page 352).

Heat the oil in a large pot over medium heat. Add the onions, bell peppers, garlic, and ½ teaspoon of the red-pepper flakes. Cook for 5 minutes, or until the onions are soft but not brown. Increase the heat to medium-high. Add the tomatoes and ¼ cup of the parsley. Cook for 3 minutes. Add the tomato paste and cook for 3 minutes. Stir in the coconut water, coconut milk, stock or clam juice and water, bay leaf, and plantains. Bring to a boil and cook for 3 minutes.

Add the crabs and cook for 5 minutes. Add the clams or mussels; cook for 5 minutes. Add the shrimp, fish, and bread crumbs. Season with salt and black pepper. Cook for 5 minutes, or until the plantains are soft and the broth is slightly thickened. (Discard any clams or mussels that remain closed or have cracked shells.)

Stir in the remaining ¼ cup parsley and simmer for 1 minute. Season with more red-pepper flakes, salt, and black pepper, if desired.

Makes 8 servings

Cooking Tips

✦ If you don't like the idea of cutting up live crabs, cook the crabs whole in rapidly boiling water for 10 minutes, or until the shells turn bright red. Cut the crabs in half. Or use 1 cup lump crabmeat, picked over and shells removed, and add it when you add the shrimp.

✦ To make ½ cup fresh bread crumbs, remove and discard the crusts from 3 slices stale white bread. Process the bread in a food processor or blender until crumbs form.

✦ Light coconut milk is available in Hispanic and Asian markets and the international section of many large supermarkets.

SPANISH-CARIBBEAN BEEF AND VEGETABLE STEW

Ajiaco

Various countries

Nutrition Snapshot	Before	After
Per serving		
Calories	814	425
Total Fat g.	34.6	11.8
Saturated Fat g.	12.2	3.6
Cholesterol mg.	136	55

Ajiaco *refers to a family of souplike stews popular in the Caribbean, Central America, and Colombia. The dish takes its name from the Spanish word aji, meaning bell or cachucha pepper. Most likely, ajiaco predates the arrival of the Spanish, as the starchy vegetables that give the stew its substance are native to the New World and were used by the Taino and Arawak Indians. Here's the Cuban version of ajiaco. Don't be intimidated by the long list of ingredients. You basically put them all in a pot and let them boil.*

12	ounces tasajo (dried beef); see tip
1¼	pounds beef brisket or flank steak, trimmed of all visible fat
1	pound lean pork loin or tenderloin, trimmed of all visible fat
2	bay leaves
16–20	cups water
1	can (14½ ounces) low-sodium or regular peeled tomatoes (with juice)
2	tablespoons olive oil
1	tablespoon Annatto Oil (page 380) or 1 tablespoon olive oil + ¼ teaspoon sweet paprika
2	medium onions, finely chopped
1	green bell pepper, finely chopped
5	cloves garlic, minced
3	tablespoons chopped fresh cilantro
1	tablespoon minced fresh ginger
1	teaspoon dried oregano
1	teaspoon ground cumin

8	ounces malanga, peeled and cut into 1" pieces
8	ounces boniato, peeled and cut into 1" pieces
8	ounces yuca, peeled (see tip) and cut into 1" pieces
8	ounces yams, peeled and cut into 1" pieces
8	ounces potatoes, peeled and cut into 1" pieces
8	ounces calabaza or butternut squash, peeled and cut into 1" pieces
8	ounces green plantains, peeled (see page 386) and cut into 1" pieces
8	ounces semi-ripe plantains (pinton), peeled and cut into 1" pieces
2	ears corn, shucked and cut crosswise into 1" pieces
¼	cup lime juice
	Salt and ground black pepper

The day before serving, scrape any fat off the tasajo. Place in a medium bowl and cover with warm water. Let soak in the refrigerator for 12 hours; change the water 3 times and rinse off the beef each time you change the water.

Cut the tasajo, beef, and pork into 1" cubes. Place in a large pot. Add the bay leaves and 16 cups of the water. Bring to a boil over high heat. Skim off any foam that rises to the surface. Reduce the heat to medium and simmer, skimming occasionally, for 1 hour.

Meanwhile, in a food processor or blender, puree the tomatoes (with juice) and set aside.

Heat the olive oil and annatto oil or olive oil and paprika in a large nonstick skillet over medium heat. Add the onions, bell peppers, garlic, cilantro, ginger, oregano, and cumin. Cook for 4 minutes, or until the onions are soft but not brown. Add the reserved tomatoes and simmer for 2 minutes. Stir into the pot after the meat has cooked for 1 hour. Add the malanga, boniato, yuca, yams, potatoes, calabaza or squash, green plantains, semi-ripe plantains, and corn. Simmer for 30 to 45 minutes, or until the vegetables and meats are very tender and the calabaza and yuca begin to disintegrate and thicken the broth. The meats and vegetables should be submerged at all times; if the stew becomes too dry, add more water.

Just before serving, remove the bay leaves and stir in the lime juice. The stew should be highly seasoned; sprinkle with salt and black pepper.

Makes 12 serving

Cooking Tips

✦ Tasajo (also known as carne seca) is salted dried beef sold at Hispanic markets. Before using tasajo, scrape off the layer of yellowish fat covering the surface. If you can't find tasajo, use more flank steak for this recipe.

✦ To peel the yuca, stand the pieces, cut side down, on a cutting board. Cut off the peel with a paring knife using downward strokes.

✦ The corn in this soup is meant to be nibbled off the cob.

COLOMBIAN CHICKEN AND VEGETABLE STEW

Ajiaco
colombiano

Colombia

Nutrition Snapshot	Before	After
Per serving		
Calories	502	374
Total Fat g.	26.5	12.5
Saturated Fat g.	9.7	2.8
Cholesterol mg.	124	81

In Colombia, ajiaco is made with chicken and cream. To trim the fat in the traditional recipe, I use skinless chicken breasts in place of whole chicken and evaporated skimmed milk instead of cream.

2	tablespoons canola oil
1	medium onion, finely chopped
5	scallions, whites finely chopped and greens sliced
4	cloves garlic, minced
2	tablespoons chopped fresh cilantro
2½	pounds boneless, skinless chicken breasts
8	cups water
1	can (14 ounces) evaporated skimmed milk
1	bay leaf
12	ounces baking potatoes, peeled and cut into 1" pieces

12	ounces Yukon gold potatoes, peeled and cut into 1" pieces
12	ounces red new potatoes, scrubbed and halved or quartered
2	ears corn, shucked and cut cross-wise into 1" rounds
1	bunch guascas, chopped, or 1 can (16 ounces) asparagus, drained and cut into ½" pieces
	Salt and ground black pepper
1	avocado
1	tablespoon lime juice
3	tablespoons rinsed and drained capers
1	cup nonfat sour cream

Heat the oil in a large pot over medium heat. Add the onions, scallion whites, half of the scallion greens, the garlic, and cilantro. Cook for 4 minutes, or until the onions are soft but not brown. Add the chicken, water, evaporated milk, and bay leaf. Increase the heat to high, bring to a boil, and skim the soup to remove any foam. Reduce the heat to medium and simmer for 15 minutes. Add all the potatoes, corn, and guascas or asparagus. Simmer for 15 minutes, or until the chicken is very tender and the potatoes are soft. Transfer the chicken to a plate and let cool. Remove and discard the bay leaf. Season with salt and pepper. Shred the chicken with a fork or finely chop with a knife. Return it to the stew and simmer for 3 minutes, or until heated through.

Peel and pit the avocado and cut into ½" cubes. Place in a small serving bowl. Toss the avocado with the lime juice. Place the capers, sour cream, and the remaining scallion greens in separate small serving bowls.

To serve, ladle the stew into serving bowls. Let each guest garnish the stew with the avocados, capers, sour cream, and scallion greens.

Makes 12 servings

CREOLE CHICKPEA STEW

Garbanzos criollos

Various countries

Nutrition Snapshot	Before	After
Per serving		
Calories	305	255
Total Fat g.	12.3	6.6
Saturated Fat g.	4.4	0.9
Cholesterol mg.	15	0

Visit a Puerto Rican, Cuban, or Dominican home, and you'll be greeted by the comforting smell of frying onions, garlic, peppers, and culantro. That's the smell of sofrito, the very soul of Spanish-Caribbean cooking and the starting point for a slew of Hispanic dishes, like this vegetarian chickpea stew, which comes together in just 30 minutes.

1½ tablespoons olive oil

1 very small onion, finely chopped

4 scallions, trimmed and finely chopped

6 rocotillo chile peppers, seeded and chopped, or ½ green bell pepper, chopped

1 red bell pepper, chopped

3 cloves garlic, minced

½ teaspoon ground cumin

½ teaspoon dried oregano

2 tomatoes, seeded and chopped

3 tablespoons chopped fresh cilantro

4 culantro leaves, finely chopped, or 1 tablespoon chopped fresh cilantro

6 tablespoons chopped fresh flat-leaf parsley

3 tablespoons tomato paste

2 cups Vegetable Stock (page 361) or fat-free reduced-sodium vegetable broth

2 medium potatoes, peeled and cut into 1" pieces

2 cans (15 ounces each) chickpeas, rinsed and drained

Salt and ground black pepper

1 tomato, seeded and thinly sliced

Heat the oil in a large nonstick skillet over medium heat. Add the onions, scallions, chile peppers or green bell peppers, red bell peppers, garlic, cumin, and oregano. Cook for 5 minutes, or until the vegetables are soft but not brown. Add the chopped tomatoes, cilantro, culantro or cilantro, and 3 tablespoons of the parsley. Cook for 5 minutes, or until most of the liquid has evaporated and the mixture is thick and fragrant.

Stir in the tomato paste; cook for 1 minute. Stir in the stock or broth and bring to a boil over high heat. Stir in the potatoes. Reduce the heat to medium and simmer for 6 minutes. Stir in the chickpeas and simmer for 6 minutes, or until the potatoes are soft and the sauce is thick and flavorful. Season with salt and black pepper. Transfer to a serving bowl and top with the tomato slices. Sprinkle with the remaining 3 tablespoons parsley.

Makes 6 servings

SALADS AND VEGETABLES
Ensaladas y verduras

Nothing matches the visual splendor of a Latin American vegetable

market. Bright red tomatoes, electric-orange squashes, and chiles in every

color of the rainbow grace the tables.

Latinos love vegetables. South of the border, vegetables are grown

for flavor and succulence rather than just picture-perfect appearance. As a re-

sult, the produce often tastes better than what you find in the United States.

It's true that many of Latin America's beloved vegetables often start

out healthy and end up soaking in loads of fat in the deep-fryer. But you can

still enjoy these classic dishes. This chapter offers heart-healthy versions of

fried potatoes, fried plantains, chile rellenos, and more.

If you don't normally like vegetables, the recipes in this chapter

will come as a revelation. Vinaigrettes and crisp-cooking methods give

them a big jolt of flavor. Even the salads are bursting with fresh tastes.

Hearts of Palm Salad (page 116) and Cactus Salad (page 117) beat the typ-

ical North American mixture of iceberg lettuce, tomatoes, and shredded

carrots by a mile.

SALAD RECIPES

VEGETABLE RECIPES

CENTRAL AMERICAN SLAW

Ensalada de repollo

Various countries

Nutrition Snapshot	Before	After
Per serving (¹/₂ cup)		
Calories	54	24
Total Fat g.	3.5	0.1
Saturated Fat g.	0.5	0
Cholesterol mg.	0	0

Enjoy this slaw with dishes like Salvadoran Stuffed Tortillas (page 206) and Honduran Enchiladas (page 218).

4	cups thinly shredded green cabbage	4–5	tablespoons white vinegar	
			Salt	
2	carrots, shredded	½	teaspoon sugar	
2–4	jalapeño chile peppers, minced (wear plastic gloves when handling)	½	teaspoon ground black pepper	

In a large bowl, combine the cabbage, carrots, chile peppers, 4 tablespoons of the vinegar, 1 teaspoon salt, the sugar, and black pepper. Toss to mix. Taste and sprinkle with more salt and vinegar, if desired.

Makes 8 servings (4 cups)

HEARTS OF PALM SALAD

Ensalada de palmitos

Various countries

Nutrition Snapshot	Before	After
Per serving		
Calories	272	138
Total Fat g.	20.8	5.6
Saturated Fat g.	2.8	0.7
Cholesterol mg.	0	0

Hearts of palm come from the center of a tropical palm tree. Look for them in the canned vegetable or international aisle of supermarkets.

2	cans (14 ounces each) hearts of palms, rinsed and drained	¼	cup chopped fresh flat-leaf parsley or cilantro
1	head Boston lettuce, broken into leaves	3	tablespoons lime juice
1	tomato, peeled (see page 383) and finely chopped (with juice)	1½	tablespoons extra-virgin olive oil
1	cup cooked or frozen and thawed corn kernels		Salt and ground black pepper

Cut any large hearts lengthwise into quarters; cut medium-size hearts in half; leave small hearts whole. Line 4 salad plates with the lettuce. Arrange the hearts of palm in neat rows on top.

In a medium bowl, combine the tomatoes (with juice), corn, parsley or cilantro, lime juice, and oil. Season with salt and pepper. Spoon the tomato mixture over the hearts of palm in a neat row down the center and over the lettuce.

Makes 4 servings

CACTUS SALAD

Ensalada de nopalitos

México

Nutrition Snapshot	Before	After
Per serving		
Calories	86	86
Total Fat g.	3.8	3.8
Saturated Fat g.	0.5	0.5
Cholesterol mg.	0	0

Nopalitos *are the fleshy paddles of a young prickly pear cactus. Popular in northern and central México, they taste somewhat like cooked green beans. If you live in an area with a large Mexican community, you may be able to find fresh cactus. Look for tender, small to medium-size paddles, 6" to 8" long, weighing about 6 ounces each. Canned nopalitos work fine for this recipe and are widely available at Hispanic markets and specialty shops. Some large supermarkets also carry them.*

3–4	nopalitos (about 1 pound) or 1 can (15 ounces) nopalitos		3	tablespoons finely chopped fresh cilantro
1	tomato, seeded and finely chopped		2–3	tablespoons lime juice
½	medium white onion, finely chopped		1	tablespoon olive oil
1	red serrano or other chile pepper, seeded and finely chopped (wear plastic gloves when handling)			Salt and ground black pepper

If using fresh nopalitos, bring a large pot of salted water to a boil over high heat. Trim the spines off the nopalitos with a paring knife and discard. Cut crosswise into ¼"-thick strips. Add to the pot and cook for 2 minutes, or until tender. Rinse and drain. If using canned nopalitos, rinse and drain.

In a large bowl, combine the nopalitos, tomatoes, onions, chile peppers, cilantro, 2 tablespoons of the lime juice, and the oil. Season with salt and black

(continued)

pepper. Toss to mix. The salad should be highly seasoned; taste and sprinkle with more salt and lime juice, if desired.

Makes 4 servings

Cooking Tip

✦ For a spicier salad, leave the seeds in the chile peppers.

Variation

Mexican Green Bean Salad: If nopalitos are unavailable, use green beans instead. They're not authentic, but they will make a good-tasting salad.

Pronto!

SOUTH AMERICAN BEAN SALAD

Ensalada de
porotos

*Various
countries*

Nutrition Snapshot	Before	After
Per serving		
Calories	408	170
Total Fat g.	32.6	5.6
Saturated Fat g.	4.4	0.8
Cholesterol mg.	0	0

This salad belongs to a roster of side dishes that accompany cocktails and steaks in the southern part of South America, particularly in Uruguay and Argentina. I prefer the earthy taste of fava beans here, but other beans will work in a pinch.

2	cups cooked or canned rinsed and drained fava beans, white kidney beans, or pigeon peas
1	small onion, finely chopped
3	tablespoons finely chopped fresh flat-leaf parsley
1½	tablespoons extra-virgin olive oil

1½–2	tablespoons red-wine vinegar
1	teaspoon dried oregano
½	teaspoon red-pepper flakes
	Salt and ground black pepper
4	leaves Boston lettuce
4	strips pimiento (optional)

In a large bowl, combine the beans, onions, parsley, oil, 1½ tablespoons of the vinegar, the oregano, and red-pepper flakes. Season with salt and pepper. Taste and sprinkle with more salt and vinegar, if desired.

Place a lettuce leaf on each of 4 salad plates. Mound the bean salad in the center. Garnish each with a strip of pimiento (if using).

Makes 4 servings

Pronto!

CHICKPEA SALAD

Ensalada de
garbanzos

Puerto Rico

Nutrition Snapshot	Before	After
Per serving		
Calories	373	154
Total Fat g.	29.2	4.5
Saturated Fat g.	3.9	0.6
Cholesterol mg.	0	0

Versions of this salad exist from one end of Latin America to the other. The type of bean used varies from region to region. In the Spanish-speaking Caribbean, garbanzos (chickpeas) are the bean of choice. Because chickpeas are so rich, you don't need a lot of oil in the dressing.

2	cups cooked or canned chickpeas, rinsed and drained
2	ribs celery, chopped
½	red bell pepper, chopped
½	green bell pepper, chopped
½	medium red onion, chopped
1	clove garlic, minced

3	tablespoons chopped fresh cilantro
2	tablespoons red-wine vinegar
1–2	tablespoons lime juice
2	teaspoons olive oil
½	teaspoon ground cumin
	Salt and ground black pepper

In a large serving bowl, combine the chickpeas, celery, bell peppers, onions, garlic, cilantro, vinegar, 1 tablespoon of the lime juice, the oil, and cumin. Season with salt and black pepper. Toss to mix. Taste and sprinkle with more salt and lime juice, if desired.

Makes 4 servings

Regional Variation

Mexican Bean Salad: Replace the chickpeas with pinto or kidney beans. Add 1 to 3 seeded and chopped jalapeño or serrano chile peppers (wear plastic gloves when handling). Increase the olive oil to 1 tablespoon. Omit the cumin.

SALADS AND VEGETABLES
119

PINTO BEAN SALAD WITH CUMIN-SCENTED SOUR CREAM

Ensalada de frijoles pintos

United States

Nutrition Snapshot	Before	After
Per serving (1 cup)		
Calories	268	196
Total Fat g.	11.4	3
Saturated Fat g.	2.4	0.4
Cholesterol mg.	4	0

Rajas *(roasted chile strips) and chipotle chiles give this salad a rich, smoky flavor.*

2 poblano chile peppers or green bell peppers

1 red bell pepper

1 yellow bell pepper

1–3 canned chipotle chile peppers, minced (wear plastic gloves when handling); see tip

3 cups cooked or canned rinsed and drained pinto beans

1 cup cooked or frozen and thawed corn kernels

½ cup chopped red onions

¼ cup chopped fresh cilantro

1 clove garlic, minced

3–4 tablespoons lime juice

1 tablespoon olive oil

Salt and ground black pepper

6 leaves lettuce

¼ cup Cumin-Scented Sour Cream (page 382)

Position a broiler rack at the highest setting. Preheat the broiler. Place the poblano chile pepper or green bell peppers, red bell peppers, and yellow bell peppers under the broiler. Roast, turning occasionally, for 6 to 8 minutes, or until charred and blackened on all sides. Transfer to a paper bag. Let cool for 15 minutes to loosen the skins. When cool enough to handle, scrape off as much of the skin (wear plastic gloves when handling chile peppers) as possible with a paring knife. Don't worry about a few charred pieces of skin; they'll add a nice smoky flavor. Discard the skin. Remove and discard the seeds and ribs. Cut the flesh into thin strips. Transfer to a large bowl.

Add the chipotle chile peppers, beans, corn, onions, cilantro, garlic, lime juice, and oil. Toss to mix. Sprinkle with salt and black pepper.

Line 6 plates with the lettuce. Spoon 1 cup of the salad onto each plate. Drizzle 2 teaspoons of the sour cream in a zigzag pattern over each serving.

Makes 6 servings (6 cups)

Cooking Tip

◆ You can also use dried chipotle chile peppers. Stem and seed the dried chiles (wear plastic gloves when handling). Place them in a small bowl. Cover with warm water. Let soak for 20 minutes, or until soft and pliable. Mince.

FAVA BEAN AND CARROT SALAD

Ensalada de
habas y zanahorias

México

Nutrition Snapshot	Before	After
Per serving		
Calories	352	262
Total Fat g.	11.2	1
Saturated Fat g.	1.5	0.2
Cholesterol mg.	0	0

first tried this salad at the covered market in Coyoacán, an artsy suburb of Mexico City and home of the Mexican artist Frieda Kahlo. It was so simple, so appealing, and so perfect a preparation for fava beans, I had to include the recipe here. For the best results, use fresh fava beans, which are available at ethnic markets and gourmet shops. You might also find fresh fava beans in supermarkets in the spring.

8	cups water
2	cups shucked fresh fava beans (see tip)
2	sprigs epazote (optional)
4	carrots, sliced ¼" thick
½–1	teaspoon salt
1	tomato, peeled (see page 383), seeded, and chopped
1–3	jalapeño chile peppers, seeded and finely chopped (wear plastic gloves when handling)
¼	cup chopped fresh cilantro
1	clove garlic, minced
3	tablespoons lime juice
¼	teaspoon ground black pepper

Bring the water to a boil in a large pot over high heat. Add the beans and epazote (if using). Cook for 6 minutes. Add the carrots and ½ teaspoon of the salt. Cook for 2 minutes, or until the beans and carrots are just tender. Drain, rinse with cold water, and drain well. Pull the skins off the beans.

Transfer the beans and carrots to a medium serving bowl. Stir in the tomatoes, chile peppers, cilantro, garlic, lime juice, and black pepper. Toss to mix. Season with more salt, if desired.

Makes 4 servings

Cooking Tip

✦ To use dried fava beans, soak 1 cup beans overnight. Drain and add fresh cold water to cover. Boil the beans for 1½ to 2 hours or pressure-cook for 30 minutes. To use canned favas, you'll need about 3 cups. Be sure to drain the beans and rinse them well with cold water before using.

QUINOA SALAD

Ensalada de
quinua

United States

Nutrition Snapshot	Before	After
Per serving (1½ cups)		
Calories	369	295
Total Fat g.	16.4	7.9
Saturated Fat g.	2.1	1
Cholesterol mg.	0	0

Here's a salad that's as colorful as it is nutritious. Quinoa (KEEN-wa) is a native grain of the Andes Mountains, where it has been cultivated for 5,000 years. Sacred to the Incas, it contains more protein than wheat, oats, or barley. It's also a good source of calcium, iron, phosphorus, and vitamin E. Quinoa can be found at most natural foods stores, gourmet shops, and in the rice aisle of many supermarkets.

1	cup quinoa, rinsed until the water runs clear
2	cups water
	Salt
1	cucumber, peeled, seeded, and chopped
1	cup cooked or frozen and thawed corn kernels
1	cup cooked or frozen and thawed peas
1	tomato, peeled (see page 383), seeded, and chopped
1	medium red bell pepper, finely chopped
1–2	jalapeño chile peppers, seeded and minced (wear plastic gloves when handling); see tip
¼	cup chopped fresh cilantro or flat-leaf parsley
3–4	tablespoons lime juice
1½	tablespoons extra-virgin olive oil
	Ground black pepper

In a medium saucepan over high heat, combine the quinoa, water, and ½ teaspoon salt. Bring to a boil. Cover the pan, reduce the heat to medium, and simmer for 15 minutes, or until all the water is absorbed and the quinoa is tender. (If any water remains, transfer the quinoa to a colander and drain.) Transfer the quinoa to a large bowl. Let cool completely.

Stir in the cucumbers, corn, peas, tomatoes, bell peppers, chile peppers, cilantro or parsley, lime juice, and oil. Toss to mix. The salad should be highly seasoned; sprinkle with black pepper and more salt, if desired.

Makes 4 servings (6 cups)

Cooking Tip

✦ For a spicier salad, do not seed the chile peppers.

FROM TOP LEFT: TORTILLA CHIPS (PAGE 70); PLANTAIN CHIPS (PAGE 71); TOMATO, ONION, AND JALAPEÑO SALSA (PAGE 296); GARLICKY PLANTAIN PUREE (PAGE 74); AND GUACAMOLE (PAGE 75)

LITTLE POTS OF RED BEANS WITH SOUR CREAM (PAGE 79)

YUCATÁN CHICKEN-LIME SOUP (PAGE 105)

HONDURAN FISH SOUP (PAGE 108)

JALAPEÑO POPPERS (PAGE 77) AND RANCH-STYLE TOMATO SALSA (PAGE 296)

PERUVIAN-STYLE CEVICHE (PAGE 90)

HEARTS OF PALM SALAD (PAGE 116)

CUBAN BLACK BEAN SOUP (PAGE 102)

SPANISH-CARIBBEAN BEEF AND VEGETABLE STEW (PAGE 110)

QUINOA SALAD (PAGE 122)

MEXICAN CORN SOUP (PAGE 98)

YUCA WITH GARLIC-LIME SAUCE

Yuca con mojo

Cuba

Nutrition Snapshot	Before	After
Per serving		
Calories	299	259
Total Fat g.	10.4	5.4
Saturated Fat g.	1.4	0.7
Cholesterol mg.	0	0

This dish is Cuban comfort food—the island version of boiled potatoes. Yuca is a starchy root vegetable with a mild, buttery flavor. Mojo (MO-ho) is a type of vinaigrette flavored with garlic, cumin, and lime juice or sour orange juice. I reduce the fat in the mojo by replacing some of the olive oil with chicken stock. I also add sliced onions to kick up the flavor and give the recipe a modern twist.

12	cups cold water
	Salt
2	pounds yuca, cut crosswise into 2"-thick pieces and peeled (see tip)
1	small white onion, thinly sliced into rings
1½	tablespoons extra-virgin olive oil
3	cloves garlic, minced

½	teaspoon ground cumin
⅓	cup lime juice or sour orange juice (see page 63)
⅓	cup Chicken Stock (page 360) or fat-free reduced-sodium chicken broth
	Ground black pepper
2	tablespoons chopped fresh flat-leaf parsley

Pour 10 cups of the water into a large pot. Lightly salt the water and bring to a boil over high heat. Halve or quarter any large yuca pieces so that all are approximately the same size. Add to the pot. Cook for 10 minutes. Add 1 cup of the remaining water. Return to a boil and cook for 5 minutes. Add the remaining 1 cup water and return to a boil. Cook for 5 minutes, or until the yuca is very soft. (The additions of cold water help tenderize the yuca.) Drain. When cool enough to handle, scrape out any fibers with a fork and discard. Arrange the yuca on a platter and scatter the onion rings on top.

While the yuca is cooking, heat the oil in a small saucepan over medium heat. Add the garlic and cumin. Cook and stir for 1 minute, or until the garlic just begins to brown. (Do not let the garlic burn, or the sauce will be bitter.) Add the lime juice or orange juice and stock or broth. Season with pepper. Increase the heat to high and boil for 2 minutes, or until the sauce is richly flavored. Season with salt.

Pour the hot sauce over the yuca and onions. Sprinkle with the parsley.

Makes 4 servings

Cooking Tip

✦ To peel the yuca, stand the pieces, cut side down, on a cutting board. Cut off the peel with a paring knife using downward strokes.

YUCA, SLAW, AND PORK CRACKLINGS

Vigorón

Costa Rica
Nicaragua

Nutrition Snapshot	Before	After
Per serving		
Calories	356	292
Total Fat g.	9.4	3.6
Saturated Fat g.	3.3	1.2
Cholesterol mg.	27	31

Most of the fat in this tasty snack comes from the chicharrones (fried pork rinds). A good-tasting low-fat version hinged on finding an alternative to these crispy bits of pork. After several experiments, I decided that oven-crisped ham steak worked best. Traditional? Not exactly. Tasty? You bet!

12	ounces lean ham steak, patted dry, trimmed of all visible fat, and cut into ½" cubes
12	cups cold water
	Salt
1½	pounds yuca, cut crosswise into 2"-thick pieces and peeled (see tip on page 139)
2	cups thinly shredded green cabbage
1	tomato, peeled (see page 383), seeded, and chopped
1	carrot, shredded
1–3	jalapeño chile peppers, minced (wear plastic gloves when handling)
3–4	tablespoons white vinegar
½	teaspoon ground black pepper

Preheat the oven to 400°F. Coat a nonstick roasting pan with nonstick spray.

Place the ham in the prepared roasting pan. Coat the top of the ham with non-stick spray. Bake, turning occasionally, for 15 minutes, or until golden brown and crisp. Transfer to a plate to cool.

Pour 10 cups of the water into a large pot. Lightly salt the water and bring to a boil over high heat. Halve or quarter any large yuca pieces so that all are approximately the same size. Add to the pot. Cook for 10 minutes. Add 1 cup of the remaining water. Return to a boil and cook for 5 minutes. Add the remaining 1 cup water and return to a boil. Cook for 5 minutes, or until the yuca is very soft. (The additions of cold water help tenderize the yuca.) Drain. When cool enough to handle, scrape out any fibers with a fork and discard. Cover to keep warm.

In a large bowl, combine the cabbage, tomatoes, carrots, chile peppers, 3 tablespoons of the vinegar, and ½ teaspoon salt. Season with black pepper. Toss to mix. Taste and add more salt and vinegar, if desired.

Arrange the yuca on plates or a platter. Spread the cabbage mixture on top. Sprinkle the ham on top and serve at once.

Makes 6 servings

BAKE-FRIED POTATOES

Papitas fritas

Various countries

Nutrition Snapshot	Before	After
Per serving		
Calories	299	91
Total Fat g.	27.1	7
Saturated Fat g.	3.6	0.5
Cholesterol mg.	0	0

Papitas fritas (French fries) are popular throughout the Spanish-speaking world, especially in the Spanish-speaking Caribbean and Central America. To make a heart-healthy version, I toss the potatoes with a small amount of oil, then bake them in a hot oven. For extra flavor, I like to season the potatoes with garlic, paprika, and cumin.

2	large or 4 medium baking potatoes, peeled and cut lengthwise into ¼" strips
2	tablespoons extra-virgin olive oil
1	clove garlic, minced

½	teaspoon salt
½	teaspoon ground black pepper
½	teaspoon paprika
¼	teaspoon ground cumin

Preheat the oven to 450°F.

Place the potatoes in a medium bowl and cover with cold water. Let soak for 10 minutes. Drain well and blot dry with paper towels.

In a nonstick roasting pan, toss together the potatoes, oil, garlic, salt, pepper, paprika, and cumin. Bake for 25 minutes, tossing occasionally, or until golden brown.

Makes 4 servings

Cooking Tip

✦ For extra-crispy fries, transfer them to a nonstick baking sheet and run them under the broiler for 1 to 3 minutes before serving.

TWICE-COOKED PLANTAINS

Tostones

Various countries

Nutrition Snapshot	Before	After
Per serving (about 4 slices)		
Calories	398	139
Total Fat g.	33.0	3.7
Saturated Fat g.	4.3	0.6
Cholesterol mg.	0	0

Tostones are a popular snack throughout the Spanish-speaking Caribbean and Central America. But talk about unhealthy! In the traditional version, plantains are fried twice: first at a low temperature to soften them, then at high heat to make them crisp and brown. To make a lighter tostón, I cook the plantains in chicken stock, then bake-fry them in the oven. Serve these as dippers for Cilantro-Pepper Sauce (page 311), Guacamole (page 75), or any of the salsas beginning on page 296.

3 cups Chicken Stock (page 360), fat-free reduced-sodium chicken broth, or water
Garlic salt
2 green plantains, peeled (see page 386) and diagonally sliced ¾" thick

1 tablespoon extra-virgin olive oil
Ground black pepper

Preheat the oven to 400°F.

Bring the stock or water to a boil in a large pot over high heat. Add a little garlic salt into the pot. Add the plantains. Reduce the heat to medium and simmer for 15 minutes, or until very tender. Drain and reserve the stock, if desired (see tip).

Place the plantains between 2 sheets of plastic wrap and flatten to a thickness of ¼" with a meat pounder or rolling pin. Remove the top sheet of plastic and brush the tops with half of the oil. Invert onto nonstick baking sheets and remove the other sheet of plastic. Brush the tops with the remaining oil.

Bake for 15 minutes, turning once with tongs, or until crisp and golden brown. Sprinkle with pepper and more garlic salt, if desired.

Makes 4 servings (about 4 slices)

Cooking Tips

✦ You can save the stock for use in the Garlicky Plantain Puree on page 74.

✦ If you live near a Hispanic market, look for a tostón press or tostonera (toe-sto-NAY-ra)—a hinged wooden press that swiftly smashes the sliced plantains to the requisite ¼" thickness. You can also buy special presses that flatten the plantains into cup-shaped tostones, which are great for filling with Cilantro-Pepper Sauce (page 311), Guacamole (page 75), or other dips.

PLANTAIN "SURFBOARDS"

Patacones

Colombia
Panamá

Nutrition Snapshot	Before	After
Per surfboard		
Calories	575	248
Total Fat g.	41.2	4
Saturated Fat g.	5.7	0.7
Cholesterol mg.	0	0

Of all the Latin American dishes made with plantain, none is as ingenious as Colombia's patacón. Named for a Spanish gold coin, traditional patacones are golden disks of twice-fried sliced green plantains. In this nifty variation, the plantains are cooked whole, rolled out to the size of a platter, then deep-fried until cracker-crisp. The result looks like a miniature surfboard, which doubles as an edible plate. To make a healthier version, I simmer the plantains in stock, then bake them in the oven. Serve these as a side dish or top with Guacamole (page 75), Turkey Picadillo (page 257), Shrimp Stew (page 234), or Colombian Shredded Chicken (page 255).

4   green plantains, peeled (see page 386)

6   cups Chicken Stock (page 360), fat-free reduced-sodium chicken broth, or water

1   tablespoon extra-virgin olive oil
    Salt

Preheat the oven to 400°F. Coat 2 large baking sheets with nonstick spray.

In a large pot over high heat, combine the plantains and stock or water. Bring to a boil. Reduce the heat to medium and cook the plantains for 20 minutes, or until soft. Drain and reserve the stock, if desired (see tip).

Place a plantain between 2 large sheets of plastic wrap. Gently flatten it by tapping with a rolling pin. Roll it out to form a large flat oval about 12" long, 5" wide, and ⅛" thick. (If the ends begin to break apart, push them back together with your fingers.) Slide the plantain onto the back of a prepared baking sheet. Lift off the top sheet of plastic wrap. Lightly brush the plantain with some of the oil and season with salt. Place another baking sheet on top, bottom side up. Invert the plantain onto it. Peel off the other piece of plastic wrap, brush the plantain with oil, and season with salt.

Bake, turning once, for 20 minutes, or until crisp and lightly browned. (To flip, place a baking sheet on top, then invert the plantain onto it.) Transfer to a large serving plate. Repeat with the remaining plantains.

Makes 4

Cooking Tip

✦ You can save the stock for use in the Sancocho on page 290.

Pronto!

GRILLED RIPE PLANTAINS

Maduros

Various countries

Nutrition Snapshot	Before	After
Per serving		
Calories	459	218
Total Fat g.	27.9	0.7
Saturated Fat g.	3.7	0.2
Cholesterol mg.	0	0

Maduros (fried ripe plantains) are a wildly popular side dish throughout Central America and the Spanish-speaking Caribbean. But how do you eliminate frying the plantains? One day, I tried cooking a ripe plantain on the barbecue grill. I got the same delectable candied sweetness without a trace of fat. Be sure to use very ripe plantains for this recipe. The skin should be completely black. If it looks like it's ready for the trash bin, it's perfect.

4   very ripe plantains

Preheat the grill to high.

Cut the ends off the plantains and cut each crosswise into 2" pieces. Coat the cut sides with nonstick spray. Grill the plantains, turning occasionally, for 10 minutes, or until the skins are charred and the cut ends are brown and caramelized. The plantains should be very soft in the center. Trim off the skins (or let your guests do it) and serve at once.

Makes 4 servings

Cooking Tip

✦ If it rains, here's an indoor method for making maduros. Preheat the oven to 450°F. Coat a nonstick baking sheet with nonstick spray. Cut the ends off the plantains and peel. Cut each plantain on the diagonal into ½"-thick slices. Arrange in a single layer on the baking sheet. Coat the tops of the plantains with nonstick spray. Bake, turning occasionally, for 10 to 15 minutes, or until the plantains are golden brown and very tender.

MINAS-STYLE COLLARD GREENS

Couve mineira *Brazil*

Nutrition Snapshot	Before	After
Per serving		
Calories	167	93
Total Fat g.	14.1	5.7
Saturated Fat g.	1.9	0.8
Cholesterol mg.	0	0

Brazilians love collard greens. And they don't cook them to death like North Americans often do. Consider the following recipe, a specialty of the Minas Gerais in north central Brazil. The secret is to slice the collard greens paper-thin using the roll-and-cut method below. Even if you don't think you like collard greens, give this simple side dish a try—you'll be pleasantly surprised.

1	bunch collard greens (about 1½ pounds), stems removed
¼	cup water
1½	tablespoons olive oil

1	small onion, finely chopped
3	cloves garlic, minced
	Salt and ground black pepper

Roll up the collard green leaves lengthwise into a tight tube. Using a sharp knife, cut the tube crosswise into extremely thin slices. Fluff the slices in a large bowl and sprinkle with the water.

Heat the oil in a large nonstick skillet over high heat. Add the onions and garlic. Cook for 20 seconds, or until fragrant but not brown. Add the collard greens and season with salt and pepper. Cook, stirring often, for 2 minutes, or until the greens are just tender. (Do not overcook; the collards should remain bright green.) Season with additional salt and pepper, if desired.

Makes 4 servings

CHILES RELLENOS WITH CORN

Chiles rellenos
con elote

México

Nutrition Snapshot	Before	After
Per chile relleno		
Calories	400	303
Total Fat g.	23.3	9.1
Saturated Fat g.	5.8	0.5
Cholesterol mg.	95	18

Chiles rellenos are one of the glories of Mexican gastronomy. But the first time I tasted the traditional version, I could almost feel my arteries hardening! Poblano chile peppers are stuffed with cheese, dipped in egg batter, and deep-fried. You can't really make traditional chiles rellenos without these high-fat ingredients. But you can make a great-tasting alternative. Here's a low-fat version of chiles rellenos that features the flavor of grilled corn with only a minimal amount of cheese. To further reduce the fat, the chiles are coated with oil and baked instead of deep-fried. The flavor is fantastic. Ranch-Style Tomato Salsa (page 296) makes a nice accompaniment.

2   large or 3 medium ears corn, shucked

Salt and ground black pepper

8   poblano chile peppers (see tip)

½   cup grated queso fresco or sharp white Cheddar cheese (4 ounces)

3   scallions, trimmed and minced

1   clove garlic, minced

¼   cup finely chopped fresh cilantro or flat-leaf parsley

3   tablespoons currants or raisins (optional)

1   cup unbleached flour

⅓   cup liquid egg substitute or 3 egg whites, lightly beaten

¾   cup unseasoned dry bread crumbs

¼   cup stone-ground yellow or blue cornmeal

Preheat a grill or broiler to high.

Coat the corn with nonstick spray and season with salt and black pepper. Grill the corn or broil 4" from the heat, turning occasionally, for 2 to 3 minutes per side, or up to 12 minutes in all, or until the kernels are well-browned. Transfer to a cutting board and let cool. When cool enough to handle, cut the kernels off the corncobs and place in a medium bowl (you should have about 1½ cups).

Meanwhile, roast the chile peppers over a flame, on the grill, or under the broiler for 3 minutes per side, or until nicely charred. Transfer to a paper bag. Let cool for 15 minutes to loosen the skins. When cool enough to handle, transfer to the cutting board and scrape off and discard the skin (wear plastic gloves when handling) using a paring knife. Set 6 of the chile peppers aside.

For the remaining 2 chile peppers, core, seed, and cut the flesh into ¼" pieces (wear plastic gloves when handling). Add to the corn kernels. Stir in the cheese, scallions, garlic, cilantro or parsley, and currants or raisins (if using). The mixture should be highly seasoned; taste and add more salt and black pepper, if desired.

Carefully make a 2"-long lengthwise cut in each of the 6 reserved chile peppers, taking care not to tear the skin (wear plastic gloves when handling). Using a melon baller or spoon, scrape out the core and seeds, leaving the stem intact. Stuff each pepper with the corn mixture.

Preheat the oven to 400°F.

Place the flour in a shallow bowl, the egg substitute or egg whites in a second bowl, and the bread crumbs and cornmeal in a third bowl (mix together the crumbs and cornmeal with your fingertips). Dip each chile first in the flour, shaking off the excess, then in the egg, then in the crumb mixture. Place the chiles on a nonstick baking sheet. Generously coat the tops of the chiles with nonstick spray. Bake for 20 minutes, or until golden brown and the filling is hot.

Makes 6 servings

Cooking Tips

✦ Poblano chile peppers are triangular-shaped, dark green chile peppers that have a definite bite. Most large supermarkets carry them in the produce section. If unavailable or if you prefer a milder dish, use Anaheim chile peppers or green bell peppers.

✦ The chile peppers can be stuffed, covered with plastic wrap, and refrigerated for up to 2 days or frozen for up to 2 months. Let them come to room temperature before breading and baking.

✦ In a pinch, you can replace the grilled corn with drained canned or frozen and thawed corn.

LATIN SUPER FOOD: CORN

Corn was originally domesticated in México and South America several thousand years ago. Now the grain is grown on every continent except Antarctica.

Because of its tremendous per-acre yield, corn (maíz) was deified by many Native American religions. Today, corn is one of our favorite vegetables, and with good reason. It's easy to prepare, tastes great, and goes with a wide variety of dishes.

Plus, eating corn is a natural way to lower your cholesterol. Each ear contains soluble fiber, which literally escorts undigested cholesterol out of your body. Corn bran (the outer layer of the corn kernel) is better than wheat bran for cutting cholesterol. When researchers at Illinois State University fed men with high cholesterol levels a low-fat diet supplemented with either 20 grams (about ½ tablespoon) of wheat bran or corn bran, both groups had cholesterol benefits from the new diet. But those taking the corn bran had an additional 5 percent drop in total cholesterol, an almost 14 percent fall in dangerous LDL cholesterol and a 13 percent decline in triglycerides, the blood fats that can contribute to heart disease. The wheat bran–eaters had no additional benefits.

You can get more than 4 grams of heart-healthy fiber just by eating 1 cup of white or yellow cooked corn. A cup of corn also provides about 13 percent of the 60 milligrams of vitamin C and the 400 micrograms of folate you need each day. Vitamin C builds healthy skin and fights viruses and infections. This potent antioxidant may also prevent cataracts and quench free radicals before they lead to heart disease and cancer. Folate not only prevents life-threatening birth defects of the spine and brain in newborn babies but it also helps lower levels of the amino acid homocysteine, which may help prevent heart disease and stroke.

Toss handfuls of sweet, juicy corn kernels in salads and soups, mix them with beans and rice, or use cornmeal tortillas for fajitas and enchiladas. For a new twist on chiles rellenos, try Chiles Rellenos with Corn (page 146).

BOLIVIAN CORN PUDDING

Humitas bolivianas

Bolivia

Nutrition Snapshot	Before	After
Per serving		
Calories	361	215
Total Fat g.	18.7	3.8
Saturated Fat g.	11.4	2
Cholesterol mg.	53	10

Humitas *is a sort of corn pudding that's popular throughout South America. Often, the pudding is baked in corn husks in the style of a tamale (known as humita en chala). Here's a simpler version cooked in a baking dish. For the best results, use fresh corn kernels. Frozen or canned corn kernels will work well, too. Either way, the sweet flavor of raisins and anise contrasted with the salty cheese and scallions is delightful.*

4 cups fresh or frozen and thawed corn kernels (see page 386)

½ cup skim milk

1¼ cups yellow cornmeal

4 scallions, finely chopped

¼ cup raisins

1–3 tablespoons sugar

2 teaspoons sweet paprika

Salt

½ teaspoon baking powder

½ teaspoon ground cinnamon

½ teaspoon anise seeds, crushed

Ground black pepper

4 egg whites

½ teaspoon cream of tartar

¾ cup coarsely grated Muenster cheese

Preheat the oven to 400°F. Coat a 2-quart baking dish with nonstick spray.

In a food processor or blender, combine 3 cups of the corn and the milk. Puree until smooth.

In a large bowl, combine the cornmeal, scallions, raisins, 1 tablespoon of the sugar, 1 teaspoon of the paprika, 1 teaspoon salt, the baking powder, cinnamon, anise seeds, ¼ teaspoon pepper, and the remaining 1 cup corn. Stir to mix. Stir in the pureed corn. Taste and add more sugar, salt, and pepper, if desired.

In another large bowl, combine the egg whites and cream of tartar. Beat with a mixer for 8 minutes, or until firm and glossy but not dry. (Begin beating on low speed and gradually increase the speed to medium, then to high.) Gently fold the corn mixture into the egg whites. Spoon the mixture into the prepared baking dish. Sprinkle with the Muenster and the remaining 1 teaspoon paprika.

Bake for 20 minutes, or until puffed and golden brown and a toothpick inserted in the center comes out clean. Let cool slightly.

Makes 8 servings

BEANS, RICE, AND OTHER GRAINS
Frijoles y granos

It makes sense that so many memorable rice and bean dishes should have originated in Latin America. The New World was the birthplace of some of the world's most popular grains and legumes: corn, amaranth, quinoa, black beans, pinto beans, and lima beans (which were named after the capital of Perú). When rice was brought from the Old World by the Spanish, the makings of heart-healthy feasts became abundant in the region.

I've trimmed the fat—while retaining the earthy flavor—in Latin America's most beloved rice and bean dishes, including Spanish Paella (page 166), Puerto Rican and Dominican Seafood Soupy Rice (page 161), Peruvian Fried Rice with Seafood (page 164), México's Refried Beans (page 155), and Cuba's ubiquitous soupy black beans (Cuban-Style Black Beans, page 152).

For more bean and grain dishes, see the appetizer recipes beginning on page 70, the soup recipes beginning on page 94, and the salad recipes beginning on page 116.

BEAN RECIPES

GRAIN RECIPES

CUBAN-STYLE BLACK BEANS

Frijoles negros al
estilo cubano

Cuba

Nutrition Snapshot	Before	After
Per serving		
Calories	341	222
Total Fat g.	17	4.8
Saturated Fat g.	2.5	0.8
Cholesterol mg.	12	4

Black beans are one of the most versatile and popular foods in Latin America, enjoyed from the Caribbean to Chile. The classic Cuban preparation is more a soup than a bean dish—designed to be ladled over white rice. Using canned beans speeds up the cooking process considerably. Cachucha chile peppers are a very mild, tiny pepper from Cuba. If unavailable, use rocotillos (see page 55), ají dulce, or red bell peppers.

1	tablespoon olive oil or lard	½	teaspoon dried oregano
6	cachucha chile peppers, seeded and chopped, or ½ green bell pepper, finely chopped	1	bay leaf
1	small onion, finely chopped	2	cans (15 ounces each) black beans, rinsed and drained
3	scallions, finely chopped	¼	cup dry white wine or nonalcoholic white wine (optional)
1	ounce Canadian bacon, minced	½	teaspoon sugar
2	cloves garlic, minced	1½–2	cups Chicken Stock (page 360) or fat-free reduced-sodium chicken broth
2	tablespoons finely chopped fresh cilantro		Salt and ground black pepper
½	teaspoon ground cumin		

Heat the oil or lard in a large nonstick skillet over medium heat. Add the chile peppers or bell peppers, onions, scallions, bacon, garlic, cilantro, cumin, oregano, and bay leaf. Cook for 5 minutes, or until the vegetables are soft but not brown. Stir in the beans and wine (if using). Bring to a boil over high heat. Stir in the sugar and 1½ cups of the stock or broth. Reduce the heat to medium and simmer for 5 minutes. Remove and discard the bay leaf.

Puree one-quarter of the bean mixture in a blender (or mash with the back of a spoon). Stir the puree into the simmering beans. Simmer for 2 minutes more, or until thick but still soupy. If the bean mixture is too thick, add more stock or broth. Season with salt and black pepper.

Makes 4 servings

Cooking Tip

✦ It may seem odd to discard the liquid from canned beans, then use chicken stock for simmering the beans. The reason is simple: Stock gives you more flavorful beans with less salt. Homemade chicken stock has a rich, meaty taste and it's salt-free. Canned beans, on the other hand, are high in sodium. A combination of rinsed and drained canned beans and chicken stock provides the most flavor with the least salt.

Regional Variation

Brazilian-Style Black Beans: After removing and discarding the bay leaf, mash the beans with the back of a wooden spoon. Stir in ¼ cup cassava flour to make a thick mixture similar in texture to mashed potatoes. Season with salt and pepper. Spoon the mixture into a serving dish in a flat layer. Sauté 1 finely chopped onion and 2 ounces finely chopped Canadian bacon in 1 tablespoon lard over medium heat for 4 minutes, or until cooked through. Spoon over the beans and serve.

Pronto!

RED BEANS AND RICE

Gallo pinto

Various countries

Nutrition Snapshot	Before	After
Per serving		
Calories	374	213
Total Fat g.	7.5	4.3
Saturated Fat g.	2.7	0.7
Cholesterol mg.	6	3

Beans and rice is a staple dish eaten throughout the Spanish-speaking Americas. Only the name and the type of bean changes from country to country. In Central America, the bean of choice is red kidneys. Pigeon peas or black beans are favored in Puerto Rico and Cuba. Traditional versions of the dish use lard and salt pork. To make healthier beans and rice, I use olive oil instead of lard. Canadian bacon gives the dish its characteristic smoky pork flavor with a minimum of fat.

1½	tablespoons olive oil	1	can (15½ ounces) small red kidney beans, rinsed and drained
1	medium onion, finely chopped	3	cups hot Basic White Rice (page 159)
1	clove garlic, minced		Salt and ground black pepper
1	ounce Canadian bacon, minced		

Heat the oil in a large nonstick skillet over medium heat. Add the onions, garlic, and bacon. Cook, stirring often, for 6 minutes, or until lightly browned.

Stir in the beans and rice. Cook for 10 minutes, or until the rice is lightly browned. Season with salt and pepper.

Makes 6 servings

LATIN SUPER FOOD: BEANS

Beans may be the best substitute for beef the world has ever known. They're economical, costing mere pennies per serving. And just ½ cup of these "meaty" morsels provides around 15 percent of the protein you need each day, with very little artery-clogging saturated fat. Beans provide almost as many health benefits as there are types of bean. Maybe that's why the Aztecs made beans a staple in their nutritional arsenal.

A half-cup of cooked beans such as kidney beans, black beans, pinto beans, or even refried beans delivers a whopping 6 grams of fiber, almost a quarter of what most experts say we need each day. Fiber provides head-to-toe benefits. It helps keep you "regular," which lowers your risk of colon cancer. And doctors say that fiber is good for people with diabetes because it helps maintain low blood sugar and normalize insulin levels. A Harvard University study of more than 47,000 men found that fiber may also reduce your risk for ulcers. And fiber has long been known to help lower your cholesterol for a healthy heart.

That's not the only good news for your heart. The amount of beans typically found in a well-stuffed burrito (about ½ cup) packs 25 to 40 percent of the Daily Value (DV) for folate, a superstar nutrient that helps lower levels of the amino acid homocysteine, thereby reducing your risk of heart disease. The same serving of beans also contains between 10 and 15 percent of the DV for magnesium, which helps lower blood pressure. Plus, beans are loaded with potent antioxidants called polyphenolics, which may be better than vitamin C (one of the most esteemed antioxidants) for preventing fat in the blood from oxidizing—the first step in the formation of artery-clogging sludge.

By current estimates, folks living north of the Río Grande eat an average of less than 2 tablespoons of beans per person each day. To help protect your heart, try tossing in a handful of beans instead of meat the next time you make burritos, enchiladas, chili, and soups.

REFRIED BEANS

Frijoles refritos   *México*

Nutrition Snapshot	Before	After
Per serving		
Calories	257	163
Total Fat g.	14.5	4.1
Saturated Fat g.	5.7	0.4
Cholesterol mg.	13	5

Refried beans are one of the glories of Mexican gastronomy. Properly prepared refried beans are soft, creamy, and loaded with complex flavors that linger in your mouth long after you've taken a bite. Alas, traditional refried beans acquire these virtues with significant amounts of rendered pork fat (lard). To make a heart-healthy version, I use just a tiny bit of lard for flavor. (For a vegetarian version, use extra-virgin olive oil instead of lard.) I also like to add a drop of liquid smoke, which bolsters the meaty lard flavor without added fat. I've updated the traditional recipe by using canned beans, which slashes the cooking time by several hours. Drain and rinse the beans to cut the sodium in half.

2   cans (15 ounces each) black beans, rinsed and drained

1   tablespoon lard or olive oil

1   small onion, minced

1   clove garlic, minced

3   sprigs fresh epazote, finely chopped (see tip)

⅛–¼   teaspoon liquid smoke (optional); see tip

   Salt and ground black pepper

2   tablespoons finely grated queso fresco or Romano cheese

Drain the beans, reserving ¼ cup of the liquid. Rinse the beans well with cold water. Coarsely mash the beans with a wooden spoon or potato masher.

Heat the lard or oil in a large nonstick skillet over medium heat. Add the onions, garlic, and epazote. Cook for 5 minutes, or until the onions begin to brown.

Stir the beans into the onion mixture. Cook for 10 minutes, or until thick and creamy. If the beans start to dry out, add the reserved bean liquid. Stir in the liquid smoke (if using) and season with salt and pepper. Transfer to a serving bowl and sprinkle with the cheese.

Makes 6 servings

Cooking Tips

✦ For authentic refried beans, use the herb epazote (see page 53). Mexicans believe that epazote helps reduce the flatulence that beans cause. There's no substitute for epazote, but fresh cilantro and oregano make tasty variations.

✦ Liquid smoke is available in the spice aisle of most supermarkets. Use it when you want to lend a rich, smoky flavor to foods without actually grilling or smoking them. This condiment also lends a meaty taste to dishes made without meat.

RICE AND BLACK BEAN PILAF

Congrí

Cuba

Nutrition Snapshot	Before	After
Per serving		
Calories	357	298
Total Fat g.	10.6	4.2
Saturated Fat g.	4.1	0.6
Cholesterol mg.	9	0

This popular Cuban rice dish won't win any beauty contests, but the depth of flavor is fantastic. To make healthier rice and black beans, I use olive oil instead of bacon fat.

1	piece (1" square) green bell pepper
2	cloves garlic
½	cup dried black beans, sorted, rinsed, and soaked in cold water to cover overnight
1	tablespoon extra-virgin olive oil
½	onion, finely chopped
¼	green bell pepper, finely chopped

¼	yellow or green bell pepper, finely chopped
¼	teaspoon ground cumin
¼	teaspoon dried oregano
1	bay leaf
1	cup long-grain white rice
1	tablespoon chopped fresh cilantro
	Salt and ground black pepper

Add the bell pepper square and 1 of the garlic cloves to the pot containing the beans. Bring to a boil over high heat. Reduce the heat to medium-low, loosely cover, and simmer, stirring occasionally, for 1 hour, or until tender. (Alternatively, cook the beans in a pressure cooker for 7 minutes.) Strain the beans, reserving the cooking liquid. You should have about 1 cup beans and 2½ cups liquid. Discard the square of bell pepper and the garlic.

Meanwhile, heat the oil in a large saucepan over medium heat. Mince the remaining clove of garlic and add to the pan. Add the onions, all the bell peppers, cumin, oregano, and bay leaf. Cook for 4 minutes, or until the vegetables are soft. Stir in the rice and cilantro. Cook for 1 minute, or until the rice is coated with the oil.

Stir in the beans and the reserved 2½ cups cooking liquid. Season with salt and black pepper. Bring to a boil over high heat. Reduce the heat to low, cover, and simmer for 20 minutes, or until the rice is tender. Remove from the heat, uncover, and drape a clean dish cloth over the pan. Recover the pan with the cloth still in place and let stand for 3 minutes. Fluff the rice with a fork and add more salt and black pepper, if desired. Remove and discard the bay leaf.

Makes 4 servings

Regional Variation

Cuban Rice and Red Beans: Replace the black beans with small red beans.

RICE WITH PIGEON PEAS

Arroz con
gandules

Puerto Rico

Nutrition Snapshot	Before	After
Per serving		
Calories	374	300
Total Fat g.	14.4	5.3
Saturated Fat g.	2.7	1
Cholesterol mg.	6	8

Pigeon peas are a dried bean native to Africa. Canned or frozen and thawed varieties work well here.

1   tablespoon Annatto Oil (page 380)

1   medium onion, finely chopped

1   yellow and/or green bell pepper, finely chopped

2   cloves garlic, minced

2   ounces Canadian bacon or serrano ham, thinly sliced

4   culantro leaves, chopped, or 2 tablespoons chopped fresh cilantro

1   tomato, finely chopped

1   cup long-grain white rice

1   cup cooked pigeon peas

2½   cups water

Salt and ground black pepper

Heat the annatto oil in a large saucepan over medium heat. Add the onions, bell peppers, garlic, and bacon. Cook over medium heat for 4 minutes, or until the vegetables are soft. Stir in the culantro or cilantro and tomato. Cook for 2 minutes, or until the juices have evaporated. Stir in the rice and cook for 1 minute.

Stir in the peas and water. Season with salt and black pepper. Bring to a boil over high heat. Reduce the heat to low, cover, and simmer for 20 minutes, or until the rice is tender. Remove from the heat, uncover, and drape a clean dish cloth over the pan. Recover the pan with the cloth still in place and let stand for 3 minutes. Fluff the rice with a fork. Add more salt and black pepper, if desired.

Makes 4 servings

¡Fiesta!
Puerto Rican New Year's Feast

This menu will be the hit of the party while helping you keep your resolutions.

Coconut Eggnog (*Coquito*, **page 352**)

Plantain Spiders (*Arañitas de plátano*, **page 73**) with **Cilantro-Pepper Sauce** (*Ají-li-mójili*, **page 311**)

Stuffed Pot Roast (*Carne asada rellena*, **page 265**)

Rice with Pigeon Peas (*Arroz con gandules*, **page 157**)

Shivering Coconut Pudding (*Tembleque*, **page 323**)

BLACK BEANS ON WHITE RICE

Moros y
cristianos

Cuba

Nutrition Snapshot	Before	After
Per serving		
Calories	327	300
Total Fat g.	6.3	3.5
Saturated Fat g.	1.6	0.7
Cholesterol mg.	5	3

Cubans have a great sense of humor. The Spanish name for this dish—literally, "Moors and Christians"—is a wry reference to the look of the black beans ladled over white rice. To reduce the fat, I cook the beans with Canadian bacon instead of belly bacon.

BEANS

1   cup dried black beans, sorted, rinsed, and soaked in cold water to cover overnight

4   cups cold water

¼   medium onion

2   cloves garlic

1   bay leaf

¼   green bell pepper

½   teaspoon ground cumin

½   teaspoon dried oregano

SOFRITO

1   tablespoon olive oil

1   slice (1 ounce) Canadian bacon, thinly slivered

¼   onion, finely chopped

¼   green bell pepper, finely chopped

2   scallions, finely chopped

1   clove garlic, minced

2   tablespoons dry white wine or nonalcoholic white wine

1   tablespoon red-wine vinegar

1   teaspoon sugar

    Salt and ground black pepper

4   cups hot Basic White Rice (page 159)

To make the beans: Add the onion, garlic, bay leaf, bell pepper, cumin, and oregano to the pot containing the beans. Bring to a boil over high heat. Skim off any foam that rises to the surface.

Reduce the heat to medium-low. Cover and gently simmer, stirring occasionally, for 45 minutes, or until the beans are tender. Add water as necessary to keep the beans submerged. Remove and discard the onion, garlic, bay leaf, and bell pepper.

To make the sofrito: Meanwhile, heat the oil in a medium nonstick skillet over medium heat. Add the bacon, onions, bell peppers, all but 2 tablespoons of the scallions, and garlic. Cook over medium heat for 4 minutes, or until the onions are soft. Stir into the beans. Add the wine, vinegar, and sugar. Season with salt and black pepper. Cover and simmer for 15 minutes, or until the beans are very soft. Add more cumin, oregano, vinegar, salt, and black pepper, if desired.

Spoon the beans over the rice. Sprinkle with the reserved scallion greens.

Makes 6 servings

BASIC WHITE RICE

Arroz blanco

Various countries

Nutrition Snapshot	Before	After
Per serving (³/₄ cup)		
Calories	283	283
Total Fat g.	3.9	3.9
Saturated Fat g.	0.6	0.6
Cholesterol mg.	0	0

Rice is one of the cornerstones of the Latin diet. Here's a great recipe for white rice that always comes out light, moist, and fluffy. The secret is rinsing the rice before cooking it.

1½   cups long-grain white rice, rinsed until the water runs clear

2¼   cups water

1   tablespoon canola oil or butter

½   teaspoon salt

Place the rice in a large heavy saucepan. Add the water, oil or butter, and salt. Bring to a boil over high heat. Tightly cover the pan, reduce the heat to low, and cook for 18 minutes, or until tender. (Check the rice after 14 minutes. If it's too moist, set the cover ajar to allow some of the liquid to evaporate. If it's too dry, add a little water.)

Remove the pan from the heat and uncover. Drape a clean dish cloth over the top of the pan and replace the lid. Let the rice stand for at least 3 minutes or up to 10 minutes. Fluff with a fork.

Makes 4 servings (3 cups)

Regional Variation

Mexican Rice: Warm the oil in a medium saucepan over medium heat. Add 2 cloves garlic, minced, and 1 small onion, finely chopped. Cook for 2 minutes. Add the rice and cook for 2 minutes more, or until the oil is absorbed. Add the water, salt, and ½ cup Ranch-Style Tomato Salsa (page 296). Bring to a boil. Proceed as directed.

RICE PILAF
WITH SHRIMP

Arroz con
camarones

Colombia

Nutrition Snapshot	Before	After
Per serving		
Calories	685	424
Total Fat g.	17.2	6.5
Saturated Fat g.	6.1	0.9
Cholesterol mg.	362	175

Here *is one of the many rice dishes enjoyed throughout Central and South America. If you can get shrimp with the heads on, use them to make a richly flavored shrimp stock. (Simmer the shrimp heads with the fish stock for 10 minutes, puree in a blender or food processor, then strain.) Cleaned shrimp also work just fine.*

1 tablespoon Annatto Oil (page 380) or 1 tablespoon olive oil + ¼ teaspoon sweet paprika

1 small red onion, finely chopped

4 scallions, finely chopped

4 rocotillo chile peppers, seeded and chopped, or ¼ red bell pepper, chopped

2 cloves garlic, minced

1 tomato, peeled (see page 383), seeded, and chopped

1 teaspoon red-wine vinegar

2¼ cups Fish Stock (page 362) or 1¾ cups bottled clam broth + ½ cup water

1 pound shrimp, peeled and deveined (shells reserved)

1½ cups long-grain white rice

Salt and ground black pepper

Heat the annato oil or olive oil and paprika in a large nonstick skillet over medium heat. Add the onions, scallions, chile peppers or bell peppers, and garlic. Cook for 5 minutes, or until the onions are soft but not brown. Increase the heat to high. Stir in the tomatoes and vinegar. Cook for 3 minutes, or until most of the tomato juices have evaporated.

Meanwhile, pour the fish stock or clam broth and water into a large saucepan. Add the shrimp shells and simmer over medium heat for 10 minutes.

While the stock is simmering, add the rice to the tomato mixture. Cook over medium heat for 2 to 3 minutes, or until the rice is shiny. Increase the heat to high and strain the fish stock into the pan. Season with salt and black pepper. Bring to a boil. Reduce the heat to low, cover, and cook for 15 minutes. Stir in the shrimp, cover, and cook for 10 minutes, or until the rice is moist but not soupy and the shrimp turn pink. If the rice is too moist, remove the cover for the last 5 minutes of cooking. Season with more salt and pepper, if desired.

Makes 4 servings

Rice Pilaf with Clams: Replace the shrimp with cleaned tiny littleneck clams. Simmer the clams in the stock for 8 minutes, or until they open. (Discard any clams with cracked shells or that remain closed.) Remove the clams from the shells and set aside. Strain the stock through cheesecloth or paper towels. Add the clams to the rice for the last 5 minutes of cooking.

SEAFOOD SOUPY RICE

Asopao de mariscos

Various countries

Nutrition Snapshot	Before	After
Per serving		
Calories	810	603
Total Fat g.	33.1	10.4
Saturated Fat g.	4.5	1.6
Cholesterol mg.	202	168

This popular Puerto Rican and Dominican main dish is a cross between bouillabaisse and paella.

2	cups Valencia-style rice or Arborio rice, rinsed until water runs clear
1	pound monkfish or swordfish, cut into 2" × 2" × ¼" pieces
1	pound shrimp, peeled and deveined
2	tablespoons lime juice
1	clove garlic, minced
	Salt and ground black pepper
2	tablespoons Annatto Oil (page 380) or 2 tablespoons olive oil + ½ teaspoon sweet paprika
1	medium onion, finely chopped
5	scallions, trimmed and chopped
6	rocotillo chile peppers or ½ green bell pepper, seeded and chopped
2	ounces Canadian bacon or lean smoked ham, finely chopped
4	cloves garlic, minced

1	teaspoon dried oregano
3	tomatoes, peeled (see page 383), seeded, and chopped
½	cup + 3 tablespoons chopped fresh flat-leaf parsley
½	cup chopped fresh cilantro
12	cups Fish Stock (page 362) or 8 cups bottled clam juice + 4 cups water
18	very small littleneck clams, scrubbed (see page 387)
18	mussels, scrubbed and debearded
1	cup cooked or frozen and thawed peas
3	pimiento-stuffed olives, sliced
2	pimientos or roasted red peppers, thinly sliced
2	tablespoons rinsed and drained capers

Place the rice in medium bowl. Cover with cold water and soak for 1 hour.

In a large glass or stainless steel bowl, combine the fish and shrimp. Add the lime juice and garlic. Toss to coat. Season with a little salt and black pepper. Cover and marinate in the refrigerator for 30 to 60 minutes.

(continued)

Meanwhile, heat the annatto oil or olive oil and paprika in a large pot over medium heat. Add the onions, scallions, chile peppers or bell peppers, bacon or ham, garlic, and oregano. Cook for 5 minutes, or until the vegetables are soft but not brown. Add the tomatoes, ½ cup of the parsley, and the cilantro. Cook for 5 minutes, or until the mixture is thick and fragrant.

Add the stock or clam juice and water to the pot. Bring to a boil over high heat. Drain the rice and add to the pot. Return to a boil, reduce the heat to medium-low, and simmer for 3 minutes. Add the clams and mussels. Cook for 5 minutes. Add the fish, shrimp, and marinade. Cook for 1 minute. Stir in the peas, olives, pimientos or roasted peppers, and capers. Cook for 1 minute more, or until the rice is tender, the clam and mussel shells are open wide, the fish is firm and white, and the shrimp are firm and pink. (Discard any clams or mussels with cracked shells or that remain closed.) Season with more salt and black pepper, if desired.

Ladle into bowls and sprinkle with the remaining 3 tablespoons parsley.

Makes 6 servings

QUINOA PILAF

Pilau de quinua

Ecuador
Perú

Quinoa (KEEN-wah) was one of the sacred grains of the Incas. Native to the Andes Mountains, it has been cultivated in the Americas for more than 5,000 years. Quinoa has a delicate, earthy, nutty flavor and a soft, somewhat crunchy consistency that reminds me a little of caviar. Talk about nutritious! Cup for cup, quinoa contains more protein than rice and more potassium than bananas. In South America, quinoa is often used for puddings (both sweet and savory). Here, it makes a quick and easy pilaf that marries well with most beef, pork, and chicken entrées. Look for quinoa at health food stores and large supermarkets.

1	tablespoon olive oil
1	medium onion, finely chopped
½	red bell pepper, finely chopped
1	clove garlic, minced
2	tablespoons pine nuts

2	cups quinoa, rinsed until the water runs clear
4	cups water (see tip)
	Salt and ground black pepper
3	tablespoons chopped fresh flat-leaf parsley

Heat the oil in a large nonstick skillet over medium heat. Add the onions, bell peppers, garlic, and pine nuts. Cook for 4 minutes, or until the onions are soft but not brown. Add the quinoa and cook for 1 minute.

Stir in the water. Season with salt and black pepper. Bring to a boil over high heat. Reduce the heat to low, cover, and simmer for 20 minutes, or until the quinoa is tender and the water is absorbed. Add the parsley and fluff the quinoa with a fork.

Makes 6 servings

Cooking Tip

✦ For a richer pilaf, cook the quinoa in chicken or vegetable stock instead of water.

FRIED RICE WITH SEAFOOD

*Arroz chaufa
de mariscos*

Perú

Nutrition Snapshot	Before	After
Per serving		
Calories	565	376
Total Fat g.	16.2	4.9
Saturated Fat g.	2	0.6
Cholesterol mg.	264	132

You might expect to find fried rice in more Chinese homes than Hispanic ones. But fried rice turns up throughout Latin America—the legacy of Chinese laborers who came to the New World in the nineteenth century to work the sugar plantations and railroads. Fried rice is especially popular in Cuba and Perú. Be sure to have all the ingredients chopped and ready before you start stir-frying. The actual cooking is only a matter of minutes.

2½ tablespoons reduced-sodium soy sauce

1 tablespoon rice vinegar or white vinegar

1 tablespoon rice wine, white wine, or water

½ teaspoon ground black pepper

4 scallions, trimmed

1 tablespoon canola oil

2 cloves garlic, minced

1 tablespoon minced fresh ginger

1 small onion, finely chopped

1 red bell pepper, finely chopped

8 ounces shrimp, peeled and deveined

8 ounces cleaned squid (see page 389), cut into ¼" rings, or sea scallops, cut into ½" pieces

4 cups hot Basic White Rice (page 159)

½ cup cooked or frozen and thawed peas

In a small bowl, combine the soy sauce, vinegar, wine or water, and black pepper. Set aside.

Mince the white part of the scallions and thinly slice the green part. Set aside.

Heat a nonstick wok or large nonstick skillet over high heat. Add the oil. When the oil is hot, add the garlic, ginger, and the reserved scallion whites. Stir-fry for 15 seconds. Add the onions and bell peppers. Stir-fry for 2 minutes more, or until fragrant. Add the shrimp and squid or scallops. Stir-fry for 3 minutes. Add the rice. Stir-fry for 2 minutes. Stir in the peas, the reserved scallion greens, and the reserved soy-sauce mixture. Stir-fry for 2 minutes, or until the shrimp is firm and pink and the squid or scallops are firm and white.

Makes 4 servings

Cooking Tip

◆ To vary the flavor, replace the squid or scallops with 8 ounces cooked octopus (see page 388 for octopus cooking directions).

HOMINY AND PORK STEW

Pozole   *México*

Nutrition Snapshot	Before	After
Per serving		
Calories	710	312
Total Fat g.	50.9	11.6
Saturated Fat g.	18.2	2.7
Cholesterol mg.	105	46

Pozole (poh-ZOH-leh) is a soulful stew made from hominy (hulled corn), pork, and red or green chile peppers. It originated in México's Pacific Coast region and is traditionally served at celebrations. The pork is used mostly as a flavoring rather than a principle ingredient. To cut back on the fat, I've slashed most of the lard in the traditional recipe but otherwise left it intact. Canned hominy makes the dish simple to prepare (look for canned hominy in the canned vegetables or rice section of most supermarkets).

2	dried red New Mexican or guajillo chile peppers, stems removed and seeded (wear plastic gloves when handling), or 2 to 3 teaspoons pure chili powder
1	tablespoon lard or canola oil
8	ounces lean pork loin or tenderloin, trimmed of all visible fat and cut into 1" cubes
1	onion, finely chopped
4	cloves garlic, minced
1	teaspoon ground cumin
1	teaspoon dried oregano
1	bay leaf
6	cups water
2	cans (14½ ounces each) hominy, rinsed and drained
	Salt and ground black pepper
¼	cup chopped scallions (optional)
¼	cup chopped fresh cilantro (optional)
	Lime wedges (optional)

If using the chile peppers, soak in hot water to cover for 20 to 30 minutes, or until softened. Transfer the chile peppers to a blender or food processor. Add ¼ cup of the soaking liquid and puree until smooth.

Heat the lard or oil in a large saucepan over medium-high heat. Add the pork and cook for 3 minutes. Add the onions and cook for 2 minutes. Add the garlic, cumin, oregano, and bay leaf. Cook for 1 minute, or until the pork and vegetables begin to brown. Add the water and hominy and bring to a boil. Reduce the heat to medium-low and simmer for 30 minutes, or until the pork is tender and the broth is thick and richly flavored. Season with salt and black pepper. Remove and discard the bay leaf. Stir in the pureed chile peppers or chili powder and simmer for 5 minutes. Taste and season with salt and black pepper.

Ladle into shallow bowls. If desired, sprinkle the scallions and cilantro on top and serve with lime wedges for squeezing.

Makes 4 servings

PAELLA

Paella

Spain

Nutrition Snapshot	Before	After
Per serving		
Calories	802	524
Total Fat g.	23	8.6
Saturated Fat g.	3.7	1.6
Cholesterol mg.	227	211

Shaped like the sun and dyed the color of fire with saffron, paella (pi-AY-yuh) is a fit gastronomic symbol of Spain. Given its prominence in Spanish cooking, it's not surprising that this rice casserole became popular in some of Spain's former New World colonies, notably Cuba, Puerto Rico, and Venezuela. In the Spanish-speaking Caribbean, paella is flavored and colored with annatto instead of saffron. To create a heart-healthy paella, I reduced the oil, replaced the skin-on chicken pieces with boneless, skinless chicken breasts, and used serrano ham (dry-cured country ham) instead of pork sausage. If you can't find serrano ham, Canadian bacon or prosciutto can be substituted. You can also use fish stock or vegetable stock in place of the chicken stock. This dish makes a stunning presentation for an everyday meal or a special occasion.

½	teaspoon saffron threads	2	cups Valencia-style rice or Arborio rice
1	tablespoon hot water	⅓	cup dry white wine or nonalcoholic white wine
2	tablespoons extra-virgin olive oil		
12	ounces boneless, skinless chicken breasts, cut into 1" pieces	3½–4	cups hot Chicken Stock (page 360) or fat-free reduced-sodium chicken broth
	Salt and ground black pepper		
1	small onion, finely chopped	12	littleneck clams, scrubbed (see page 387)
1	red or yellow bell pepper, cut into ¼" strips	12	mussels, scrubbed and debearded
1	ounce serrano ham or Canadian bacon, cut into ¼" strips	8	ounces shrimp, peeled and deveined
2	cloves garlic, minced	8	ounces cleaned squid (see page 389), cut into ½" rings, or shrimp, peeled and deveined
1	tomato, seeded and cut into ¼" pieces		
3	tablespoons finely chopped fresh flat-leaf parsley	⅓	cup cooked or frozen and thawed peas

In a cup, combine the saffron and water. Let soak for 15 minutes.

Meanwhile, heat 1 tablespoon of the oil in a very large heavy skillet or paella pan over medium heat. Season the chicken with salt and black pepper. Add to the skillet and cook, stirring often, for 2 to 4 minutes, or until lightly browned. Transfer the chicken to a plate and set aside.

Add the remaining 1 tablespoon oil to the skillet. Add the onions, bell peppers, ham or bacon, and garlic. Cook, stirring often, for 5 minutes, or until golden brown. Increase the heat to high. Add the tomatoes and 2 tablespoons of the parsley. Cook for 1 minute.

Preheat the oven to 400°F.

Add the rice to the skillet and cook for 1 minute, or until the grains are shiny. Add the wine and bring to a boil. Add 3½ cups of the stock or broth and the reserved saffron (with liquid). Return to a boil. Reduce the heat to medium-low and simmer for 10 minutes. Stir in the clams, mussels, and the reserved chicken. Return to a boil. Stir in the shrimp and squid or shrimp.

Cover the skillet and transfer to the oven. Bake for 20 to 25 minutes, or until the rice is tender, almost all the liquid is absorbed, the clams and mussels are open wide, and the shrimp and squid are firm and cooked through. (Discard any clams or mussels that are cracked or remain closed.) Stir in the peas. The paella should be quite moist; if the rice starts to dry out during cooking, add a little more stock or broth.

Season with salt and black pepper and sprinkle with the remaining 1 tablespoon parsley.

Makes 6 servings

Regional Variation

Cuban Paella: Replace the saffron, hot water, and olive oil with 2 tablespoons Annato Oil (page 380) or 2 tablespoons olive oil mixed with 1 teaspoon sweet paprika.

TAMALES, BREADS, AND SANDWICHES
Tamales, panes y sándwiches

Tamales are savored from the Río Grande to the Cape of Good Hope. Traditional Mexican and Cuban tamales are made with cornmeal masa cooked in dried corn husks. Nicaraguan Tamales (page 174) and Venezuelan Mushroom Tamales (page 176) are both wrapped and boiled in banana leaves. Tamales are endlessly variable.

These cornmeal turnovers are a big part of the Latin American corn story but not the whole tale. Some other essential cornmeal dishes include México's Fresh Corn Tortillas (page 178), Colombia's Cornmeal Flatcakes (page 179) and Paraguay's soufflé-like cornbread (page 180).

This chapter also includes a recipe for an irresistible dinner roll made with yuca, and recipes for simple Cuban sandwiches that really satisfy.

MEXICAN TAMALES

Tamales mexicanos   *México*

Nutrition Snapshot	Before	After
Per tamale		
Calories	259	163
Total Fat g.	16.4	6
Saturated Fat g.	5.9	1.8
Cholesterol mg.	35	23

Mexican tamales have three basic ingredients in the dough: water, masa harina (hulled, dried, and ground corn), and lard. The corn for masa harina is soaked in limewater prior to grinding, which gives it a unique texture and flavor. The filling often consists of ground beef and chopped vegetables. To reduce the fat without sacrificing flavor, I use less lard than traditional recipes call for and add chicken or vegetable stock to moisten and enrich the dough. The filling uses chopped chicken or turkey breast instead of fatty ground beef. If you usually use ground beef, try the recipe with half ground beef and half ground chicken or turkey breast at first to give your taste buds time to adjust to the flavor.

MASA

- 24 dried corn husks (see tip)
- ¼ cup fresh or frozen and thawed corn kernels (see page 386)
- 2 cups masa harina
- 1 teaspoon salt
- 1 teaspoon baking powder
- 1 cup hot water
- 1 cup Chicken Stock (page 360) or fat-free reduced-sodium chicken or vegetable broth
- 3 tablespoons lard or shortening, at room temperature

FILLING

- 1 tablespoon olive oil
- ½ small onion, finely chopped
- ¼ red bell pepper, finely chopped
- 2–3 jalapeño chile peppers, seeded and minced (wear plastic gloves when handling)
- 1 clove garlic, minced
- ¼ teaspoon ground cumin
- ¼ teaspoon dried oregano
- ¼ teaspoon ground cinnamon
- 8 ounces finely chopped boneless, skinless chicken or turkey breast
- 2 tablespoons chopped fresh cilantro
- ¼ cup dry white wine or nonalcoholic white wine

Salt (optional)

To make the masa: Place the corn husks in a large bowl and cover with cold water. Let soak for 2 hours.

Meanwhile, puree the corn kernels in a food processor or blender. In a large bowl and using a wooden spoon, combine the masa harina, salt, and baking powder. Gradually add the hot water, stock or broth, pureed corn, and lard or shortening. Stir vigorously for 5 to 15 minutes, or until the dough is moist and pliable but not sticky. The consistency should resemble that of Play-Doh. (The longer you beat, the more air will be incorporated into the dough, making lighter-tasting tamales. Alternatively, you can make the dough in a standing mixer fitted with a paddle or dough hook. Beat the dough at high speed for 15 minutes.)

To make the filling: Heat the oil in a nonstick skillet over medium heat. Add the onions, bell peppers, chile peppers, garlic, cumin, oregano, and cinnamon. Cook for 3 minutes, or until the vegetables are soft but not brown. Stir in the chicken or turkey and cilantro. Cook, stirring often, for 3 minutes, or until the chicken or turkey is cooked through. Add the wine and cook for 5 minutes, or until all the liquid has been absorbed. Season with salt, if desired.

To assemble: Place 1 of the corn husks flat on a work surface, tapered end toward you. Mound 3 heaping tablespoons of the masa mixture in the center of the top half of the corn husk. (The mound should be oblong and run the length of the corn husk.) Make a shallow groove the length of the corn mixture. Place a spoonful of the filling mixture in the groove. Pinch the sides of the groove together to encase the filling. Fold the tapered half of the corn husk over the top to enclose the filling. Lay another corn husk flat on the work surface, tapered end away from you. Place the first husk in the center of the bottom half of the second husk. Fold the tapered end over the bottom to encase the tamale. Tie the bundle into a neat rectangle, using strips of corn husk or string. Repeat to use the remaining corn husks and filling.

Insert a steamer basket into a large pot. Add 1" of water and bring to a simmer over medium heat. Stack the tamales to the basket, cover, and simmer for 1 hour and 30 minutes, or until the dough is set and comes away easily from the corn husks when tested. Remove the string before serving.

Makes 12

Cooking Tip

✦ Dried corn husks are available at many Hispanic markets. Or, see the source list on page 66.

CUBAN TAMALES

Tamales cubanos

Cuba

Nutrition Snapshot	Before	After
Per tamale		
Calories	150	120
Total Fat g.	8.8	2.9
Saturated Fat g.	4	0.8
Cholesterol mg.	22	15

No one makes better tamales than my Cuban friend, Elida Proenza. Her tamales are mercifully low in fat—the result of using pureed fresh corn instead of lard or oil to moisten the cornmeal. To be strictly authentic, you'd use freshly ground autumn corn (sometimes called horse corn or maíz tierno para tamal). Autumn corn is a harder, drier corn than North American corn on the cob (it's similar to feed corn). You can buy preground autumn corn at Cuban markets. To simplify things, I call for North American–style corn on the cob and cornmeal. The cachucha chile peppers are a very mild, tiny pepper from Cuba. If unavailable, use rocotillos (see page 55), ají dulce, or bell peppers.

MASA

48	dried corn husks (see tip)
4	cups fresh or frozen and thawed corn kernels (see page 386)
2–2½	cups stone-ground yellow cornmeal
2	teaspoons sugar
	Salt and ground white or black pepper

FILLING

10	cachucha chile peppers or ½ green bell pepper, seeded and minced
8	cloves garlic
1½	teaspoons ground cumin

	Ground white or black pepper
1	tablespoon olive oil
1	small onion, minced
2	tablespoons finely chopped fresh cilantro
1	tomato, peeled (see page 383), seeded, and chopped
1	pound very lean boneless pork loin, chops, or tenderloin, trimmed of all visible fat and cut into ½" cubes
	Salt
8	cups water
2	bay leaves
4	sprigs fresh cilantro

To make the masa: Place the corn husks in a large bowl and cover with cold water. Let soak for 2 hours.

Puree the corn kernels in a food processor or blender. Transfer to a large bowl. Using a wooden spoon, stir in 2 cups of the cornmeal to obtain a soft, thick, pliable dough. The consistency should resemble that of Play-Doh; add more cornmeal, if needed. Stir in the sugar. Season with salt and pepper.

To make the filling: In a mortar and pestle or food processor, pound or process the chile peppers or bell peppers and garlic to a coarse paste. Add ½ teaspoon of the cumin and ½ teaspoon white or black pepper. Process or pound until combined.

Heat the oil in a small nonstick skillet over medium heat. Add the onions and the chile-pepper or bell-pepper paste. Cook for 3 minutes, or until the onions are soft but not brown. Stir in the chopped cilantro, tomatoes, and pork. Cook for 5 minutes, or until the pork is no longer pink in the center. Season with salt and white or black pepper. Remove from the heat and let cool.

To assemble: Place 1 of the corn husks flat on a work surface, tapered end toward you. Mound 2 heaping tablespoons of the corn mixture in the center of the top half of the corn husk. (The mound should be oblong and run the length of the corn husk.) Make a shallow groove the length of the corn mixture. Place a spoonful of the pork mixture in the groove. Pinch the sides of the groove together to encase the filling. Fold the tapered half of the corn husk over the top to encase the tamale. Lay another corn husk flat on the work surface, tapered end away from you. Place the first husk in the center of the bottom half of the second husk. Fold the tapered end over the bottom to encase the first bundle. Tie the bundle into a neat rectangle with strips of corn husk or string. Repeat to use the remaining corn husks and filling.

In a large saucepan over high heat, combine the water, the remaining 1 teaspoon cumin, 1 teaspoon white or black pepper, bay leaves, and cilantro sprigs. Season with salt and bring to a boil. Reduce the heat to medium and add the tamales. Simmer for 1 hour.

Transfer the packages to a colander and drain well. Remove the string and serve in the packages.

Makes 24

Cooking Tip

✦ Dried corn husks are available at many Hispanic markets. Or, refer to the source list on page 66.

NICARAGUAN TAMALES

Nacatamales

Nicaragua

Nutrition Snapshot	Before	After
Per tamale		
Calories	666	435
Total Fat g.	31.6	8.4
Saturated Fat g.	16.7	1.6
Cholesterol mg.	98	31

Nacatamal is the national snack of Nicaragua—and the most lavish tamale in Latin America. Like a Mexican tamale, it's made with masa harina, but like a Puerto Rican pastel, it's cooked in a banana leaf. The generous garnish of annatto-flavored pork, onions, tomatoes, olives, raisins, prunes, and even spearmint makes the nacatamal a light meal in itself. The only drawback is the melted butter or lard called for in the traditional recipe. To make a healthier version, I replaced the lard with chicken stock and used annatto-marinated pork loin instead of bacon. If you like sauce, serve these with Central American Tomato Sauce (page 301). Start the tamales a day ahead to get the most flavor from the marinade.

PORK AND MARINADE

⅔ cup long-grain white rice

1 cup cold water

1 teaspoon annatto seeds

1 clove garlic, minced

¾ teaspoon salt

½ teaspoon ground black pepper

½ cup sour orange juice (see page 63), or 6 tablespoons lime juice + 2 tablespoons orange juice

1 pound lean pork loin or boneless, skinless chicken breasts, trimmed of all visible fat

MASA

½ onion, minced

½ red bell pepper, minced

1 clove garlic, minced

1½ cups warm Chicken Stock (page 360) or fat-free reduced-sodium chicken broth

1 cup warm skim milk

2 tablespoons Annatto Oil (page 380) or 2 tablespoons olive oil + ½ teaspoon sweet paprika

2¼ teaspoons salt

½ teaspoon ground black pepper

3–3½ cups masa harina

FILLING

8 pieces (12" × 12" each) banana leaves, plantain leaves, or foil

1 potato, peeled and cut into 8 slices

1 onion, peeled and cut into 8 slices

1 tomato, peeled (see page 383) and cut into 8 slices

8 pimiento-stuffed green olives, halved

8 pitted prunes, halved

⅓ cup raisins

8 sprigs spearmint

To make the pork and marinade: In a small bowl, combine the rice and water. Let soak for 4 to 12 hours. Drain.

Grind the annatto seeds to a powder in a spice mill or crush with a mortar and pestle. Transfer to a medium bowl. Stir in the garlic, salt, pepper, and sour orange juice or lime juice and orange juice. Add the pork or chicken and turn to coat.

Cover and marinate in the refrigerator for at least 1 hour or overnight. Turn a few times while marinating.

To make the masa: In a large bowl, combine the onions, bell peppers, garlic, stock or broth, milk, oil, salt, and black pepper. Using a wooden spoon, stir in 4 cups of the masa harina to obtain a soft, thick, pliable dough. The consistency should resemble that of Play-Doh; add more masa harina, if needed. Cover the dough with plastic wrap and let stand for 20 minutes.

To assemble: Slice the pork or chicken into 8 slices, reserving the marinade.

Arrange the banana leaves, plantain leaves, or foil on a large work surface. Divide the dough into 8 pieces. Place 1 piece in the center of each square. Pat it into a rectangle about 3½" long × 2½" wide × ¾" thick.

Tuck a slice of potato, onion, and tomato under each dough rectangle. Press the dough on top of them. Place 1½ tablespoons rice, 1 slice pork or chicken, 1 olive, 1 prune, a few raisins, and 1 sprig spearmint on top of the dough. Press into the dough. Drizzle the reserved marinade on top. Fold the left side and right side of the leaves or foil over the dough, then fold over the top and bottom to form a neat package. Wrap each in a piece of foil. Tie the bundles closed with string.

Place the packages in a large pot and set over medium heat. Pour in water to cover by 4". Simmer for 3 hours, adding more water as needed to keep the packages submerged.

Transfer the packages to a colander and drain well. Remove the string and foil and serve in the packages.

Makes 8

VENEZUELAN MUSHROOM TAMALES

Hallacas
venezolanas

Venezuela

Nutrition Snapshot	Before	After
Per tamale		
Calories	214	184
Total Fat g.	13	5
Saturated Fat g.	3.5	0.6
Cholesterol mg.	27	0

Hallacas (ay-YAH-kas) belong to that great family of wrapped boiled cornmeal dishes that includes Mexican Tamales (page 170) and Nicaraguan Tamales (page 174). The Venezuelan version features fine white corn-flour masa flavored with annatto oil, raisins, capers, and olives. The whole bundle is wrapped and cooked in banana leaves. The idea for these vegetarian hallacas comes from Luis Contreras, affable chef of the celebrated Yuca restaurant in Miami. He stuffs his hallacas with a guiso (stew) made of portobello mushrooms instead of the traditional pork. To further lighten the hallacas, I like to add pureed corn to the dough in place of some of the oil.

STEW

½ medium onion, thinly sliced lengthwise

½ red bell pepper, thinly sliced lengthwise

1 large portobello mushroom or 8 ounces button mushrooms, thinly sliced

1 plum tomato, peeled (see page 383) and thinly sliced lengthwise

1 clove garlic, thinly sliced

¼ teaspoon dried oregano

¼ teaspoon ground cumin

½ cup Vegetable Stock (page 361) or water

Salt and ground black pepper

DOUGH

1 cup fresh, frozen and thawed, or drained canned corn kernels

2 cups arepa flour (see "Masa" on page 60)

1¾–2 cups hot Vegetable Stock (page 361) or hot water

2 tablespoons Annatto Oil (page 380) or 2 tablespoons olive oil + ½ teaspoon sweet paprika

1¼ teaspoons salt

½ teaspoon ground black pepper

FILLING

16 pieces (12" × 12" each) banana leaves, plantain leaves, or foil

½ cup cooked or canned chickpeas, rinsed and drained (optional)

3 tablespoons raisins

2 tablespoons drained and rinsed capers

1 tablespoon chopped pimiento-stuffed green olives

12 cups water

1 onion, quartered

2 cloves garlic

4 culantro leaves or cilantro sprigs

To make the stew: In a large heavy saucepan over high heat, combine the onions, bell peppers, mushrooms, tomatoes, garlic, oregano, cumin, and stock or water. Bring to a boil. Reduce the heat to medium, cover the pan, and cook for 5 minutes. Uncover the pan and simmer, stirring occasionally, for 10 minutes, or until most of the liquid has evaporated and the vegetables are very tender. Season with salt and black pepper. Let the mixture cool to room temperature.

To make the dough: Puree the corn kernels in a food processor. Add the flour, 1¾ cups of the stock or water, 1 tablespoon of the annatto oil or olive oil and paprika, salt, and pepper. Process for 2 to 3 minutes, or until the dough is soft, moist, and pliable. The mixture should be the consistency of soft ice cream; add more stock or water, if needed. (Alternatively, puree the corn in a blender and knead the ingredients for the dough together with your fingers.)

To assemble: Arrange the banana leaves, plantain leaves, or foil on a large work surface. Lightly brush the centers with the remaining 1 tablespoon annatto oil or olive oil and paprika. Divide the dough into 8 pieces and roll each into a ball. Place 1 ball in the center of each square. Pat it into a flat disk about 5½" across.

Divide the stew, chickpeas (if using), raisins, capers, and olives among the disks of dough. Fold the left side and right side of the leaves or foil over each disk of dough, then fold over the top and bottom to form a neat package approximately 4" × 4". Wrap each in another leaf or piece of foil. Tie the packages closed with string.

Pour the water into a large pot. Lightly salt the water and add the onions, garlic, and culantro or cilantro. Bring to a boil over high heat. Reduce the heat to medium and add the packages. Cover the pot and cook for 1 hour, or until the filling is firm but tender when tested with a skewer. Transfer the hallacas to a colander and let drain. Remove the string and foil and serve in the packages.

Makes 8

Cooking Tip

✦ The packages can be assembled up to 3 days ahead and stored in the refrigerator before cooking.

FRESH CORN TORTILLAS

Tortillas frescas

México

Nutrition Snapshot	Before	After
Per tortilla		
Calories	67	52
Total Fat g.	2.2	0.5
Saturated Fat g.	0.7	0.1
Cholesterol mg.	2	0

Tortilla-making is as old as Mexican civilization itself. A ball of dough made from masa harina (hulled, dried, ground corn) and water, is pressed as flat as a compact disk, then toasted on a hot comal (a griddle for cooking tortillas). Tortillas are easy to make at home and taste vastly superior to the store-bought variety. You'll need one special piece of equipment: a tortilla press, which can be found at Mexican markets or mail-ordered from one of the sources on page 66. Most presses are fairly inexpensive.

> 2 cups masa harina
> 1¼ cups hot water

In a medium bowl, combine the masa harina and water. Mix and knead with a wooden spoon or your fingers for 3 to 4 minutes, or until the dough is smooth and thick. The consistency should resemble that of Play-Doh; add a spoonful of water, if needed. Cover the dough with plastic wrap and let rest for 20 minutes.

Heat a comal, griddle, or cast-iron or nonstick skillet over medium-high heat until a drop of water sprinkled in the pan evaporates in 10 seconds. Pinch off a 1½" piece of the dough. Roll it between the palms of your hands into a ball. Sandwich the ball between 2 pieces of plastic (see tip) and place in a tortilla press. Flatten the ball in the press to make a 5" tortilla. (Alternatively, you can flatten the dough with a large heavy object such as a cast-iron skillet or very large can of tomatoes. Be sure to flatten evenly to a ¹⁄₁₆" thickness.)

Gently peel off the top layer of plastic, then the bottom layer, and place the tortilla in the hot pan. Cook for 30 to 60 seconds per side, or until the top of the tortilla puffs and the bottom begins to brown. Transfer the tortilla to a bread basket lined with a cloth napkin. As you make and cook each tortilla, transfer it to the basket and cover with the napkin. (The cloth helps steam the tortillas, making them soft and tender.) Keep covered for at least 5 minutes before serving.

Makes 16

Cooking Tip

✦ In the old days, tortillas were pressed between 2 banana leaves. I simply cut off the edges of a large resealable plastic bag to make 2 large pieces of plastic.

CORNMEAL FLATCAKES

Arepas

Colombia
Venezuela

Nutrition Snapshot	Before	After
Per arepa		
Calories	139	134
Total Fat g.	9.6	3.7
Saturated Fat g.	5.5	0.9
Cholesterol mg.	26	2

What do you get when you cross polenta with a pancake? Arepas. Look for arepa flour (masarepa), or fine white corn flour, in Hispanic markets and the international aisle of large supermarkets.

2–2¼	cups warm water (105° to 115°F)	2	cups arepa flour
1	teaspoon salt	1	tablespoon canola oil

Combine 2 cups of the water and the salt in a large bowl. Stir in the flour and knead for 2 minutes, or until the dough is firm yet pliable. The consistency should resemble that of mashed potatoes; if it is too firm, add a little more water.

Divide the dough into 8 balls. Wet your hands and pat the dough into patties about ¼" thick and 4" across.

Heat 1½ teaspoons of the oil in a large nonstick skillet or on a griddle over medium heat. Add 4 of the patties and cook for 3 minutes per side, or until lightly browned. Transfer to a plate and cover to keep warm. Repeat with the remaining patties.

Makes 8

Cooking Tips

✦ To make fat-free arepas, omit the oil and skillet and cook the flatcakes on a nonstick baking sheet in a 400°F oven for 5 to 10 minutes instead.

✦ Arepas keep well in the refrigerator. To store, wrap each arepa in plastic and refrigerate for up to 3 days. Reheat in the toaster.

Regional Variations

Colombian Cheese and Herb Arepas: Add ¼ cup grated Muenster or Parmesan cheese, 2 tablespoons chopped fresh herbs (such as flat-leaf parsley, oregano, and cilantro), and 1 clove garlic, minced, to the dough.

North American Fresh Corn Arepas: Warm 1½ teaspoons olive oil in a large non-stick skillet over medium heat. Add 1 small onion, finely chopped, and 1 clove garlic, minced. Cook for 3 minutes. Add 1 cup fresh or frozen and thawed corn kernels and cook for 3 minutes, or until soft. Add the 2 cups warm water. Remove the pan from the heat. Stir in the salt, flour, and 3 tablespoons chopped fresh cilantro or flat-leaf parsley. Proceed as directed.

PARAGUAYAN CORNBREAD

Sopa Paraguaya   *Paraguay*

Nutrition Snapshot	Before	After
Per serving		
Calories	440	226
Total Fat g.	26	6.5
Saturated Fat g.	13.8	2.1
Cholesterol mg.	143	10

Despite the name, this dish has more in common with corn puddings than with North American cornbread. The traditional version is loaded with butter, cheese, and egg yolks. To reduce the fat, I omitted the butter, cut back on the cheese, and used egg whites in place of the yolks. I like to beat the egg whites to give the cornbread a light, soufflélike texture.

2	tablespoons grated Parmesan cheese	½	cup grated Muenster or sharp Cheddar cheese
2	tablespoons canola oil	1½	cups yellow cornmeal
1	small onion, finely chopped	1	teaspoon salt
½	green bell pepper, finely chopped	½	teaspoon ground black pepper
2	cups fresh or frozen and thawed corn kernels (see page 386)	4	large egg whites
½	cup low-fat cottage cheese	½	teaspoon cream of tartar
½	cup skim milk		

Preheat the oven to 400°F. Coat a nonstick 9" cake pan with nonstick spray. Dust the pan with the Parmesan.

Heat the oil in a small nonstick skillet over medium heat. Add the onions and bell peppers. Cook for 4 minutes, or until the onions are soft but not brown. Transfer to a food processor or blender. Add 1½ cups of the corn kernels and the cottage cheese. Puree. Transfer to a large bowl. Stir in the remaining ½ cup corn kernels, the milk, Muenster or Cheddar, cornmeal, salt, and black pepper.

In another large bowl, combine the egg whites and cream of tartar. Beat with a mixer for 8 minutes, or until firm and glossy but not dry. (Begin beating on low speed and gradually increase the speed to medium, then to high.) Gently fold the corn mixture into the egg-white mixture. Spoon the mixture into the prepared cake pan.

Bake for 20 minutes, or until the top is puffed and browned, the center is set, and a toothpick inserted in the center comes out clean. Let cool for 3 minutes. Invert onto a platter and cut into 8 wedges.

Makes 8 servings

YUCA ROLLS

Panecitos de
yuca

United States

Nutrition Snapshot	Before	After
Per roll		
Calories	199	188
Total Fat g.	4.4	2.5
Saturated Fat g.	1.7	0.4
Cholesterol mg.	4	0

These moist, chewy rolls have become the star of the bread basket at Nuevo Latino restaurants.

1	pound yuca, peeled and cut into 3" × ½" strips	1	tablespoon salt
3	tablespoons honey	1½	cups whole-wheat flour
1	package (¼ ounce) active dry yeast	4–4½	cups unbleached or all-purpose flour
¼	cup warm water (105° to 115°F)	2	tablespoons skim milk
3	tablespoons canola oil		

Place the yuca in a large saucepan and cover with cold water. Bring to a boil over high heat. Reduce the heat to medium and simmer for 15 minutes, or until the yuca is very soft. Drain, reserving 1½ cups of the cooking liquid. Using a fork, remove and discard any fibers from the yuca. Return the yuca to the pan. Add 1 tablespoon of the honey. Mash with a potato masher or fork.

Meanwhile, in a very large bowl, combine the yeast, warm water, and the remaining 2 tablespoons honey. Let stand for 5 minutes, or until foamy. Add the oil, salt, reserved cooking liquid, and mashed yuca to the yeast mixture. Stir in the whole-wheat flour. Stir in the unbleached or all-purpose flour, ½ cup at time, to obtain a sticky dough that comes away from the sides of the bowl but is soft enough to knead. Turn onto a floured work surface and knead for 6 to 8 minutes, or until smooth.

Wash and lightly oil the bowl. Transfer the dough to the bowl and press plastic wrap on top. Cover with a dish towel. Place in a warm, draft-free spot and let rise for 1½ to 2 hours, or until doubled in bulk.

Lightly oil two 8" springform pans or baking pans. With oiled hands, punch down the dough and divide into 20 pieces. Shape into 2" balls. Place 10 balls in each pan, ½" apart. Cover with plastic wrap or a damp dish towel. Place in a warm, draft-free spot and let rise for 1 hour, or until doubled in bulk.

Preheat the oven to 375°F. Brush the tops of the rolls with the milk. Bake for 25 minutes, or until puffed and browned. Let cool slightly before serving.

Makes 20

MIDNIGHTER SANDWICH

Medianoche   *Cuba*

Nutrition Snapshot	Before	After
Per sandwich		
Calories	661	339
Total Fat g.	37.4	10
Saturated Fat g.	16.6	4.2
Cholesterol mg.	131	44

The midnighter is Cuba's most famous sandwich—a satisfying combination of ham, pork, pickles, and cheese on a sweet roll. It takes its name from the time it is traditionally eaten, typically after a movie or show. In Cuba, the sandwich is made with slightly sweet pan suave bread. Nonfat sour cream stands in for the more conventional mayonnaise.

1   slightly sweet roll (about 7" long) or 1 section (7" long) French or Italian bread, halved lengthwise

1   tablespoon nonfat sour cream

1   tablespoon Dijon mustard

2   thin slices (1½ ounces total) cold roast pork, trimmed of all visible fat

2   thin slices (1½ ounces total) prosciutto or lean cooked ham, trimmed of all visible fat

1   thin slice (½ ounce) low-fat Swiss cheese such as Jarlsberg

4   thin slices tomato

2   leaves iceberg lettuce

4   thin slices pickle

Spread the bottom of the roll with the sour cream and the top with the mustard. Layer the pork, prosciutto or ham, cheese, tomatoes, lettuce, and pickles on the bottom. Close up the sandwich and coat both sides with nonstick spray.

Preheat a sandwich press or heat a medium nonstick skillet over medium heat. Add the sandwich and cook for 6 minutes, or until crusty and golden brown. If using a skillet, place a heavy weight, such as another heavy skillet, on top of the sandwich. Flip once halfway through the cooking time. Slice in half on the diagonal.

Makes 1

TURKEY TEA SANDWICH

Elena Ruz

Cuba

Nutrition Snapshot	Before	After
Per sandwich		
Calories	504	330
Total Fat g.	24.1	7
Saturated Fat g.	14.1	1.2
Cholesterol mg.	133	47

Here is Cuba's most unusual sandwich, named for a Havana socialite of the 1930s. The combination of sliced turkey, strawberry jam, and cream cheese may seem strange to some. Then again, North Americans eat turkey with cranberry sauce. In Cuba, a slightly sweet bread called pan suave and turkey sliced from a whole bird would be used in this recipe.

1   slightly sweet roll (about 7" long) or 1 section (7" long) French or Italian bread, halved lengthwise

2   tablespoons low-fat or nonfat cream cheese

2   tablespoons strawberry jam

2   ounces sliced turkey breast

    Spread the bottom of the roll with the cream cheese and the top with the jam. Place the turkey on the bottom. Close up the sandwich and coat both sides with nonstick spray.

    Preheat a sandwich press or heat a medium nonstick skillet over medium heat. Add the sandwich and cook for 6 minutes, or until crusty and golden brown. If using a skillet, place a heavy weight, such as another heavy skillet, on top of the sandwich. Flip once halfway through the cooking time. Slice in half on the diagonal.

Makes 1

TORTILLA SPECIALTIES
Especialidades de tortillas

Standing at a market in Chiapas, México, I see a woman pat a ball

of dough into a thin, round flatbread. This scene is as old as Central Amer-

ican civilization itself: the making of a tortilla.

To millions of Latin Americans, a meal just wouldn't be complete

without tortillas. These flatbreads are the staff of life to the peoples of

México, Guatemala, El Salvador, and Honduras. Their healthfulness, conve-

nience, and flavor have made them one of the most popular foods in North

America as well. Almost every North American supermarket carries tortillas.

Without them, there would be no burritos, enchiladas, fajitas, or tostadas.

The recipes that follow are updated versions of classic tortilla

dishes. From México, savor Quesadillas (page 212) and Huevos Rancheros

(page 186) as well as the lesser-known (but just as delectable) Yucatán

Open-Faced Sandwiches (page 210). Specialties from Central America in-

clude the Bean Tortilla with Honduran "Butter" (page 208) and Salvadoran

Stuffed Tortillas (page 206), an irresistible handheld snack. To make fresh

corn tortillas, see the recipe on page 178.

RECITES

HUEVOS RANCHEROS

Huevos
rancheros modernos

México

Nutrition Snapshot	Before	After
Per serving		
Calories	796	200
Total Fat g.	61.3	3.7
Saturated Fat g.	18.6	0.5
Cholesterol mg.	482	0

This traditional Mexican breakfast is made with fried eggs, fried tortillas, and spicy salsa ranchera. Delicious, but deadly. To slash the fat, I use scrambled egg substitute instead of fried eggs. (You can also use egg whites, which are the main ingredient in egg substitute.) Onions, tomatoes, and cilantro pump up the flavor of the egg scramble. To cut fat further, the tortillas are baked instead of fried. I like to cut some of the tortillas into long, thin triangles and stand them upright in the eggs. I also char the vegetables in the salsa to hint at the smoky flavor of eggs and tortillas fried in lard.

6	fat-free flour tortillas (6" diameter)
1	tablespoon extra-virgin olive oil
1	medium onion, finely chopped
1	clove garlic, minced
1–2	jalapeño or serrano chile peppers, seeded and finely chopped (wear plastic gloves when handling)

1	tomato, seeded and finely chopped
¼	cup chopped fresh cilantro
1	cup liquid egg substitute or 8 egg whites
	Salt and ground black pepper
1	cup Ranch-Style Tomato Salsa (page 296)

Preheat the oven to 350°F.

Using a sharp knife, cut 2 of the tortillas into wedges or long, thin triangles. (To make long triangles, place a tortilla flat on a work surface. Starting from one side, make 8 diagonal cuts at sharp angles to one another across the length of the tortilla. The cuts will look like two Ws. For each tortilla, you should be left with 7 long, thin triangles and 2 semicircular pieces. See the photo on page 193.) Place the tortilla pieces and the remaining 4 whole tortillas on nonstick baking sheets. Bake for 10 minutes, or until lightly browned and crisp. Transfer to a rack to cool.

Heat the oil in a large nonstick skillet over medium heat. Add the onions. Cook for 2 minutes. Add the garlic and chile peppers. Cook for 2 minutes, or until the onions are soft but not brown. Add the tomatoes and cilantro. Cook for 2 minutes more. Add the egg substitute or egg whites. Cook and stir for 3 minutes, or until the eggs are scrambled but still moist. Season with salt and black pepper.

Place 1 whole tortilla in the center of each of 4 plates. Divide the egg mixture among the tortillas. Stand the tortilla pieces in the egg mixture so that the points rise up dramatically. Ladle the salsa around the egg mixture and serve.

Makes 4 servings

BAKE-FRIED POTATOES (PAGE 141)

BOLIVIAN CORN PUDDING (PAGE 149)

NICARAGUAN TAMALES (PAGE 174) AND VENEZUELAN MUSHROOM TAMALES (PAGE 176)

CHILES RELLENOS WITH CORN (PAGE 146)

GRILLED RIPE PLANTAINS (PAGE 144)

PAELLA (PAGE 166)

HUEVOS RANCHEROS (PAGE 186)

RICE PILAF WITH SHRIMP (PAGE 160)

MIDNIGHTER SANDWICH (PAGE 182)

MEXICAN TAMALES (PAGE 170) AND CUBAN TAMALES (PAGE 172)

MEXICO CITY TOSTADAS (PAGE 205)

TORTILLA, EGG, AND GREEN SALSA CASSEROLE (PAGE 204)

PORK AND PINEAPPLE SOFT TACOS (PAGE 217)

QUESADILLAS (PAGE 212)

SALVADORAN STUFFED TORTILLAS (PAGE 206), CENTRAL AMERICAN SLAW (PAGE 116), AND CENTRAL AMERICAN TOMATO SALSA (PAGE 300)

FRESH CORN TORTILLAS (PAGE 178)

Pronto!

TEX-MEX EGGS AND TORTILLAS

Migas texanas

Tex-Mex

Nutrition Snapshot	Before	After
Per serving		
Calories	453	244
Total Fat g.	32.5	8.4
Saturated Fat g.	7.5	0.5
Cholesterol mg.	462	7

Whenever I visit my relatives in Corpus Christi, Texas, our first stop is a local breakfast joint for steaming platters of migas (eggs scrambled with fried tortillas). To make a heart-healthy version of this popular Tex-Mex breakfast, I bake the tortillas instead of frying them and substitute egg whites (or liquid egg substitute) for the whole eggs.

4	corn tortillas (6" diameter), each cut into 8 wedges
1½	tablespoon canola oil or lard
1	onion, finely chopped
2	cloves garlic, minced
16	egg whites or 2 cups liquid egg substitute

3	tablespoons chopped fresh cilantro Salt and ground black pepper
2	cups Ranch-Style Tomato Salsa (page 296) or your favorite salsa
2	tablespoons grated queso fresco, sharp white Cheddar cheese, or Romano cheese

Preheat the oven to 350°F.

Arrange the tortilla pieces in a single layer on nonstick baking sheets. Coat with nonstick spray. Bake for 10 minutes, or until lightly browned and crisp. Transfer to a rack to cool.

Heat the oil or lard in a large nonstick skillet over medium heat. Add the onions and garlic. Cook and stir for 4 minutes, or until the onions are soft but not brown.

In a medium bowl, beat together the egg whites or egg substitute and cilantro. Season with salt and pepper. Stir in the crisped tortilla pieces. Pour the egg mixture into the skillet. Cook, stirring often, for 3 minutes, or until scrambled. Season with more salt and pepper, if desired.

Divide the eggs among 4 plates and top each serving with ½ cup salsa and 1½ teaspoons cheese.

Makes 4 servings

TORTILLA, EGG, AND GREEN SALSA CASSEROLE

Chilaquiles   *México*

Nutrition Snapshot	Before	After
Per serving		
Calories	524	195
Total Fat g.	41.3	4.9
Saturated Fat g.	10.6	0.4
Cholesterol mg.	442	0

This is another one of my favorite Mexican breakfasts. Crisp tortillas are simmered in salsa verde, then served with eggs and sour cream. The traditional version is a nutritional nightmare, laden with artery-clogging deep-fried tortillas, fried eggs, and full-fat sour cream. To make a healthier version, I crisp the tortillas in the oven, use scrambled egg whites instead of fried eggs, and top with dollops of nonfat sour cream.

4	corn tortillas (6" diameter), each cut into 1" × 2" strips
¾	cup finely chopped onions
½	cup + 2 tablespoons chopped fresh cilantro
2	cups Salsa Verde (page 302) or your favorite salsa
1	tablespoon lard or canola oil
1	clove garlic, minced
½	teaspoon dried oregano
12	egg whites or 1½ cups liquid egg substitute, lightly beaten
	Salt and ground black pepper
¼	cup nonfat or low-fat sour cream

Preheat the oven to 350°F.

Arrange the tortilla pieces in a single layer on nonstick baking sheets. Coat with nonstick spray. Bake for 10 minutes, or until lightly browned and crisp. Transfer to a rack to cool.

Combine ¼ cup of the onions and ¼ cup of the cilantro in a small serving bowl. Set aside.

Heat the salsa in a large nonstick skillet over medium heat. Stir in the crisped tortilla pieces and another ¼ cup of the cilantro. Simmer for 5 minutes.

While the salsa is simmering, heat the lard or oil in a medium nonstick skillet over medium heat. Add the remaining ½ cup onions, garlic, and oregano. Cook and stir for 4 minutes, or until the onions are soft but not brown. Stir in the egg whites or egg substitute. Season with salt and pepper. Cook, stirring often, for 3 minutes, or until scrambled. Stir into the salsa and tortillas.

Spoon the egg mixture onto individual plates or into an earthenware casserole. Top with dollops of the sour cream and the remaining 2 tablespoons cilantro.

Serve with the reserved onion and cilantro mixture.

Makes 4 servings

MEXICO CITY TOSTADAS

Tostadas
de la ciudad
de México

México

Nutrition Snapshot	Before	After
Per serving		
Calories	482	90
Total Fat g.	34.4	3.3
Saturated Fat g.	7.2	0.1
Cholesterol mg.	57	8

The best tostadas I ever tasted were served by street vendors outside Mexico City's enormous cathedral. They were striking in their simplicity. These open-faced sandwiches were put together with handmade corn tortillas and just a light topping of refried beans and vegetables. They were a far cry from the cheese-laden, fat-drenched tostadas served at Mexican restaurants in North America.

6 yellow or blue corn tortillas (6" diameter)

1 cup warm Refried Beans (page 155) or fat-free canned refried beans

1 small white onion, finely chopped

1 small tomato, seeded and finely chopped

3 scallions, finely chopped

¼ cup chopped cooked nopalitos (see page 60) or chopped cooked green beans

¼ cup coarsely chopped fresh cilantro

Juice of 1 lime

3 tablespoons finely grated queso fresco or Parmesan cheese

Preheat the oven to 350°F.

Arrange the tortillas in a single layer on 2 large nonstick baking sheets. Bake for 10 minutes, or until lightly browned and crisp. Transfer to a rack to cool.

Spread about 2½ tablespoons of the refried beans over the surface of each tortilla. Divide the onions, tomatoes, scallions, nopalitos or green beans, cilantro, lime juice, and cheese among the tortillas.

Makes 6 servings

Variations

Chicken Tostadas: Add ¼ cup shredded cooked chicken breast to each tortilla.

Picadillo Tostadas: Add ¼ cup Turkey Picadillo (page 257) to each tortilla.

SALVADORAN STUFFED TORTILLAS

Pupusas
salvadoreñas

El Salvador

Pupusas rank with pizza and hamburgers among the world's great handheld snacks. Incredibly, few people outside Central America have ever heard of them. These stuffed tortillas traditionally come with one of four fillings: chicharrones (pork cracklings), queso (cheese and scallions), frijoles (mashed red kidney or black beans), and revueltos (a combination of all three). Because I'm married to a vegetarian, I'm partial to the bean filling. The only remotely challenging aspect to the recipe is shaping the pupusas. Don't be frustrated if your first few fail—with a little practice, you'll be turning out pupusas like a Salvadoran grandmother. These tortillas are traditionally served with Central American Slaw (page 116) and Central American Tomato Salsa (page 300).

MASA

2½ cups masa harina

1½–1¾ cups hot water

FILLING

1 cup cooked or canned red kidney beans, rinsed and drained

1 tablespoon minced onions

1 clove garlic, minced

¼ teaspoon ground cumin

1 cup Chicken Stock (page 360) or fat-free reduced-sodium chicken broth

Salt and ground black pepper

1–2 teaspoons canola oil

4 cups Central American Slaw (page 116)

1 cup Central American Tomato Salsa (page 300) or your favorite salsa

To make the masa: In a medium bowl, combine the masa harina and water. Mix and knead with a wooden spoon or your fingers for 3 to 4 minutes, or until the dough is smooth and thick. The consistency should resemble that of Play-Doh; add a little more water, if needed. Cover the dough with plastic wrap and let rest for 20 minutes.

To make the filling: In a medium nonstick skillet over high heat, combine the beans, onions, garlic, cumin, and stock or broth. Bring to a boil, reduce the heat to medium, and simmer for 6 to 8 minutes, or until all the stock has been absorbed. Season with salt and pepper. Remove from the heat and let cool for 2 to 3 minutes. Mash the beans with the back of a spoon and let cool.

To assemble: Divide the dough into 16 portions. With wet hands, roll 1 portion into a ball (cover the remaining portions with plastic to keep them from drying out as you work). Using your thumb, make a depression in the center of the ball. Gradually enlarge this depression to turn each masa ball into a cup. (Rotate the masa as you shape it with your thumb to keep the sides of the cup even. The walls of the cup should be about ¼" thick.) Repeat with the remaining dough.

Place a spoonful of the filling in the center of each masa cup. Bring the top sides of the cup together over the filling to enclose it and pinch the top shut. Remoisten your hands and gently pat the resulting ball into a disk. (If necessary, pat the pupusas between sheets of plastic to avoid sticking). Continue patting the disk to obtain a pupusa about 4" across and ¼" thick. Repeat to make a total of 16 pupusas.

Heat a large nonstick skillet or griddle over medium heat. Brush both sides of each pupusa with oil. Working in batches, cook for 2 minutes per side, or until puffed, hot, and just beginning to brown. Keep warm in a 250°F oven until all of the pupusas are cooked. Serve with the slaw and salsa.

Makes 16

Variation

Cheese-and-Scallion-Stuffed Tortillas: Omit the bean filling. Instead, combine 2½ ounces grated queso fresco or sharp Cheddar cheese and 3 tablespoons finely chopped scallions in a small bowl. Proceed as directed, using the cheese filling in place of the bean filling.

BEAN TORTILLA WITH HONDURAN "BUTTER"

Baleada
hondureña

Honduras

Nutrition Snapshot	Before	After
Per tortilla		
Calories	316	213
Total Fat g.	17.2	3.8
Saturated Fat g.	8.6	1
Cholesterol mg.	50	9

The baleada belongs to a popular family of Central American antojitos (appetizers). This recipe is simplicity itself, consisting of flour tortillas stuffed with mashed red beans and slathered with a rich, clotted cream–like condiment known as mantequilla hondureña (Honduran "butter"). The real challenge was coming up with a low-fat version of this rich, creamy dairy product.

FILLING

1½ cups cooked or canned red kidney beans, rinsed and drained

3 tablespoons minced onions

1 clove garlic, minced

¼ teaspoon ground cumin

1 cup Chicken Stock (page 360) or fat-free reduced-sodium chicken broth

Salt and ground black pepper

SLAW

2 cups shredded green cabbage

1 carrot, shredded

1 pickled jalapeño chile pepper, minced (wear plastic gloves when handling)

2–3 tablespoons white vinegar

½ teaspoon sugar

Salt

½ teaspoon ground black pepper

8 fat-free flour tortillas (6" diameter)

½ cup Honduran "Butter" (opposite page)

To make the filling: In a medium nonstick skillet over high heat, combine the beans, onions, garlic, cumin, and stock or broth. Bring to a boil, reduce the heat to medium, and simmer for 5 minutes, or until all the stock has been absorbed. Season with salt and pepper. Remove from the heat and let cool for 2 to 3 minutes. Mash the beans with the back of a spoon.

To make the slaw: In a large bowl, combine the cabbage, carrots, chile peppers, 2 tablespoons of the vinegar, the sugar, ½ teaspoon salt, and black pepper. Toss to mix. Taste and season with more vinegar and salt, if desired.

To assemble: Warm the tortillas in a comal (a griddle for cooking tortillas) or small nonstick skillet over high heat for 15 seconds per side, or until soft and pliable. Lay the tortillas on a work surface and spread each with 3 tablespoons of the bean mixture. Roll each tortilla into a tube. Arrange on plates or a platter and serve with the Honduran butter and slaw.

Makes 8 servings

HONDURAN "BUTTER"

Mantequilla
hondureña

Honduras

Nutrition Snapshot	Before	After
Per 2 tablespoons		
Calories	103	29
Total Fat g.	11	0.7
Saturated Fat g.	6.9	0.5
Cholesterol mg.	41	3

Mantequilla *is the Spanish word for butter, yet this dairy product looks and tastes more like Scottish clotted cream or French crème fraîche. It's thick and creamy, with a sweet butter flavor followed by a slightly sour, fermented taste. To reduce the fat in the traditional recipe, I use a combination of low-fat sour cream, feta cheese, and low-fat cream cheese. Honduran butter is great served with dishes like bean tortillas (opposite page).*

1 ounce feta cheese

2 ounces low-fat or nonfat cream cheese, at room temperature

¾ cup low-fat sour cream

Press the feta through a sieve or mash it to a smooth paste with a fork. Transfer to a serving bowl and whisk in the cream cheese and sour cream until smooth and well-blended.

Makes 1 cup

Cooking Tips

◆ Feta cheese is Greek sheep's-milk cheese with a sharp, slightly sour flavor. Look for it in the dairy section of your supermarket.

◆ To save time, you could also puree the feta cheese and cream cheese in a food processor or blender. Transfer to a bowl and whisk in the sour cream.

YUCATÁN OPEN-FACED SANDWICHES

Panuchos del Yucatán   *México*

Nutrition Snapshot	Before	After
Per serving		
Calories	506	163
Total Fat g.	23.5	3.7
Saturated Fat g.	3.6	1.7
Cholesterol mg.	59	32

Panuchos are the Yucatán version of a tostada. The dish originated at the San Sebastián bar in Mérida. The proprietor, Señor Ucho, so the story goes, was about to close for the evening, when he was besieged by a busload of travelers. He was just about out of food, except for a few leftover tortillas, some refried black beans, lettuce, and a bit of turkey. So he stacked them up to make an open-face sandwich, which was promptly christened "pan Ucho," or "Ucho's bread." Today, panuchos are served everywhere in Mérida, and they make a novel alternative to traditional Mexican tostadas.

4	corn tortillas (6" in diameter)		1	tomato, cut into 12 wedges
½	cup warm Refried Beans (page 155) or fat-free canned refried beans		2	pickled jalapeño chile peppers, quartered lengthwise (wear plastic gloves when handling)
½	cup warm shredded cooked turkey or chicken breast		2	tablespoons grated queso fresco or white Cheddar cheese
½	cup shredded lettuce			

Heat a comal (a griddle for cooking tortillas) or large nonstick skillet over medium heat. Add the tortillas and cook until warm, about 1 minute per side. (You can also warm the tortillas on a baking sheet in a 300°F oven or on a grill.)

Spread each tortilla with 2 tablespoons of the refried beans. Divide the turkey or chicken, lettuce, tomatoes, chile peppers, and cheese among the tortillas.

Makes 4 servings

Cooking Tip

✦ To be strictly authentic, you'd warm the tortillas in a dry skillet while patting them with a damp cloth. This causes the tortillas to puff so that you can put the beans inside. But a perfectly delectable panucho can be made by spreading the beans on top of the tortillas, which is quicker and easier.

Variation

Open-Faced Sandwiches with Eggs: Slice one hard-cooked egg white and divide among the sandwiches. Using only the white of the egg adds no fat to the sandwiches (all the fat is in the yolk).

FLAUTAS

Flautas   *México*

Nutrition Snapshot	Before	After
Per flauta		
Calories	798	152
Total Fat g.	45.5	3.3
Saturated Fat g.	8.2	1
Cholesterol mg.	127	26

Flautas are a popular snack both in México and in Tex-Mex restaurants in the United States. The name literally means "flute"—an apt description of these long, slender, deep-fried tortilla tubes filled with chicken or cheese. To make a low fat version with all the rich flavor of the original, I lightly brush the tortillas with melted lard, tie them into tubes, and crisp them in the oven instead of deep-frying them. The low-fat sour cream replaces the traditional cheese. The resulting snack has only 3 grams of fat—instead of the original 45 grams—but with the same snap, crackle, and poppingly crisp texture.

8 corn tortillas (6" diameter)	1 cup warm Refried Beans (page 155)
1 tablespoon melted lard or nonstick spray	1½ cups shredded green cabbage or iceberg lettuce
1 cup shredded cooked chicken breast	1½ cups Ranch-Style Tomato Salsa (page 296) or your favorite salsa
¼ cup Chicken Stock (page 360) or fat-free reduced-sodium chicken broth	½ cup low-fat sour cream

Preheat the oven to 400°F.

Lightly brush the tops of the tortillas with the lard or coat with nonstick spray. Roll each tortilla, coated side out, into a slender tube that measures 1" in diameter. Tie with a piece of kitchen string to hold closed. Place on a large baking sheet. Bake the tortillas for 6 minutes, or until lightly browned and crisp. Transfer to a rack to cool. Remove the string.

Just before serving, heat the chicken and stock or broth in a small skillet over high heat for 5 minutes, or until all the stock has been absorbed. Using a teaspoon, stuff each tortilla tube with the chicken. Arrange the tubes on a platter or plates. Spoon the refried beans on top of the flautas and sprinkle with the cabbage or lettuce. Spoon a little salsa over each flauta and garnish each with dollop of sour cream.

Makes 8

Variation

Vegetarian Flautas: Replace the chicken with an additional 1 cup refried beans. Stuff the additional beans inside the tortilla tubes.

QUESADILLAS

Quesadillas

México

Nutrition Snapshot	Before	After
Per quesadilla (8 wedges)		
Calories	516	175
Total Fat g.	34	6
Saturated Fat g.	16.4	2.6
Cholesterol mg.	75	11

Quesadillas are México's answer to the North American grilled cheese sandwich. In many parts of México, quesadillas are called sincronizadas. To keep the fat content low, I reduce the amount of cheese and add low-fat sour cream for richness. Cumin, cilantro, and chile peppers kick up the flavor. Serve these with your favorite salsa for dipping.

¾	cup low-fat sour cream
2	ounces sharp Cheddar cheese or queso fresco, grated
1	tomato, peeled (see page 383), seeded, and chopped
4	scallions, thinly sliced
2–4	pickled jalapeño chile peppers, thinly sliced (wear plastic gloves when handling)

¼	cup coarsely chopped fresh cilantro
½	teaspoon ground cumin
	Salt and ground black pepper
8	fat-free flour tortillas (8" diameter)

Preheat the oven to 400°F.

In a medium bowl, combine the sour cream, cheese, tomatoes, scallions, chile peppers, cilantro, and cumin. Stir to mix. Season with salt and black pepper.

Arrange 4 of the tortillas on 2 nonstick baking sheets. Divide the sour-cream mixture among the tortillas and spread evenly. Top each with 1 of the remaining tortillas.

Bake, turning once, for 10 minutes, or until lightly browned and heated through. Cut each quesadilla into 8 wedges.

Makes 4 (32 wedges)

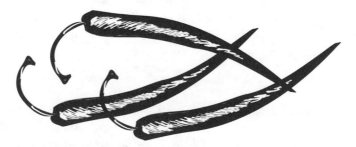

Pronto!

POTATO QUESADILLAS

Quesadillas
de papa

México

Nutrition Snapshot	Before	After
Per quesadilla (8 wedges)		
Calories	286	166
Total Fat g.	17.9	4.3
Saturated Fat g.	2.4	0.6
Cholesterol mg.	0	0

Here's one way to reduce the fat in a quesadilla: Eliminate the cheese entirely. That's what street vendors in Mexico City do when they serve potato quesadillas. Unfortunately, the vendors fry their potatoes in a sea of corn oil, lard, or sausage fat. To make a low-fat version, I simmer the spuds in chicken stock.

1 tablespoon olive oil or lard

2 small white onions, thinly sliced

1 large baking potato, peeled and cut into ¼" cubes

1 cup Chicken Stock (page 360) or fat-free reduced-sodium chicken broth

Salt and ground black pepper

8 fat-free flour tortillas (8" diameter)

1 cup low-fat sour cream

1 tomato, chopped

2 fresh or pickled jalapeño chile peppers, thinly sliced (wear plastic gloves when handling)

Heat the oil or lard in a medium nonstick skillet over medium heat. Add half of the onions and cook, stirring often, for 6 minutes, or until golden brown. Stir in the potatoes and cook for 1 minute. Stir in the stock or broth and simmer for 8 minutes, or until the potatoes are very soft and the liquid has been absorbed. Season with salt and black pepper.

Preheat the oven to 400°F. Coat 2 nonstick baking sheets with nonstick spray.

Arrange 4 of the tortillas on the baking sheets. Divide the potato mixture among the tortillas and spread evenly. Top each with 1 of the remaining tortillas. Coat the tops of the quesadillas with nonstick spray.

Bake, turning once, for 10 minutes, or until lightly browned and heated through. Cut each quesadilla into 8 wedges.

Arrange the sour cream, tomatoes, chile peppers, and the remaining onions in separate serving bowls. Serve with the quesadillas and pass at the table.

Makes 4 (32 wedges)

BEEF FAJITAS

Fajitas de res

Tex-Mex

Nutrition Snapshot	Before	After
Per 2 fajitas		
Calories	761	459
Total Fat g.	31	13.4
Saturated Fat g.	14	5.3
Cholesterol mg.	136	62

This Tex-Mex classic takes its name from the Spanish word faja, which translates as "girdle"—a colorful nickname for skirt steak. Skirt steak is an inexpensive, stringy, and exceptionally flavorful cut of beef. Look for it in specialty butcher shops and Hispanic supermarkets. If unavailable, use beef sirloin. I like to grill the beef and vegetables over mesquite wood chunks or chips. (If using chips, soak the chips in cold water for 1 hour before tossing on the coals). It also helps to use a fine-holed grill tray so that the vegetables don't fall through the bars of the grill grate. If you prefer, cook the meat and vegetables under the broiler instead of on the grill.

3	tablespoons + 1 cup chopped fresh cilantro
2	cloves garlic, minced
½	teaspoon ground cumin
½	teaspoon ground black pepper
½	teaspoon salt
1	pound beef skirt steak, trimmed of all visible fat
½	cup lime juice
1	red bell pepper, cut into ½" strips
1	green bell pepper, cut into ½" strips

1	medium onion, cut into 8 wedges
5	scallions
8	fat-free flour tortillas (8" diameter)
1	large tomato, seeded and finely chopped
1	red onion, finely chopped
1	cup low-fat sour cream
1	cup Charred Tomato Salsa with Chipotle Chiles (page 298) or your favorite salsa (optional)

In a medium glass or stainless steel bowl, combine 3 tablespoons of the cilantro, the garlic, cumin, black pepper, and salt. Rub into the steaks and let stand in the bowl for 5 minutes. Pour the lime juice over the steaks. Cover and marinate in the refrigerator for 1 hour.

Preheat the grill or broiler.

Grill the steak or broil 4" from the heat for 3 to 4 minutes per side for medium-rare to medium, or until cooked to taste. At the same time, grill or broil the bell peppers, onion wedges, and scallions for 6 to 8 minutes, or until nicely charred. Thinly slice the steak and arrange on a platter with the grilled vegetables.

Warm the tortillas on the grill or under the broiler for 10 seconds per side, or until soft and pliable. Place in a basket. Place the tomatoes, red onions, the remaining 1 cup cilantro, sour cream, and salsa in individual serving bowls.

To serve, let diners place some of the sliced beef and grilled vegetables on a tortilla and spoon some of the tomatoes, red onions, cilantro, sour cream, and salsa on top. Roll up the tortilla like an envelope and eat with your hands.

Makes 8

Cooking Tip

✦ Fajitas are often served in hot, sizzling skillets at the table. Preheat a cast-iron skillet in a 400°F oven for 15 minutes. Just before serving, transfer the beef and vegetables to the skillet. They will immediately start sizzling. Warn your guests not to touch the hot skillet.

CHICKEN FAJITAS

Fajitas de pollo   *Tex-Mex*

Nutrition Snapshot	Before	After
Per 2 fajitas		
Calories	953	476
Total Fat g.	48.1	8.2
Saturated Fat g.	14.7	1.8
Cholesterol mg.	170	96

Skirt steak may have been the original meat for fajitas, but many of today's health-conscious cooks prefer boneless, skinless chicken breasts. I like the smoky flavor imparted by grilling, but you could also cook the ingredients in a skillet.

1	pound boneless, skinless chicken breasts, trimmed of all visible fat
3	tablespoons orange juice
3	tablespoons + ½ teaspoon lime juice
3	tablespoons chopped fresh cilantro
1	small onion, quartered
1	jalapeño chile pepper, seeded and chopped (wear plastic gloves when handling)
2	cloves garlic, minced
	Salt and ground black pepper
1	small avocado

½	cup non-fat or low-fat sour cream
1	large tomato, seeded and finely chopped
1½	cups Tomato, Onion, and Jalapeño Salsa (page 296) or your favorite salsa
2	poblano chile peppers
2	red or yellow bell peppers
2	medium onions, cut crosswise into 1" slices
10	scallions
8	fat-free flour tortillas (8" diameter)

Arrange the chicken in a 13" × 9" baking dish. In a food processor or blender, combine the orange juice, 3 tablespoons of the lime juice, the cilantro, onion quarters, jalapeño chile peppers, and garlic. Puree until smooth. Season with salt and black pepper. Pour over the chicken. Cover and marinate in the refrigerator for 30 to 60 minutes. Turn twice while marinating.

Pit the avocado and cut into small cubes. Transfer to a small serving bowl. Sprinkle with the remaining ½ teaspoon lime juice and toss. Place the sour cream, tomatoes, and salsa in separate small serving bowls.

Preheat the grill or broiler.

Grill the poblano chile peppers and bell peppers or broil 4" from the heat, turning occasionally, for 6 to 8 minutes, or until nicely charred. Transfer to a cutting board. Grill or broil the onion slices on a grill tray or broiler pan for 3 to 4 minutes per side, or until nicely charred. Transfer to the cutting board. Grill the scallions for 1 to 2 minutes per side, or until charred and wilted. Transfer to the cutting board. Scrape any burnt skin off the peppers (wear plastic gloves when handling). Remove and discard the cores and seeds. Cut the flesh into long thin strips. Thinly slice the onions. Leave the scallions whole. Arrange the vegetables on a platter and cover to keep warm.

Grill or broil the chicken 4" from the heat for 3 to 4 minutes per side, or until no longer pink in the center. Discard the marinade. Transfer the chicken to the cutting board and thinly slice against the grain.

Warm the tortillas on the grill or under the broiler for 10 seconds per side, or until soft and pliable. Place in a basket.

To serve, let diners place some chicken and vegetables on a tortilla. Spoon the avocados, sour cream, tomatoes, and salsa on top. Roll the tortilla like an envelope and eat with your hands.

Makes 8

Cooking Tip

✦ Fajitas are often served in hot, sizzling skillets at the table. Preheat a cast-iron skillet in a 400°F oven for 15 minutes. Just before serving, transfer the grilled chicken and vegetables to the skillet. They will immediately start sizzling. Warn your guests not to touch the hot skillet.

PORK AND PINEAPPLE SOFT TACOS

Tacos al pastor   *México*

Nutrition Snapshot	Before	After
Per taco		
Calories	257	197
Total Fat g.	8.6	3.4
Saturated Fat g.	2.7	0.9
Cholesterol mg.	42	30

This summery dish was inspired by a popular Mexico City street food called tacos al pastor—literally, "shepherd's tacos." Thinly sliced marinated pork is roasted on a vertical spit in the style of Middle Eastern shwarma (grilled shredded meat). It's customary to place the pineapple on top of the pork so that the sweet juices marinate and flavor the meat. The traditional version is hard to make at home (after all, who has a vertical rotisserie?). For an easier, homestyle version, I mix pineapple juice into the marinade and thread the pork and pineapple pieces onto skewers, then grill them kabob-style. You can use a broiler for this recipe, but the pork tastes best cooked on a grill.

1	small ripe pineapple (see tip on page 218)		¼	teaspoon ground cumin
1	pound lean pork loin, trimmed of all visible fat and cut into ½" cubes		1	medium onion, halved crosswise
			2	tablespoons red-wine vinegar
2	cloves garlic, minced		1	cup finely shredded cabbage
1½	teaspoons pure chili powder or hot paprika		½	cup finely chopped fresh cilantro
½	teaspoon salt		½	cup Charred Tomato Salsa with Chipotle Chiles (page 298) or your favorite salsa
½	teaspoon ground black pepper		8	corn tortillas (6" diameter)

Working over a medium bowl to catch the juices, trim the leaves and rind off the pineapple, core the flesh, and cut into ½" cubes. Place the cut pineapple in a separate bowl.

In a large bowl, mix together the pork, garlic, chili powder or paprika, salt, pepper, and cumin. Let stand for 5 minutes. Thinly slice half the onion. Add to the bowl along with the vinegar and reserved pineapple juice. Stir briefly. Cover and marinate in the refrigerator for 1 hour.

Preheat the grill or broiler.

Thread the pork and reserved pineapple alternately onto 8 bamboo or metal skewers (see tip on page 218). Discard the marinade. Grill the kabobs or broil 4" from the heat for 2 minutes per side (8 minutes total), or until the pork is no longer pink in the center. Transfer to a platter.

While the pork is cooking, finely chop the remaining onion half. Place the onions, cabbage, cilantro, and salsa in individual serving bowls. Warm the tor-

(continued)

tillas on the grill or under the broiler for 10 seconds per side, or until soft and pliable. Place in a basket.

To serve, let diners unskewer the meat and pineapple into a tortilla (use the tortilla as a pot holder) and spoon some of the onions, cabbage, cilantro, and salsa on top. Roll the tortilla like an envelope and eat with your hands.

Makes 8

Cooking Tips

✦ A ripe pineapple should be slightly soft to the touch with a vibrant gold color and little green. Overripe pineapples will have soft or dark spots on the skin.

✦ To prevent the bamboo skewers from burning on the grill, soak them in cold water for 15 minutes before using.

✦ If you're in a hurry, you can replace the fresh pineapple with 2 cups well-drained canned pineapple chunks. Add ¼ cup pineapple juice to the marinade.

Pronto!

HONDURAN ENCHILADAS

Enchiladas
hondureñas

Honduras

Nutrition Snapshot	Before	After
Per enchilada		
Calories	536	169
Total Fat g.	43.6	5.5
Saturated Fat g.	13.4	0.9
Cholesterol mg.	88	26

Enchilada means different things in different parts of Latin America. In the Spanish-speaking Caribbean, it refers to shellfish stew. In México, it describes a dish of rolled stuffed tortillas. In Honduras and in this recipe, it refers to a type of open-faced sandwich made from crispy fried tortillas topped with shredded chicken or enchilada (a sort of hash). To trim the fat in the traditional Honduran recipe, I crisp the tortillas in the oven and use a low-fat enchilada (see Honduran Turkey Hash on the opposite page). The fat savings is 38 grams total fat and 12 grams saturated fat.

8	corn tortillas (6" diameter)	2	tomatoes, finely chopped
2	teaspoons melted lard or canola oil	½	avocado, chopped (optional)
2	cups warm Honduran Turkey Hash (opposite page) or 8 ounces shredded cooked chicken breast	1	hard-cooked egg white, finely chopped
4	cups finely shredded green cabbage	2	tablespoons grated queso fresco or Romano cheese
		1	cup Central American Tomato Salsa (page 300) or your favorite salsa

Preheat the oven to 350°F.

Lightly brush the tortillas on 1 side with the lard or oil. Arrange on a baking sheet, coated side up. Bake for 10 minutes, or until lightly browned. Transfer to a rack to cool. (The tortillas will crisp as they cool.)

Arrange the crisped tortillas on plates or a platter. Top each with ¼ cup of the turkey hash or chicken and ½ cup of the cabbage. Divide the tomatoes, avocados (if using), egg whites, and cheese among the enchiladas. Serve with the salsa.

Makes 8

Pronto!

HONDURAN TURKEY HASH

Picadillo de
pavo al estilo
hondureño

Honduras

Nutrition Snapshot	Before	After
Per ½ cup		
Calories	139	73
Total Fat g.	10	3.6
Saturated Fat g.	2.7	0.8
Cholesterol mg.	24	22

This recipe is great with Honduran Enchiladas (opposite page).

2 teaspoons canola oil	1 medium potato, peeled and cut into ¼" pieces
¼ onion, minced	8 ounces lean ground turkey breast
¼ green bell pepper, minced	Salt and ground black pepper
1 clove garlic, minced	1 cup Chicken Stock (page 360), fat-free reduced-sodium chicken broth, or water
¼ teaspoon cumin	
1 small tomato, halved and grated (discard the skin)	

Heat the oil in a large saucepan over medium heat. Add the onions, bell peppers, garlic, and cumin. Cook for 4 minutes, or until the onions are soft but not brown. Stir in the tomatoes and potatoes. Cook for 1 minute. Stir in the turkey. Season with salt and black pepper. Cook, breaking the turkey up with a spoon, for 3 minutes, or until the turkey is white and crumbly.

Add the stock, broth, or water. Simmer for 12 minutes, or until the potatoes are soft and most of the liquid has been absorbed. The enchilada should be highly seasoned; season with more salt and black pepper, if desired.

Makes 2 cups

CHICKEN ENCHILADAS WITH RED SAUCE

Enchiladas de
pollo con
salsa roja

*México
United States*

Nutrition Snapshot	Before	After
Per serving (3 enchiladas)		
Calories	693	442
Total Fat g.	34.2	9.4
Saturated Fat g.	7	3.1
Cholesterol mg.	159	118

This is one of México's most popular enchiladas. There are probably as many recipes as there are individual cooks. This particular version comes from the Juárez/El Paso border region and is equally beloved by Mexicans and Texans. Calories, fat, and cholesterol were dramatically reduced by using chicken instead of beef and eliminating much of the cheese. I also cook the tortillas in chicken stock instead of lard. The new enchiladas contain 75 percent less fat. To speed up the preparation, you can use 12 ounces cooked chicken in place of the uncooked chicken breasts and begin the recipe by making the sauce. You can also use water in place of the stock.

CHICKEN

1	pound boneless, skinless chicken breasts, trimmed of all visible fat
¼	onion
½	tomato
1	sprig fresh cilantro
4–4¼	cups Chicken Stock (page 360) or fat-free reduced-sodium chicken broth

SAUCE

15	dried New Mexico red chile peppers or chile colorados

½	tomato, seeded and cut into 1" pieces
¼	medium onion, cut into 1" pieces
1	clove garlic
2	sprigs fresh cilantro
½	teaspoon dried oregano
	Salt and ground black pepper
12	corn tortillas (6" diameter)
¼	cup minced white onions
3	tablespoons grated white Cheddar or Monterey Jack cheese

To make the chicken: In a large saucepan over medium heat, combine the chicken, onion, tomato, cilantro, and 4 cups of the stock or broth. Simmer for 10 minutes, or until the chicken is no longer pink in the center. Remove the chicken from the pan and let cool to room temperature. When cool, shred or cut the chicken into thin slivers. Strain the cooking liquid into a measuring cup and reserve for the sauce (you should have about 3½ cups).

To make the sauce: Meanwhile, coat a 13" × 9" baking dish with nonstick spray.

Stem the chile peppers, tear open, and remove and discard the ribs and seeds (wear plastic gloves when handling). In the same saucepan, combine the chile peppers and 3 cups of the reserved chicken cooking liquid. Let soak for 5 minutes. Cook over low heat for 10 minutes, or until softened.

Transfer the chile peppers and 2¾ cups of the cooking liquid to a blender. Add the tomatoes, onion pieces, garlic, cilantro, and oregano. Puree until smooth. The sauce should be thick but pourable; add a little more stock or broth, if necessary. Season with salt and black pepper. Pour one-third of the sauce into the prepared baking dish.

Preheat the oven to 400°F.

Bring the remaining chicken cooking liquid to a boil in the same saucepan over high heat. Add the tortillas, one at a time, and cook for 10 seconds, or until soft and pliable. Remove to a plate and keep warm.

To assemble: Place 2 to 3 tablespoons of the chicken on each tortilla. Top with 1 teaspoon of the minced onions and roll each into a tube. Arrange the enchiladas, seam side down, in the prepared baking dish and spoon the remaining sauce on top. Sprinkle with the cheese.

Bake the enchiladas for 10 to 15 minutes, or until the cheese is melted and the sauce is bubbling hot.

Makes 4 servings

Cooking Tip

✦ This dish can be fully assembled and refrigerated before the final baking time. To store, let cool to room temperature, cover with plastic wrap, and refrigerate for up to 2 days. Let the dish come to room temperature, then bake for 15 to 20 minutes, or until heated through.

TURKEY IN CHILE-CHOCOLATE SAUCE

Mole poblano

México

Nutrition Snapshot	Before	After
Per serving (3 tortillas)		
Calories	621	457
Total Fat g.	28.1	12.4
Saturated Fat g.	9.2	2.8
Cholesterol mg.	149	47

Mole poblano (MOH-leh poh-BLAH-no) is one of the most famous dishes in classical Mexican cooking, invented, so the story goes, by the nuns of the Santa Rosa Convent in the town of Puebla de los Ángeles in central México. The truth is that the Aztecs made complex mole sauces with nuts, chiles, and chocolate long before the arrival of the Spanish. When people first hear about mole poblano, they often envision a thick, sweet chocolate sauce that would be better suited for dessert than for turkey. Actually, the chocolate is used more as a spice than a sweetener. To reduce the fat, I've slashed the amount of lard and nuts in the traditional recipe. You could replace the original turkey with chicken, if desired. This recipe may look complicated, but the ingredients are mostly spices that are added quickly.

TURKEY

1½   cups Chicken Stock (page 360) or fat-free reduced-sodium chicken broth

2   sprigs fresh cilantro

1   pound lean, thinly sliced uncooked turkey breast

SAUCE

6   dried Mexican chile peppers (preferably 2 ancho chile peppers, 2 mulato chile peppers, and 2 pasilla chile peppers)

13   corn tortillas (6" diameter)

2   tablespoons slivered almonds, lightly toasted (see tip)

1   onion, finely chopped

1   tomato, quartered

¼   cup chopped fresh cilantro

3   tablespoons golden raisins

2   cloves garlic, minced

1   tablespoon sesame seeds, lightly toasted (see tip)

½   teaspoon ground coriander

¼   teaspoon anise seeds, crushed

¼   teaspoon ground cinnamon

⅛   teaspoon ground cloves

1   tablespoon lard or olive oil

1½   tablespoons unsweetened cocoa powder

2   teaspoons honey

2–3   teaspoons lime juice

   Salt and ground black pepper

    To make the turkey: In a medium nonstick skillet over medium heat, bring the stock or broth and cilantro to a gentle simmer. Add the turkey and poach for 3 minutes, or until the turkey is white and firm. Transfer the turkey to a cutting board. When cool enough to handle, thinly sliver or shred the meat. Reserve the poaching liquid in the skillet.

    To make the sauce: Tear the chile peppers in half (wear plastic gloves when handling). Remove and discard the stems, ribs, and seeds. Place the chile peppers in a small bowl and cover with warm water. Let soak for 30 minutes, or until pliable. Drain.

Cut 1 of the tortillas into 1" squares. Place in a blender or food processor. Add the chile peppers, almonds, onions, tomatoes, cilantro, raisins, garlic, 1½ teaspoons of the sesame seeds, the coriander, anise seeds, cinnamon, and cloves. Puree until smooth, scraping down the sides of the container several times.

Heat the lard or oil in a large deep skillet over medium heat. Add the chile mixture. Cook and stir for 5 minutes, or until thick and fragrant. Reduce the heat to medium-low. Stir in the cocoa, honey, 2 teaspoons of the lime juice, and 1 cup of the reserved poaching liquid. Season with salt and black pepper. Simmer the sauce, stirring occasionally, for 10 minutes, or until thickened. The sauce should be very flavorful; sprinkle with more lime juice and salt, if desired.

To assemble: Preheat the oven to 400°F. Coat a 13" × 9" baking dish with nonstick spray.

Bring the remaining poaching liquid to a boil over high heat. Add the remaining 12 tortillas, one at a time, and cook for 10 seconds, or until soft and pliable. Remove to a plate and keep warm.

Stir 1 cup of the sauce into the poaching liquid. Add the turkey and cook until warmed through. Place 3 tablespoons of the turkey on each tortilla and roll it into a tube. Spread ¼ cup of the remaining sauce in the prepared baking dish. Arrange the tortillas on top, seam side down, and spoon the remaining sauce over the tortillas. Bake for 10 minutes, or until heated through. Sprinkle with the remaining 1½ teaspoons sesame seeds.

Makes 4 servings

Cooking Tips

✦ To toast the almonds and sesame seeds, place them separately in a dry nonstick skillet and cook, shaking the pan often, for 2 to 3 minutes, or until golden and fragrant.

✦ This dish can be fully assembled and refrigerated before the final baking time. To store, let cool to room temperature, cover with plastic wrap, and refrigerate for up to 2 days. Let the dish come to room temperature, then bake for 10 to 15 minutes, or until heated through.

FISH AND SHELLFISH
Pescados y mariscos

Seafood makes a big splash in Latin American cooking. The region is a fisherman's paradise, boasting plenty of sweet-fleshed warm-water fish, like grouper and snapper.

Shellfish also abound. In fact, some of the best seafood dishes create flavor intrigue by mixing multiple mollusks or crustaceans in a single pot. Peruvian Seafood Stew (page 240) combines mussels, clams, shrimp, octopus, and squid in a chile- and herb-infused broth.

The seafood dishes in this chapter display a versatile range of styles, from the hearty informality of grilled Mexican Swordfish with Roasted Fruit and Chile Sauce (page 227), nicknamed "tablecloth stainer," to a sophisticated Plantain-Crusted Grouper (page 229) inspired by the young Turks of Nuevo Latino cooking.

High in flavor, low in fat, and often loaded with beneficial omega-3 fatty acids, seafood fits perfectly into the mosaic of healthy Latin dining.

FISH RECIPES

SHELLFISH RECIPES

SNAPPER IN VERACRUZ-STYLE SPICY TOMATO SAUCE

Huachinango
a la veracruzana

México

Nutrition Snapshot	Before	After
Per serving		
Calories	410	264
Total Fat g.	18.2	7.3
Saturated Fat g.	2.7	1.1
Cholesterol mg.	83	62

Veracruz, a fishing port on the Caribbean coast of México, is home to some of the country's best seafood. It's also the birthplace of this classic Mexican fish dish. The sauce is a study in counterpoint; the sweetness of the cloves and cinnamon offset the piquancy of the pickled peppers and capers. To make a low-fat dish, I simply reduced the amount of oil used for pan-frying. Don't be intimidated by the number of ingredients; they're mostly seasonings. This recipe comes together in less than 45 minutes.

4   snapper fillets (6 ounces each), skinned, rinsed, and patted dry

3   tablespoons lime juice

     Salt and ground black pepper

1   tablespoon olive oil

1   medium onion, thinly sliced

2   cloves garlic, thinly sliced

1   fresh jalapeño chile pepper, seeded and thinly sliced (wear plastic gloves when handling)

4   large tomatoes, peeled (see page 383), seeded, and coarsely chopped, or 1 can (28 ounces) peeled tomatoes, drained and coarsely chopped

2   tablespoons rinsed and drained capers

1   tablespoon chopped green olives

1   pickled jalapeño chile pepper, finely chopped (wear plastic gloves when handling)

2–3   teaspoons pickled jalapeño chile pepper juice

3   tablespoons chopped fresh cilantro or flat-leaf parsley

½   teaspoon dried marjoram

½   teaspoon dried oregano

2   bay leaves

1   stick cinnamon (3" long)

2   whole cloves

1   strip orange peel

1   cup Fish Stock (page 362) or bottled clam juice (see tip)

Place the fish in a shallow 13" × 9" glass baking dish. Sprinkle both sides with the lime juice and season with salt and black pepper.

Heat the oil in a large nonstick skillet over medium heat. Add the onions. Cook, stirring often, for 4 minutes. Add the garlic and fresh chile peppers. Cook, stirring often, for 4 minutes, or until the onions are soft but not brown. Add the tomatoes, capers, olives, pickled chile peppers, and 2 teaspoons of the pickled chile pepper juice. Cook for 1 minute. Stir in 1½ tablespoons of the cilantro or parsley, the marjoram, oregano, bay leaves, and cinnamon stick. Stick the cloves into the orange peel and add to the skillet. Cook for 5 minutes. Add the stock or clam juice and simmer for 10 minutes, or until thick and flavorful.

Add the fish and spoon the sauce on top. Cook for 4 to 5 minutes per side, or until the fish flakes easily when tested with a fork. Season with more salt, black pepper, and pickled chile pepper juice, if desired. Remove and discard the bay leaves, cinnamon stick, and orange peel with the cloves. Sprinkle the remaining 1½ tablespoons cilantro or parsley over the fish.

Makes 4 servings

Cooking Tips

✦ You can use chicken stock, vegetable stock, tomato juice (reserved from the canned tomatoes), or water in place of the fish stock or clam juice.

✦ Snapper, called *pargo* (PAHD-go) in Cuba and *chillo* (CHEE-yo) in Puerto Rico, is the traditional fish used in this dish. You can also use bluefish, cod, haddock, or shrimp.

SWORDFISH WITH ROASTED FRUIT AND CHILE SAUCE

Manchamanteles de pez espada con salsa de frutas y chiles

México

Nutrition Snapshot	Before	After
Per serving		
Calories	563	425
Total Fat g.	24.4	15.8
Saturated Fat g.	7.6	3.3
Cholesterol mg.	130	86

Here's a recipe with an inventive name—literally, "tablecloth stainer." That's just what the fruit sauce does if you drip it on the table. This sauce has so much flavor that the recipe didn't need a complete overhaul to make it more healthy. I simply reduced the fat by swapping olive oil for the lard. I like to use swordfish, but the sauce goes equally well with chicken breasts, turkey cutlets, and pork loin.

6 swordfish steaks (6 ounces each)
  Salt and ground black pepper
2 tablespoons lime juice
1 clove garlic, minced
5 ancho chile peppers
3 guajillo chile peppers
3 cups warm Chicken Stock (page 360) or fat-free reduced-sodium chicken broth
2 tomatoes
2 jalapeño chile peppers

3 tablespoons slivered almonds
3 tablespoons sesame seeds
1 tablespoon olive oil
1 stick cinnamon (3" long)
1 ripe plantain, peeled (see page 386) and chopped
1 cup chopped fresh or drained canned pineapple
½ cup chopped jícama (see page 59)
3 tablespoons finely chopped fresh cilantro

Season the swordfish with salt and black pepper. Place in a 13" × 9" glass baking dish. Sprinkle both sides with the lime juice and garlic. Cover and marinate in the refrigerator for 30 to 60 minutes.

Meanwhile, tear open the ancho and guajillo chile peppers (wear plastic gloves when handling). Remove and discard the stems and seeds. Roast the chile peppers under the broiler or in a large, dry nonstick skillet over high heat for 10 seconds; do not let burn. Place in a medium bowl. Add the stock or broth. Place a small pot lid or dish on the chile peppers to keep them submerged. Let soak for 15 minutes, or until softened. Transfer the chile peppers and stock to a food processor or blender.

Roast the tomatoes and jalapeño chile peppers under the broiler or in the skillet over high heat for 5 minutes, or until the skins blister. Scrape off the burnt skin and seed the tomatoes and chile peppers (wear plastic gloves when handling). Transfer to the food processor or blender.

In a large, dry nonstick skillet over medium heat, roast the almonds and sesame seeds for 3 to 4 minutes, or until lightly browned. (Do not let the nuts and seeds brown too much, or they will become bitter. Transfer to the food processor or blender. Puree until smooth, working in batches if necessary.

Heat the oil in the same skillet over medium heat. Add the cinnamon stick, plantains, pineapple, and the pureed sauce. Simmer, stirring often, for 20 minutes, or until thick and flavorful and the plantains are cooked. Season with more salt and black pepper, if desired. Remove and discard the cinnamon stick.

Preheat the grill or broiler. Grill or broil the swordfish 4" from the heat for 4 minutes per side, or until firm and white and the fish flakes easily when tested with a fork. Transfer the fish to a platter and spoon the sauce over the top. Top with the jícama and cilantro.

Makes 6 servings

Cooking Tip

✦ If you like your food fiery, leave the seeds in the jalapeño chiles after roasting.

PLANTAIN-CRUSTED GROUPER

Mero empanizado
con mariquitas
molidas

United States

Nutrition Snapshot	Before	After
Per serving		
Calories	673	290
Total Fat g.	24.9	2.9
Saturated Fat g.	3.1	0.6
Cholesterol mg.	249	62

Not long ago, no one had ever heard of Nuevo Latino cooking. Today, some of the hottest chefs in North America are first-generation Hispanics who have revolutionized the cuisines of their ancestors. Nuevo Latino cuisine blends traditional Hispanic ingredients and cooking techniques with the unexpected flavor combinations and dramatic plate presentations of contemporary American cooking. No one does it better than Douglas Rodríguez, owner-chef of the sizzling Patria restaurant in New York City. When Doug was working at another hot Nuevo Latino restaurant, he developed a dish that has become a contemporary Hispanic classic: grouper crusted with crunchy plantain chips.

4	grouper fillets (6 ounces each)	36	Plantain Chips (page 71)
1	clove garlic, minced	¾	cup unbleached or all-purpose flour
½	teaspoon ground cumin	2	egg whites, lightly beaten
¼	cup lime juice	1	lime, cut into 4 wedges
	Salt and ground black pepper		

Place the fish in a 13" × 9" glass baking dish and sprinkle both sides with the garlic, cumin, and lime juice. Season with salt and pepper. Cover and marinate in the refrigerator for 30 to 60 minutes.

Meanwhile, preheat the oven to 400°F. Coat a nonstick baking sheet with nonstick spray.

Coarsely grind the plantain chips in a food processor or crush in a plastic bag with a rolling pin. Transfer to a shallow bowl. Pour the flour into a second shallow bowl and the egg whites into a third.

Dip each fish fillet in the flour and shake off the excess. Dip in the egg whites, then in the plantain chips. Transfer the fish to the prepared baking sheet and coat the tops with nonstick spray.

Bake for 20 minutes, or until the crust is golden brown and the fish flakes easily when tested with a fork. Serve with the lime wedges for squeezing over the fish.

Makes 4 servings

Cooking Tip

✦ For a quick alternative, use store-bought plantain chips. Look for a low-fat brand.

YUCATÁN-BAKED POMPANO

Tikenxik

México

Nutrition Snapshot	Before	After
Per serving		
Calories	505	323
Total Fat g.	32.3	16.8
Saturated Fat g.	9.4	6.1
Cholesterol mg.	115	86

Tikenxik *(tee-ken-SHEEK) is an ancient Mayan dish that predates the arrival of the Spanish. Annatto seeds and sour orange juice give it a stunning color and flavor. Other good fish choices include snapper, porgy, black bass, and sea trout.*

MARINADE
- ½ teaspoon annatto seeds
- ½ cup sour orange juice (see page 63) or lime juice
- ¼ onion, minced
- 2 cloves garlic, minced
- ½ teaspoon dried oregano
- 1 teaspoon salt
- ½ teaspoon ground black pepper
- ¼ teaspoon ground cinnamon
- ¼ cup water

FISH
- 1–1¼ pounds whole pompano fish or 4 fish fillets (6 ounces each), skinned
- 1 small onion, thinly sliced
- 1 tomato, seeded and chopped
- 4 sprigs epazote (see page 53)
- 4 lime wedges

To make the marinade: In a small saucepan over medium heat, combine the annatto seeds and orange juice or lime juice. Simmer for 2 minutes. Remove from the heat and let cool for 10 minutes. Transfer to a blender or food processor and puree. Add the onions, garlic, oregano, salt, pepper, cinnamon, and water. Process just enough to mix; do not puree.

To make the fish: If using a whole fish, make 4 diagonal slashes in the side of each fish to the bone. Place the whole fish or fish fillets in a 13" × 9" glass baking dish. Pour the marinade on top. Cover and marinate in the refrigerator for 30 to 60 minutes, turning once. Drain and transfer the fish to a plate.

Preheat the oven to 400°F.

Coat the baking dish with nonstick spray. Arrange half of the onions and half of the tomatoes in the prepared dish. Place the fish on top and sprinkle with the epazote and the remaining onions and tomatoes. Coat the top of the fish with nonstick spray.

Bake for 20 to 25 minutes, or until no longer translucent and the fish flakes easily when tested with a fork. Serve with the lime wedges for squeezing over the fish.

Makes 4 servings

SALT COD A LA VIZCAÍNA

Bacalao
a la vizcaína

*Various
countries*

Nutrition Snapshot	Before	After
Per serving		
Calories	488	381
Total Fat g.	14.4	2.3
Saturated Fat g.	2	0.4
Cholesterol mg.	114	114

Vizcaína *is a city in Spain's Basque region. This dish serves as a reminder of the profound influence that Spain has had on Latin American cooking. Variations of this dish turn up throughout the Americas. The Mexican version contains pickled yellow chiles. The Cuban and Puerto Rican renditions feature oregano, cumin, and cilantro. To make the recipe healthier, I use a minimum of oil for sautéing and increase the number of soakings and boilings to remove the excess salt from the cod.*

1	pound skinless salt cod		2	tablespoons rinsed and drained capers
1	can (28 ounces) plum tomatoes (with juice)		1	tablespoon coarsely chopped pimiento-stuffed green olives
1½	tablespoons olive oil		1	bay leaf
1	medium onion, finely chopped			Ground black pepper
½	green bell pepper, finely chopped		½	cup water
3	cloves garlic, minced		1	pound baking potatoes, peeled and cut into ¼" slices
2	tablespoons chopped fresh cilantro		2	medium onions, peeled and cut crosswise into ¼" slices
½	teaspoon dried oregano			
3	tablespoons raisins			

Place the cod in a medium bowl. Cover with cold water. Let soak in the refrigerator for 24 hours. Change the water 3 times and rinse off the cod each time.

Place the cod in a large saucepan and cover with cold water. Bring to a boil over high heat. Drain and rinse with cold water. Return the cod to the pan and cover with cold water. Bring to a boil again, drain, and rinse. Return the cod to the pan and cover again with cold water. Bring to a boil, reduce the heat to medium, and simmer for 10 minutes, or until tender. Drain and rinse with cold water. Pull the fish into large flakes with your fingers, removing and discarding any bones.

Coarsely puree the tomatoes (with juice) in a food processor or blender.

Heat the oil in a large nonstick saucepan over medium heat. Add the chopped onions, bell peppers, garlic, cilantro, and oregano. Cook for 4 minutes, or until the onions are soft but not brown. Add the pureed tomatoes, raisins, capers, olives, bay leaf, ¼ teaspoon black pepper, and water. Simmer for 10 minutes, or until thick and richly flavored. Taste and add more black pepper, if desired. Remove and discard the bay leaf.

(continued)

Preheat the oven to 400°F. Coat a 13" × 9" baking dish with nonstick spray.

Spoon one-quarter of the sauce over the bottom of the prepared baking dish. Arrange the cod over the sauce. Arrange the potatoes over the cod. Arrange the sliced onions over the potatoes. Spoon the remaining sauce on top. Bake for 20 minutes, or until the sauce is bubbling and the potatoes and onions are tender.

Makes 6 servings

Regional Variation

Mexican Salt Cod a la Vizcaína: Add 3 to 4 ounces sliced pickled yellow chile peppers along with the potatoes and onions. Garnish with ¼ cup chopped pimientos and 8 slices toasted bread.

CHILEAN FISH STEW

Caldillo

Chile

Nutrition Snapshot	Before	After
Per serving		
Calories	511	376
Total Fat g.	15.3	4.8
Saturated Fat g.	2	0.6
Cholesterol mg.	84	63

Chileans know seafood. And they know chowder. This chowder traditionally features conger eel (look for it frozen in some Hispanic markets). You can also use cod or halibut.

1½	pounds conger eel, cod, or halibut
3	cloves garlic, minced
	Salt and ground black pepper
3	tablespoons lemon juice
1	tablespoon extra-virgin olive oil
1	onion, finely chopped
1	green bell pepper, finely chopped
1	cup dry white wine or nonalcoholic white wine

1	pound potatoes, peeled and cut into ½" × 1" pieces
2	large carrots, cut into ½" slices
1	bay leaf
4	cups Fish Stock (page 362) or 3 cups bottled clam juice + 1 cup water
½	cup finely chopped fresh flat-leaf parsley or cilantro

Place the seafood in a 13" × 9" glass baking dish. Sprinkle with one-third of the garlic. Season with salt and black pepper. Pour the lemon juice over the top. Cover and marinate in the refrigerator for 1 hour.

Heat the oil in a large saucepan over medium heat. Add the onions, bell peppers, and the remaining garlic. Cook, stirring often, for 4 minutes, or until the onions are soft but not brown. Increase the heat to high. Add the wine. Bring to a boil. Add the potatoes, carrots, bay leaf, and stock or clam juice and water. Return to a boil. Reduce the heat to medium and simmer for 5 minutes, or until the vegetables begin to soften. Add the seafood. Simmer for 10 minutes, or until the seafood flakes easily when tested with a fork and the vegetables are tender.

Stir in the parsley or cilantro and simmer for 1 minute. The mixture should be highly seasoned; sprinkle with more salt and black pepper, if desired. Remove and discard the bay leaf before serving.

Makes 4 servings

Pronto!

MEXICAN STEAMED MUSSELS

Caldo
de mejillones   *México*

Nutrition Snapshot	Before	After
Per serving		
Calories	110	110
Total Fat g.	1.4	1.4
Saturated Fat g.	0	0
Cholesterol mg.	32	32

This is the most simple and tasty way I know to cook mussels. It's extremely low in fat and yields a highly aromatic broth. It's best served with warm tortillas or bread for dunking.

1 cup dry white wine or nonalcoholic white wine

1½ cups water

1 onion, finely chopped

1 tomato, seeded and finely chopped

1 poblano chile pepper, peeled (see page 382), seeded, and cut into thin strips (wear plastic gloves when handling)

1–2 serrano or jalapeño chile peppers, thinly sliced (wear plastic gloves when handling)

2 cloves garlic, minced

1 bunch fresh cilantro, stemmed and coarsely chopped

½ teaspoon salt

½ teaspoon ground black pepper

4 pounds very small mussels, scrubbed and debearded (see page 387)

Bring the wine to a boil in a large pot over high heat. Add the water, onions, tomatoes, chile peppers, garlic, cilantro, salt, and black pepper. Return to a boil. Add the mussels and cover the pan. Cook, stirring once or twice, for 8 minutes, or until all the shells open wide. (Discard any mussels that have cracked shells or remain closed.)

Transfer the mussels and broth to serving bowls. Provide additional bowls for the empty shells.

Makes 4 servings

Pronto!

SHRIMP STEW

Enchilado
de camarones

Various countries

Nutrition Snapshot	Before	After
Per serving		
Calories	245	211
Total Fat g.	7.3	3.9
Saturated Fat g.	1	0.5
Cholesterol mg.	172	172

In the Spanish-speaking Caribbean, enchilado refers not to a dish made with tortillas, but to a soulful seafood stew. Depending on the cook and the region, this dish might be simmered in wine, beer, or a mixture of the two. A lobster, crab, scallop, fish, or even chicken or tofu enchilado can be prepared the same way. Serve with Basic White Rice (page 159) to soak up the rich tomato broth.

SHRIMP

1	pound shrimp, peeled and deveined
2	tablespoons lime juice
¼	teaspoon ground cumin
	Salt and ground black pepper

SAUCE

1	tablespoon olive oil
1	onion, finely chopped
1	small red bell pepper, finely chopped
3	cloves garlic, minced
½–¾	teaspoon ground cumin
½	cup tomato paste
½–¾	cup dry white wine or nonalcoholic white wine
½–¾	cup beer or nonalcoholic beer
1	bay leaf
3	tablespoons finely chopped fresh cilantro or flat-leaf parsley
	Salt and ground black pepper

To make the shrimp: In a medium glass or stainless steel bowl, combine the shrimp, lime juice, cumin, salt, and pepper. Stir to mix. Cover and marinate in the refrigerator for 30 to 60 minutes.

To make the sauce: While the shrimp is marinating, heat the oil in a large non-stick skillet over medium heat. Add the onions, bell peppers, garlic, and ½ teaspoon of the cumin. Cook for 4 minutes, or until lightly browned. Increase the heat to high and stir in the tomato paste. Cook for 1 minute. Stir in the wine, ½ cup of the beer, and the bay leaf. Bring to a boil. Stir in the shrimp and reduce the heat to medium-low. Simmer for 3 to 5 minutes, or until the shrimp is firm and pink and the sauce is richly flavored. If the sauce is too dry, add a little more wine or beer. Remove and discard the bay leaf. Season with salt, black pepper, and more cumin, if desired. Sprinkle the cilantro or parsley on top.

Makes 4 servings

Dominican Crab Stew: Replace the shrimp with 1 pound lump crabmeat. Add 1 to 4 seeded and minced jalapeño chile peppers along with the bell peppers for the sauce. Replace the beer with ½ cup dry sherry or nonalcoholic white wine.

SEAFOOD STEW

Mariscada   *Venezuela*

Nutrition Snapshot	Before	After
Per serving		
Calories	401	326
Total Fat g.	14.8	6.4
Saturated Fat g.	2.1	0.9
Cholesterol mg.	267	182

Mariscada *is a seafood stew of Spanish origin that's popular throughout Latin America. As the recipe crossed the Atlantic Ocean, it picked up New World flavorings, such as cilantro and jalapeño chiles. The seafood varies. Feel free to use the freshest seafood available in your area.*

12	ounces shrimp, peeled and deveined
12	ounces sea scallops, halved
12	ounces cleaned squid (see page 389), cut into ¼" rings (see tip)
3	cloves garlic, minced
3	tablespoons lime juice
	Salt and ground black pepper
1½	tablespoons olive oil
1	medium onion, finely chopped
1	red bell pepper, finely chopped
2	large tomatoes, peeled (see page 383) and chopped
3	tablespoons chopped fresh flat-leaf parsley
1	tablespoon sweet paprika
2	bay leaves
1	tablespoon tomato paste
½	cup dry white wine or nonalcoholic white wine
6	cups Fish Stock (page 362) or 4 cups bottled clam juice + 2 cups water
1	jalapeño chile pepper, thinly sliced (wear plastic gloves when handling); optional
18	littleneck clams, scrubbed (see page 387)
18	mussels, scrubbed and debearded
½	cup chopped fresh cilantro

In a large glass or stainless steel bowl, combine the shrimp, scallops, squid, one-third of the garlic, and the lime juice. Season with salt and black pepper. Toss to mix. Cover and marinate in the refrigerator for 30 to 60 minutes.

Meanwhile, heat the oil in a large nonstick skillet over medium heat. Add the onions, bell peppers, and the remaining garlic. Cook for 4 minutes, or until the onions are soft but not brown. Increase the heat to high. Add the tomatoes, parsley, paprika, and bay leaves. Cook for 1 minute. Add the tomato paste and

(continued)

cook for 1 minute more. Add the wine and bring to a boil. Add the fish stock or clam juice and water and chile peppers (if using). Boil for 3 minutes.

Add the clams and mussels and cook for 8 minutes. Add the shrimp, scallops, and marinade and cook for 2 minutes. Add the squid and cook for 2 minutes more, or until the clam and mussel shells open wide and the shrimp, scallops, and squid are opaque. (Discard any clams or mussels that remain closed or have cracked shells.) Stir in the cilantro. The dish should be highly seasoned; season with more salt and black pepper, if desired.

Makes 6 servings

Cooking Tips

✦ You can use 12 ounces additional shrimp or scallops in place of the squid. Or try cooked octopus cut into ½" chunks. See page 388 for octopus cooking instructions.

✦ If you want to add more heat, use up to 3 jalapeño chiles.

✦ For a meaty variation of this recipe, see the Sancocho recipe on page 290.

LATIN SUPER FOOD: SHRIMP

Latin America is flanked on all sides by the briny waters of the sea—four bodies of water to be exact—the Pacific Ocean, Atlantic Ocean, Caribbean Sea, and the Gulf of México. No wonder Latino cooking is teeming with so many wonderful seafood dishes. One of the region's most popular delights from the sea is shrimp.

Despite shrimp's reputation for containing boatloads of cholesterol, it turns out that this shellfish is actually good for you. One of the things that makes shrimp so healthful is its fat. This shellfish contains a type of fat called omega-3 fatty acids, which help protect you from heart disease. Researchers from the University of Washington in Seattle found that people who ate 5.5 grams of omega-3's a month (that's only about 3 ounces of seafood a week) had half the risk of heart attacks than those who ate no seafood. Plus, shrimp contains only trace amounts of artery-clogging saturated fat.

A 3-ounce serving of shrimp does contain about 165 milligrams of cholesterol. But research from Rockefeller University in New York City and Harvard School of Public Health shows that the cholesterol in shrimp does not significantly raise your blood cholesterol. Saturated fat is the bigger culprit in raising blood cholesterol. Because shrimp is so low in saturated fat, moderate shrimp consumption does not worsen your total cholesterol profile. The study concludes that shrimp can be included as part of a heart-healthy diet.

Shrimp are also a smorgasbord of essential minerals. Three ounces of this fan-tailed fare boasts almost 15 percent of the Daily Value (DV) for blood-building iron as well as about 9 percent of the DV for immune system–boosting zinc and 8 percent of the DV for copper, a mineral that your body uses to form strong, flexible connective tissue. Shrimp are surprisingly high in protein, too; a typical 3-ounce serving contains a whopping 18 grams of protein, which is 35 percent of the DV.

The next time you want to toss some steak or chicken on the grill, think shrimp instead. Or try shrimp in some of Latin America's best-tasting dishes like Mexican Shrimp Cocktail (page 83), Shrimp Soup (page 107), Shrimp Stew (page 234), or Rice Pilaf with Shrimp (page 160).

BRAZILIAN SEAFOOD STEW

Moqueca de peixe

Brazil

Nutrition Snapshot	Before	After
Per serving		
Calories	678	345
Total Fat g.	35.1	9.7
Saturated Fat g.	20.1	1.1
Cholesterol mg.	329	194

Moqueca de peixe (moo-KAY-ka dje PESH-ee) is a tropical fish stew from the province of Bahia in northern Brazil. Bahia is the New Orleans of South America, where Brazil's African heritage is more pronounced and delicious than anywhere else in the country. To lower the fat in the traditional recipe, I use light coconut milk instead of the full-fat variety. Light coconut milk is available at gourmet shops and in the international aisle of many supermarkets.

2	pounds fish fillets, cut into 2" pieces (see tip)
1	pound large shrimp, peeled and deveined
2	tablespoons lime juice
8	cloves garlic, minced
	Salt and ground black pepper
1	tablespoon olive oil
2	cups finely chopped onions
5	scallions, trimmed and finely chopped
1	green bell pepper, finely chopped
1	red bell pepper, finely chopped
3	tomatoes, peeled (see page 383), seeded, and chopped
3	cups Fish Stock (page 362) or bottled clam juice
½	cup chopped fresh cilantro
1	cup light coconut milk
	Ground red pepper

In a shallow 13" × 9" glass baking dish, combine the fish and shrimp. Add the lime juice and one-quarter of the garlic. Season with the salt and black pepper. Toss to coat. Cover and marinate in the refrigerator for 30 to 60 minutes.

Meanwhile, heat the oil in a large, nonstick skillet over medium heat. Add the onions, scallions, bell peppers, and the remaining garlic. Cook, stirring often, for 6 to 8 minutes, or until the vegetables are soft and translucent but not brown.

Increase the heat to high. Add the tomatoes. Cook for 2 minutes, or until most of the juice from the tomatoes has evaporated. Stir in the stock or clam juice and ¼ cup of the cilantro. Cook for 10 to 15 minutes, or until slightly reduced and richly flavored. Remove from the heat.

Transfer the vegetable mixture to a blender. Puree until smooth. Return to the skillet. Add the coconut milk and reduce the heat to medium. Simmer for 3 minutes. Add the fish and simmer for 3 minutes. Add the shrimp and simmer for 2 minutes more, or until the fish and shrimp are opaque. Sprinkle with a pinch of

¡Fiesta!
Brazilian Carnaval

Traditionally, *carnaval* is a time for feasting and merrymaking during the season just before Lent. The word *carnaval* literally means "without meat." It comes from the Latin words *carne* (meat) and *levare* (to remove). Here's a *carnaval* menu that features one of Brazil's most famous fish stews, *Moqueca de peixe.*

Hearts of Palm Salad (*Ensalada de palmitos*, **page 116**)

Brazilian Seafood Stew (*Moqueca de peixe*, **page 238**)

Basic White Rice (*Arroz blanco*, **page 159**)

Minas-Style Collard Greens (*Couve mineira*, **page 145**)

Apricot Meringue Flan (*Pudim do claras*, **page 319**)

ground red pepper. The mixture should be highly seasoned; season with more ground red pepper, salt, and black pepper, if desired. Sprinkle the remaining ¼ cup cilantro on top.

Makes 6 servings

Cooking Tip

◆ When choosing fish for this stew, let freshness—not specific type—be your guide. Some good choices include snapper, bluefish, mahi mahi, and even salmon.

PERUVIAN SEAFOOD STEW

Caucau
   de mariscos

Perú

Nutrition Snapshot	Before	After
Per serving		
Calories	425	336
Total Fat g.	16.1	6
Saturated Fat g.	2.2	0.9
Cholesterol mg.	163	163

Caucau (COW-cow) refers to a family of bold Peruvian stews. The classic caucau contains tripe. Seafood caucaus, like the one below, are equally popular. This recipe comes from a Peruvian restaurant in Miami called El Chalón. It's so loaded with spices and aromatic vegetables that it doesn't need a lot of fat to taste great. Vary the seafood according to what looks freshest and smells best at your market. You'll need about 1½ pounds in all. Serve the stew with hot cooked white rice.

1	tablespoon olive oil
1	medium onion, thinly sliced
1	red bell pepper, thinly sliced
3	cloves garlic, minced
1	tablespoon minced fresh ginger
½	teaspoon powdered ají amarillo or ají paste or ½ teaspoon hot paprika mixed with ¼ teaspoon ground turmeric
½	teaspoon dried oregano
¼	teaspoon ground cumin
½	cup dry white wine or nonalcoholic white wine
1½	cups Fish Stock (page 362) or 1 cup bottled clam juice + ½ cup water
2	medium potatoes, peeled and cut into ½" pieces
12	mussels, scrubbed and debearded
12	littleneck clams, scrubbed (see page 387)
6	ounces shrimp, peeled and deveined
6	ounces cooked octopus or sea scallops (see tip)
6	ounces cleaned squid (see page 389), cut into ¼" rings
1	teaspoon lime juice
¼	teaspoon garlic powder
¼	cup cooked or frozen and thawed peas
¼	cup chopped fresh cilantro or mint
	Salt and ground black pepper

Heat the oil in a large nonstick skillet over medium heat. Add the onions, bell peppers, garlic, and ginger. Cook for 4 minutes, or until the onions are soft but not brown. Increase the heat to high and add the ají or paprika and turmeric, the oregano, and cumin. Cook for 1 minute. Add the wine and bring to a boil. Add the stock or clam juice and water and return to a boil. Add the potatoes and cook for 5 minutes, or until the potatoes are soft and the sauce is thick and flavorful.

Add the mussels and clams and cook for 5 minutes. Add the shrimp, octopus or scallops, and squid. Cook for 3 to 5 minutes, or until the mussel and clam shells open wide, the shrimp are firm and pink, and the octopus or scallops and squid are firm and white. (Discard any mussels or clams that remain closed or have cracked shells.) Stir in the lime juice, garlic powder, peas, and cilantro or mint. Cook for 1 minute. Season with the salt and black pepper.

Makes 4 servings

Cooking Tips

✦ If using octopus, see the cooking instructions on page 388.

✦ To be strictly traditional, use ají amarillo, Perú's distinctive yellow chile pepper, which comes dried, powdered, and in paste form. It's quite hot and highly aromatic. Look for ají amarillo at Latin markets or use the resources on page 66. If unavailable, the color and flavor can be approximated by using a combination of hot paprika and turmeric.

CHICKEN AND TURKEY
Pollo y pavo

When the conquistadores landed in México, they encountered a large bird with a strange wattle under its beak: the turkey. Within a century, the turkey and another New World bird, the guinea fowl, had sailed to Europe and become incorporated into Old World cuisine.

The Europeans completed the culinary exchange by exporting the chicken to the Americas. Today, all kinds of poultry are prized throughout Latin America and enjoyed in dishes as varied as Mexican enchiladas, Panamanian stews, and Uruguayan pamplonas (grilled stuffed chicken breast rolls).

Poultry's neutral flavor makes it an ideal canvas for the colorful flavor combinations of Latin cooks. Mexican *moles* (complex chile and fruit sauces) and Dominican *guisados* (stews flavored with onions, tomatoes, bell peppers, capers, and olives) illustrate the diversity.

Many Latin poultry recipes don't need a complete overhaul to make them healthier. Choosing skinless chicken and turkey breast can dramatically slash the fat in any of your favorite poultry recipes. By using boneless cuts, the dishes also become easier to serve.

CHICKEN RECIPES

TURKEY RECIPES

CHICKEN WITH RICE

Arroz
  con pollo

*Various
countries*

Nutrition Snapshot	Before	After
Per serving		
Calories	553	486
Total Fat g.	21	8.3
Saturated Fat g.	4.8	1.7
Cholesterol mg.	89	86

Arroz con pollo (ah-rose-con-POY-yo) is paella for people who don't like seafood. Like paella, it's made with short-grain Valencia-style rice. Unlike the Spanish dish, however, it contains only chicken and it's colored and flavored with annatto seeds (achiote) instead of saffron. To slim down the traditional version, I replaced the lard with olive oil and used boneless, skinless chicken breasts instead of whole chickens. If you prefer to use dark meat or a whole chicken, keep fat to a minimum by removing the skin before eating.

2½ pounds boneless, skinless chicken breasts, trimmed of all visible fat and cut into 3" squares

1 teaspoon dried oregano

1 teaspoon ground cumin

Ground black pepper

2 tablespoons lime juice

2 tablespoons olive oil

2 teaspoons annatto seeds

1 medium onion, chopped

1 red bell pepper, chopped

3 cloves garlic, minced

3 tablespoons finely chopped fresh cilantro

1 small tomato, seeded and chopped

1 cup dry white wine or nonalcoholic white wine

½ cup beer or nonalcoholic beer

1 tablespoon tomato paste

3½-4 cups Chicken Stock (page 360), fat-free reduced-sodium chicken broth, or water

Salt

1 pound Valencia-style rice or Arborio rice, rinsed until the water runs clear

¼ cup pimiento-stuffed green olives

1 can (8½ ounces) peas, drained

1 can (6½ ounces) red pimientos, chopped

In a large glass or stainless steel bowl, combine the chicken, oregano, cumin, ½ teaspoon black pepper, and lime juice. Cover and marinate in the refrigerator for 20 minutes.

Heat the oil in a large, deep, ovenproof skillet over medium heat. Add the annatto seeds. Cook for 3 minutes, or until the oil turns red and the seeds begin to crackle. Remove the seeds with a metal spatula or slotted spoon and discard. Add the onions, bell peppers, garlic, and cilantro. Cook for 3 minutes, or until the onions are softened. Add the tomatoes and cook for 1 minute more. Add the chicken and cook for 3 minutes, or until it begins to turn white. Add the wine and beer. Bring to a boil over high heat. Add the tomato paste and 3½ cups of the stock, broth, or water. Return to a boil. Season with salt and additional black pepper, if desired.

Stir in the rice and return to a boil. Reduce the heat to medium-low. Cover and simmer for 20 to 25 minutes, or until the rice is tender. If the rice starts to dry out, add more stock or broth. If the mixture looks too soupy, remove the cover during the last 5 minutes of cooking time.

Just before the rice is finished, stir in most of the olives, peas, and pimientos. Sprinkle the remainder on top just before serving.

Makes 8 servings

Regional Variations

Panamanian Chicken with Rice: Add ½ teaspoon curry powder along with the other spices to marinate the chicken.

Venezuelan Chicken with Rice: Omit the annatto seeds. Soak ½ teaspoon crushed saffron threads in 1 tablespoon hot water. Add the saffron and soaking liquid along with the stock.

Pronto!

STUFFED CHICKEN BREASTS

Pamplona
de pollo

*Uruguay
Argentina*

Nutrition Snapshot	Before	After
Per serving		
Calories	542	372
Total Fat g.	18.2	7.2
Saturated Fat g.	5.8	2.1
Cholesterol mg.	293	151

first tasted this stuffed chicken at a steakhouse in Uruguay. A similar dish is found across the Río de la Plata in Argentina. When the chicken rolls are sliced, they reveal a beautiful spiral of color. Top with Chimichurri (page 310), if desired. This dish can also serve 8 as an appetizer.

2	whole boneless, skinless chicken breasts (12 ounces each), trimmed of all visible fat	2	ounces Canadian bacon (2 slices), cut into ¼"-thick strips
1	teaspoon dried oregano	2	hard-cooked egg whites, quartered lengthwise
	Salt and ground black pepper	8	pitted prunes
1	red bell pepper, cut into ¼"-thick strips	24	golden raisins

Preheat the oven to 400°F.

Using a meat pounder or rolling pin, pound the chicken breasts between sheets of plastic wrap to a ¼" thickness. Sprinkle both sides of the chicken with the oregano and season with salt and pepper. Lay each breast flat on a work surface, smooth side down. Arrange the bell peppers, bacon, egg whites, prunes, and raisins on top of each breast, running the length of the breast. Starting at one side, roll each breast into a tight cylinder and secure with kitchen string.

Place the rolls on a nonstick baking sheet and coat with nonstick spray. Bake for 20 minutes, or until the chicken is no longer pink and a meat thermometer registers 165°F when inserted in a roll.

Transfer the rolls to a cutting board and remove the string. Cut each roll crosswise into ½"-thick slices.

Makes 4 servings

ORANGE-MARINATED GRILLED CHICKEN WITH SMOKY TOMATO SALSA

Pollo adobado
    a la parrilla
    con salsa de chipotle   *México*

Nutrition Snapshot	Before	After
Per serving		
Calories	624	377
Total Fat g.	31.4	10.3
Saturated Fat g.	7.9	2
Cholesterol mg.	161	96

Citrus, chiles, and smoked tomatoes are the key flavors in these grilled chicken breasts.

CHICKEN AND MARINADE

4	boneless, skinless chicken breast halves (4 ounces each)
	Salt and ground black pepper
½	cup orange juice
2	tablespoons lime juice
1	clove garlic, minced
1	tablespoon extra-virgin olive oil (optional)

SALSA

2	large tomatoes
1	small onion, quartered
2	cloves garlic
1–2	canned chipotle chile peppers, minced (wear plastic gloves when handling); see tip
¼	cup coarsely chopped fresh cilantro
2–3	tablespoons lime juice
	Salt and ground black pepper
4	fat-free flour tortillas (8" diameter)
4	sprigs fresh cilantro

To make the chicken and marinade: Season each chicken breast with salt and pepper. Arrange in a 13" × 9" baking dish.

In a small bowl, combine the orange juice, lime juice, garlic, and oil (if using). Whisk to mix. Pour over the chicken. Cover and marinate in the refrigerator for 60 minutes.

To make the salsa: While the chicken is marinating, preheat the grill or a comal (a griddle for cooking tortillas) over high heat.

Place the tomatoes on the grill or in the comal and roast, turning occasionally, for 6 to 8 minutes, or until the skins are charred and blistered. Transfer to a plate to cool. Place the onions and garlic on the grill or in the comal and roast, turning occasionally, for 6 to 8 minutes, or until charred. (If you grill the garlic cloves, skewer them to keep them from falling through the grate.) Transfer to the plate to cool.

When the vegetables are cool enough to handle, peel off most of the burnt skin. Don't worry about a few charred pieces of skin; they'll add a nice smoky flavor. In a blender or food processor, combine the tomatoes, onions, garlic, and chile peppers. Puree until smooth. Stir in the chopped cilantro and 2 tablespoons of the lime juice. Season with salt and black pepper. Taste and add more lime juice, if desired. Let cool to room temperature.

To assemble and cook: Just before serving, preheat the grill or broiler. Grill the chicken or broil 4" from the heat for 3 minutes per side, or until no longer pink in the center and a meat thermometer inserted in the center of a breast half registers 165°F. Warm the tortillas on the grill or under the broiler for 10 seconds per side.

Spoon one-quarter of the salsa in a pool on each of 4 plates. Place a grilled chicken breast in the center of each and garnish with a cilantro sprig. Serve with the tortillas.

Makes 4 servings

Cooking Tip
◆ You can use dried chipotle chile peppers instead of canned. If using the dried variety, remove and discard the stems and seeds (wear plastic gloves when handling). Place the chiles in a small bowl. Cover with warm water and let soak for 20 minutes, or until soft and pliable. Mince the chile peppers.

ROASTED SPICED CHICKEN

Pollo pibil

México

Nutrition Snapshot	Before	After
Per serving		
Calories	651	314
Total Fat g.	51	6.7
Saturated Fat g.	18.3	1.8
Cholesterol mg.	144	144

*P*ebil *(PEH-bil) describes an ancient family of Yucatán meat dishes that were traditionally cooked in a pib, or fire pit. The meat is marinated in a tangy spice paste flavored with annatto seeds (achiote) and sour orange juice, then wrapped in banana leaves and baked in the pit. Today, most Mexicans cook this dish in the oven. If banana leaves are unavailable, use foil, minus the distinctive nutty flavor imparted by the leaves. Serve with warm tortillas and Roasted Habanero Salsa (page 306).*

4	large boneless, skinless chicken breast halves (6 ounces each), trimmed of all visible fat
1	teaspoon annatto seeds
½	teaspoon black peppercorns
3	whole cloves
2	whole allspice berries
1	piece (½" long) cinnamon stick

¾	cup sour orange juice (see page 63) or ½ cup lime juice + ¼ cup orange juice
¼	cup orange juice
2	cloves garlic, minced
1	teaspoon salt
4	pieces (12" × 8" each) banana leaves, plantain leaves, or foil

Arrange the chicken breasts in a 13" × 9" glass or ceramic baking dish just large enough to hold them.

In a spice mill or with a mortar and pestle, grind the annatto seeds, peppercorns, cloves, allspice, and cinnamon stick to a fine powder. Transfer the spices to a medium bowl. Stir in the sour orange juice or lime juice and orange juice. Add the orange juice, garlic, and salt. Pour the mixture over the chicken. Cover and marinate in the refrigerator for 2 hours. Turn the chicken twice while marinating.

Preheat the oven to 350°F.

Arrange the banana leaves, plantain leaves, or foil on a work surface. Place a chicken breast in the center of each and top with a spoonful of the marinade. Fold the top and bottom of each leaf or piece of foil over the chicken, then fold over the sides to form a package. Secure with toothpicks if using leaves.

Place the packages on a baking sheet. Bake for 25 minutes, or until the chicken is no longer pink in the center. (To test for doneness without opening the packages, insert a meat thermometer; the internal temperature should register 165°F.) Serve the chicken in the packages.

Makes 4 servings

PANAMANIAN STEWED CHICKEN

Pollo guisado
estilo panameño   *Panamá*

Nutrition Snapshot	Before	After
Per serving		
Calories	668	342
Total Fat g.	36.3	9.9
Saturated Fat g.	6.3	2
Cholesterol mg.	217	145

Rosario Solez may not be the most famous chef in Miami, but if you come to South Florida and miss her cheerful restaurant, Las Molas, in the Miami suburb of Sweetwater, you'll pass up some of the most soulful Panamanian cooking this side of the Canal. Ever mindful of health, Solez uses skinless chicken breasts for stewing but leaves the bones in for flavor. She piles on layer after layer of flavor by adding culantro (see page 53), mustard, and even curry. I've trimmed some of the oil from her recipe, but otherwise followed her instructions to the letter.

1½	tablespoons canola oil
6	bone-in chicken breast halves (8 ounces each), skin removed
3	cloves garlic, minced
1	tablespoon coarse mustard
1½	teaspoons curry powder
½	teaspoon dried oregano
1	onion, finely chopped
1	rib celery, finely chopped
1	red bell pepper, thinly slivered
1	green bell pepper, thinly slivered
3	leaves culantro or 3 sprigs cilantro
3	tablespoons chopped fresh flat-leaf parsley
⅔	cup dry white wine or water
⅓	cup tomato puree
1	chicken bouillon cube (½"), crumbled
	Salt and ground black pepper

Heat the oil in a large nonstick skillet over medium heat. Add the chicken, garlic, mustard, curry, and oregano. Cook for 5 minutes, or until the chicken is browned. Add the onions, celery, bell peppers, culantro or cilantro, and 2 tablespoons of the parsley. Cook over medium heat for 8 minutes, or until the vegetables are soft. Increase the heat to high, add the wine or water, and bring to a boil. Stir in the tomato puree and bouillon cube and bring to a boil. Reduce the heat to medium and simmer for 5 minutes. Season with salt and black pepper.

Cover the skillet, reduce the heat to low, and simmer for 5 minutes, or until the chicken is very tender and no longer pink and a meat thermometer inserted in the center of a breast half registers 165°F. Season with more salt and black pepper, if desired. Sprinkling the remaining 1 tablespoon parsley on top.

Makes 6 servings

CHICKEN FRICASSE

Fricasé de pollo

Puerto Rico
Dominican Republic

Nutrition Snapshot	Before	After
Per serving		
Calories	793	417
Total Fat g.	38.5	10.4
Saturated Fat g.	9.1	2.2
Cholesterol mg.	206	124

The name of this dish may be French, but Spanish-Caribbean cooks make it their own special way. Cubans favor a simple fricasse, relying on cumin and olives for flavor (see the regional variation on the opposite page). Puerto Ricans add a sweet touch with prunes and raisins. To trim the fat from the traditional Puerto Rican version, I use Canadian bacon instead of salt pork and boneless, skinless chicken breasts instead of whole chicken. The cachucha chile peppers are a very mild tiny pepper from Cuba. If unavailable, use rocotillos (see page 55), ají dulce, or red bell peppers.

1¼	pounds boneless, skinless chicken breasts, trimmed of all visible fat and cut into 3" pieces
2	tablespoons lime juice
2	cloves garlic, minced
½	teaspoon ground cumin
1	tablespoon olive oil
½	medium onion, finely chopped
6	cachucha chile peppers, seeded, or ½ red bell pepper, finely chopped
½	green bell pepper, finely chopped
1	ounce Canadian bacon (1 slice), thinly slivered
3	culantro leaves or 2 tablespoons chopped fresh cilantro

1	teaspoon dried oregano
1	bay leaf
½	cup dry white wine or nonalcoholic white wine
½	cup tomato puree
2	cups Chicken Stock (page 360), fat-free reduced-sodium chicken broth, or water
1	large baking potato, peeled and cut into 1" cubes
2	carrots, cut into 1" pieces
	Salt and ground black pepper
8	pimiento-stuffed green olives
3	tablespoons raisins
8	pitted prunes (optional)

In a medium bowl, combine the chicken, lime juice, garlic, and cumin. Stir to mix. Cover and marinate in the refrigerator for 15 minutes.

Meanwhile, heat the oil in a large nonstick skillet over medium heat. Add the onions, chile peppers or red bell peppers, green bell peppers, bacon, culantro or cilantro, oregano, and bay leaf. Cook and stir for 5 minutes, or until the vegetables are soft but not brown. Stir in the chicken and cook for 3 minutes, or until the chicken turns white. Add the wine and tomato puree and bring to a boil over high heat. Add the stock, broth, or water. Add the potatoes and carrots. Season with salt and black pepper. Reduce the heat to medium-low and simmer for 20 minutes, or until the chicken is no longer pink in the center, the potatoes and carrots are tender, and the sauce is thick and flavorful.

About 5 minutes before the chicken and vegetables are finished cooking, stir in the olives, raisins, and prunes (if using). Season with more salt and black pepper, if desired. Remove and discard the bay leaf before serving.

Makes 4 servings

Regional Variations

Cuban Chicken Fricasse: Omit the Canadian bacon, raisins, and prunes. Add 2 tablespoons drained capers and 2 tablespoons chopped pimientos along with the olives.

Guatemalan Chicken Fricasse: Replace the potato with finely chopped chayote.

CHICKEN IN GREEN PUMPKIN SEED SAUCE

Pollo en mole verde de pepitas   *México*

Nutrition Snapshot	Before	After
Per serving		
Calories	800	376
Total Fat g.	58.5	13.2
Saturated Fat g.	17.4	2.7
Cholesterol mg.	258	120

*G*reen pumpkin seed sauce is one of the seven classic moles (gravies) of Oaxaca, México. Like most nuts and seeds, pepitas (pumpkin seeds) are high in fat, so I've reduced the amount in the traditional recipe and increased the amount of green vegetables.

CHICKEN

- 4 boneless, skinless chicken breast halves (1¼ pounds total), trimmed of all visible fat
- 1 small onion, quartered
- 3 cloves garlic
- 1 2" piece poblano chile pepper (wear plastic gloves when handling) or green bell pepper
- 1 sprig fresh cilantro
- 3 cups Chicken Stock (page 360) or fat-free reduced-sodium chicken broth

SAUCE

- 8 fresh or canned tomatillos, husked and rinsed
- 2–4 jalapeño chile peppers, halved lengthwise and seeded (wear plastic gloves when handling)
- 3 scallions, cut into 1" pieces
- ⅓ cup chopped fresh cilantro
- ⅓ cup chopped fresh flat-leaf parsley
- 2 leaves romaine lettuce, thinly sliced
- ¼ cup hulled pumpkin seeds, toasted (see tip)
- ½ teaspoon ground cumin
- 2 tablespoons lime juice
- 1 tablespoon lard or olive oil
- 2 sprigs epazote, finely chopped (optional)
- Salt and ground black pepper
- 4 sprigs fresh cilantro

To make the chicken: In a large nonstick saucepan over medium heat, combine the chicken, onions, garlic, chile pepper or bell pepper, cilantro sprig, and stock or broth. Simmer for 10 minutes, or until the chicken is no longer pink in the center. Transfer the chicken to a plate and cover to keep warm. Keep 2½ cups of the broth and the vegetables in the saucepan. (Remove the remaining broth and save for another use.)

To make the sauce: Add the tomatillos, chile peppers, and scallions to the saucepan. Simmer over medium heat for 8 minutes, or until the tomatillos are softened. Remove from the heat. Stir in half of the chopped cilantro, half of the parsley, the lettuce, pumpkin seeds, cumin, and 1 tablespoon of the lime juice. Working in batches, transfer to a blender or food processor. Puree until smooth.

Heat the lard or oil in a large deep saucepan over medium heat. Add the pureed pumpkin-seed mixture. Cook, stirring occasionally, for 10 minutes. Stir in the epazote (if using), the remaining chopped cilantro, the remaining parsley, and the remaining 1 tablespoon lime juice. Cook for 5 minutes, or until thick and fragrant. Season with salt and black pepper.

Add the chicken to the sauce. Cook for 3 to 5 minutes, or until a meat thermometer inserted in the center of a breast half registers 165°F. Transfer to plates or a platter. Garnish each chicken breast with a cilantro sprig.

Makes 4 servings

Cooking Tips

✦ To toast hulled pumpkin seeds, place them in a small dry skillet over medium heat. Cook, shaking the pan often, for 3 minutes, or until the seeds begin to brown and pop. Transfer to a shallow bowl and let cool.

✦ The chicken can be cooked and the sauce can be prepared up to 6 hours ahead and stored in the refrigerator. Just before serving, warm the chicken breasts in the sauce.

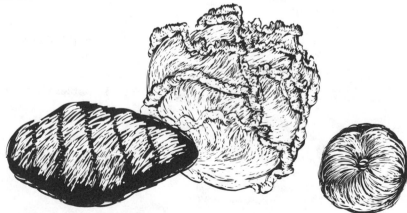

CHICKEN IN RED SESAME SEED SAUCE

Pollo en mole colorado

México

Nutrition Snapshot	Before	After
Per serving		
Calories	623	383
Total Fat g.	45.9	11.9
Saturated Fat g.	14	2.4
Cholesterol mg.	177	128

Here's another classic Oaxacan mole. This one is flavored with tomatoes, cinnamon, and sesame seeds. To cut back on the fat, I use boneless, skinless chicken breasts instead of whole chickens and a lot less lard in the sauce. To bolster the flavor, I rely on an age-old Mexican technique: roasting the vegetables in a comal (a griddle for cooking tortillas).

CHICKEN

6 boneless, skinless chicken breast halves (2 pounds total), trimmed of all visible fat

2½ cups Chicken Stock (page 360) or fat-free reduced-sodium chicken broth

SAUCE

5 ancho chile peppers, stems removed and seeded (wear plastic gloves when handling)

3 guajillo chile peppers, stems removed and seeded (wear plastic gloves when handling)

2 tablespoons raisins

1 cup hot water

3 tomatoes

1 medium onion, quartered

3 cloves garlic

1 corn tortilla (6" diameter), torn into 1" pieces

3 tablespoons sesame seeds

2 tablespoons sliced almonds

1 slice darkly toasted white bread

½ teaspoon dried oregano

½ teaspoon dried marjoram

⅛ teaspoon ground cloves

1 tablespoon lard or olive oil

1 stick cinnamon

1 avocado leaf (optional); see tip

Salt and ground black pepper

6 sprigs fresh flat-leaf parsley

To make the chicken: Combine the chicken and stock or broth in a large non-stick skillet over medium heat. Simmer for 10 minutes, or until the chicken is no longer pink in the center. Transfer the chicken to a plate and cover to keep warm. Reserve the stock.

To make the sauce: In a medium bowl, combine the chile peppers, raisins, and water. Let soak for 20 minutes, or until softened.

Heat a comal or medium nonstick skillet over medium heat. Add the tomatoes and roast, turning occasionally, for 8 minutes, or until the skins are charred and blistered. Transfer to a plate. Add the onions and garlic to the pan. Roast, turning occasionally, for 8 minutes, or until slightly charred. Transfer to the plate with the tomatoes. Add the tortilla pieces to the pan and roast, stirring, for 5 minutes, or until lightly browned. Transfer to the plate. Separately add the sesame seeds and

(continued)

almonds to the pan and roast, stirring often, for 2 minutes each, or until lightly browned.

Drain the chile peppers and raisins. Working in batches, combine the chile peppers, raisins, tomatoes, onions, garlic, tortilla pieces, 1½ tablespoons of the sesame seeds, the almonds, bread, oregano, marjoram, and cloves in a food processor or blender. Puree until smooth.

Heat the lard or oil in a large deep saucepan over medium heat. Add the pureed tomato mixture, cinnamon stick, and avocado leaf (if using). Cook, stirring occasionally, for 5 minutes, or until thick and fragrant. Add the reserved stock and cook, stirring occasionally, for 10 minutes. Season with salt and black pepper.

Add the chicken to the sauce. Cook for 3 to 5 minutes, or until a meat thermometer inserted in the center of a breast half registers 165°F. Remove and discard the cinnamon stick and avocado leaf. Transfer to plates or a platter. Sprinkle the remaining 1½ tablespoons sesame seeds over the chicken and garnish with the parsley.

Makes 6 servings

Cooking Tips

✦ Avocado leaves are available at Mexican markets. They add a very subtle licorice-like flavor.

✦ The chicken can be cooked and the sauce can be prepared up to 6 hours ahead and stored in the refrigerator. Just before serving, warm the chicken breasts in the sauce.

COLOMBIAN SHREDDED CHICKEN

Pollo desmechado   *Colombia*

estilo colombiano

Nutrition Snapshot	Before	After
Per serving		
Calories	360	237
Total Fat g.	24.6	7.6
Saturated Fat g.	5.6	1.5
Cholesterol mg.	106	96

This simple chicken recipe belongs to a large family of shredded meat dishes that includes Spanish-Caribbean Braised Skirt Steak (page 260). To reduce the fat, I use boneless, skinless chicken breasts instead of dark meat. This chicken makes a great topping for Plantain "Surfboards" (page 143).

1	tablespoon Annatto Oil (page 380) or 1 tablespoon olive oil + ¼ teaspoon sweet paprika
1	small onion, finely chopped
2	cloves garlic, minced
4	scallions, finely chopped
4	rocotillo chile peppers, seeded and chopped, or ¼ red bell pepper, chopped
1	tomato, peeled (see page 383), seeded, and chopped
1	teaspoon red-wine vinegar
1	pound boneless, skinless chicken breasts, trimmed of all visible fat
1¾–2¼	cups water
	Salt and ground black pepper

Heat the annatto oil or olive oil and paprika in a large deep skillet over medium heat. Add the onions, garlic, scallions, and chile peppers or bell peppers. Cook for 5 minutes, or until the onions are soft but not brown. Increase the heat to high and stir in the tomatoes and vinegar. Cook for 3 minutes, or until most of the tomato juices have evaporated.

Add the chicken and water to cover. Season with salt and black pepper. Reduce the heat to medium, cover the pan, and simmer for 30 minutes, or until the chicken is very tender when tested with a knife. Transfer the chicken breasts to a cutting board and let cool. Increase the heat to high and boil the cooking liquid until only 1 cup remains.

Using 2 forks, pull the chicken along the grain of the meat into fine shreds. Place the chicken in a medium saucepan and strain the cooking liquid on top. Simmer for 5 minutes, or until the chicken has absorbed most of the cooking liquid. Season with more salt and black pepper, if desired.

Makes 4 servings

DOMINICAN TURKEY STEW

Pavo guisado
estilo dominicano

*Dominican
Republic*

Nutrition Snapshot	Before	After
Per serving		
Calories	751	415
Total Fat g.	36.7	4.8
Saturated Fat g.	7.9	0.8
Cholesterol mg.	158	126

If your experience of turkey is limited to a roasted bird, you're in for a revelation.

2 pounds skinless turkey breast, trimmed of all visible fat and diagonally sliced into ½"-thick slices

4 cloves garlic, minced

1 teaspoon dried oregano

2 tablespoons red-wine vinegar

Salt and ground black pepper

1 tablespoon olive oil

1 onion, finely chopped

1 green bell pepper, finely chopped

¼ cup chopped fresh flat-leaf parsley

1 tomato, peeled (see page 383), seeded, and finely chopped

1 cup dry white wine or nonalcoholic white wine

1 cup tomato sauce

1–2 cups Chicken Stock (page 360), fat-free reduced-sodium chicken broth, or water

1½ pounds potatoes, peeled and cut into 1" cubes

2 tablespoons rinsed and drained capers

12 pimiento-stuffed green olives

1 cup cooked or frozen and thawed peas

Place the turkey in a medium bowl. Add half of the garlic, the oregano, and vinegar. Season with salt and black pepper. Toss to coat. Cover and marinate in the refrigerator for 30 minutes.

Heat the oil in a large saucepan over medium heat. Add the onions, bell peppers, the remaining garlic, and 2 tablespoons of the parsley. Cook for 4 minutes, or until the vegetables are soft. Increase the heat to high. Add the tomatoes. Cook for 1 minute. Add the turkey (reserving any marinade). Cook for 2 minutes, or until no longer pink in the center. Add the wine, tomato sauce, and the reserved turkey marinade. Bring to a boil. Add 1 cup of the stock, broth, or water and the potatoes. Return to a boil. Reduce the heat to medium-low, cover, and simmer for 10 minutes.

Stir in the capers and olives. Cook for 12 minutes. Add more stock, broth, or water, if needed, to keep the turkey and potatoes covered. Stir in the peas. Cook for 3 minutes, or until the turkey and potatoes are tender.

Transfer to a platter and sprinkle with the remaining 2 tablespoons parsley.

Makes 6 servings

TURKEY PICADILLO

Picadillo
de pavo

*Various
countries*

Nutrition Snapshot	Before	After
Per serving		
Calories	685	294
Total Fat g.	46.7	5
Saturated Fat g.	17.4	0.9
Cholesterol mg.	155	142

Picadillo *(pee-ka-DEE-yo) turns up all over Latin America as a filling for empanadas and as a light dish by itself. My heart-healthy version uses ground turkey instead of ground beef.*

1½	pounds lean ground turkey breast		8	pimiento-stuffed green olives, finely chopped
½–1	teaspoon ground cumin		¼	cup dark raisins
	Salt and ground black pepper		3	tablespoons rinsed and drained capers
1	tablespoon olive oil			
3	cloves garlic, minced		1	tablespoon caper juice
1	medium onion, finely chopped		¾	cup dry white wine or nonalcoholic white wine
1	red bell pepper, finely chopped			
1	tomato, seeded and finely chopped		1	tablespoon tomato paste

In a medium bowl, combine the turkey, ½ teaspoon of the cumin, 1 teaspoon salt, and 1 teaspoon black pepper. Mix well with a spoon. Let stand for 5 minutes.

Heat the oil in a large nonstick skillet over medium-high heat. Add the garlic, onions, and bell peppers. Cook for 4 minutes, or until the onions are just beginning to brown. Stir in the tomatoes and cook for 2 minutes. Crumble the turkey into the skillet. Cook, breaking up the turkey with a wooden spoon, for 3 minutes, or until it starts to turn white.

Stir in the olives, raisins, and capers. Cook for 2 minutes more. Stir in the caper juice, wine, and tomato paste and bring to a boil over high heat. Reduce the heat to medium-low and simmer for 6 to 8 minutes, or until the turkey is tender and no longer pink in the center and most of the liquid has evaporated. (The picadillo should be moist but not soupy.) Season with more salt, black pepper, and cumin, if desired.

Makes 4 servings

Regional Variation

Mexican Turkey Picadillo: Add 1 teaspoon pure chili powder and ¼ teaspoon ground cinnamon along with the cumin. Add ⅓ cup chopped fresh mushrooms to the sauté along with the turkey. Omit the capers. Replace the caper juice with 1 teaspoon cider vinegar.

BEEF, PORK, AND LAMB
Res, cerdo y cordero

Latinos love meat. Pork reigns supreme in México and in the Spanish-speaking Caribbean. Some of the world's finest-flavored beef is raised on the grassy Pampas (plains) of Argentina, Paraguay, and southern Brazil.

A healthy approach to meat consumption includes three strategies. First, use lean cuts of meat, such as pork loin, beef tenderloin, and beef eye of round. Be sure to trim all visible fat from the meat before cooking. Second, enjoy sensible portions. Four to five ounces of lean meat satisfies the appetite without clogging the arteries. Finally, use meat as a condiment to accompany and flavor the more lean and nutritious foods in the Latin American pantry: beans, grains, vegetables, and fruit.

Some of Latin America's best meat dishes can be made healthier simply by cutting back on the fats used in marinades and cooking. These include Nicaraguan Grilled Beef Tenderloins (page 263) and Puerto Rico's Stuffed Pot Roast (page 265). To make Cuba's Spiced Pork Bites (page 285) a bit leaner, I grill the pork instead of deep-frying it. Grilling imparts a robust, smoky flavor to the traditional recipe.

BEEF RECIPES

PORK RECIPES

LAMB RECIPE

BRAISED SKIRT STEAK

Ropa vieja

Various countries

Nutrition Snapshot	Before	After
Per serving		
Calories	633	378
Total Fat g.	34.1	12.5
Saturated Fat g.	9.2	4.2
Cholesterol mg.	99	46

The Spanish name of this popular dish literally means "old clothes." The "clothes" here are meaty shreds of skirt steak, which—with a little imagination—do look sort of raglike. Skirt steak is available at butcher shops and most supermarkets. In a pinch, you could substitute flank steak. To trim the fat in the traditional recipe, I reduce the proportion of meat and increase the proportion of vegetables.

1	tablespoon olive oil
1	onion, thinly sliced
1	green bell pepper, thinly sliced
1	red bell pepper, thinly sliced
2	cloves garlic, minced
½	teaspoon ground cumin
1	large tomato, peeled (see page 383) and chopped
1	pound beef skirt steak, trimmed of all visible fat
	Salt and ground black pepper

½	cup dry white wine or nonalcoholic white wine
3–3½	cups Chicken Stock (page 360) or fat-free reduced-sodium chicken broth
¼	cup tomato puree or tomato sauce
4	carrots, cut into 1" pieces
2	potatoes, cut into 1" pieces
2	teaspoons rinsed and drained capers
1	tablespoon finely chopped fresh flat-leaf parsley (optional)

Heat the oil in a large, wide saucepan over medium heat. Add the onions, bell peppers, garlic, and cumin. Cook, stirring often, for 5 minutes, or until the onions are just beginning to brown. Add the tomatoes and cook for 1 minute.

Season the steak with salt and black pepper. Add it to the vegetables and cook for 2 minutes per side. Increase the heat to high, add the wine, and bring to a boil. Add 3 cups of the stock or broth and return to a boil. Reduce the heat to medium-low and simmer for 30 to 40 minutes, or until the steak is very tender. Skim off any foam that rises to the surface.

Stir in the tomato puree or tomato sauce, carrots, and potatoes. Simmer for 15 to 20 minutes, or until the vegetables are tender and the sauce is reduced and flavorful. If too much liquid evaporates, add a little more stock or broth. Stir in the capers.

Using 2 forks, tear the meat along the grain into very thin shreds. (You should be able to do this right in the pan.) Simmer for 3 minutes more, or until the meat soaks up the sauce. Season with more salt and black pepper, if desired. Sprinkle with the parsley (if using).

Makes 4 servings

CREOLE STEAK

Bistec a la criolla *Colombia*

Nutrition Snapshot	Before	After
Per serving		
Calories	662	373
Total Fat g.	37.3	16.3
Saturated Fat g.	9	5
Cholesterol mg.	189	118

Colombians certainly know how to dress up a steak. These steaks are fragrant, colorful, and full of flavor. If you're feeling generous, use beef tenderloin. For a more economical cut, look to sirloin. To reduce the fat, I grill the steaks instead of pan-frying them, which also provides a jolt of smoky flavor.

4	beef tenderloin or sirloin steaks (4 ounces and ½" thick each)		2	onions, finely chopped
	Salt		2	cloves garlic, minced
	Ground black pepper		4	scallions, finely chopped
½	teaspoon ground cumin		2	large tomatoes, peeled (see page 383), seeded, and chopped
1	tablespoon + 2 teaspoons red-wine vinegar		3	tablespoons chopped fresh flat-leaf parsley
1½	tablespoons Dijon mustard		1	tablespoon chopped fresh oregano or 1 teaspoon dried
1	tablespoon canola oil			

Rub the steaks with ½ teaspoon salt, ½ teaspoon pepper, and cumin. Let stand for 10 minutes. Sprinkle the steaks with 1 tablespoon of the vinegar and spread the mustard on top. Cover and marinate in the refrigerator for 20 minutes.

Heat the oil in a large nonstick skillet over medium heat. Add the onions, garlic, and scallions. Cook for 5 minutes, or until the onions are soft but not brown. Increase the heat to high and stir in the tomatoes and the remaining 2 teaspoons vinegar. Cook for 3 minutes, or until most of the tomato juices have evaporated. Stir in the parsley and oregano. Cook for 3 minutes. The sauce should be highly seasoned; sprinkle with more salt and pepper, if desired.

Preheat the grill or broiler to high.

Grill the steaks or broil 4" from the heat for 2 to 3 minutes per side for medium-rare or until a meat thermometer inserted in the center of a steak registers 160°F for medium. Spoon the sauce onto plates and set the steaks on top. Alternatively, serve the sauce spooned over the steaks.

Makes 4 servings

SALVADORAN BEEF STEW

Carne
guisada estilo
salvadoreño

El Salvador

Nutrition Snapshot	Before	After
Per serving		
Calories	597	367
Total Fat g.	21.6	9.5
Saturated Fat g.	5.4	2.5
Cholesterol mg.	142	71

This peppery beef stew is Salvadoran soul food. To speed up the cooking time, I use a pressure cooker (see the tip below).

1 tablespoon olive oil

1 pound lean stew beef, trimmed of all visible fat and cut into 1" cubes

1 small onion, thinly sliced

½ green bell pepper, thinly sliced

2 cloves garlic, minced

Ground black pepper

Salt

1 pound tomatoes, peeled (see page 383) and finely chopped

1 bay leaf

2 cups water

6 carrots, cut into 1" pieces

2 large baking potatoes (10 ounces each), cut into 1" pieces

Heat the oil in a pressure cooker over medium-high heat. Add the beef, onions, bell peppers, garlic, and ½ teaspoon black pepper. Season with salt. Cook and stir for 5 minutes, or until lightly browned. Add the tomatoes and cook for 1 minute more. Add the bay leaf and water.

Put the lid on the cooker and pressure-cook for 10 minutes. Transfer to the sink and run cold water over the lid to cool it down. Remove the lid and stir in the carrots and potatoes. Re-cover the cooker, return to the heat, and pressure-cook for 6 to 8 minutes, or until the meat and vegetables are tender. Season with more black pepper and salt, if desired. Remove and discard the bay leaf before serving.

Makes 4 servings

Cooking Tip

✦ To cook the stew in a conventional pot, replace the pressure cooker with a 4-quart soup pot. Proceed as directed. After adding the bay leaf and water, bring to a boil over high heat. Cover, reduce the heat to medium-low, and simmer for 45 minutes. Add the carrots and potatoes. Cover and cook for 30 to 45 minutes, or until the meat and vegetables are very tender.

NICARAGUAN GRILLED BEEF TENDERLOINS

Churrasco
nicaragüense

Nicaragua

Nutrition Snapshot	Before	After
Per serving		
Calories	578	338
Total Fat g.	26	13.4
Saturated Fat g.	9.6	4.2
Cholesterol mg.	189	78

Churrasco (chur-AS-ko) is a general term referring to grilled beef. The Nicaraguan version uses paper-thin slices of beef tenderloin. Accompaniments include Pickled Onion Relish (page 313), Central American Tomato Sauce (page 301), and Red Beans and Rice (page 153).

1	pound beef tenderloin, cut from the center, trimmed of all visible fat
	Salt and ground black pepper
½	onion, thinly sliced
¼	cup chopped fresh flat-leaf parsley
2	cloves garlic, minced

3	tablespoons dry sherry or nonalcoholic white wine (optional)
2	bay leaves
3	tablespoons red-wine vinegar
4	large sweet onions, cut crosswise into ½"-thick slices
½	cup Chimichurri (page 310)

Lay the beef on a cutting board with the long side facing you. Holding a sharp knife parallel to the cutting board, cut the beef through the side lengthwise into 4 flat, even slices. Place each slice between 2 sheets of plastic wrap and pound with a meat pounder or the side of a cleaver or to a thickness of ¼". Season each slice with salt and pepper and arrange in a 13" × 9" baking dish.

In a small bowl, combine the thinly sliced onions, parsley, garlic, sherry or wine, and bay leaves. Whisk to mix. Pour over the meat. Cover and marinate for 15 minutes. Turn once while marinating.

Preheat the grill or broiler to high.

Coat the sweet onions with nonstick spray. Place on a grill tray or broiler pan. Grill the onions or broil 4" from the heat for 4 minutes per side, or until nicely browned. Turn carefully with a metal spatula. Transfer the onions to a platter.

Drain the beef and discard the marinade. Grill the beef or broil 4" from the heat for 2 minutes per side for medium-rare, or until a meat thermometer inserted in the center registers 160°F for medium. Arrange the beef on top of the onions. Serve with the chimichurri.

Makes 4 servings

CENTRAL AMERICAN GRILLED SIRLOIN

Churrasco
centroamericano

*Various
countries*

Nutritional Snapshot	Before	After
Per serving		
Calories	604	314
Total Fat g.	26.4	10.4
Saturated Fat g.	8.9	4.1
Cholesterol mg.	202	101

Nicaragua's neighbors like to serve their grilled beef with chirmol (a type of tomato salsa) instead of chimichurri (a garlic and parsley sauce similar to pesto). They also prefer beef sirloin steak and like to use a dry rub instead of a marinade.

½ teaspoon salt
½ teaspoon ground black pepper
½ teaspoon garlic powder
½ teaspoon dried oregano
¼ teaspoon ground cumin

4 sirloin steaks (each 4 ounces and ½" thick), trimmed of all visible fat
4 sweet onions, cut crosswise into ½"-thick slices
1 cup Central American Tomato Salsa (page 300) or your favorite salsa

In a small bowl, mix together the salt, pepper, garlic powder, oregano, and cumin. Rub over the steaks and let stand for 5 minutes.

Preheat the grill or broiler to high.

Coat the onions with nonstick pray. Place on a grill tray or broiler pan. Grill the onions or broil 4" from the heat for 4 minutes per side, or until nicely browned. Turn carefully with a metal spatula. Transfer the onions to a platter.

Grill the steaks or broil 4" from the heat for 3 to 5 minutes per side for medium-rare, or until a meat thermometer inserted in the center of a steak registers 160°F for medium. Arrange the beef on top of the onions. Serve with the salsa.

Makes 4 servings

STUFFED POT ROAST

Carne asada rellena

Puerto Rico

Nutrition Snapshot	Before	After
Per serving		
Calories	773	533
Total Fat g.	30.4	12.3
Saturated Fat g.	10.7	3.9
Cholesterol mg.	225	120

Puerto Rican pot roast features a lively stuffing of raisins, peppers, olives, and country ham. Cubans like to stuff their roast with chorizo sausages. Venezuelans often stew the roast in a rich, black sauce made with Coca-Cola. Here's the Puerto Rican version with less fat. I increased the proportion of vegetables to beef, but left the robust flavorings the same. This dish makes a great holiday centerpiece.

¼	cup raisins
¼	cup dry sherry or nonalcoholic white wine
1	medium onion, finely chopped
½	red bell pepper, finely chopped
1	ounce serrano ham or prosciutto, finely chopped
4	pimiento-stuffed green olives, chopped
4	cloves garlic, minced
1	tablespoon rinsed and drained capers
1	eye of round beef roast (3 pounds), trimmed of all visible fat
½	teaspoon salt
½	teaspoon ground black pepper
½	teaspoon dried oregano
½	teaspoon ground cumin
½	teaspoon garlic powder
2	tablespoons red-wine vinegar

1	tablespoon olive oil
6	rocotillo chile peppers, seeded and chopped, or ½ red bell pepper, chopped
½	green bell pepper, finely chopped
2	tablespoons chopped fresh cilantro
3	culantro leaves, thinly slivered, or 2 tablespoons chopped fresh cilantro
1	cup dry white wine or nonalcoholic white wine
2	cups tomato sauce
3–4	cups fat-free reduced-sodium beef broth or water
2	pounds potatoes, peeled and cut into 1" pieces
8	carrots, peeled and cut into 1" pieces
	Salt and ground black pepper
2	tablespoons chopped fresh flat-leaf parsley or cilantro

In a medium bowl, combine the raisins and sherry or wine. Let soak for 15 minutes. Drain the liquid and reserve. To the bowl with the raisins, stir in half of the onions, the red bell peppers, ham, olives, half of the garlic, and the capers.

Using a long slender knife, cut a tunnel 1" in diameter through the center of the roast, running from narrow end to narrow end. Spoon the raisin mixture into the tunnel, pushing it in from both ends with your fingers.

In a cup, stir together the salt, black pepper, oregano, cumin, and garlic powder.

(continued)

Sprinkle over the roast and rub it into the meat. Transfer to a roasting pan and let stand for 10 minutes. Sprinkle the vinegar over the roast. Cover and marinate in the refrigerator for 40 minutes.

Preheat the oven to 350°F.

Heat the oil in a Dutch oven over medium heat. Drain the roast, reserving the marinade, and blot dry. Add the roast to the Dutch oven. Cook, turning to brown on all sides, for 10 to 15 minutes. Transfer to a plate.

Add the remaining onions, the remaining garlic, chile peppers or red bell peppers, green bell peppers, cilantro, and culantro or cilantro to the Dutch oven. Cook over medium heat for 4 minutes, or until the vegetables are soft but not brown.

Return the roast to the Dutch oven and increase the heat to high. Add the wine, reserved soaking liquid, and reserved marinade. Bring to a boil. Add the tomato sauce and bring to a boil. Add enough broth or water to cover the roast and return to a boil. Cover the pan and transfer to the oven. Bake for 1½ hours. Add the potatoes and carrots. Cook for 1 hour. Uncover and cook for 35 to 45 minutes, or until the meat and vegetables are very tender.

Transfer the beef to a cutting board. Thinly slice crosswise. Arrange the beef and vegetables on a platter. Set the Dutch oven over high heat. Boil the sauce for 5 to 10 minutes, or until thick and flavorful. Season with salt and black pepper. Pour over the meat (or strain the sauce over the meat, if desired). Sprinkle with the parsley or cilantro.

Makes 8 servings

FLAUTAS (PAGE 211)

SNAPPER IN VERACRUZ-STYLE SPICY TOMATO SAUCE (PAGE 226)

CHICKEN ENCHILADAS WITH RED SAUCE (PAGE 220)

MEXICAN STEAMED MUSSELS (PAGE 233)

ORANGE-MARINATED GRILLED CHICKEN WITH SMOKY TOMATO SALSA (PAGE 246)

BRAZILIAN SEAFOOD STEW (PAGE 238)

CHICKEN WITH RICE (PAGE 244)

STUFFED CHICKEN BREASTS (PAGE 245)

NICARAGUAN GRILLED BEEF TENDERLOINS (PAGE 263) AND CHIMICHURRI (PAGE 310)

BRAISED SKIRT STEAK (PAGE 260)

CHICKEN IN GREEN PUMPKIN SEED SAUCE (PAGE 251)

**CHILE-MARINATED PORK TENDERLOIN AND BLACK BEAN SALSA (PAGE 289) WITH
PLANTAIN SPIDERS (PAGE 73) AND ORANGE AND CARROT JUICE (PAGE 354)**

281

STUFFED POT ROAST (PAGE 265)

ARGENTINIAN MIXED GRILL

Parillada
   argentina completa   *Argentina*

Nutrition Snapshot	Before	After
Per serving		
Calories	1,098	315
Total Fat g.	69.4	12.5
Saturated Fat g.	17.4	4.4
Cholesterol mg.	302	101

Argentina is probably the most carnivorous country in the Western Hemisphere. Order a mixed grill in Buenos Aires, and you'll start with a heaping plateful of assorted grilled sausages and organ meats. That's just the appetizer. The main course consists of beef, beef, and more beef. To create a healthy mixed grill, I keep the beef as the centerpiece, but reduce the serving size and round out the meal with the grilled vegetables often served as an appetizer. The result is a plateful of smoky, meaty flavor and bearable levels of cholesterol and saturated fat.

½   cup dry white wine or nonalcoholic white wine

3   tablespoons lemon juice

1   tablespoon olive oil

2   cloves garlic, minced

2   red bell peppers

2   green bell peppers

12   mushroom caps

2   large onions, cut crosswise into ½"-thick slices

1   eggplant, cut crosswise into ½"-thick slices

2   teaspoons dried oregano

2   teaspoons red-pepper flakes

   Coarse salt (see tip on page 284) and ground black pepper

1½   pounds beef sirloin steak (at least 1" thick), trimmed of all visible fat

1½   cups Creole Tomato Salsa (page 299), optional

Preheat the grill to high.

In a small bowl, combine the wine, lemon juice, oil, and garlic. Place the bell peppers, mushrooms, onions, and eggplant on a grill tray. Brush the wine mixture on the vegetables. Grill the vegetables for 4 to 6 minutes per side, or until nicely charred. Sprinkle with the oregano, red-pepper flakes, salt, and black pepper. Baste with any leftover marinade. Transfer the vegetables to a platter.

Grill the steak for 4 minutes per side for medium-rare, or until a meat thermometer inserted in the center registers 160°F for medium. Cut into 6 portions and transfer to the platter with the vegetables.

Serve the steak and vegetables with the salsa (if using).

Makes 6 servings

Cooking Tips

✦ For a more intense smoky flavor, soak 2 cups oak or hickory chips in cold water for 1 hour. Toss the chips on the coals just before grilling.

(continued)

✦ This dish can also be broiled. To capture some of the live-fire flavor of out-door grilling, add ¼ teaspoon liquid smoke to the marinade. Broil the vegetables and meat 4" from the heat for 4 to 5 minutes per side, or until cooked to taste. The broiling may take several batches.

✦ Coarse salt is the salt of choice for seasoning the steak as it cooks. If un-available in your local grocery store, regular table salt works fine.

✦ Traditionally, the bell peppers are grilled whole and the cores are cut off at the table. You could also remove the cores before grilling.

Regional Variations

Uruguayan Mixed Grill: Serve the mixed grill with toasted manioc or cassava flour (available at Brazilian and Argentinian markets). To toast the flour, cook it in a dry skillet over medium heat, shaking the pan often, for 3 minutes. Sprinkle over the meat before serving.

Chilean Mixed Grill: Season the sirloin with salt, black pepper, and garlic powder prior to grilling.

¡Fiesta!
South American Barbecue

Grilled meats are a regular part of South American festivities. Wow your guests this summer with an outdoor menu that's full of surprises. Cool and hot combine for a fantastic outdoor feast.

Kiwifruit Cooler (*Jugo de lulo*, **page 354**)

Peruvian-Style Ceviche (*Ceviche a lo peruano*, **page 90**)

Argentinian Mixed Grill (*Parillada argentina completa*, **page 283**)

Creole Tomato Salsa (*Salsa criolla*, **page 299**)

Tropical Fruit Salad (*Ensalada de frutas*, **page 332**)

SPICED PORK BITES

Masitas de puerco   *Cuba*

Nutrition Snapshot	Before	After
Per serving		
Calories	658	254
Total Fat g.	34	6.8
Saturated Fat g.	8.7	2.3
Cholesterol mg.	154	89

These crisp, garlicky cubes of pork were my first introduction to Spanish-Caribbean cooking. I loved them to the last bite. Too bad they were deep-fried and loaded with artery-clogging fat. To make a healthier version, I use boneless pork loin roast instead of fatty pork shoulder and grill the pork kabob-style instead of using the deep fryer. The results are so flavorful, you'll never miss the fat. Serve these with Refried Beans (page 155), Basic White Rice (page 159), or Grilled Ripe Plantains (page 144). They also make a great appetizer for 8 people.

4	cloves garlic, minced
6	tablespoons chopped fresh cilantro
3	tablespoons chopped fresh flat-leaf parsley
1	teaspoon ground cumin
1	teaspoon ground oregano
1	teaspoon ground black pepper
1	teaspoon salt
¾	cup sour orange juice (see page 63) or lime juice
¼	cup orange juice
1½	pounds boneless pork loin roast or tenderloin, trimmed of all visible fat and cut into 1" cubes
1	tablespoon olive oil or nonstick spray
1	small onion, thinly sliced
1	lime, cut into 4 wedges

In a large bowl, whisk together the garlic, 3 tablespoons of the cilantro, the parsley, cumin, oregano, pepper, salt, sour orange juice or lime juice, and orange juice. Add the pork and toss to coat. Cover and marinate in the refrigerator for 4 hours. Stir once or twice while marinating.

Preheat the grill or broiler to high.

Drain the pork and thread the cubes onto metal skewers. Brush with the oil or coat with nonstick spray.

Grill the pork or broil 4" from the heat for 8 minutes, or until browned and no longer pink in the center. Turn the kabobs occasionally to ensure even cooking. Unskewer the kabobs onto plates or a platter. Top with the onions and the remaining 3 tablespoons cilantro. Serve with the lime wedges for squeezing onto the pork.

Makes 4 servings

ROAST PORK

Lechón asado

Cuba
Puerto Rico

Nutrition Snapshot	Before	After
Per serving		
Calories	606	247
Total Fat g.	40.8	6.8
Saturated Fat g.	14.6	2.3
Cholesterol mg.	145	90

Lechón asado *(garlicky roast pork) is often the centerpiece of the Spanish-Caribbean Nochebuena (Christmas Eve feast). Tradition calls for a whole pig to be roasted in a backyard barbecue pit—a delectable but fatty meal that requires an experienced cook and very resilient arteries. To trim the fat and make the recipe easier for the home cook, I use pork loin roast. For the most flavor, start marinating the pork the night before.*

1	boneless pork loin roast (3 pounds), trimmed of all visible fat
4	cloves garlic
1	teaspoon salt
½	teaspoon dried oregano
½	teaspoon ground cumin
½	teaspoon ground black pepper

¼	teaspoon ground bay leaves or 1 whole bay leaf, crumbled
½	cup sour orange juice (see page 63) or 6 tablespoons lime juice + 2 tablespoons orange juice
3	tablespoons dry sherry or nonalcoholic white wine
1	large onion, thinly sliced

Using the tip of a sharp knife, make shallow slits all over the pork.

With a mortar and pestle or in a food processor or blender, mash the garlic, salt, oregano, cumin, pepper, and bay leaf to a paste. Rub the mixture all over the pork, forcing it into the slits. Place the pork in a large resealable plastic bag. Add the sour orange juice or lime juice and orange juice, sherry or wine, and onions. Seal the bag and marinate in the refrigerator overnight, turning the bag several times.

Preheat the oven to 400°F.

Drain the pork and pat dry, reserving the marinade. Place the pork in a heavy nonstick roasting pan. Roast for 20 minutes, turning occasionally to ensure even browning.

Reduce the heat to 325°F. Pour the reserved marinade and onions over the pork. Loosely cover the pan with foil and roast, basting occasionally with the pan juices, for 1 to 1¼ hours, or until no longer pink and the internal temperature reads 160°F on a meat thermometer. (Many Cubans prefer their pork very well done, about 180°F.) Add a little water if the pan starts to dry out. Uncover the roast for the last 15 minutes of cooking.

Let the roast stand for 10 minutes before carving.

Makes 8 servings

PORK IN OAXACAN MOLE

Mole negro carne con
de cerdo   *México*

Nutrition Snapshot	Before	After
Per serving		
Calories	555	278
Total Fat g.	44.9	10.2
Saturated Fat g.	15	2.2
Cholesterol mg.	85	60

Here's another of the great moles (MOH-lehs) of Oaxaca, México. This one features a rich, complex gravy flavored with chiles, almonds, peanuts, dried fruits, spices, and chocolate. To trim the fat in the traditional recipe, I reduced the amount of lard and nuts and substituted cocoa powder for the chocolate. The bread is toasted instead of deep-fried. There's still so much flavor, you won't miss the fat for a second. Don't be intimidated by the long list of ingredients; they're mostly spices that are added quickly. This dish is best served with warm tortillas.

2	pounds pork loin roast, trimmed of all visible fat and cut into 1½" pieces		1	slice French bread, darkly toasted and broken into 1" pieces
10	cups water		2	tablespoons slivered almonds
	Salt and ground black pepper		2	tablespoons dry-roasted unsalted peanuts
4	guajillo chile peppers		2	tablespoons sesame seeds
2	ancho chile peppers		1	teaspoon dried oregano
2	pasilla chile peppers		1	teaspoon dried thyme
1	chipotle chile pepper		½	teaspoon anise seeds, crushed
3	dried apricots		¼	teaspoon ground cloves
2	tablespoons raisins		1	tablespoon lard or olive oil
1	cup hot water		1	piece (1" long) cinnamon stick
2	tomatoes		1	avocado leaf (optional); see tip on page 288
4	tomatillos, peeled and rinsed		2	tablespoons honey
1	small onion, quartered		2	tablespoons unsweetened cocoa powder
2	cloves garlic			

In a large saucepan over high heat, combine the pork and 10 cups water. Season with salt and black pepper. Bring to a boil, skimming off any fat or foam that rises to the surface. Reduce the heat to medium-low and simmer, skimming occasionally, for 40 to 60 minutes, or until tender. Set a strainer in a large bowl. Drain the pork in the strainer and reserve the cooking liquid.

Stem the chile peppers. Tear in half and remove and discard the seeds (wear plastic gloves when handling).

Heat a comal (a griddle for cooking tortillas) or large nonstick skillet over medium-high heat. Add the chile peppers and roast for 20 seconds per side, or

(continued)

until fragrant and toasted. (Alternatively, you can roast the chile peppers under the broiler.) Transfer to a medium bowl. Add the apricots, raisins, and hot water. Let soak for 30 minutes, or until softened. Drain. Chop the apricots.

Reheat the comal or skillet over medium-high heat. Add the tomatoes and roast, turning occasionally, for 8 minutes, or until charred and blistered. Transfer to a food processor or blender. Add the tomatillos, onions, and garlic to the pan. Roast, turning occasionally, for 8 minutes, or until charred. Transfer to the food processor or blender along with the toast. Add the almonds, peanuts, and sesame seeds to the pan. Cook, stirring, for 2 minutes, or until toasted and brown. Transfer all but 1 tablespoon of the sesame seeds to the food processor or blender. Add the chile-pepper mixture, oregano, thyme, anise seeds, ½ teaspoon black pepper, and cloves to the food processor or blender. Puree the mixture until smooth. If the mixture is not wet enough to puree, add up to 1 cup of the reserved cooking liquid.

Heat the lard or oil in a large deep nonstick skillet over medium heat. Add the chile-pepper puree, cinnamon stick, and avocado leaf (if using). Cook and stir for 5 minutes, or until thick and fragrant. Stir in the honey, cocoa, and 4 cups of the reserved cooking liquid. Simmer, stirring often, for 10 minutes, or until thick and flavorful.

Stir in the pork and simmer for 10 minutes, or until the pork is tender and the sauce is flavorful. Season with salt and black pepper, if desired. If the sauce gets too thick, add a little more cooking liquid. Before serving, remove and discard the cinnamon stick and avocado leaf.

Makes 8 servings

Cooking Tip

✦ Avocado leaf adds a subtle licorice-like flavor to Mexican dishes. It is available at Hispanic markets and through the sources on page 66.

Variation

Chicken in Oaxacan Mole: Replace the pork loin with 2 pounds boneless, skinless chicken breasts.

CHILE-MARINATED PORK WITH BLACK BEAN SALSA

Puerco en
adobo con
salsa de frijoles
negros

México
United
States

Nutrition Snapshot	Before	After
Per serving		
Calories	661	357
Total Fat g.	41.7	8.5
Saturated Fat g.	14.1	3.6
Cholesterol mg.	113	66

Here's a quick and easy dish that's bursting with the smoky flavors of chipotle chiles (smoked jalapeño chile peppers). It features the leanest, most tender cut of pork there is: tenderloin. Accompanying the pork is a colorful black bean salsa. For extra color and crunch, I sprinkle the pork with fresh pomegranate seeds. If pomegranate is unavailable, use finely chopped red bell peppers.

2	small pork tenderloins (1 pound total), trimmed of all visible fat
2–4	canned chipotle chile peppers, coarsely chopped (wear plastic gloves when handling)
3	cloves garlic, coarsely chopped
1	shallot or ¼ small red onion, coarsely chopped
½	cup orange juice
¼	cup lime juice
3	tablespoons red-wine vinegar
1	teaspoon dried oregano
¼	teaspoon ground allspice
	Salt and ground black pepper
3	cups Black Bean Salsa (page 303)
¼	cup Cumin-Scented Sour Cream (page 382) or nonfat sour cream
1	pomegranate, cut and broken into individual seeds

Arrange the pork in a 13" × 9" glass or ceramic baking dish.

In a food processor or blender, combine the chile peppers, garlic, shallots or onions, orange juice, lime juice, vinegar, oregano, and allspice. Puree until smooth.

Spoon the marinade evenly over the pork. Cover and marinate in the refrigerator for 8 to 12 hours. Turn 2 or 3 times while marinating.

Preheat the grill or broiler to medium-high.

Season the pork with salt and black pepper. Grill or broil the pork 4" from the heat for 6 to 8 minutes per side, or until the internal temperature registers 160°F on a meat thermometer. Transfer the pork to a cutting board and let stand for 3 minutes. Thinly slice on the diagonal.

Mound ⅔ cup of the salsa in the center of each of 4 dinner plates. Divide the pork among the plates, fanning out the slices around the salsa. Squirt or dollop the sour cream over the pork. Sprinkle each dish with the pomegranate seeds.

Makes 4 servings

SANCOCHO

Sancocho

Various countries

Nutrition Snapshot	Before	After
Per serving		
Calories	756	488
Total Fat g.	36.1	13.4
Saturated Fat g.	13.8	3.8
Cholesterol mg.	130	91

This rib-sticking stew is a favorite throughout the Spanish-speaking Caribbean and Colombia. In the Dominican Republic, it's a popular Sunday supper. Sancocho is so popular that there's even a Spanish verb, sancochar, which means "to stew." To make a healthier stew, I use leaner cuts of meat and cut back on the oil for sautéing. Feel free to customize the recipe using different cuts of meat or vegetables. Serve with Basic White Rice (page 159).

MEAT AND MARINADE

- 12 ounces lean pork tenderloin, cut into 1" pieces
- 12 ounces boneless, skinless chicken breasts, cut into 1" pieces
- 8 ounces lean beef (such as chuck) or lamb, cut into 1" pieces
- ½ cup sour orange juice (see page 63) or 6 tablespoons lime juice + 2 tablespoons orange juice
- 3 cloves garlic, minced
- 2 bay leaves

SOFRITO

- 2 tablespoons olive oil
- 1 large onion, finely chopped
- 5 scallions, trimmed and finely chopped
- 1 green bell pepper, finely chopped
- 4 cloves garlic, minced
- 3–6 jalapeño chile peppers, seeded, if desired, and finely chopped (wear plastic gloves when handling)

- 6 leaves culantro or 6 sprigs fresh cilantro
- 6 tablespoons chopped fresh flat-leaf parsley
- 6 tablespoons chopped fresh cilantro
- 12 cups water
  - Salt and ground black pepper
- 12 ounces taro, peeled and cut into 1" pieces
- 12 ounces yuca, peeled (see tip) and cut into 1" pieces
- 12 ounces calabaza, peeled and cut into 1" pieces
- 12 ounces yams or potatoes, peeled and cut into 1" pieces
- 1 green plantain, cut crosswise into 8 pieces
- 2 ears corn, shucked and cut crosswise into 1" pieces
- 1–2 tablespoons red-wine vinegar

To make the meat and marinade: In a large glass or stainless steel bowl, combine the pork, chicken, and beef or lamb. Add the sour orange juice or lime juice and orange juice, garlic, and bay leaves. Toss to coat. Cover and marinate in the refrigerator for 30 to 60 minutes.

To make the sofrito: Heat the oil in a large stockpot over medium heat. Add the onions, scallions, bell peppers, garlic, chile peppers, culantro or cilantro, 4 tablespoons of the parsley, and 4 tablespoons of the cilantro. Cook, stirring occasionally, for 4 minutes, or until the onions are soft but not brown. Add the meat and marinade. Cook for 5 minutes. Increase the heat to high, add the water, and bring to a boil. Skim off any foam that rises to the surface. Reduce the heat to medium and simmer, skimming occasionally, for 30 minutes. Season with salt and black pepper.

Add the taro, yuca, calabaza, yams or potatoes, plantains, and corn. Simmer for 1 hour, or until the calabaza has disintegrated and the meat is soft and tender. Stir in 1 tablespoon of the vinegar, the remaining 2 tablespoons parsley, and the remaining 2 tablespoons cilantro. The broth should be highly seasoned; add more vinegar, salt, and black pepper, if desired. Divide the mixture among 8 serving bowls.

Makes 8 servings

Cooking Tip

✦ To peel the yuca, stand the pieces, cut side down, on a cutting board. Cut off the peel with a paring knife using downward strokes

Variation

Seafood Sancocho: Substitute 1 pound white fish (such as grouper, snapper, or pompano) and 1 pound shrimp, peeled and deveined, for the meat. Cook all the vegetables first, then add the fish and shrimp toward the end of the cooking time. Cook the seafood for 10 minutes, or until the fish breaks into pieces when pressed and the shrimp turn bright pink.

Regional Variations

Puerto Rican Sancocho: Omit the scallions and jalapeño chile peppers from the sofrito. Add 1 red bell pepper and 1 tomato to the sofrito. Substitute 2 sliced green plantains for the taro. Add ½ cup tomato sauce when adding the vegetables to the stew.

Colombian Sancocho: Use 2 pounds of beef instead of the pork, chicken, beef or lamb. Omit the jalapeño chile peppers and culantro from the sofrito. Substitute white and yellow potatoes for the taro and calabaza.

LAMB FRICASSE

Fricasé de cordero   *Cuba*
Puerto Rico

Nutrition Snapshot	Before	After
Per serving		
Calories	645	452
Total Fat g.	38.9	13.4
Saturated Fat g.	11.6	3.6
Cholesterol mg.	198	101

Fricasses are popular throughout the Spanish-speaking Caribbean. This one—a specialty of my Cuban friend, Elida Proenza—features lamb instead of the usual chicken. To cut the fat in the traditional recipe, I replace some of the lamb with potatoes and chickpeas. To shorten the cooking time, the fricasse is done in a pressure cooker. Stove-top cooking instructions are included in the tip on the opposite page.

1	pound lean lamb (from the leg), cut into 2" × ¼" pieces
½	red bell pepper, cut into ¼" strips
2	cloves garlic, thinly sliced
½	teaspoon dried oregano
¼	teaspoon ground cumin
	Salt and ground black pepper
1	bay leaf
½	cup dry white wine or nonalcoholic white wine
1	tablespoon canola oil

1	medium onion, finely chopped
2	cloves garlic, minced
3	tablespoons chopped fresh cilantro
1	cup tomato sauce
1	pound baking potatoes, peeled and cut into 1" cubes
1	cup cooked or canned chickpeas, rinsed and drained
2	tablespoons chopped fresh flat-leaf parsley

In a large glass or ceramic bowl, combine the lamb, bell peppers, sliced garlic, oregano, cumin, ¼ teaspoon salt, ½ teaspoon black pepper, bay leaf, and wine. Cover and marinate in the refrigerator for 30 to 60 minutes.

Drain the lamb and bell peppers, reserving the marinade. Blot the lamb and bell peppers dry with a paper towel.

Heat the oil in a pressure cooker over high heat. Add the lamb and cook, stirring often, for 5 minutes, or until lightly browned. Transfer the lamb to a plate. Discard all but 1 tablespoon of the fat. Add the onions, minced garlic, cilantro, and the reserved bell pepper pieces to the cooker. Reduce the heat to medium and cook, stirring often, for 4 minutes, or until the onions are soft but not brown. Stir in the lamb, the reserved marinade, and the tomato sauce. Increase the heat to high and bring to a boil. Reduce the heat to medium, place the lid on the pressure cooker, and cook for 18 minutes.

Transfer to the sink and run cold water over the lid to cool it down. Uncover and add the potatoes and chickpeas. Re-cover the pressure cooker and cook over medium-low heat for 5 minutes, or until the lamb is very tender and the potatoes are cooked. Season with more salt and black pepper, if desired. Transfer to a platter and garnish with the parsley.

Makes 4 servings

Cooking Tip

✦ If you don't have a pressure cooker, you can use a 4-quart soup pot instead and proceed as directed. After bringing the fricasse to a boil, cover, reduce the heat to medium-low, and simmer for 1½ hours. Check occasionally and add water as necessary to keep the fricasse from drying out during cooking.

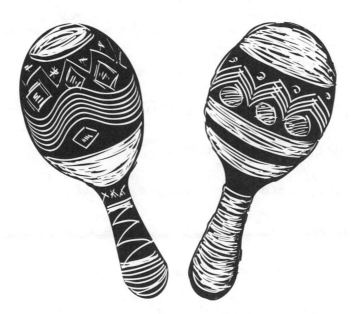

SAUCES AND SALSAS
Salsas

Is any word more evocative of the bold, dynamic flavors of Latin America than *salsa*? The term embraces an endless range of vibrant condiments, from the Yucatán's Roasted Habanero Salsa (page 306) to the smoky chipotle salsas of central México to the versatile chirmols (tomato salsas) of El Salvador.

Not all salsas are based on tomatoes or chiles. Puerto Rico's Cilantro-Pepper Sauce (page 311) is a type of salsa. So is Chimichurri (page 310). Even Cuba's universal table condiment, mojo—a tart, garlicky vinaigrette fragrant with cumin and oregano—is a type of salsa.

Not all salsas are served raw. Some are cooked, like México's Ranch-Style Tomato Salsa (page 296), and Central American Tomato Sauce (page 301).

So dig in! Like the music that sets your feet on fire, salsa will make your taste buds dance. Best of all, most salsas are naturally healthy and quick to assemble.

RECIPES

Pronto!

TOMATO, ONION, AND JALAPEÑO SALSA

Pico de gallo

México

Nutrition Snapshot	Before	After
Per ¼ cup		
Calories	13	13
Total Fat g.	0.1	0.1
Saturated Fat g.	0	0
Cholesterol mg.	0	0

Pico de gallo *literally means "rooster beak" in Spanish—a wry reference, perhaps, to its lively bite.*

2	tomatoes, finely chopped	1	clove garlic, minced
2–3	jalapeño chile peppers, finely chopped (wear plastic gloves when handling)	¼	cup finely chopped fresh cilantro
		2–3	tablespoons lime juice
1	small onion, finely chopped		Salt and ground black pepper

In a medium bowl, combine the tomatoes, chile peppers, onions, garlic, cilantro, and 2 tablespoons of the lime juice. Season with salt and black pepper. Toss to mix. Season with more lime juice and salt, if desired.

Makes 2 cups

Pronto!

RANCH-STYLE TOMATO SALSA

Salsa ranchera

México
United States

Nutrition Snapshot	Before	After
Per ½ cup		
Calories	32	32
Total Fat g.	0.3	0.3
Saturated Fat g.	0.1	0.1
Cholesterol mg.	0	0

Here's a cooked salsa that should be part of your basic repertoire. Charring the vegetables gives them a rich, smoky flavor. Serve the sauce with egg dishes like Huevos Rancheros (page 186). Or stir it into Basic White Rice (page 159). You could even serve it over pasta. Use as many chile peppers as you like.

4	tomatoes	3	cloves garlic
1–3	jalapeño or serrano chile peppers, seeded (wear plastic gloves when handling)	¼	cup chopped fresh cilantro
		3–4	tablespoons lime juice
1	large onion, quartered		Salt and ground black pepper

LATIN SUPER FOOD: CHILE PEPPERS

Chile peppers have been around for almost 9,000 years. Despite their long history, the spicy pods are only just beginning to catch on in the United States. And it's not just the chiles' flavor that Americans are after. Chile peppers have some important healing properties, too. One medium-size red chile packs 3 milligrams of beta-carotene (about 20 percent of what experts recommend you should get each day), almost 100 percent of the Daily Value (DV) for vitamin A, and almost twice the DV for vitamin C. These nutrients make chile peppers a sure bet against a host of diseases. Research shows that diets high in nutrient-rich fruits and vegetables like chiles can protect against many types of cancer. One study of more than 1,500 men in Chicago found that eating an additional 12 to 24 milligrams of beta-carotene (4 to 8 chiles) and another 50 to 100 milligrams of vitamin C each day (just 1 chile) lowered risk of death by 31 percent.

Capsaicin, the substance that gives chiles their heat, has a healing power all its own. According to conventional wisdom, people with sensitive stomachs should avoid eating spicy foods. But scientists have found that chile peppers don't cause ulcers. What's more, they can help prevent them. Canadian researchers discovered that capsaicin stunts the growth of the *Helicobacter pylori* bacteria that may be responsible for many ulcers. And a study of 190 Chinese people found that those who ate the most chile peppers had the fewest incidences of ulcers, while those who ate the least chiles had more ulcers.

It's well-known that chile peppers can also help open your sinuses when you have a cold. There's no better remedy for a stuffy nose than a bowl of spicy soup or a few bites of fresh chile pepper, says Hector Balcazar, Ph.D., associate professor of community nutrition and public health in the department of family resources and human development and a member of the affiliated faculty at the Hispanic Research Center at Arizona State University in Tempe. So don't be afraid to turn up the heat with a little spicy food. Next time you're looking for a burst of flavor, fire up with chile peppers.

Preheat a grill or broiler to high.

Place the tomatoes, chile peppers, onions, and garlic on a grill tray or broiler pan. Grill or broil 4" from the heat. The tomatoes and chile peppers will take 2 minutes per side, or until the skins are blistered and charred. The onions will take 3 minutes per side, or until browned. The garlic will take 4 to 5 minutes per side, or until softened.

In a food processor, combine the chile peppers, onions, and garlic. Puree to a coarse paste. Add the tomatoes, cilantro, and 3 tablespoons of the lime juice. Season with salt and black pepper. Process briefly to combine. (To make the salsa in a blender, add all the ingredients at once and puree.) Transfer to a medium saucepan. Simmer over medium heat for 5 minutes, or until richly flavored. The salsa should be highly seasoned; add more salt or lime juice, if desired.

Makes 3 cups

Cooking Tip

✦ You can also char the vegetables in a comal (a griddle for cooking tortillas) or heavy skillet. Set the pan over medium-high heat. When hot, add the tomatoes, onions, garlic, and chile peppers. Cook, turning occasionally, for 5 minutes, or until the vegetables are lightly browned.

Pronto!

CHARRED TOMATO SALSA WITH CHIPOTLE CHILES

Salsa de chipotle   *México*

Nutrition Snapshot	Before	After
Per 1/3 cup		
Calories	18	18
Total Fat g.	0.2	0.2
Saturated Fat g.	0	0
Cholesterol mg.	0	0

Here's a bold, smoky salsa that's perfect for serving at a barbecue. To heighten the smoke flavor, I char the tomatoes on the grill and use chipotle (smoked jalapeño) chile peppers.

1–3	dried or canned chipotle chile peppers		3	tablespoons chopped fresh cilantro
2	large tomatoes		2–3	tablespoons lime juice
½	medium onion			Salt and ground black pepper
1	clove garlic			

If using dried chile peppers, for a mild salsa, tear open the chile peppers and remove and discard the ribs and seeds (wear plastic gloves when handling). For a spicier salsa, leave the seeds in. Place the chile peppers in a small bowl with hot water. Let soak for 15 to 20 minutes, or until pliable. If using canned chile peppers, leave them as they are.

Preheat the grill or broiler to high.

Grill the tomatoes or broil 4" from the heat for 2 minutes per side, or until the skins are blistered and charred. Grill or broil the onion for 3 minutes per side, or until browned.

In a food processor, combine the onion, garlic, and chile peppers. Puree to a coarse paste. Add the tomatoes, cilantro, and 2 tablespoons of the lime juice. Season with salt and black pepper. Process briefly to combine. (To make the salsa in a blender, add all the ingredients at once and puree.) The salsa should be highly seasoned; add more salt or lime juice, if desired.

Makes 2 cups

Pronto!

CREOLE TOMATO SALSA

Salsa criolla

Various countries

Nutrition Snapshot	Before	After
Per 2 tablespoons		
Calories	47	9
Total Fat g.	4.6	0.3
Saturated Fat g.	0.6	0.1
Cholesterol mg.	0	0

Part salsa and part salad, this colorful relish is a traditional accompaniment to grilled meats in the southern part of South America. I use considerably less olive oil than in the traditional recipe. The relish is so loaded with flavor, you won't miss the fat.

2	tomatoes, finely chopped	1	teaspoon red-pepper flakes
1	sweet onion, finely chopped	1	teaspoon dried oregano
1	green bell pepper, finely chopped	2–3	tablespoons red-wine vinegar
¼	cup finely chopped fresh flat-leaf parsley	1½	teaspoons extra-virgin olive oil
1	clove garlic, minced		Salt and ground black pepper

In a large bowl, combine the tomatoes, onions, bell peppers, parsley, garlic, red-pepper flakes, oregano, 2 tablespoons of the vinegar, and the oil. Season with salt and black pepper. Toss to mix. The salsa should be highly seasoned; add more salt and vinegar, if desired.

Makes 3 cups

Cooking Tip

✦ This salsa tastes best when served within 1 hour of preparation.

Pronto!

CENTRAL AMERICAN TOMATO SALSA

Chirmol

Various countries

Nutrition Snapshot	Before	After
Per ½ cup		
Calories	96	16
Total Fat g.	9.1	0.1
Saturated Fat g.	1.2	0
Cholesterol mg.	0	0

Chirmol refers to a family of Central American sauces that can be served raw, like Mexican salsa, or cooked, like a European tomato sauce. Here's the salsa-style version. Serve it with grilled meats, chicken, seafood, or Salvadoran Stuffed Tortillas (page 206).

2 tomatoes, peeled (see page 383), seeded, and finely chopped	1 clove garlic, minced
1 small white onion, finely chopped	¼ cup chopped fresh cilantro
4 radishes, finely chopped (optional)	2–3 tablespoons lime juice or lemon juice
2 scallions, trimmed and finely chopped	2–3 tablespoons white vinegar
2 jalapeño chile peppers, seeded and finely chopped (wear plastic gloves when handling)	2 tablespoons water
	Salt and ground black pepper

In a large serving bowl, combine the tomatoes, onions, radishes (if using), scallions, chile peppers, garlic, cilantro, 2 tablespoons of the lime juice or lemon juice, 2 tablespoons of the vinegar, and the water. Season with salt and black pepper. Stir to mix. The salsa should be highly seasoned; add more lime juice or lemon juice and vinegar, if desired.

Makes 2 cups

Pronto!

CENTRAL AMERICAN TOMATO SAUCE

Chirmol frito

Various countries

Nutrition Snapshot	Before	After
Per ¼ cup		
Calories	28	28
Total Fat g.	1.8	1.8
Saturated Fat g.	0.2	0.2
Cholesterol mg.	0	0

Here's Central America's version of cooked tomato sauce. The vegetables are roasted in a dry skillet to give them a smoky flavor. Serve the sauce with grilled meat, broiled fish, or Salvadoran Stuffed Tortillas (page 206).

2	large tomatoes		2	tablespoons chopped fresh flat-leaf parsley
1	small onion, halved		1	tablespoon lime juice
1	jalapeño chile pepper, seeded (wear plastic gloves when handling)		½	teaspoon dried oregano
2	cloves garlic			Salt and ground black pepper
1	tablespoon olive oil			

Heat a large, heavy nonstick skillet over medium heat. Add the tomatoes and onions. Cook, turning occasionally, for 4 minutes. Add the chile peppers and garlic. Cook, turning occasionally, for 8 to 10 minutes, or until all the vegetables are browned on all sides. Peel off as much of the vegetable skins as possible. Don't worry about a few charred pieces of skin; they'll add a nice smoky flavor. Transfer the vegetables to a food processor or blender. Puree until smooth.

Heat the oil in the skillet. Add the parsley, lime juice, oregano, and vegetable puree. Cook, stirring often, for 5 minutes, or until thick and flavorful. Season with salt and black pepper.

Makes 1½ cups

SALSA VERDE

Salsa verde

México

Nutrition Snapshot	Before	After
Per ¼ cup		
Calories	28	28
Total Fat g.	0.6	0.6
Saturated Fat g.	0	0
Cholesterol mg.	0	0

Salsa verde is one of the cornerstones of Mexican cuisine. It's a tangy green salsa made from piquant tomatillos—a fruit related to the gooseberry that is recognizable by its papery husk. Tomatillos look and taste somewhat like green tomatoes crossed with tart strawberries. You can find fresh ones in Mexican markets and most large supermarkets. The following recipe is done in the style of the Yucatán. The ingredients are pan-roasted to add an extra dimension of flavor (you could also grill or broil them). Elsewhere in México, the tomatillos may be boiled instead of roasted.

1	pound tomatillos, husked and rinsed
1	small onion, quartered
1–3	serrano or jalapeño chile peppers, seeded (wear plastic gloves when handling)
2	cloves garlic

⅓	cup chopped fresh cilantro
½	teaspoon sugar or honey (optional)
⅓–½	cup Chicken Stock (page 360), fat-free reduced-sodium chicken broth, or water
	Salt and ground black pepper

Heat a comal (a griddle for cooking tortillas) or large nonstick skillet over medium-high heat. Add the tomatillos, onions, chile peppers, and garlic. Cook, turning as needed, for 5 minutes, or until the vegetables are lightly browned. (You may wish to wear oven mitts to protect your hands and arms because the tomatillos may split, releasing hot juices.) Don't worry if the vegetables char in a few spots.

Transfer the vegetables to a blender or food processor. Puree to a smooth paste. Add the cilantro, sugar or honey (if using), and ⅓ cup of the stock, broth, or water. Season with salt and black pepper. The salsa should be pourable; add more stock, broth, or water, if needed.

Makes 2 cups

Cooking Tips

✦ If you can't find fresh tomatillos, use canned tomatillos from the international aisle of your supermarket. In a blender or food processor, puree the canned tomatillos (with juice), onions, chile peppers, and garlic. Transfer to a medium saucepan over medium heat. Simmer for 5 minutes. Stir in the cilantro and sugar or honey (if using). Omit the stock, broth, or water. Season with salt and black pepper.

✦ For extra spice, leave the seeds in the chiles.

Pronto!

BLACK BEAN SALSA

Salsa de
frijoles negros

*United
States*

Nutrition Snapshot	Before	After
Per ¼ cup		
Calories	102	43
Total Fat g.	6.3	0.2
Saturated Fat g.	0.5	0.04
Cholesterol mg.	0	0

If you're accustomed to black beans in soups and refried beans, this refreshing salsa will come as a pleasant surprise.

2	cups cooked or rinsed and drained canned black beans
½	small red onion, finely chopped
½	red bell pepper, finely chopped
1	rib celery, finely chopped
1	poblano chile pepper or ½ green bell pepper, finely chopped (wear plastic gloves when handling)

½–1	habanero chile pepper or 1–2 jalapeño chile peppers, seeded and minced (wear plastic gloves when handling)
¼	cup chopped fresh cilantro
3	tablespoons lime juice
	Salt and ground black pepper

In a medium bowl, combine the beans, onions, red bell peppers, celery, poblano chile peppers or green bell peppers, habanero or jalapeño chile peppers, cilantro, and lime juice. Toss to mix. Season with salt and black pepper.

Makes 3½ cups

MANGO SALSA

Salsa de mango *United States*

Nutrition Snapshot	Before	After
Per ½ cup		
Calories	68	68
Total Fat g.	0.3	0.3
Saturated Fat g.	0.1	0.1
Cholesterol mg.	0	0

You won't find this recipe in any traditional Latin American cookbook. But visit a cutting-edge Latino restaurant in Houston, Miami, or New York City, and you'll experience all sorts of fruit salsas—a natural fusion of the Latin American passion for flavor and the North American obsession with health. Naturally low in fat, mango salsa makes the perfect pick-me-up for a simple grilled chicken breast, fish fillet, or lean cut of pork. Or try it with Tortilla Chips (page 70).

2 mangoes

1 habanero or jalapeño chile pepper, minced (wear plastic gloves when handling)

1 cucumber, peeled, seeded, and finely chopped

½ red bell pepper, finely chopped

¼ red onion, finely chopped

1 tablespoon minced fresh or crystallized ginger

¼ cup finely chopped fresh cilantro

3–4 tablespoons lime juice

1–2 tablespoon light brown sugar (optional)

Peel the mangoes and cut the flesh off the seeds. Cut the mango into ¼" pieces. You should have about 1½ cups. Transfer to a serving bowl. Add the chile peppers, cucumbers, bell peppers, onions, ginger, cilantro, lime juice, and brown sugar (if using). Toss to mix. The salsa should be a little tart, a little sweet, and very highly seasoned; add more lime juice and brown sugar, if desired.

Makes 3 cups

Cooking Tips

✦ The easiest way to seed a cucumber is to halve it lengthwise and scrape out the seeds with a melon baller or spoon.

✦ This salsa tastes best when served within 20 minutes of preparation.

✦ For a milder salsa, remove the seeds from the chile pepper.

Variation

Pineapple Salsa: Replace the mango with 1½ cups chopped pineapple.

SPANISH-CARIBBEAN SALSA

Mojito
isleño

*Puerto Rico
Dominican
Republic*

Nutrition Snapshot	Before	After
Per ¼ cup		
Calories	149	59
Total Fat g.	13.7	3.6
Saturated Fat g.	1.8	0.5
Cholesterol mg.	0	0

Salsa *is a recurring theme throughout the cuisines of Latin America, even when it's not strictly called salsa. Puerto Rico's Cilantro-Pepper Sauce (page 311) is a sort of salsa made with garlic and parsley. Mojito (mo-HEE-toe) is the Spanish-Caribbean version, traditionally served as a dip for Plantain Chips (page 71) and Twice-Cooked Plantains (page 142). But don't overlook serving mojito with tortilla chips or even as a cocktail sauce for shrimp and other seafood. I've reduced the oil in the traditional recipe, letting the bold flavors of the peppers and seasonings speak for themselves.*

6	rocotillo chile peppers (see page 55) or 2 tablespoons chopped red bell peppers	2	tablespoons rinsed and drained capers	
1	large tomato, peeled (see page 383) and seeded	1	teaspoon dried oregano	
½	green bell pepper, chopped	¼	cup tomato paste	
½	cup fresh cilantro leaves	2	tablespoons extra-virgin olive oil	
¼	onion, chopped	1–1½	tablespoons red-wine vinegar	
4	cloves garlic, chopped		Salt and ground black pepper	

In a food processor or blender, combine the chile peppers or red bell peppers, tomatoes, green bell peppers, cilantro, onions, garlic, capers, and oregano. Puree to a smooth paste. Add the tomato paste, oil, and 1 tablespoon of the vinegar. Process briefly to combine. Taste and add more vinegar, if desired. Season with salt and black pepper.

Makes 2 cups

ROASTED HABANERO SALSA

X'nipec

México

Nutrition Snapshot	Before	After
Per 2 tablespoons		
Calories	13	13
Total Fat g.	0.1	0.1
Saturated Fat g.	0	0
Cholesterol mg.	0	0

X'*nipec (shnee-PECK) is one of the hottest salsas on Earth. It comes from the Yucatán region of México and owes its firepower to the habanero chile, which is 50 times hotter than a jalapeño. The name of the salsa literally means "dog's nose"—perhaps because of its ferocious bite.*

8 habanero chile peppers, stems removed (wear plastic gloves when handling)

1 medium tomato

1 medium onion, quartered

2 tablespoons chopped fresh cilantro

¼ cup sour orange juice (see page 63) or lime juice

Salt

Heat a comal (a griddle for cooking tortillas) or medium nonstick skillet over medium-high heat. Add the chile peppers and roast, turning occasionally, for 3 to 5 minutes, or until lightly charred. Transfer to a plate. Add the tomato to the pan and roast, turning occasionally, for 6 to 8 minutes, or until the skin is charred and blistered. Transfer to the plate with the chile peppers. Add the onions to the pan and roast, turning occasionally, for 6 to 8 minutes, or until lightly charred. Transfer to the plate. When cool enough to handle, remove and discard as much of the tomato and chile skins (wear plastic gloves when handling the habaneros) as possible with a paring knife or your fingers. Don't worry about a few charred pieces of skin; they'll add a nice smoky flavor.

Coarsely chop the chile peppers, tomatoes, and onions. Transfer to a serving bowl. Stir in the cilantro and sour orange juice or lime juice. Season with salt.

Makes 1 cup

Cooking Tip

✦ For a little less heat, seed the chiles before chopping.

Pronto!

TAMARIND SAUCE

Salsa de
tamarindo

United States

Nutrition Snapshot	Before	After
Per 2 tablespoons		
Calories	412	412
Total Fat g.	0.5	0.5
Saturated Fat g.	0.1	0.1
Cholesterol mg.	0	0

Tamarind is a warm-climate seed pod grown widely in India and loved by Caribbean and Mexican cooks. Dark in color and sweet-and-sour in flavor, it is a key ingredient in Worcestershire sauce. In this Caribbean-inspired sauce, tamarind lends a pleasantly rich fruity flavor. Try it with almost any seafood—especially grouper.

⅓ cup tamarind water or puree (see tip)

4–6 tablespoons light brown sugar

3–4 tablespoons soy sauce

3 tablespoons pineapple juice

1 small onion, minced

1 clove garlic, minced

1 jalapeño chile pepper, minced (wear plastic gloves when handling)

3 tablespoons chopped fresh cilantro

Ground black pepper

In a small saucepan over medium heat, combine the tamarind water or puree, 4 tablespoons of the brown sugar, 3 tablespoons of the soy sauce, the pineapple juice, onions, garlic, and chile peppers. Simmer for 5 minutes, or until richly flavored. Stir in the cilantro and season with black pepper. The sauce should be a little sweet, sour, and salty; add more brown sugar and soy sauce, if desired.

Makes 1 cup

Cooking Tip

✦ Look for tamarind water or puree (*pulpa de tamarindo*) in Latin American, Asian, and Indian markets. Some large supermarkets carry it in the international aisle. Or make it at home using the recipe on page 381.

VENEZUELAN AVOCADO SAUCE

Guasacaca

Venezuela

Nutrition Snapshot	Before	After
Per ¼ cup		
Calories	147	36
Total Fat g.	15	3
Saturated Fat g.	1.8	0.5
Cholesterol mg.	0	0

Guasacaca (wa-sa-KA-ka) is Venezuela's answer to guacamole. It's a creamy avocado puree spiced with cilantro and bell peppers. Unlike its Mexican cousin, guasacaca is traditionally served as a sauce for grilled meats, not as a dip. Of course, there's no reason why you couldn't serve guasacaca with tortilla chips or even with sliced fresh vegetables.

1	large avocado, pitted, peeled, and coarsely chopped
1	small onion, coarsely chopped
½	green bell pepper, coarsely chopped
½	cup chopped fresh cilantro

1	clove garlic
1½–2	tablespoons white vinegar
	Salt
½	teaspoon black pepper
1	cup water

In a food processor or blender, combine the avocados, onions, bell peppers, cilantro, garlic, 1½ tablespoons of the vinegar, 1 teaspoon salt, black pepper, and water. Puree until smooth. The mixture should be highly seasoned; taste and add more vinegar and salt, if desired.

Makes 3 cups

Cooking Tip

✦ This sauce should be eaten within a few hours of preparation, as the avocados tend to lose their flavor over time. In a pinch, you can store the sauce in an airtight container for up to a day.

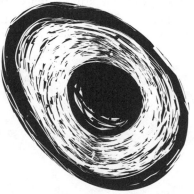

Pronto!

CUBAN MOJO

Mojo cubano

Cuba

Nutrition Snapshot	Before	After
Per 2 tablespoons		
Calories	129	50
Total Fat g.	13.6	4.6
Saturated Fat g.	1.8	0.6
Cholesterol mg.	0	0

Mojo (MO-ho) is Cuba's national table sauce—a tart, garlicky vinaigrette fragrant with cumin and oregano. No Cuban meal would be complete without mojo. Cubans splash it on everything from seafood to vegetables to sandwiches. This mojo goes particularly well with pork and boiled yuca. The citrus fruit of choice is naranja agria, or sour orange (see page 63 for a full description). You can also use a combination of lime juice and orange juice, as many Cuban cooks do in the United States where sour orange is hard to come by. To trim the fat, I reduced the amount of olive oil and added a little vegetable stock.

¼	cup olive oil		½	teaspoon ground cumin
8	cloves garlic, very thinly sliced		½	teaspoon ground oregano
¾	cup sour orange juice (see page 63) or ½ cup lime juice + ¼ cup orange juice		½	teaspoon ground black pepper
				Salt
½	cup Vegetable Stock (page 361) or reduced-sodium vegetable broth		3	tablespoons chopped fresh cilantro or flat-leaf parsley

Heat the oil in a small saucepan over medium heat. Add the garlic and cook for 2 to 4 minutes, or until fragrant and pale golden brown. (Be careful not to let the garlic burn or it will become bitter.)

Remove the pan from the heat and stir in the sour orange juice or lime juice and orange juice, stock or broth, cumin, oregano, and pepper. Return the pan to the stove. Bring the sauce to a boil over high heat. (Be careful; the mixture may splatter.) Reduce the heat to medium and simmer for 3 minutes, or until the flavor has mellowed. Season with salt. Remove from the heat and let cool to room temperature. Stir in the cilantro or parsley.

Store in a glass bottle in the refrigerator for up to a week. Shake well before using.

Makes 1½ cups

MANGO MOJO

Mojo de mango

United States

Nutrition Snapshot	Before	After
Per 2 tablespoons		
Calories	19	19
Total Fat g.	0.1	0.1
Saturated Fat g.	0	0
Cholesterol mg.	0	0

Here's a fruit mojo inspired by contemporary Latino chefs. Try it with grilled fish and poultry.

- 1 large or 2 small mangoes, peeled, seeded, and cubed (1 cup)
- ½ cup chopped fresh mint leaves
- 1 jalapeño chile pepper, seeded and minced (wear plastic gloves when handling)
- 1 clove garlic, minced
- 1 tablespoon light brown sugar
- ½ cup lime juice

In a food processor or blender, combine the cubed mangoes, mint, chile peppers, garlic, brown sugar, and lime juice. Puree until smooth. Serve within a few hours, or refrigerate in a glass bottle for one day.

Makes 1½ cups

CHIMICHURRI

Chimichurri

Various countries

Nutrition Snapshot	Before	After
Per 2 tablespoons		
Calories	129	51
Total Fat g.	13.6	4.5
Saturated Fat g.	1.8	0.6
Cholesterol mg.	0	0

This pungent garlic-parsley sauce accompanies grilled meats throughout Latin America.

- 1 bunch fresh flat-leaf parsley, stemmed and minced
- 1 carrot, minced or grated
- 1 small onion, minced or grated
- ½ red bell pepper, minced or grated
- 4–8 cloves garlic, minced
- ⅔ cup Vegetable Stock (page 361) or fat-free vegetable broth
- ⅓ cup extra-virgin olive oil
- 3–5 tablespoons white-wine vinegar or white vinegar
- 1 teaspoon dried oregano
- 1 teaspoon red-pepper flakes
- Salt
- ½ teaspoon ground black pepper

In a large bowl, combine the parsley, carrots, onions, bell peppers, garlic, stock or broth, oil, 3 tablespoons of the vinegar, the oregano, red-pepper flakes, 1 teaspoon salt, and black pepper. Whisk to mix. The sauce should be highly seasoned; add more salt and vinegar, if desired. Refrigerate for up to 3 days.

Makes 2 cups

Pronto!

CILANTRO-PEPPER SAUCE

Ají-li-mójili   *Puerto Rico*

Nutrition Snapshot	Before	After
Per 1/4 cup		
Calories	175	78
Total Fat g.	18.1	6.9
Saturated Fat g.	2.4	0.9
Cholesterol mg.	0	0

▌ *like to think of this sauce as Puerto Rican pesto. It makes a delectable dip for Tortilla Chips (page 70), Plantain Chips (page 71), and Plantain Spiders (page 73). You can also use it as a marinade. Or spoon it over grilled fish, chicken, or even steak. To make a low-fat version, I cut back on the oil and use more vegetables instead.*

1	small onion, peeled and quartered		1	bunch fresh cilantro, stemmed
6	rocotillo chile peppers, stemmed and seeded, or 1/4 red bell pepper, cut into 1" pieces		4	culantro leaves or 2 tablespoons chopped fresh cilantro (optional)
2	scallions, trimmed and cut into 1" pieces		1/2	teaspoon dried oregano
			1/4	cup extra-virgin olive oil
1/2	red bell pepper, cut into 1" pieces		3–5	tablespoons red-wine vinegar
1/2	green bell pepper, cut into 1" pieces		1/4	cup water
3	cloves garlic			Salt and ground black pepper

In a food processor, combine the onions, chile peppers or bell peppers, scallions, bell peppers, garlic, cilantro, culantro or cilantro (if using), and oregano. Puree until coarsely chopped. Add the oil, 3 tablespoons of the vinegar, and the water. Puree until smooth. Season with salt and black pepper. Season with more vinegar, if desired. (To make the sauce in a blender, add all the ingredients at once and puree.)

Transfer the mixture to clean glass jars. Refrigerate for up to 3 weeks.

Makes 2 cups

Pronto!

HOTHEAD HOT SAUCE

Salsa pica pica

United States

Nutrition Snapshot	Before	After
Per tablespoon		
Calories	17	17
Total Fat g.	0.9	0.9
Saturated Fat g.	0.1	0.1
Cholesterol mg.	0	0

The Caribbean and Central America are home to the world's hottest chile pepper, the habanero. A cousin of Jamaica's infamous Scotch bonnet, the habanero chile is 50 times hotter than a jalapeño chile. This recipe is dedicated to the original hothead, my editor, David Joachim, who loves hot sauces. I like to think of it as the ultimate flavor booster. It can be stirred into soups and stews or served over grilled meats and fish. This may be the hottest hot sauce you have ever tasted. A little goes a long way.

1	mango
12	habanero chile peppers, stemmed (wear plastic gloves when handling)
5	cloves garlic, coarsely chopped
½	cup water
⅓	cup lime juice

⅓	cup white vinegar
2	tablespoons olive oil
1	tablespoon Dijon mustard
1–2	tablespoons sugar
1–1½	teaspoons molasses
	Salt

Peel the mango. Cut the flesh off the seeds and chop the flesh. You should have about ¾ cup.

In a food processor or blender, combine the chile peppers, mangoes, garlic, water, lime juice, vinegar, oil, mustard, 1 tablespoon of the sugar, 1 teaspoon of the molasses, and 1 tablespoon salt. Puree until smooth. Transfer the mixture to a medium saucepan. Simmer over medium heat for 5 minutes, or until heated through. Taste and add more molasses and salt, if desired.

Pour the warm sauce into a 16-ounce bottle that has been sterilized in boiling water. Screw on the lid and let cool to room temperature. Store in the refrigerator. Once opened, the sauce will keep in the refrigerator for up to a month. (You can use the sauce right away, but the flavor will improve if you refrigerate it for a few days. Shake well before using.)

Makes 2 cups

Variation

Tongue-Scorching Habanero Hot Sauce: Use red Caribbean habanero chiles, which check in at 450,000 Scoville units. That's nearly twice as hot as a typical habanero and 100 times hotter than a jalapeño.

PICKLED ONION
RELISH

Encurtido

Nicaragua
Costa Rica

Nutrition Snapshot	Before	After
Per ½ cup		
Calories	45	45
Total Fat g.	0.2	0.2
Saturated Fat g.	0.1	0.1
Cholesterol mg.	0	0

This tangy condiment is used throughout coastal Central America as an all-purpose table sauce for empanadas, rice and bean dishes, grilled and roasted fare, and just about everything between. Spicy food–lovers will like the habanero chiles. The more tender of tongue might want to stick with jalapeño chiles. Either way, encurtido has an electrifying effect on virtually any dish that it touches.

3	large white onions, chopped
1–3	habanero or jalapeño chile peppers, thinly sliced (wear plastic gloves when handling)
3	tablespoons chopped fresh cilantro
3	tablespoons chopped fresh oregano or 1 tablespoon dried

8	whole allspice berries
8	black peppercorns
1	tablespoon salt
2–2½	cups white vinegar

In a large bowl, combine the onions, chile peppers, cilantro, oregano, allspice, peppercorns, salt, and 2 cups of the vinegar. Stir with a wooden spoon until the salt is completely dissolved. Spoon the mixture into clean glass jars. Add more vinegar, if necessary, to cover the onions. Cover the tops of the jars with plastic wrap and screw on the lids. (The plastic wrap will prevent the vinegar from corroding the metal lids.)

Let the onions pickle in the refrigerator for 24 hours before serving. Refrigerate for up to 3 weeks.

Makes 4 cups

DESSERTS, JAMS, AND SYRUPS
Postres, jaleas y almíbares

Latin Americans have been sweet on sugar ever since Christopher Columbus brought the tropical cane to the Dominican Republic in 1493. By the nineteenth century, vast sugar plantations stretched from Cuba to Brazil, and soon Latino cooks began to use the sweetener extensively in their desserts.

One of the most inventive desserts is *tres leches*, a rich cake soaked in a syrup made from three different kinds of milk. Others include creamy *natillas* (puddings), which are as sensuous as a tropical night. Golden caramel-coated Flan (page 316) is the most widely enjoyed dessert in South America.

To keep the soul of Latino desserts but shed the fat and cholesterol, evaporated skimmed milk, sweetened condensed skim milk, and reduced-fat coconut milk are a godsend. Replacing egg yolks with egg whites or fruit purees also cuts fat and cholesterol in custards and ice creams.

Need a unique holiday gift? Look no further than Sweet Potato Jam (page 340) or the distinctive Tomatoes Candied in Syrup (page 335) from the Dominican Republic.

RECIPES

FLAN

Various countries

Nutrition Snapshot	Before	After
Per serving		
Calories	509	423
Total Fat g.	7.2	0.1
Saturated Fat g.	2.9	0.1
Cholesterol mg.	221	1

Flan is universally popular in Latin America—so popular that every country in the Spanish-speaking Americas has a version. To trim the fat and cholesterol from traditional flan, I use egg substitute (or egg whites, which are the main ingredient in egg substitute) and sweetened condensed skim milk. Lemon peel and extra spices make up for the missing flavor of the egg yolks.

1½	cups sugar		2	teaspoons vanilla extract
¼	cup water		1½	teaspoons grated lemon peel or orange peel
1	can (14 ounces) sweetened condensed skim milk		½	teaspoon grated nutmeg
1	cup skim milk		½	teaspoon ground cinnamon
1¼	cups liquid egg substitute or 10 egg whites			Pinch of salt

Preheat the oven to 350°F. Bring 4 cups water to a boil.

In a small heavy saucepan over high heat, combine the sugar and water. Cover and cook for 2 minutes. Uncover the pan and reduce the heat to medium. Cook, without stirring, for 5 to 8 minutes, or until the sugar has caramelized (it will turn a dark golden brown).

Quickly divide the caramelized sugar among six 6-ounce ramekins or custard cups, rotating each to coat the bottom and sides. Avoid touching the hot caramel. Let the caramel cool until hardened.

In a large bowl, whisk together the condensed milk, skim milk, egg substitute or egg whites, vanilla extract, lemon peel or orange peel, nutmeg, cinnamon, and salt. Spoon on top of the hardened caramel in each ramekin or cup. Set the ramekins or cups in a roasting pan and pour ½" of the boiling water around them. Bake for 45 minutes, or until the custard is set. Transfer to a rack to cool. Refrigerate for at least 4 hours or overnight.

To unmold, run the tip of a knife around the inside edge of each ramekin or cup. Cover with a small plate and invert. Shake until the custard slips loose. Spoon any caramel left in the ramekin or cup around the custard.

Makes 6 servings

¡Fiesta!
Cuban Christmas Eve Feast

Christmas Eve in Cuba is celebrated with good food and family togetherness. The star of the Christmas meal is usually Lechón asado (Roast Pork). For the crowning touch, flan is a popular dessert. Here's a traditional Nochebuena (Christmas Eve) menu that celebrates the season without piling on the pounds.

White Bean and Collard Green Soup (*Caldo gallego*, **page 101**)

Roast Pork (*Lechón asado*, **page 286**) **with Cuban Mojo** (*Mojo cubano*, **page 309**)

Rice and Black Bean Pilaf (*Congrí*, **page 156**)

Grilled Ripe Plantains (*Maduros*, **page 144**)

Flan (page 316)

Regional Variations

Cuban Pumpkin Flan: Replace the skim milk with ¾ cup cooked and pureed pumpkin or calabaza mixed with ¼ cup skim milk.

Venezuelan Pineapple Flan: Replace the skim milk with 1 cup drained pureed pineapple (fresh or canned).

QUINOA FLAN

Flan de quinua   *Ecuador*

Nutrition Snapshot	Before	After
Per serving		
Calories	280	250
Total Fat g.	8.1	2.3
Saturated Fat g.	3.7	0.4
Cholesterol mg.	123	2

Most North Americans think of quinoa as a grain meant for savory dishes. But in Ecuador, quinoa is often served as a pudding, cake, or dessert. The following recipe was inspired by a book called Foods of Ecuador *by Michelle Fried. Unlike most desserts, it's high in protein and low in fat.*

1	cup sugar
2¼	cups water
½	cup raisins
¼	cup rum or 1 teaspoon rum extract + ¼ cup water
1	cup quinoa, rinsed until the water runs clear
1	can (14 ounces) sweetened condensed skim milk
2	eggs + 4 egg whites, or 1 cup liquid egg substitute

1	tablespoon lemon juice
1½	teaspoons grated lemon peel
1½	teaspoons grated orange peel
1	teaspoon vanilla extract
½	teaspoon ground cinnamon
½	teaspoon ground nutmeg
	Pinch of salt

In a heavy medium saucepan over high heat, combine the sugar and ¼ cup of the water. Cover the pan and cook for 2 minutes. Uncover the pan, reduce the heat to medium, and cook for 5 to 8 minutes, or until dark golden brown. Do not stir.

Pour the caramelized sugar into an 8" baking pan or cake pan. Rotate the pan to coat the bottom and sides. (Take care not to burn yourself. It's a good idea to wear oven mitts to protect your hands.) Let cool until the caramel is hardened.

In a small bowl, combine the raisins and rum or rum extract and water. Let soak for 10 minutes.

Meanwhile, preheat the oven to 350°F. Bring 4 cups water to a boil.

In a large heavy saucepan over high heat, combine the quinoa and the remaining 2 cups water. Bring to a boil. Reduce the heat to medium and simmer for 15 minutes, or until the quinoa is very soft and all the water is absorbed. Remove the pan from the heat and let cool slightly. Stir in the condensed milk, eggs and egg whites or egg substitute, lemon juice, lemon peel, orange peel, vanilla extract, cinnamon, nutmeg, salt, and the raisins with their liquid. Spoon into the caramel-lined pan.

Set the pan in a roasting pan. Pour the boiling water in the outer pan until it reaches ½" up the sides of the pan. Bake for 40 minutes, or until the mixture no longer jiggles when the pan is tapped. Remove the pan from the roasting pan and transfer to a rack to cool. Refrigerate for at least 4 hours or overnight.

To unmold, run the tip of a knife around the edge of the pan. Place a platter over the pan, invert, and give a firm shake. The flan should slide out easily. Spoon any caramel left in the pan around the flan. Cut into 8 wedges.

Makes 8 servings

APRICOT MERINGUE FLAN

Pudim do claras   *Brazil*

Nutrition Snapshot	Before	After
Per serving		
Calories	301	277
Total Fat g.	0.1	0
Saturated Fat g.	0	0
Cholesterol mg.	0	0

This popular Brazilian dessert works best with a pan that is one solid piece to prevent leakage.

1¾ cups sugar	1 teaspoon grated orange peel
¾ cup dried apricots	6 large egg whites
5 cups water	½ teaspoon cream of tartar
2 tablespoons chopped crystallized ginger	1 teaspoon vanilla extract
1 teaspoon grated lemon peel	

Preheat the oven to 350°F. Bring 4 cups water to a boil.

Sprinkle ¾ cup of the sugar into an 8" metal ring mold or Bundt pan with an 8-cup capacity. Place the mold directly on the burner and cook over medium-low heat for 10 minutes, or until the sugar melts into a golden brown caramel (turn the mold often to ensure even melting). Using a spoon, rotate the mold to completely coat the interior with the caramel (wear oven mitts to protect your hands). Let cool.

Place the apricots in a small saucepan with 1 cup of the water. Bring to a simmer over medium heat. Cook for 6 minutes, or until the apricots are very tender. Transfer 3 tablespoons of the cooking liquid to a food processor or blender. Drain the apricots and add to the food processor or blender. Puree until smooth. Add the ginger, lemon peel, and orange peel. Process briefly to combine.

In a large, dry clean bowl, using an electric mixer, beat the egg whites on low speed for 1 minute. Add the cream of tartar. Gradually increase the speed to medium, then medium-high and beat for 4 to 5 minutes, or until soft peaks form. Gradually add the remaining 1 cup sugar and the vanilla extract in a thin stream.

(continued)

Continue beating for 3 to 5 minutes, or until the whites are firm and glossy but not dry. Fold the apricot puree into the egg whites. Spoon into the caramel-lined mold. Set the mold in a roasting pan. Add the boiling water to the outer pan until it reaches 1" up the sides of the pan.

Bake for 40 minutes (do not open the oven door). Turn off the oven and let the meringue cool in the oven for 1 hour without opening the oven door.

Run the tip of a knife around the edge of the mold. Place a platter over the mold and invert. The meringue should slide out easily. If not, give the mold a gentle shake. Spoon any caramel that remains in the mold on top. Slice into 6 wedges.

Makes 6 servings

SPICED MILK PUDDING

Natilla

Various countries

Nutrition Snapshot	Before	After
Per serving		
Calories	208	143
Total Fat g.	11.1	4.3
Saturated Fat g.	5.3	2.3
Cholesterol mg.	233	63

No dessert is quite as comforting as natilla, a simple milk pudding. To lighten the traditional recipe, I use fewer eggs and boost the flavor with cinnamon, anise, and lemon.

1½	cups skim milk		¼	teaspoon anise seeds, crushed
1	stick cinnamon (3" long)		¼	cup sugar
1	piece vanilla bean (3" long), halved lengthwise, or 1 teaspoon vanilla extract		1½	tablespoons cornstarch
			1	egg + 1 egg white, lightly beaten
2	strips orange peel		1	tablespoon unsalted butter
2	strips lemon peel			Ground cinnamon (optional)

In a medium saucepan over medium heat, combine the milk, cinnamon stick, vanilla bean or vanilla extract, orange peel, lemon peel, anise seeds, and 1 tablespoon of the sugar. Bring to a boil, stirring often. Remove the pan from the heat. Let stand for 10 minutes.

In a medium bowl, whisk together the remaining 3 tablespoons sugar and the cornstarch. Strain the egg and egg white into the cornstarch mixture and whisk to combine. While continuing to whisk, strain the milk mixture into the egg mixture in a thin, steady stream.

Return the mixture to the saucepan and set over medium-high heat. Bring to a boil, whisking constantly. Reduce the heat to medium and simmer for 2 minutes, or until thickened. Remove the pan from the heat and whisk in the butter.

Spoon the mixture into 4 custard cups or compote glasses. Let cool to room temperature. Refrigerate for 3 to 4 hours, or until cold. Lightly dust with ground cinnamon (if using) before serving.

Makes 4 servings

Regional Variations

Puerto Rican Milk Pudding: Replace the lemon peel and orange peel with lime peel.

Mexican Milk Pudding: Replace the white sugar with piloncillo, or brown sugar.

SPICED CHOCOLATE PUDDING

Natilla de chocolate

Various countries

Nutrition Snapshot	Before	After
Per serving		
Calories	356	203
Total Fat g.	25.2	7.4
Saturated Fat g.	13.7	3.4
Cholesterol mg.	241	63

There are times when nothing but chocolate will do. Here's a dark, rich pudding for those times.

1½	cups skim milk	6	tablespoons sugar
1	stick cinnamon (3" long)	3	tablespoons unsweetened cocoa powder
1	piece vanilla bean (3" long), halved lengthwise, or 1 teaspoon vanilla extract	1½	tablespoons cornstarch
2	strips orange peel	1	egg + 1 egg white, lightly beaten
4	whole cloves	½	ounce unsweetened chocolate, chopped
¼	teaspoon anise seeds, crushed	1	tablespoon unsalted butter

In a medium saucepan over medium heat, combine the milk, cinnamon stick, vanilla bean or vanilla extract, orange peel, cloves, anise seeds, and 2 tablespoons of the sugar. Bring to a boil, stirring often. Remove the pan from the heat. Let stand for 10 minutes.

In a medium bowl, whisk together the remaining 4 tablespoons sugar, the cocoa, and cornstarch. Strain the egg and egg white into the cocoa mixture. Whisk

(continued)

to combine. While continuing to whisk, strain the milk mixture into the egg mixture in a thin, steady stream.

Return the mixture to the saucepan and set over medium-high heat. Bring to a boil, whisking constantly. Whisk in the chocolate. Reduce the heat to medium and simmer for 4 minutes, or until the mixture is thickened. Remove the pan from the heat and whisk in the butter.

Spoon the mixture into 4 custard cups or compote glasses. Let cool to room temperature. Refrigerate for 3 to 4 hours, or until cold.

Makes 4 servings

Cooking Tip
✦ For a pudding with even less fat, omit the butter. Without the butter, each serving has only 177 calories, 4.5 grams of total fat, 1.6 grams of saturated fat, and 55 milligrams of cholesterol.

RUM-RAISIN RICE PUDDING

Arroz con leche

Various countries

Nutrition Snapshot	Before	After
Per serving		
Calories	348	185
Total Fat g.	15.4	0.2
Saturated Fat g.	11.5	0.1
Cholesterol mg.	0	1

This rice pudding owes its incredible creaminess to the type of rice used: short-grain Valencia-style rice, which is similar to Italian Arborio rice. The cholesterol goes up slightly in the new recipe because low-fat dairy products replace the high-fat (but cholesterol-free) coconut milk used in the original recipe.

½	cup golden or dark raisins	1	cup sweetened condensed skim milk
¼	cup light rum or 1 teaspoon rum extract + ¼ cup water	1	cup evaporated skimmed milk
1	cup Valencia-style rice or Arborio rice, rinsed until the water runs clear	4–6	tablespoons light brown sugar
1	stick cinnamon (3" long)	1	teaspoon grated lemon peel
1	piece vanilla bean (3" long), halved lengthwise, or 1 teaspoon vanilla extract	1	teaspoon grated orange peel
			Pinch of salt
3	cups water		Ground cinnamon or grated nutmeg (optional)

In a small bowl, combine the raisins and rum or rum extract and water. Let soak for 15 minutes, or until softened.

In a large saucepan over high heat, combine the rice, cinnamon stick, vanilla bean or vanilla extract, and water. Bring to a boil, reduce the heat to medium-low, and simmer for 20 minutes, or until the rice is tender and most of the liquid is absorbed.

Stir in the condensed milk, evaporated milk, and the raisins with their liquid. Simmer for 10 minutes, or until the rice is very soft. Stir in 4 tablespoons of the brown sugar, the lemon peel, orange peel, and salt. Cook for 5 minutes (the pudding will seem wet; it firms as it cools). Taste and add more brown sugar, if desired.

Let the pudding cool to room temperature. Remove and discard the cinnamon stick and vanilla bean (if using). Spoon the pudding into 8 martini glasses or serving bowls. Refrigerate until cold. Sprinkle each serving with cinnamon or nutmeg (if using).

Makes 8 servings

Regional Variations

Puerto Rican Rice Pudding: Replace the lemon peel and orange peel with 2 teaspoons grated lime peel.

Brazilian Coconut-Rice Pudding: Replace the evaporated skimmed milk with 1 cup light coconut milk. Sprinkle each serving with 1 tablespoon toasted shredded unsweetened dried coconut.

SHIVERING COCONUT PUDDING

Tembleque   *Puerto Rico*

Nutrition Snapshot	Before	After
Per serving		
Calories	465	189
Total Fat g.	35.8	2.6
Saturated Fat g.	31.7	0.1
Cholesterol mg.	0	2

Tembleque *(tem-BLAY-kay) is a famous Puerto Rican dessert. It's a soft coconut pudding that "trembles" or "shivers" when you serve it. Skim milk adds a negligible amount of cholesterol.*

3	ripe (brown) coconuts	¼	teaspoon salt
1½–2	cups skim milk	1	tablespoon coconut-flavored rum or ½ teaspoon rum extract
6	tablespoons cornstarch		
1	cup light coconut milk	1	tablespoon orange flower water or orange liqueur (optional); see tip on page 324
1	cup sweetened condensed skim milk		
3	strips lemon peel		

Coat a 9" pie pan or 8 small custard cups or ramekins with nonstick spray.

Punch the eyes out of the coconuts with a screwdriver. Drain the coconut water into a 4-cup measuring cup. (You should have about 1½ cups coconut water.) Add enough skim milk to make 3 cups.

Place the cornstarch in a heavy medium saucepan. Add ½ cup of the coconut water mixture. Whisk until smooth. Whisk in the coconut milk, condensed milk, lemon peel, and salt. Set the pan over high heat and bring the mixture to a boil, whisking constantly. Reduce the heat to medium and simmer for 3 minutes, or until the mixture is very thick. Remove the pan from the heat and whisk in the coconut rum or rum extract and orange flower water or orange liqueur (if using). Remove and discard the lemon peel.

Pour the mixture into the prepared pan, custard cups, or ramekins. Let cool to room temperature. Refrigerate for 6 to 24 hours.

Run the tip of a knife around the edge of the pan or each custard cup or ramekin. Invert onto a platter or plates and shake vigorously to release the pudding. (If the pudding does not slide out easily, dip the bottom of the mold in a pan of boiling water for 15 seconds and try again.)

Makes 8 servings

Cooking Tip

✦ The orange flower water is optional, but I love the floral aroma that it adds to the pudding—a trick I learned from Puerto Rican cooking authority Carmen Aboy Valldejuli. Look for it in Hispanic and Middle Eastern markets.

MILK CARAMEL

Dulce de leche   *Various countries*

Nutrition Snapshot	Before	After
Per serving		
Calories	318	280
Total Fat g.	8.6	0
Saturated Fat g.	5.5	0
Cholesterol mg.	34	4

A*mong Latin American sweets, this one is universally beloved. It's found as far north as Cuba and México and as far south as Argentina and Chile. The preparation is so simple, I hesitate to call it a recipe. You simply boil a can of sweetened condensed milk. Sweetened condensed skim milk makes it fat-free.*

1   can (14 ounces) sweetened
    condensed skim milk

Place the unopened can of milk in a medium bowl. Cover with hot water and let stand for 10 minutes, or until the label is loosened. Scrape off the label and discard.

Place the can in a large saucepan. Cover with water by 5". Bring to a boil over high heat. Reduce the heat to medium and simmer for 2 hours. Add water as needed to keep the can covered. (Alternatively, cook the can in a pressure-cooker for 25 minutes.)

Remove the can with tongs and let cool to room temperature. Open the can. Divide the contents among 4 small bowls.

Makes 4 servings

Cooking Tip

✦ I like to spoon the caramel over bananas and/or frozen yogurt. Mexicans like to serve dulce de leche in crêpes.

MEXICAN MILK GELATIN

Gelatina de leche   *México*

Nutrition Snapshot	Before	After
Per serving		
Calories	363	289
Total Fat g.	8.8	0.4
Saturated Fat g.	5.3	0
Cholesterol mg.	33	3

If you like fruit gelatin, you'll love these deliciously different milk gelatins. Vendors in Mexico City sell them on street corners everywhere. The strawberry sauce in the recipe below isn't traditional, but it turns a simple street food into an elegant dessert.

¼	cup dark raisins		2	strips lemon peel
¼	cup golden raisins		2	strips orange peel
1¾	cups hot water		1	teaspoon vanilla extract
3	tablespoons cold water		½	teaspoon almond extract
1½	envelopes (0.4 ounces or 4 teaspoons) unflavored gelatin		2	pints strawberries, hulled
1	can (14 ounces) sweetened condensed skim milk		3–4	tablespoons lime juice
1	stick cinnamon (3" long)		3–4	tablespoons honey

Coat 6 custard cups or ramekins with nonstick spray.

Combine the dark raisins, golden raisins, and hot water in a large saucepan. Let stand for 15 minutes, or until softened.

(continued)

Meanwhile, place the cold water in a 1-cup measuring cup and sprinkle the gelatin on top. Let stand for 10 minutes, or until spongy.

Stir the condensed milk, cinnamon stick, lemon peel, and orange peel into the saucepan with the raisins. Simmer over medium-high heat for 2 minutes, or until scalded and just under the boiling point. Remove from the heat and whisk in the gelatin, vanilla extract, and almond extract. Remove and discard the cinnamon stick, lemon peel, and orange peel.

Transfer the mixture to a large bowl and let cool to room temperature. Place the bowl in another large bowl filled with ice. Stir the mixture with a spatula until it starts to gel. Spoon into the prepared custard cups or ramekins. Refrigerate for 6 to 12 hours, or until set.

Set 6 whole strawberries aside. In a food processor or blender, puree the remaining strawberries, 3 tablespoons of the lime juice, and 3 tablespoons of the honey. Taste and add more lime juice and honey, if desired.

Pour a pool of strawberry sauce on each of 6 dessert plates. Run the tip of a knife around the edge of each custard cup or ramekin. Invert the mold onto a metal spatula and shake vigorously to release the custard. (If the custard does not slide out, dip the bottom of the mold in a pan of boiling water for 15 seconds and try again.) Set a custard in the center of each plate and top with one of the reserved strawberries.

Makes 6 servings

Cooking Tips

✦ For a fanciful touch, make a series of thin parallel slices in each of the 6 whole strawberries almost to, but not through, the green cap. Push on the strawberry to fan out the slices.

✦ Stirring the mixture over ice until it starts to gel helps distribute the raisins evenly throughout the gelatin.

GUAVA CHEESECAKE

Torta cremosa
de queso y
guayaba

United States

Nutrition Snapshot	Before	After
Per serving		
Calories	474	234
Total Fat g.	35	9.5
Saturated Fat g.	21.1	5.4
Cholesterol mg.	228	61

Here's a contemporary twist on a Latino classic. Guava paste and cheese is a popular combination in Latin America—it is used as a stuffing for empanadas in the Spanish-speaking Caribbean and eaten straight as a dessert throughout South America. The piquancy of cheese is the perfect counterpoint to the sweetness of guava. This dessert scores big with cheesecake-lovers.

16	ounces low-fat cottage cheese
16	ounces low-fat cream cheese, at room temperature
10	ounces guava paste (see tip on page 328)
¾	cup sugar
2	eggs + 4 egg whites, or 1 cup liquid egg substitute
¼	cup lemon juice
1	tablespoon grated lemon peel
1	tablespoon vanilla extract
	Pinch of salt

Position a rack in the lower third of the oven. Preheat the oven to 350°F. Coat an 8" springform pan with nonstick spray. Wrap a piece of foil around the bottom and sides of the pan. Bring 4 cups water to a boil.

Puree the cottage cheese in a food processor, occasionally scraping down the sides, for 2 to 3 minutes, or until very smooth. Add the cream cheese and guava paste. Puree until smooth. Add the sugar and process until combined. Add the eggs and egg whites or egg substitute, lemon juice, lemon peel, vanilla extract, and salt. Process until well-combined. Strain the mixture into the prepared pan. (Straining creates a smoother cheesecake.) Tap the pan a few times on the work surface to knock out any bubbles.

Set the pan in a roasting pan. Pour the boiling water into the roasting pan until it reaches 1" up the sides of the pan. Bake for 35 minutes, or until set and a skewer inserted into the center comes out clean. (Do not overcook, or the cheesecake will become watery.) Transfer to a rack. Let cool to room temperature. Refrigerate for 3 to 4 hours, or until cold.

Run the tip of a knife around the inside of the springform pan. Remove the pan side. Cut the cheesecake into 10 wedges.

Makes 10 servings

(continued)

✦ Guava paste can be found at Hispanic markets and in the canned fruit or international aisles of some supermarkets.

✦ Top the cheesecake with fresh strawberries. For a jazzier cheesecake, make a jelly glaze. Combine ⅓ cup guava jelly or currant jelly and 3 to 4 tablespoons lemon juice in a small saucepan over medium heat. Cook, whisking constantly, until the jelly is melted. If the mixture is too thick, add a little water. Strain into a small bowl to remove any lumps of jelly. Gently brush the melted jelly on top of the cold cheesecake. Refrigerate for 30 minutes or up to 3 days before serving.

NICARAGUAN THREE MILKS CAKE

Tres leches
nicaragüense

Nicaragua

Nutrition Snapshot	Before	After
Per serving		
Calories	607	399
Total Fat g.	21.2	3.7
Saturated Fat g.	12.1	1.9
Cholesterol mg.	200	51

Tres leches (trays-LETCHEZ) is Nicaragua's national dessert. You can also find versions of it in southern México. The rich cake is soaked in a syrup made from three different kinds of milk: fresh milk, evaporated milk, and sweetened condensed milk. I've whittled down the fat by reducing the amount of eggs and butter in the cake and using nonfat milks for the syrup. I like the tropical fruit flavor of bananas in the cake, but to be strictly traditional, you'd make the cake without them.

CAKE

- 3 tablespoons unseasoned dry bread crumbs or unbleached flour
- 2 eggs
- 4 egg whites
- ⅔ cup sugar
- 2 teaspoons vanilla extract
- 1 cup cake flour, sifted twice
- 2 tablespoons unsalted butter, melted
- 2 bananas (optional)
- 1 teaspoon lime juice (optional)

SYRUP

- 1 can (12 ounces) evaporated skimmed milk
- 1 can (14 ounces) sweetened condensed skim milk
- ½ cup skim milk
- 2 teaspoons vanilla extract
- 1 tablespoon light rum or 3 drops rum extract
- 1 tablespoon banana liqueur or 3 drops banana extract (optional)

MERINGUE

- 1 cup sugar
- ½ teaspoon cream of tartar
- ½ cup water
- 3 egg whites

To make the cake: Preheat the oven to 350°F. Coat a 9" cake pan with nonstick spray and freeze for 5 minutes. Line the bottom of the pan with parchment or waxed paper and coat with nonstick spray. Sprinkle the inside of the pan with the bread crumbs or unbleached flour.

In a large bowl, using an electric mixer, beat the eggs, egg whites, and sugar for 10 minutes, or until thick and foamy. (Start beating the mixture on low speed and gradually increase the speed to medium, then to high.) The mixture should be pale yellow and tripled in volume. Add the vanilla extract and beat for 10 seconds.

Sift the cake flour into the egg mixture in three batches, gently folding in each batch. Whisk about ½ cup of the batter into the melted butter. Return the mixture to the bowl and fold gently. Spoon the batter into the prepared pan.

Bake for 20 minutes, or until a toothpick inserted in the center of the cake comes out clean. Remove the pan from the oven and let cool slightly. Invert the cake onto a rack and gently tap the pan to release the cake. Peel off and discard the parchment or waxed paper. Let cool to room temperature.

If not using the bananas, poke holes in the top of the cake with a fork.

If using the bananas, peel and thinly slice them. Place in a small bowl and toss with the lime juice to prevent browning. Cut the cake in half through the side with a serrated knife. Place the bottom half of the cake, cut side up, on a deep cake platter. Arrange the bananas over the cake half that is on the platter. Place the other half of the cake, cut side down, on top. Poke holes in the top of the cake with a fork.

To make the syrup: In a large bowl, combine the evaporated milk, condensed milk, skim milk, vanilla extract, rum or rum extract, and banana liqueur or banana extract (if using). Whisk to mix. Pour the syrup over the cake, spooning the overflow back on top until all is absorbed.

To make the meringue: In a heavy medium saucepan over high heat, combine all but 3 tablespoons of the sugar, ¼ teaspoon of the cream of tartar, and the water. Cover and cook for 2 minutes. Uncover the pan and cook for 6 minutes, or until the mixture reaches the soft-ball stage (a candy thermometer will register 239°F, and a spoonful of the mixture dropped into a bowl of cold water will form a soft, gummy ball).

In a medium bowl, beat the egg whites and the remaining ¼ teaspoon cream of tartar for 4 to 6 minutes, or until soft peaks form. Add the remaining 3 tablespoons sugar and beat for 10 minutes, or until stiff peaks form. Gradually pour the sugar mixture into the egg-white mixture and beat until cool.

To assemble: Using a wet rubber spatula, thickly spread the top and sides of the cake with the meringue. Refrigerate the cake for 2 hours before serving.

Makes 10 servings

(continued)

✦ Don't be alarmed by the wet bottom of this cake. You did everything right! The rich, creamy syrup is supposed to soak to the bottom of the pan.

✦ The egg-white topping for this cake is known as an Italian meringue. According to the U.S. Department of Agriculture, this type of meringue is safe to eat because the egg whites from the boiling sugar syrup that is poured over them reach a temperature of more than 160°F, which is enough to eliminate any harmful bacteria.

Variation

Pineapple-Milk Cake: In a small saucepan, bring 2 cups pineapple juice to a boil. Boil until reduced to 1 cup. Substitute the boiled-down pineapple juice for the evaporated skimmed milk in the syrup.

MANGO ICE CREAM

Helado de mango

Puerto Rico

Nutrition Snapshot	Before	After
Per serving		
Calories	721	118
Total Fat g.	32.8	0.3
Saturated Fat g.	18.3	0.1
Cholesterol mg.	364	0

In Puerto Rico, fruit sorbets and ice creams are a way of life. The region's hot climate and luscious tropical fruits make chilled desserts especially refreshing. To cut fat and calories, I reduced the sugar in the traditional recipe and replaced the heavy cream with sweetened condensed skim milk. To vary the flavor, replace the mango with strawberries, papaya, pineapple, mamey, or soursop (guanábana).

2–3	mangoes		½	cup sweetened condensed skim milk
1½	cups water			
4–6	tablespoons sugar		2–3	tablespoons lime juice

Peel the mangoes and cut the flesh off the seeds. Puree the flesh in a food processor or blender. You should have about 2 cups puree.

In a heavy medium saucepan over high heat, combine the water, 4 tablespoons of the sugar, and the condensed milk. Bring to a rolling boil and boil for 5 minutes, or until the sugar has completely dissolved and the mixture is syrupy. Remove the pan from the heat and let cool to room temperature. Stir in the mango puree and 2 tablespoons of the lime juice. Taste and add more sugar and lime juice, if desired.

Transfer the mixture to an ice cream maker. Freeze according to the manufacturer's instructions (see tip).

Makes 4 servings

Cooking Tips

✦ When buying mangoes, use your sense of smell and touch. (The mangoes should be softly yielding and very fragrant.) Some varieties remain green even when ripe. Also, if you have sensitive skin, wear rubber gloves when handling mangoes, as some people are allergic to the sap.

✦ If you don't have an ice cream maker, transfer the mixture to a medium metal bowl. Cover and freeze, scraping occasionally with a fork or whisking to break up the ice crystals, for 2 hours, or until solid.

AMARANTH FRUIT TARTLETS

Postre
alegría

United States

Nutrition Snapshot	Before	After
Per serving		
Calories	440	271
Total Fat g.	22.9	0.2
Saturated Fat g.	7.5	0
Cholesterol mg.	74	0

One of the great challenges of healthy cooking is creating a good-tasting pie crust that's not loaded with fat. Mexican culinary guru Rick Bayless (owner of the Frontera Grill and Topolobampo restaurants in Chicago) has come up with an ingenious and nutritious crust that contains less than a single gram of fat. His secret? He combines popped amaranth with boiled-down sugar or honey. Amaranth has the unique ability to be popped just like popcorn. You can buy prepopped, or puffed, amaranth through the resources on page 66.

½	cup dark brown sugar	3	cups nonfat vanilla frozen yogurt
⅓	cup granulated sugar	3	cups chopped or sliced fruit (such as strawberries, bananas, papaya, or mango)
1	teaspoon lime juice		
½	cup water	6	sprigs fresh mint
2½	cups popped amaranth (see tip on page 332)		

Coat 6 tartlet pans or 6-ounce custard cups with nonstick spray.

In a large saucepan over high heat, combine the brown sugar, granulated sugar, lime juice, and water. Cover the pan and cook for 3 minutes. Uncover the pan and cook for 5 minutes, or until the hard-ball stage is reached. (When sugar is cooked to the hard-ball stage, a candy thermometer will register 245°F, and a spoonful of

(continued)

the mixture dropped into a bowl of cold water will form a hard, glassy ball.) Remove the pan from the heat. Stir in the amaranth with a wooden spoon.

Spoon the mixture into the prepared custard cups. Let cool slightly. Quickly press the amaranth mixture into the bottom and up the sides of each custard cup, using the back of the spoon or your fingers (work quickly, as the mixture hardens as it cools). Let cool to room temperature. Remove the tartlet shells from the molds (you can also serve tartlets in the molds).

Just before serving, spoon ½ cup frozen yogurt into each tartlet shell. Top each with ½ cup of the fruit and a mint sprig.

Makes 6 servings

Cooking Tip

✦ To pop amaranth, place 1 tablespoon seeds in a large, deep, dry pot over medium-high heat. Shake the pot to keep the seeds moving. They will pop in seconds like popcorn. Transfer to a bowl and repeat the process.

Pronto!

TROPICAL FRUIT SALAD

Ensalada de frutas

Various countries

Nutrition Snapshot	Before	After
Per serving		
Calories	269	159
Total Fat g.	6	0.5
Saturated Fat g.	5	0.1
Cholesterol mg.	0	0

Every country in Latin America has a version of fruit salad. For this one, I use the tropical fruits of the Caribbean—mangos, papaya, star fruits, and bananas. Choose whatever tropical fruits you like best. For a fanciful presentation, I serve the fruit salad in hollowed-out coconut shells. Reserve the coconut water in the refrigerator for up to 3 days for making Honduran Fish Soup (page 108).

3   ripe (brown) coconuts
3   tablespoons lime juice
3   tablespoons honey
2   tablespoons coconut-flavored rum
    or 1 teaspoon rum extract
    (optional)
2   tablespoons chopped crystallized
    ginger
2   star fruits, peeled and thinly
    sliced

1   mango, peeled, seeded, and
    chopped
1   papaya, peeled, seeded, and
    chopped
1   orange or tangerine, peeled, cut
    or broken into segments, and
    seeded
2   apple bananas (plátanos man-
    zanos), peeled and thinly sliced
6   sprigs mint

Working over a large bowl, crack the coconuts in half by tapping the shell repeatedly with the back of a cleaver along an imaginary line going around the middle. Drain the coconut water into a bowl (you should have about 1½ cups). Reserve for another use, if desired. Rinse the coconut shells and set aside.

In a large bowl, whisk together the lime juice, honey, rum or rum extract (if using), and ginger. Set aside 6 slices of the star fruit. Stir in the remaining star fruit, the mangoes, papayas, oranges or tangerines, and apple bananas.

Place the coconut shells in large shallow bowls filled with crushed ice to hold the shells upright. Spoon the fruit salad into the coconut shells and garnish each with a starfruit slice and a mint sprig.

Makes 6 servings

Pronto!

CINNAMON-SUGAR CRISPS

Buñuelos   *México*

Nutrition Snapshot	Before	After
Per crisp		
Calories	259	225
Total Fat g.	17.6	5.4
Saturated Fat g.	2.9	2.2
Cholesterol mg.	12	8

Buñuelos (boon-WAY-lows) are one of the triumphs of Mexican pastry—crisply fried pastry disks sprinkled with anise seeds, cinnamon, sugar, and honey. Here's a low-fat version using flour tortillas that are baked instead of deep-fried. Best of all, these low-fat buñuelos are ready in minutes.

4	fat-free flour tortillas (8" diameter)		1	tablespoon ground cinnamon
1	tablespoon butter or lard, melted		1	teaspoon anise seeds, crushed
¼	cup sugar		2	tablespoons honey

Preheat the oven to 400°F.

Place the tortillas on a large baking sheet. Lightly brush the top side of each tortilla with the butter or lard.

In a small bowl, combine the sugar, cinnamon, and anise seeds. Sprinkle 1 tablespoon of the mixture over each tortilla.

Bake the tortillas for 5 minutes, or until crisp (watch closely so that they don't burn). Transfer to a rack or plate and let cool slightly. Just before serving, drizzle the honey over the tortillas.

Makes 4

BAKE-FRIED BREAD IN SPICE-SCENTED SYRUP

Caballeros pobres   *México*

Nutrition Snapshot	Before	After
Per serving		
Calories	360	208
Total Fat g.	9.8	0.9
Saturated Fat g.	3.7	0.2
Cholesterol mg.	80	0

I've always loved the name of this Mexican dessert, literally, "poor horseman." It's a sort of French toast (actually, deep-fried bread) that's served in spice-scented syrup. To make a heart-healthy version, I use egg whites instead of egg yolks in the batter and crisp the bread in the oven instead of the deep-fryer.

1	cup water
½	cup sugar
3	tablespoons piloncillo (page 61) or dark brown sugar
¼	cup raisins
1	stick cinnamon (3" long)
4	whole cloves
2	strips lemon peel
3	egg whites or ⅓ cup liquid egg substitute

½	cup skim milk
3	tablespoons sweet wine (such as Marsala or Málaga) or 2 tablespoons skim milk
½	teaspoon vanilla extract
¼	teaspoon almond extract
¼	teaspoon ground cinnamon
6	slices day-old French bread (1" thick each)

In a medium saucepan over high heat, combine the water, sugar, piloncillo or brown sugar, raisins, cinnamon stick, cloves, and lemon peel. Bring to a boil. Reduce the heat to medium and simmer for 5 minutes, or until the sugar is dissolved and the mixture is slightly thickened. Pour into a large shallow bowl. Let cool to room temperature. Refrigerate the syrup for 2 hours, or until cold.

In another large shallow bowl, whisk together the egg whites or egg substitute, milk, wine or milk, vanilla extract, almond extract, and ground cinnamon. Add the bread and let soak, turning once or twice, for 10 to 15 minutes.

Preheat the oven to 400°F. Coat a nonstick baking sheet with nonstick spray.

Arrange the bread on the prepared baking sheet. Coat the tops with nonstick spray. Bake for 10 minutes per side, or until nicely browned and crisp. Transfer the bread to a rack to cool.

Transfer the bread to the bowl with the syrup. Let soak, turning once or twice, for 30 minutes. Remove and discard the cinnamon stick, cloves, and lemon peel.

Transfer 1 slice into a small shallow serving bowl and spoon a little syrup and some raisins on top. Repeat with the remaining slices.

Makes 6 servings

TOMATOES CANDIED IN SYRUP

Dulce de tomate

Dominican Republic

Nutrition Snapshot	Before	After
Per serving (about 2 tomato halves and 2½ tablespoons syrup)		
Calories	235	186
Total Fat g.	0.4	0.4
Saturated Fat g.	0.1	0.1
Cholesterol mg.	0	0

The notion of serving tomatoes for dessert may strike North Americans as bizarre. But, botanically speaking, the tomato is a fruit, not a vegetable. And that's how it's treated in the Dominican Republic, where tomatoes candied in syrup is a popular dessert. The traditional way to serve dulce de tomate is with slices of queso fresco or cream cheese. The saltiness and tartness of the cheese offsets the sweetness of the tomatoes. You could also serve the tomatoes over frozen yogurt. Choose tomatoes that are firm and not too ripe.

2	sticks cinnamon (3" long each)		1	star anise
1	piece vanilla bean (3" long), halved lengthwise, or 1 teaspoon vanilla extract		2	cups sugar
			2	cups water
4	whole cloves		1	cup raisins
4	whole allspice berries		2	pounds firm plum tomatoes, halved lengthwise
4	strips orange peel			

Tie the cinnamon sticks, vanilla bean, cloves, allspice, orange peel, and star anise in a cheesecloth bag or wrap in a piece of foil and pierce with a fork. In a large heavy saucepan over high heat, combine the sugar, water, raisins, and cheesecloth bag. Bring to a boil, reduce the heat to medium, and add the tomatoes. Simmer for 10 minutes, or until the tomatoes are soft but not mushy. Remove and discard the cheesecloth bag. If using vanilla extract instead of whole vanilla, stir into the syrup after discarding the spice bag.

Spoon the tomatoes and their syrup into 3 hot 1-pint canning jars that have been sterilized in boiling water. Leave ¼" headspace. Wipe the rims clean and screw on the lids. Invert the jars for 5 minutes. Turn the jars upright and let cool to room temperature. Store in the refrigerator. Once opened, the tomatoes will keep in the refrigerator for up to 2 weeks.

Makes 12 servings (3 pints)

Cooking Tip

✦ If you can't find whole star anise in your area, it could be omitted from the recipe.

GUAVA SHELLS

Casquitos
de guayaba
en almíbar

*Various
countries*

Nutrition Snapshot	Before	After
Per ¾ cup		
Calories	925	622
Total Fat g.	3	2.3
Saturated Fat g.	0.8	0.6
Cholesterol mg.	0	0

Guavas have a haunting aroma and perfumed flavor suggestive of lemons, bananas, strawberries, and honey. But try eating one out of hand and you'll be left with a mouthful of tiny, rock-hard seeds. Centuries ago, Spanish-Caribbean cooks devised an ingenious way to enjoy the guava: They poached the shells in syrup and cooked the seedy flesh into jam. Whenever I prepare guava, I make both preparations (see Guava Jam on page 338). These make especially festive gifts for the holidays.

6	pounds guavas, rinsed and peeled		1	piece vanilla bean (3" long), halved lengthwise
2	lemons		2	sticks cinnamon (3" long each)
6	cups water		6	whole cloves
3–4	cups sugar		6	whole allspice berries

Cut each guava in half lengthwise and scrape out the seeds with a melon baller or spoon. You should be left with ¼"-thick shells. (Reserve the skins and seeds for the Guava Jam on page 338.)

Using a vegetable peeler, remove the outer peel in strips from 1 of the lemons. Place the peels in a large heavy saucepan. Cut both lemons in half and squeeze the juice into the pan. Add the water, 3 cups of the sugar, vanilla bean, cinnamon sticks, cloves, and allspice. Bring to a boil over high heat. Reduce the heat to medium-low and add the guava shells. Simmer for 8 to 10 minutes, or until the shells are very tender. Skim off any foam that rises to the surface during cooking. Taste and add more sugar, if desired.

Spoon the guava shells and their syrup into 4 hot 8-ounce canning jars that have been sterilized in boiling water. Leave ¼" headspace. Wipe the rims clean and screw on the lids. Invert the jars for 5 minutes. Turn the jars upright and let cool to room temperature. Store in the refrigerator. Once opened, the shells will keep in the refrigerator for up to 2 weeks.

Makes 4 cups

Cooking Tip

✦ Guava shells are traditionally served with thin slivers of queso fresco or cream cheese to balance the sweetness of the guava. Guava shells also make a delectably different topping for frozen yogurt.

LATIN SUPER FOOD: GUAVA

A guava a day may keep the doctor away. This sweet, tropical fruit helps ward off colds and flu and can even help protect you from diseases like cancer and heart disease.

One guava contains about 5 grams of fiber, which helps protect against colon cancer and the high blood sugar associated with diabetes. All that fiber combined with guava's good vitamin-A content may reduce the risk for certain kinds of ulcers, according to one study. Plus, guavas are great for lowering artery-hardening cholesterol. Researchers in India compared cholesterol levels among people who ate guava throughout the day with folks who didn't eat guava. They found that after 12 weeks, the guava-eaters had a 10 percent reduction in total cholesterol, an 8 percent drop in triglycerides (blood fats that can contribute to heart disease), and an 8 percent rise in healthy HDL cholesterol.

Looking to ward off that winter cold or flu? A shot of guava may help boost your immunity against infection, say researchers. One guava contains 165 milligrams of vitamin C—that's 275 percent of the Daily Value and triple the amount of vitamin C found in oranges. As a big bonus, all that vitamin C may also lower your cancer risk.

Because guavas contain compounds that are natural stomach relaxants, G-U-A-V-A may be the best way to spell digestive relief, says Hector Balcazar, Ph.D., associate professor of community nutrition and public health in the department of family resources and human development and a member of the affiliated faculty at the Hispanic Research Center at Arizona State University in Tempe. If you're battling a bout of indigestion or heartburn, a cup of guava juice should do the trick, he says.

Though guava sounds exotic and hard to find, most large supermarkets stock them. For a nice change of pace from apples and bananas, pick up a few guavas the next time you're in the produce aisle.

GUAVA JAM

Jalea de
guayaba

*Various
countries*

Nutrition Snapshot	Before	After
Per 2 tablespoons		
Calories	88	41
Total Fat g.	0.2	0
Saturated Fat g.	0.4	0
Cholesterol mg.	0	0

Guavas are sold at Hispanic markets and at large supermarkets. They usually come hard and green. Let them ripen in a sealed paper bag at room temperature. A ripe guava will be intensely fragrant and soft but not mushy to the touch.

6 pounds guavas, rinsed and peeled (skins reserved)

5 cups water

1–1½ cups sugar

1 piece vanilla bean (2" long), halved lengthwise

1 stick cinnamon (3" long)

4 whole cloves

2 teaspoons grated lemon peel

Cut each guava in half lengthwise and scrape out the seeds with a melon baller or spoon. Reserve the seeds. (You should be left with ¼"-thick shells. Reserve the shells for the Guava Shells on page 336.)

In a large heavy saucepan over high heat, combine the guava skins, seeds, and any pulp with the water. Bring to a boil, reduce the heat to medium, and simmer for 10 minutes, or until the skins are very tender. Remove the pan from the heat and let cool slightly.

Transfer the mixture to a blender or food processor and puree. Wipe out the saucepan. Pour the puree through a fine-meshed strainer or a colander lined with several layers of cheesecloth back into the saucepan, pressing with a rubber spatula or the back of wooden spoon to extract as much liquid as possible. (You should have 5½ to 6 cups puree.)

Stir in 1 cup of the sugar, the vanilla bean, cinnamon stick, cloves, and lemon peel. Simmer, stirring often, for 20 minutes, or until thick and concentrated. Taste and add more sugar, if desired.

Spoon the hot jam into 4 hot 8-ounce canning jars that have been sterilized in boiling water. Leave ¼" headspace. Wipe the rims clean and screw on the lids. Invert the jars for 5 minutes. Turn the jars upright and let cool to room temperature. Store at room temperature for up to 3 months. Once opened, the jam will keep in the refrigerator for up to 2 weeks.

Makes 4 cups

BANANA JAM

Jalea de
Banana

Guatemala

Nutrition Snapshot	Before	After
Per 2 tablespoons		
Calories	130	82
Total Fat g.	0.2	0.2
Saturated Fat g.	0.1	0.1
Cholesterol mg.	0	0

This jam is a tongue tickler. The citrus and sweet spices enhance the tropical flavor of the bananas. Around the holidays, I like to make a big batch, pack it into decorative jars, and give the jam away as gifts.

6	bananas (see tip)		1	stick cinnamon (3" long)
1¼	cups orange juice		1	piece vanilla bean (3" long), halved lengthwise
¼	cup lime juice			Pinch of salt
1½–2	cups sugar			

Peel and thinly slice the bananas. In a large heavy saucepan over high heat, combine the bananas, orange juice, lime juice, 1½ cups of the sugar, the cinnamon stick, vanilla bean, and salt. Bring to a boil. Reduce the heat to medium-low and simmer, stirring often, for 30 minutes, or until thick. Taste and add more sugar, if desired.

Spoon the hot jam into 4 hot 6-ounce canning jars that have been sterilized in boiling water. Leave ¼" headspace. Wipe the rims clean and screw on the lids. Invert the jars for 5 minutes. Turn the jars upright and let cool to room temperature. Store in the refrigerator. Once opened, the jam will keep in the refrigerator for up to 3 weeks.

Makes 3 cups

Cooking Tip

✦ My favorite type of banana for this jam is the apple banana (manzano plátano). It has a pleasant tartness reminiscent of apples.

SWEET POTATO JAM

Boniatillo

Various countries

Nutrition Snapshot	Before	After
Per 2 tablespoons		
Calories	192	96
Total Fat g.	0.1	0.1
Saturated Fat g.	0	0
Cholesterol mg.	0	0

Latin American sweet potatoes are called boniatos (bone-ee-AH-toes). Boniatos are quite different from North American sweet potatoes. They have a patchy purple skin and firm white flesh, and they taste similar to roasted chestnuts. (They are only slightly sweet.) Look for boniatos (also known as batatas) in the produce section of large supermarkets or in Hispanic and West Indian markets. If you can't find them, replace the boniatos with American-style sweet potatoes and reduce the sugar to 1 to 1½ cups.

1	lemon
4	cups water
1½	pounds boniatos, peeled and finely chopped
1½–2	cups sugar

1	stick cinnamon (3" long)
1	piece vanilla bean (3" long), halved lengthwise
4	whole cloves
4	whole allspice berries

Remove 5 strips (2" × ½" each) of the outer peel from the lemon with a vegetable peeler and place in a large saucepan. Cut the lemon in half and squeeze the lemon juice into the pan. Add the water, boniatos, 1½ cups of the sugar, cinnamon stick, vanilla bean, cloves, and allspice. Bring to a boil over high heat. Reduce the heat to medium-low and simmer for 30 minutes, or until the consistency of soft ice cream. Skim off any foam that rises to the surface as the jam cooks. The boniatos should disintegrate into a chunky puree; mash with the back of a wooden spoon, if necessary. Taste and add more sugar, if desired.

Spoon the hot jam into 4 hot 8-ounce canning jars that have been sterilized in boiling water. Leave ¼" headspace. Wipe the rims clean and screw on the lids. Invert the jars for 5 minutes. Turn the jars upright and let cool to room temperature. Store in the refrigerator. Once opened, the jam will keep in the refrigerator for up to 1 week.

Makes 4 cups

Cooking Tip

✦ Cubans often eat this jam as a dessert. Spoon it into bowls or compote glasses and pour a little skim milk or evaporated skimmed milk on top. Or serve the jam over frozen yogurt.

LATIN SUPER FOOD: SWEET POTATOES

Sweet potatoes are tubular root vegetables native to the Americas. They're also bursting with health-protecting antioxidants. Here's the scoop on why antioxidants are so good for you. Many diseases are helped along by certain oxygen molecules known as free radicals. Free radicals plunder your body's healthy cells, leading the way for heart disease, cataracts, cancer, and maybe even aging itself. Antioxidants, like vitamins C and E and beta-carotene, fend off free radicals before they can do their dirty deeds.

Bright orange fruits and vegetables like sweet potatoes are some of nature's richest sources of antioxidants. Just ½ cup of mashed sweet potatoes delivers 13 milligrams of beta-carotene, nearly 100 percent of what you should eat each day. The same amount also yields 40 percent of the Daily Value (DV) for vitamin C.

All this antioxidant, disease-fighting potential just might add up to a longer life, according to a study of more than 1,500 men in Chicago. The study's researchers found that men who increased their daily vitamin C and beta-carotene intake by the amount found in just a bit more than a cupful of sweet potatoes could slash their risk of dying from cancer or heart disease by almost a third.

Sweet potatoes are also a respectable source of fiber, with 3 grams in every ½ cup. Fiber lowers cholesterol, stabilizes blood sugar, helps prevent colon cancer, and may even fend off certain types of ulcers.

Folate is another super-nutrient found in sweet potatoes. One half-cup serving provides about 6 percent of the 400 micrograms you need each day. Folate helps lower levels of the amino acid homocysteine, which research shows can be dangerous to your heart in high levels. Plus, folate may help you think better. Researchers at Tufts University in Medford, Massachusetts, found that high levels of homocysteine were linked to poor performance on certain tests that measure brain function.

If you like baked potatoes, try a baked sweet potato. They taste a bit sweeter, but most folks love them with a small amount of butter, a little maple syrup, or a dash of cinnamon. Or try a Spanish-Caribbean favorite, Sweet Potato Jam (opposite page).

HOT AND COLD BEVERAGES
Bebidas

Latin Americans make the most distinctive and nutritious thirst quenchers on the planet. Cinnamon-Almond Cooler (page 349), made from sweetened blended rice, is enjoyed throughout Central America. It's creamy, refreshing, and quite low in fat. Ecuador favors a soothing Pineapple, Carrot, and Oat Drink (page 350). In Mexico, the morning often starts with Chocolate Breakfast Drink (page 347), an ingenious combination of chocolate and corn-meal. And throughout Latin America, milkshakes consist of frosty pureed fruit minus the high-fat ice cream. One particularly hearty version, Puffed Wheat Milkshake (page 348), makes an outstanding liquid breakfast or mini-meal for hectic days.

Perhaps the most legendary Latin American drink is Mexican Hot Chocolate (page 344), passed down from the Aztecs. For festive occasions, there's Spiced Tomato Juice (page 357) to sip during the cocktail hour and Coconut Eggnog (page 352), a luscious Puerto Rican nog to toast the New Year.

Whether rustic or refined, Latino beverages retain a healthful appeal because they're based on fresh fruits, vegetables, and grains.

RECIPES

LEMONGRASS TEA

Té de limoncillo   *Cuba*

Nutrition Snapshot	Before	After
Per serving		
Calories	212	212
Total Fat g.	0	0
Saturated Fat g.	0	0
Cholesterol mg.	0	0

Like many Latinas, my Cuban friend Elida Proenza prizes foods not only for their flavor but also for their medicinal properties. Whenever anyone in the family has a cold, she prepares this soothing tea.

4	stalks lemon grass			Juice of 1 lemon
5	cups water		3–4	tablespoons honey

Trim the roots and leafy tips off the lemon grass and thinly slice the stalks.

In a large pot over medium heat, combine the lemon grass and water. Simmer for 20 minutes, or until the tea is richly flavored.

Stir in the lemon juice and 3 tablespoons of the honey. Taste and add more honey, if desired. Strain the tea into mugs.

Makes 4 servings

MEXICAN HOT CHOCOLATE

Chocolate mexicano   *México*

Nutrition Snapshot	Before	After
Per serving		
Calories	440	291
Total Fat g.	33.1	2.8
Saturated Fat g.	20.4	0.3
Cholesterol mg.	61	6

Thick and frothy, spicy and sweet—such is the luscious hot chocolate served in Oaxaca (wah-HA-ka), México. To pare down the saturated fat, I use cocoa powder instead of hard chocolate. Evaporated skimmed milk provides creamy thickness, while sweet spices and extracts add flavor.

½	cup skim milk		¼	teaspoon ground cinnamon
½	cup evaporated skimmed milk			Pinch of ground cloves
1½	tablespoons unsweetened cocoa powder		½	teaspoon vanilla extract
1–2	tablespoons sugar		3	drops almond extract

In a small heavy saucepan over medium-high heat, bring the milk and evaporated milk to a boil, stirring constantly.

In a small bowl, whisk together the cocoa, 1 tablespoon of the sugar, cinnamon, and cloves. Whisk the hot milk into the cocoa mixture. Return it to the pan. Bring to a boil, whisking steadily. Cook for 1 minute, or until thick and frothy. Taste and add more sugar, if desired.

Pour the hot chocolate into a mug and stir in the vanilla extract and almond extract.

Makes 1 serving

Cooking Tip

✦ Traditionally, Mexican hot chocolate is cooked in a metal coffeepot and beaten with a molinillo, a handsomely carved wooden beater.

Pronto!

CHOCOLATE CORNMEAL MILKSHAKE

Pinolillo   *Nicaragua*

Nutrition Snapshot	Before	After
Per serving		
Calories	253	178
Total Fat g.	11.8	2
Saturated Fat g.	7.0	0.2
Cholesterol mg.	16	2

Pinolillo *(Pee-no-LEE-yo) is Nicaragua's version of a milkshake. With chocolate, milk, and cornmeal, it's as nourishing as it is satisfying. The combination of two New World foods (cornmeal and chocolate) suggests that pinolillo was enjoyed long before the arrival of the Spanish.*

2   tablespoons cornmeal

2   tablespoons unsweetened cocoa powder

3   tablespoons sugar or honey

¼   teaspoon ground cinnamon

¼   teaspoon ground allspice

     Pinch of ground cloves

1   cup skim milk

1   cup cold water

Warm a small skillet over medium heat. Add the cornmeal. Cook and stir for 2 minutes, or until lightly toasted. Transfer to a blender. Add the cocoa, sugar or honey, cinnamon, allspice, cloves, milk, and water. Blend until frothy.

Makes 2 servings

LATIN SUPER FOOD: CHOCOLATE

Scientists have finally discovered what everyday folks have been saying all along: Chocolate is good for you (in moderation, of course).

Hailing from ore-rich Latin America, chocolate is a good source of the trace mineral copper. The U.S. Department of Agriculture recommends that we get 2 milligrams of this shiny orange mineral daily for optimum health. Yet surveys show that most people routinely get only half that amount. Without enough copper, we risk hampering our immune systems. And some experts believe that women with low levels of copper may be at increased risk for osteoporosis.

Well, it just so happens that 2 tablespoons of either powdered cocoa mix or chocolate syrup can provide between 10 and 15 percent of the Daily Value for this important mineral, with virtually no fat. As if that weren't enough reason to savor your Mexican hot cocoa, chocolate also contains the same antioxidant compounds, called phenols, that make red wine a winner against heart disease. Phenols prevent bad LDL cholesterol from oxidizing, which scientists believe is the first step to plaque buildup in your arteries. Researchers from the University of California, Davis, found that a 1½ ounce piece of chocolate contains nearly as many of these protective compounds as a 5-ounce glass of red wine.

Plus, a little chocolate simply makes you feel good. According to researchers at the Neurosciences Institute in San Diego, eating chocolate stimulates brain chemicals that create a temporary feeling of well-being. Even the aroma of chocolate stimulates what scientists call theta brain waves, producing a relaxing effect.

All that said, solid chocolate is still a high-fat, high-sugar food. Reach for cocoa powder and chocolate syrup instead, says Hector Balcazar, Ph.D., associate professor of community nutrition and public health in the department of family resources and human development and a member of the affiliated faculty at the Hispanic Research Center at Arizona State University in Tempe. These foods are virtually fat-free and have all the health benefits of hard chocolate. For those times when nothing but solid chocolate will do, eat it in moderation.

CHOCOLATE BREAKFAST DRINK

Champurrado   *México*

Nutrition Snapshot	Before	After
Per serving		
Calories	201	135
Total Fat g.	6	2.1
Saturated Fat g.	2.6	0.2
Cholesterol mg.	16	2

Visit Mexico City's Central Market, and you'll find vendors with huge pots ladling out steaming mugs of champurrado (chahm-poo-RAH-dough) and atole (ah-TOE-lay). Atole is flavored with spices (see the variation below), while champurado boasts chocolate. Both drinks are a cross between hot milk and porridge. They owe their rib-sticking consistency to an ingredient that few North Americans would think of as a component of a breakfast drink: masa harina. Here's the chocolate version. I can't imagine a better way to take the chill off a winter morning.

2	tablespoons masa harina
2	tablespoons unsweetened cocoa powder
2–3	tablespoons piloncillo (see page 61) or dark brown sugar
½	teaspoon ground cinnamon
¼	teaspoon anise seeds, crushed
1	cup water
1	cup skim milk

In a medium saucepan, whisk together the masa harina, cocoa, piloncillo or brown sugar, cinnamon, and anise seeds. Whisk in ¼ cup of the water to make a thick paste. Whisk in the remaining ¾ cup water and the milk.

Set the saucepan over medium heat and bring to a boil, whisking constantly. Reduce the heat to medium-low and simmer, whisking occasionally, for 5 minutes, or until thick and richly flavored. Taste and add more piloncillo or brown sugar, if desired.

Makes 2 servings

Variation

Spiced Breakfast Drink: Omit the cocoa powder. Add 1 teaspoon vanilla extract, ¼ teaspoon ground allspice, and ⅛ teaspoon ground cloves.

STRAWBERRY-PINEAPPLE MILKSHAKE

Batido de
fresas y
piña

*Various
countries*

Nutrition Snapshot	Before	After
Per serving		
Calories	195	140
Total Fat g.	2.3	0.7
Saturated Fat g.	1.1	0
Cholesterol mg.	7	1

Here's a switch from the usual North American strawberry-banana smoothie.

½	cup chopped fresh or frozen and thawed strawberries	1	tablespoon sweetened condensed skim milk
½	cup chopped fresh or drained canned pineapple	1	teaspoon lime juice
3	tablespoons pineapple juice	1	cup crushed ice

Combine all of the ingredients in a blender. Blend until smooth.

Makes 1 serving

PUFFED WHEAT MILKSHAKE

Batido de trigo

Cuba

Nutrition Snapshot	Before	After
Per serving		
Calories	293	207
Total Fat g.	5.9	0.4
Saturated Fat g.	3.6	0.1
Cholesterol mg.	23	3

This batido (milkshake) makes a great grab 'n' go breakfast with complex carbohydrates.

1	cup puffed wheat	1	tablespoon honey
½	cup skim milk		Pinch of salt
½	cup crushed ice		
1	tablespoon sweetened condensed skim milk		

Combine all of the ingredients in a blender. Blend until smooth.

Makes 1 serving

MANGO-BANANA MILKSHAKE

Batido de
mango y
plátano

Various countries

Nutrition Snapshot	Before	After
Per serving		
Calories	231	176
Total Fat g.	2.2	0.6
Saturated Fat g.	1.2	0.2
Cholesterol mg.	7	1

Batidos (bah-TEA-dose) are Latino milkshakes: fruit, ice, and sweetened condensed milk whipped to a refreshing puree. They're a lot healthier than American milkshakes because they're mostly fruit, not ice cream. The richness comes from sweetened condensed milk. Apple bananas (plátanos manzanos) are my favorite variety for this recipe.

½	cup chopped mangoes	1–2	teaspoons lime juice
½	cup chopped bananas	1	cup crushed ice
1	tablespoon sweetened condensed skim milk	2–3	tablespoons water (optional)
			Sugar (optional)

In a blender, combine the mangoes, bananas, condensed milk, 1 teaspoon of the lime juice, and the ice. Blend until smooth. If the batido is too thick, add the water. Taste and add more lime juice and a touch of sugar, if desired.

Makes 1 serving

CINNAMON-ALMOND COOLER

Agua de horchata

México

Nutrition Snapshot	Before	After
Per serving		
Calories	480	136
Total Fat g.	26	0.3
Saturated Fat g.	2.5	0.1
Cholesterol mg.	0	0

Horchata is one of the most refreshing beverages ever to grace a glass. It looks like milk, but it's made with rice and spices. It's the perfect drink for people who don't drink milk.

½	cup uncooked white rice	3–4	tablespoons sugar or honey
2	strips orange peel (2" long)	4½	cups water
2	sticks cinnamon (3" long each)	½	teaspoon vanilla extract
3	whole cloves	½	teaspoon almond extract
3	whole allspice berries		

In a large bowl, combine the rice, orange peel, cinnamon sticks, cloves, allspice, 3 tablespoons of the sugar or honey, and the water. Let stand in the refrigerator for 1½ hours, or until the rice is soft. Transfer to a blender or food processor and puree until smooth.

Pour the mixture through a strainer lined with cheesecloth or paper towels into a pitcher. Stir in the vanilla extract and almond extract. Taste and add more sugar or honey, if desired. Refrigerate for at least 4 hours or up to 4 days.

Makes 4 servings

Variation

Fruited Cinnamon-Almond Cooler: Add 1 cup chopped or pureed melon to the horchata. You can also add fresh berries, orange segments, or other cut-up fruit for color.

PINEAPPLE, CARROT, AND OAT DRINK

Quáker   *Ecuador*

Nutrition Snapshot	Before	After
Per serving		
Calories	196	181
Total Fat g.	1	1
Saturated Fat g.	0.2	0.2
Cholesterol mg.	0	0

Thick, rich, and supremely satisfying, quaker (pronounced "quacker") is the ultimate fruit nectar. The drink is named after the manufacturer of its principle ingredient, oats. Quáker belongs to an extended family of sweet, nonalcoholic grain-based drinks that includes Mexican Aqua de horchata (Cinnamon-Almond Cooler, page 349). In Ecuador, the beverage would be made with a South American fruit called naranjilla. For an easy alternative, I use an orange. Honey replaces the traditional sugar.

1	orange	5–7	tablespoons honey
½	cup quick-cooking oats	1	stick cinnamon (3" long)
2	carrots, chopped	5	cups water
1½	cups chopped fresh or canned pineapple (with juice)		

With a vegetable peeler, remove the orange peel in 2" × ½" strips. Place in a large saucepan. Cut the orange in half and squeeze the juice into the saucepan. Add the oats, carrots, pineapple (with juice), 5 tablespoons of the honey, the cinnamon stick, and water. Bring to a boil over high heat and boil for 10 minutes, or until the oats are very soft. Remove from the heat and let cool for 5 minutes.

Remove and discard the cinnamon stick and orange peel. Transfer the mixture to a blender and puree. Strain through a fine-meshed strainer into a pitcher. Refrigerate for at least 4 hours or up to 3 days.

Makes 4 servings

YELLOW CORN DRINK

Chicheme a la
Chorrera

Panamá

Nutrition Snapshot	Before	After
Per serving		
Calories	266	209
Total Fat g.	8.9	1.3
Saturated Fat g.	4.9	0.3
Cholesterol mg.	29	3

This unusual drink is a southern Central American specialty. It's a sort of unblended milkshake made from corn. The corn of choice would be maíz amarillo trillado, a dried, hulled yellow corn similar to hominy. This product is available at Hispanic markets and many supermarkets. You can also make the drink with canned hominy, which is available in the international aisle of most supermarkets. If using dried corn, begin the recipe a day before serving.

½ cup dried hulled yellow corn or drained canned hominy

4 cups water

1 stick cinnamon (3" long)

1 can (14 ounces) evaporated skimmed milk

4–6 tablespoons sugar

1 teaspoon vanilla extract

½–¾ teaspoon ground nutmeg

In a small bowl, combine the corn and 1 cup of the water. Cover and let soak for 6 hours or overnight in the refrigerator. The next day, in a large heavy saucepan, combine the corn and its soaking water, the remaining 3 cups water, and the cinnamon stick. (If using drained canned hominy, combine the hominy with 4 cups water and the cinnamon stick in a large heavy saucepan.)

Bring to a boil over high heat. Reduce the heat to medium, loosely cover, and simmer for 30 minutes, or until the corn is soft. Remove and discard the cinnamon stick. Stir in the evaporated milk and 4 tablespoons of the sugar. Simmer for 5 minutes. Remove from the heat and let cool to room temperature. Refrigerate for at least 4 hours or up to 3 days.

Stir in the vanilla extract and ½ teaspoon of the nutmeg. Taste and add more sugar and nutmeg, if desired. Serve in tall glasses with ice cubes.

Makes 4 servings

COCONUT EGGNOG

Coquito   *Puerto Rico*

Nutrition Snapshot	Before	After
Per serving		
Calories	407	250
Total Fat g.	22.6	3.2
Saturated Fat g.	17.1	0.2
Cholesterol mg.	129	29

Holiday time already? Don't forget to include this traditional Puerto Rican drink. In this low-fat version, the richness comes from coconut water (the liquid inside a coconut), light coconut milk, and sweetened condensed skim milk. One egg provides just enough eggy flavor and thickness for the nog, but you can omit it, if desired. Don't worry; the eggnog is cooked (then chilled) to avoid the risk of food-borne illness. For a festive touch, serve this drink in coconut shells. If you have any extra coconut water, reserve it for making the Shivering Coconut Pudding on page 323.

4   ripe (brown) coconuts

1   can (14 ounces) sweetened condensed skim milk

1   cup light coconut milk (see page 53)

1   cup light rum or 4 teaspoons rum extract + 1 cup water

½   teaspoon ground cinnamon

¾   teaspoon ground nutmeg

1   egg, beaten

Punch the eyes out of the coconuts with a screwdriver. Strain 1½ cups of the coconut water into a large saucepan. Reserve any remaining coconut water for another use. On a cutting board, crack the coconuts in half with a cleaver (see tip). Rinse the coconut shells and set aside.

Set the saucepan over medium heat. Whisk in the condensed milk, coconut milk, rum or rum extract and water, cinnamon, ½ teaspoon of the nutmeg, and the egg. Cook, stirring often with a wooden spoon, for 3 minutes, or until the mixture thickly coats the back of the spoon. Do not let the mixture boil or even simmer because the egg will become scrambled. Immediately pour the mixture through a strainer into a medium bowl or pitcher. Let cool to room temperature. Refrigerate for 3 to 4 hours, or until chilled.

Pour into the coconut shells or coquito glasses (tiny glasses that look like egg cups). Sprinkle each with a little of the remaining nutmeg.

Makes 8 servings

Cooking Tip

✦ To crack a coconut in half, tap the shell repeatedly with the back of a cleaver along an imaginary line going around the middle. After 10 to 20 taps, the shell should break neatly in half.

PINEAPPLE CIDER

Garapiña

Cuba

Nutrition Snapshot	Before	After
Per serving		
Calories	75	43
Total Fat g.	0.1	0.1
Saturated Fat g.	0	0
Cholesterol mg.	0	0

Here's a recipe for people who can't stand to waste food. It's made from the rind of a fresh pineapple. It takes only a few minutes of hands-on time. Then, the pineapple steeps for a few days, infusing the water with a refreshingly sweet-tart flavor. This drink is naturally low in fat. By boosting the flavor with ginger and spices, I cut back on the amount of sweetener and reduce the calories.

	Rind of 1 pineapple (see tip)	2	whole cloves
1	piece fresh ginger (2" long), cut into ¼" slices	8	cups water
2	sticks cinnamon (3" long each)	4–6	tablespoons honey

In a large jar, combine the pineapple rind, ginger, cinnamon sticks, cloves, and water. Loosely cover with the lid. Let steep at room temperature for 2 to 3 days.

Strain the mixture into a pitcher. Stir in 4 tablespoons of the honey. Taste and add more honey, if desired. Refrigerate for 3 to 4 hours, or until chilled.

Makes 8 servings

Cooking Tip

✦ To remove the rind from a pineapple, cut the pineapple lengthwise into eighths with a sharp knife. Run the knife along the inside edge of the rind on each eighth to cut the rind away from the fruit. Rinse the rind, then coarsely chop and use as directed.

Regional Variations

Guatemalan Cider: Replace the pineapple rind with 4 cups chopped mixed fruit, such as apples, apricots, cherries, peaches, and quinces.

Venezuelan Cider: Add ½ cup fresh or frozen and thawed corn kernels along with the pineapple rind.

KIWIFRUIT COOLER

Jugo de lulo

Colombia

Nutrition Snapshot	Before	After
Per serving		
Calories	168	139
Total Fat g.	0.7	0.7
Saturated Fat g.	0	0
Cholesterol mg.	0	0

The fruit traditionally used for this drink is lulo, a luscious green fruit with a berrylike tartness. It is virtually impossible to find in the United States, so I began making the drink with something similar: kiwifruit.

2	kiwifruits, peeled	½	cup crushed ice
2–3	teaspoons lime juice	½	cup cold water
2–3	teaspoons sugar or honey		

In a blender, combine the kiwifruit, 2 teaspoons of the lime juice, 2 teaspoons of the sugar or honey, the ice, and water. Puree until smooth. The drink should be quite tart; taste and add more lime juice and sugar or honey, if desired.

Makes 1 serving

ORANGE AND CARROT JUICE

Jugo de
naranja y
zanahoria

*Various
countries*

Nutrition Snapshot	Before	After
Per serving		
Calories	105	105
Total Fat g.	0.4	0.4
Saturated Fat g.	0.1	0.1
Cholesterol mg.	0	0

Here's a glassful of refreshing flavor and color. Never before have a fruit and a vegetable had such an affinity for one another. To save time, use bottled orange juice and carrot juice (½ cup of each).

1	large or 2 medium oranges, halved	3	ice cubes
2	carrots, cut into ½"-thick slices	½–¾	cup water

Squeeze the juice from the orange(s). In a blender, combine the orange juice, carrots, ice, and ½ cup of the water. Puree until smooth. If the juice is too thick, add more water. Strain into a tall glass.

Makes 1 serving

LATIN SUPER FOOD: CITRUS FRUITS

North Americans often reserve citrus fruits for breakfast (and eat only a fraction of the fruit that they should). But folks in Latin America take full advantage of oranges, limes, and lemons to perk up everything from salsas and marinades to drinks and desserts. As a result, they add a plateful of flavor and health benefits to their diets.

Citrus fruits are an outstanding source of vitamin C, with most citrus providing above and beyond the Daily Value. As an antioxidant, one of the things that vitamin C does best is wipe out harmful oxygen molecules known as free radicals. These molecules are notorious for pillaging your body's healthy cells and paving the way for heart disease, cancer, cataracts, and other diseases. Vitamin C is so effective that it may even help your heart heal more quickly after a heart attack. Researchers in India found that people who ate fruits and vegetables high in vitamin C soon after a heart attack had lower levels of an enzyme that indicates heart damage than those who ate little vitamin C. Eating lots of vitamin C may also protect against the cartilage loss associated with osteoarthritis, according to researchers in Boston. A study in Israel found that the vitamin may even help calm the airways in some people who have exercise-induced asthma.

In a ground-breaking Canadian study, researchers found that they could halt the growth of breast cancer tumors in animals by giving them daily doses of orange juice. Citrus fruits, particularly oranges and grapefruits, contain special flavonoid compounds, called hesperetin and naringenin, that appear to have powerful anticancer properties, scientists say.

When you peel and eat a whole orange, you're also treating your body to a good source of fiber—more than 3 grams of fiber in a single fruit. The soluble fiber in citrus helps lower cholesterol levels, while the insoluble fiber helps prevent constipation and may reduce colon cancer risk. Add a squirt of lime to your favorite Latin dishes to start getting more of these benefits. Or replace some of the oil in your marinades and salad dressings with citrus juice.

SUNRISE VEGETABLE JUICE

Jugo de
un nuevo
amanecer

*México
El Salvador*

Nutrition Snapshot	Before	After
Per serving		
Calories	77	77
Total Fat g.	0.2	0.2
Saturated Fat g.	0	0
Cholesterol mg.	0	0

The taste of this colorful juice drink is light years ahead of canned vegetable juices. It's incredibly low in sodium and makes a great morning pick-me-up.

2	carrots, cut into ½"-thick pieces	¼	cup beet juice (if using canned beets) or water
2	ribs celery, cut into ½"-thick slices	¾	cup water
1–2	cooked or canned beets (about 3 ounces total), cut into ½"-thick slices	3	ice cubes
1–2	tablespoons honey		

In a blender, combine the carrots, celery, beets, 1 tablespoon of the honey, the beet juice or water, water, and ice. Blend until smooth. Taste and add more honey, if desired. Strain the juice into tall glasses.

Makes 2 servings

SPICED TOMATO JUICE

Sangrita   *México*

Nutrition Snapshot	Before	After
Per serving		
Calories	18	18
Total Fat g.	0.1	0.1
Saturated Fat g.	0	0
Cholesterol mg.	0	0

Mexican meals often start with a small glass of this turbocharged tomato juice. It usually accompanies appetizers and tequila. The traditional recipe calls for lime juice, but I like the bittersweet flavor provided by fresh grapefruit juice.

¾   cup tomato juice

¾   cup grapefruit juice or ½ cup lime juice

½   cup lime juice

2   tablespoon pickling juice from pickled jalapeño chile peppers

1   tablespoon grenadine or nonalcoholic grenadine

In a pitcher, combine the tomato juice, grapefruit juice or lime juice, lime juice, pickling juice, and grenadine. Stir to mix. Serve in cordial glasses.

Makes 8 servings

STOCKS, SEASONINGS, AND BASICS
Caldos, condimentos y recetas básicas

In Laura Esquivel's best-selling novel *Like Water for Chocolate*, the heroine, Tita, is a cook of tremendous passion and astounding attention to the details that turn good food into great food.

Basic recipes were the foundation of Tita's cooking. Peeling tough-skinned plantains, roasting tomatoes, scrubbing mussels, selecting avocados at their peak of ripeness—these and other basics are the building blocks that make Latin American cooking so unique.

A perfect example is homemade chicken, fish, and vegetable stocks. These are essential for making full-bodied soups, stews, sauces, moles, and casseroles. And for the health-conscious cook, stocks can make a satisfying substitute for lard, oil, and even cream.

Fortunately for us modern cooks, we have refrigeration and electrical appliances to make things faster and easier. It takes very little effort to simmer up stocks and mix up other basic recipes on a lazy weekend or a quiet evening. Then these basics are ready when you are.

STOCK RECIPES

SEASONING RECIPES

BASIC RECIPES

CHICKEN STOCK

Caldo de
pollo

*Various
countries*

Nutrition Snapshot	Before	After
Per cup		
Calories	110	28
Total Fat g.	2.2	0.2
Saturated Fat g.	0.6	0
Cholesterol mg.	49	0

A *good chicken stock is the cornerstone of great Latin American soups, sauces, and gravies. You can also use the chicken meat off the bone to make stuffings and tortilla dishes. Stock is especially useful for the health-conscious cook. It makes a great fat-free substitute for lard, oil, and even cream. (I soften tortillas in stock instead of in lard.) To reduce the fat in traditional chicken stock, skin the chicken before simmering. For a clean, clear stock, skim the foam off the stock as it simmers.*

1	bay leaf
2	whole cloves
10	black peppercorns
1	chicken (about 3½ pounds), skin removed, trimmed of all visible fat, and rinsed (see tip)
1	onion, unpeeled and quartered
2	carrots, cut into 1" pieces

2	ribs celery, cut into 1" pieces
1	tomato, quartered
½	green bell pepper
2	cloves garlic, halved
4	sprigs fresh cilantro or flat-leaf parsley
12–14	cups water

Tie the bay leaf, cloves, and peppercorns in a piece of cheesecloth (or wrap tightly in foil and pierce the bundle in several places with a fork).

In a large stockpot over high heat, combine the spice bundle, chicken, onions, carrots, celery, tomatoes, peppers, garlic, cilantro or parsley and 12 cups of the water. Bring to a boil. Skim off any foam that rises to the surface. Reduce the heat to low and simmer for 50 to 60 minutes, or until the chicken is falling off the bone and is no longer pink. Add water as needed to keep the chicken covered. Occasionally skim the foam from the stock.

Pour the stock through a fine-meshed strainer into a large bowl, pressing the solids with the back of a spoon to extract as much liquid as possible; discard the solids. (For a clearer stock, strain it through paper towels or coffee filters.) Let cool to room temperature. Transfer the stock to airtight containers and refrigerate for up to 5 days or freeze for up to 3 months. Pull the chicken meat off the bone and reserve for another use.

Makes 8 cups

Cooking Tip

✦ For a super-lean stock, use 2 pounds boneless, skinless chicken breasts.

VEGETABLE STOCK

Caldo de
vegetal

*Various
countries*

Nutrition Snapshot	Before	After
Per cup		
Calories	21	21
Total Fat g.	0.2	0.2
Saturated Fat g.	0	0
Cholesterol mg.	0	0

You can use almost any vegetable for stock, from corncobs to collard greens. Use strong-tasting vegetables like eggplant, turnips, and cabbage in moderation. Avoid beets, which will turn a stock red. Steer clear of asparagus and artichokes, too. They'll make your stock bitter. I like this particular stock because it makes a great base for Latin American soups, stews, and sauces.

8 cups chopped vegetables or vegetable trimmings	6 cloves garlic, unpeeled and halved
1 large onion, unpeeled and quartered	2 tablespoons tomato paste
2 carrots, cut into 1" pieces	3 sprigs fresh flat-leaf parsley
2 ribs celery, cut into 1" pieces	3 sprigs fresh cilantro
2 tomatoes, cut into 1" pieces	12–14 cups water
	Salt and ground black pepper

In a large stockpot over high heat, combine the chopped vegetables or vegetable trimmings, onions, carrots, celery, tomatoes, garlic, tomato paste, parsley, cilantro, and 12 cups of the water. Bring to a boil, reduce the heat to medium-low, and simmer, uncovered, for 1 hour, or until richly flavored. Add water as needed to keep the vegetables covered. Season with salt and pepper.

Pour the stock through a fine-meshed strainer into a large bowl, pressing the vegetables with the back of a spoon to extract as much liquid as possible; discard the solids. Let cool to room temperature. Transfer the stock to airtight containers and refrigerate for up to 5 days or freeze for up to 3 months.

Makes 8 cups

Cooking Tip

✦ Freeze vegetable peelings in resealable plastic bags. Most peels keep frozen for up to 3 months. Add these along with whole vegetables when making stock.

Variation

Roasted Vegetable Stock: For a slightly sweeter, richer-tasting stock, roast the vegetables before simmering. In a large roasting pan, toss the vegetables with 1 tablespoon olive oil. Bake, stirring occasionally, at 450°F for 30 to 40 minutes, or until the vegetables are browned. Proceed as directed.

FISH STOCK

Caldo de
pescado

*Various
countries*

Nutrition Snapshot	Before	After
Per cup		
Calories	39	30
Total Fat g.	2.3	0.3
Saturated Fat g.	0.3	0
Cholesterol mg.	0	0

Fish stock is the secret to many Latin American fish stews and soups. Any light-colored, non-oily fish can be used to make stock. Try snapper, grouper, cod, halibut, hake, cusk, or sea bass. The more different types of fish you use, the richer your stock will be. To save money, use fish frames (bones still attached to one another) or heads. You can also use chowder fish (chunks) or scrap fish.

2	pounds scraps, frames, or heads from fine-flavored non-oily white fish
1	tablespoon olive oil
1	medium onion, finely chopped
½	red or green bell pepper, finely chopped
4	scallions, finely chopped

1	rib celery, finely chopped
1	clove garlic, minced
1	tomato, finely chopped
2	bay leaves
2	sprigs fresh flat-leaf parsley
2	sprigs fresh cilantro
5	cups cold water

If using fish heads, remove the gills. (Wear gloves or use a dish cloth to protect your fingers.) Rinse the fish thoroughly. Using a cleaver, cut the frames into 3" pieces.

Heat the oil in a stockpot over medium heat. Add the onions, peppers, scallions, celery, and garlic. Cook for 5 minutes, or until the onions are soft but not brown. Add the tomatoes and cook for 1 minute. Add the bay leaves, parsley, cilantro, and fish. Cook for 3 minutes. Add the water. Bring to a boil over high heat and skim off any foam that rises to the surface. Reduce the heat to medium-low and simmer for 20 minutes, or until richly flavored. Do not overcook, or the stock will become bitter.

Pour the stock through a fine-meshed strainer lined with paper towels into a large bowl, pressing the solids with the back of a spoon to extract as much liquid as possible. Let cool to room temperature. Transfer the stock to airtight containers and refrigerate for up to 3 days or freeze for up to 3 months.

Makes 4 cups

Cooking Tip

✦ In a pinch, you can use bottled clam juice in place of fish stock. Clam juice is quite salty, however, so if you're using a large amount (more than 1 cup) add 1 part water to every 2 parts clam juice.

PORK IN OAXACAN MOLE (PAGE 287)

BEEF FAJITAS (PAGE 214) AND BLACK BEANS ON WHITE RICE (PAGE 158) WITH SALSAS
(PAGES 296 AND 298), GUACAMOLE (PAGE 75), AND PLANTAIN CHIPS (PAGE 71)

CENTRAL AMERICAN SLAW (PAGE 116), CORNMEAL FLATCAKES (PAGE 179), AND
CREOLE STEAK (PAGE 261) WITH PORK EMPANADAS (PAGE 80) AND FLAN (PAGE 316)

SANCOCHO (PAGE 290)

ROAST PORK (PAGE 286)

SPICED PORK BITES (PAGE 285)

FLAN (PAGE 316)

SPICED CHOCOLATE PUDDING (PAGE 321)

MEXICAN HOT CHOCOLATE (PAGE 344)

SHIVERING COCONUT PUDDING (PAGE 323)

BAKE-FRIED BREAD IN SPICE-SCENTED SYRUP (PAGE 334)

AMARANTH FRUIT TARTLETS (PAGE 331)

**PITCHERS OF CINNAMON-ALMOND COOLER (PAGE 349) AND KIWIFRUIT COOLER
(PAGE 354)**

SUNRISE VEGETABLE JUICE (PAGE 356) AND SPICED TOMATO JUICE (PAGE 357)

NICARAGUAN THREE MILKS CAKE (PAGE 328)

SEASONED SALT

Sazón

Various countries

Nutrition Snapshot	Before	After
Per ¹⁄₂ teaspoon		
Calories	3	3
Total Fat g.	0.1	0.1
Saturated Fat g.	0	0
Cholesterol mg.	0	0

This tangy spiced salt is an indispensable seasoning in Puerto Rico. It's easy to make, and it's healthier than most commercial blends because it's free of MSG (monosodium glutamate). Come holiday time, I like to make a large batch of sazón and package it in attractive bottles for gift giving. Sprinkle sazón on your favorite meats and seafood prior to cooking. Or use it in place of salt at the table.

¼	cup cumin seeds		¾	cup salt
2	tablespoons white peppercorns		¼	cup garlic powder
2	tablespoons black peppercorns		¼	cup dried oregano

In a small dry skillet, combine the cumin seeds, white peppercorns, and black peppercorns. Roast over medium heat for 3 minutes, or until lightly toasted and very fragrant. Transfer to a small bowl to cool.

In a spice mill or with a mortar and pestle, grind the roasted spices to a fine powder. Stir in the salt, garlic powder, and oregano. Store the sazón in airtight containers in a cool, dark place. It will keep its maximum flavor for up to 6 months.

Makes 2 cups

PINEAPPLE VINEGAR

Vinagre de piña

México

Nutrition Snapshot	Before	After
Per ¹⁄₂ cup		
Calories	30	30
Total Fat g.	0.1	0.1
Saturated Fat g.	0	0
Cholesterol mg.	0	0

Use fruit vinegars to add a touch of flavor to foods at the table and in marinades. This pineapple vinegar is perfect for gift giving. Look for decorative bottles at houseware stores.

24	1" chunks fresh pineapple	12–13	cups white vinegar
8	small red serrano or jalapeño chile peppers		

Thread 6 pineapple chunks and 2 chile peppers onto each of four 8" bamboo skewers, alternating the ingredients for color.

Using boiling water, wash out 4 attractive bottles with a 3½-cup capacity and a mouth at least 1" wide (to accommodate the skewers). Carefully lower 1 skewer into each bottle. Fill the bottle with the vinegar. Cover tightly and let steep in the refrigerator for at least 3 days before using. Store in the refrigerator for up to 3 months. Add more vinegar as necessary to keep the pineapple pieces submerged.

Makes 14 cups (including pineapple)

Cooking Tip

✦ For the best results, use a super-ripe, juicy pineapple for this recipe. Use any extra pineapple to make Pork and Pineapple Soft Tacos (page 217).

Pronto!

ANNATTO OIL

Aceite de
achiote

*Various
countries*

Nutrition Snapshot	Before	After
Per teaspoon		
Calories	39	41
Total Fat g.	4.3	4.6
Saturated Fat g.	1.7	0.3
Cholesterol mg.	4	0

Annatto *(also known as achiote) is a hard, rust-colored seed with an earthy, almost mineral-like flavor. Native to Central America, it's used throughout the Caribbean Basin as a flavoring and natural food coloring. Chicken with Rice (page 244) and Seafood Soupy Rice (page 161) would look pale as ghosts without this essential ingredient. In the old days, annatto "oil" was made with rendered lard. Here's a more contemporary (and healthier) version made with canola oil.*

1	cup canola oil
½	cup annatto seeds

Heat the oil in a heavy medium saucepan over medium heat. Add the annatto seeds. Cook, stirring occasionally, for 3 minutes, or until the oil becomes reddish gold and the seeds begin to crackle. Do not overcook, or the oil will become bitter. Remove the pan from the heat and strain the oil into a medium heat-proof bowl. Let cool.

Transfer the oil to a clean glass bottle. Cover tightly and store in the refrigerator for up to 3 months.

Makes 1 cup

TAMARIND PUREE

Pulpa de tamarindo

Puerto Rico

Nutrition Snapshot	Before	After
Per 2 tablespoons		
Calories	68	68
Total Fat g.	0.1	0.1
Saturated Fat g.	0.1	0.1
Cholesterol mg.	0	0

Tamarind has a pleasing sweet-and-sour flavor that hints at prunes doused with lime juice. The fruit takes its name from the Arabic words tamr hindi, *literally, "Indian date." If you live near a neighborhood with a large Hispanic or Indian community, you may be able to find whole tamarind pods, which are arched and dusty brown. Otherwise, look for peeled tamarind pulp, which is sold in plastic packages at Hispanic markets and some supermarkets. Because the fruit is stringy and riddled with seeds, it's often pureed with boiling water to make tamarind water or tamarind puree. Alternatively, you can buy tamarind puree in Hispanic markets and some supermarkets.*

8	ounces tamarind pods (8 to 10 pods) or peeled tamarind pulp	1½ cups hot water

If using tamarind pods, peel the skin off the pods with a paring knife. Break the pulp into 1" pieces and place in a blender. Add 1 cup of the water. Let stand for 5 minutes, or until the tamarind is soft.

Blend on low speed with on/off turns for 15 to 20 seconds, or until the mixture is a thick brown liquid. (Do not overblend, or you'll break up the seeds.) Pour through a strainer set over a medium bowl, pressing hard and scraping the bottom of the strainer with a wooden spoon to extract the juices. Discard the seeds.

Return the pulp in the strainer to the blender and add the remaining ½ cup water. Blend again on low speed with on/off turns. Pour the mixture through the strainer into the bowl, pressing well to extract the juices.

Transfer the tamarind water in the bowl to an airtight container. It will keep in the refrigerator for up to 5 days or in the freezer for several months.

Makes 1 cup

Cooking Tip

✦ I like to freeze tamarind water in plastic ice-cube trays so that I have convenient premeasured portions.

CUMIN-SCENTED SOUR CREAM

Crema agria
a lo comino   *United States*

Nutrition Snapshot	Before	After
Per tablespoon		
Calories	31	9
Total Fat g.	3	0
Saturated Fat g.	1.9	0
Cholesterol mg.	6	0

A *free and artistic hand with a squirt bottle is one of the calling cards of modern Latino chefs. Brightly colored sauces are placed in plastic squirt bottles, then squirted like paint in decorative squiggles and zigzags over soups, salads, and main dishes. Here's a cumin-scented sour cream that goes well with bean and pork dishes. (Look for plastic squirt bottles, such as restaurant-style ketchup bottles, in supermarkets and cookware shops.)*

1   cup nonfat or low-fat sour cream
1   teaspoon ground cumin

Salt and ground white or black pepper

In a small bowl, combine the sour cream and cumin. Whisk to mix. Season with salt and pepper. Whisk to combine. Spoon into a squirt bottle. Invert the bottle and gently squeeze to squirt decorative squiggles of sour cream.

Makes 1 cup

HOW TO ROAST AND PEEL A CHILE PEPPER

Nutrition Snapshot	Before	After
Per pepper		
Calories	60	60
Total Fat g.	0.3	0.3
Saturated Fat g.	0.03	0.03
Cholesterol mg.	0	0

Many *Mexican recipes call for peeled chiles. Traditionally, the chiles are deep-fried to blister the skin. In New Mexico, cooks char the chiles over a direct flame, under the broiler, or on the grill. Fire charring has two advantages: It's fat-free, and it imparts a wonderful sweet-smoky flavor to the chiles.*

1   poblano chile pepper, New Mexican chile pepper, or green bell pepper (wear plastic gloves when handling chile peppers)

TO ROAST A CHILE PEPPER

Burner method: Preheat a gas or electric burner to high. Place the pepper directly on top of the burner. Roast, turning with tongs, for 6 to 8 minutes, or until charred and blackened on all sides.

Broiler method: Position a rack at the highest setting. Preheat the broiler. Place the pepper under the broiler. Roast, turning with tongs, for 6 to 8 minutes, or until charred and blackened on all sides.

Grill method: Preheat the grill to high. Place the pepper on the grill. Roast, turning with tongs, for 10 to 12 minutes, or until charred and blackened on all sides.

TO PEEL A ROASTED CHILE PEPPER

Whichever roasting method you use, once the skin is charred and blackened, place the chile pepper or bell pepper in a paper bag and seal, or wrap in a wet paper towel, or place in a bowl and cover with plastic wrap. Let stand for 15 minutes to sweat and loosen the skin. When cool enough to handle, scrape off and discard as much of the skin as possible with a paring knife or your fingers (wear plastic gloves when handling chile peppers). Don't worry about a few charred pieces of skin; they'll add a nice smoky flavor. Remove and discard the seeds and ribs. Cut the flesh into long, thin strips, or chop.

One large peeled and seeded pepper (5 ounces) yields about ⅔ cup chopped

Cooking Tip

✦ In México, cooked and peeled poblano chile strips are called *rajas*. They're used as a garnish for a variety of dishes.

Pronto!

HOW TO ROAST, PEEL, AND SEED A TOMATO

Nutrition Snapshot	Before	After
Per tomato		
Calories	26	26
Total Fat g.	0.4	0.4
Saturated Fat g.	0.1	0.1
Cholesterol mg.	0	0

Mexicans are particularly fond of roasting tomatoes to impart a rich, smoky flavor. In South America, cooks often remove the skin after blanching the tomatoes in boiling water.

1   tomato

TO ROAST A TOMATO

Pan method: Heat a comal (a griddle for cooking tortillas) or dry skillet over medium-high heat until very hot. Add the tomato. Roast, turning with tongs, for 6 to 8 minutes, or until browned and blistered.

Burner method: Preheat a gas or electric burner to high. Spear the tomato with a carving fork. Roast like a marshmallow in the gas flames or on the electric burner, turning the fork, for 6 to 8 minutes, or until browned and blistered on all sides. Be careful not to touch the fork.

Broiler method: Position a rack at the highest setting. Preheat the broiler. Core the tomato and slice in half lengthwise. Place on a baking sheet or broiler pan and roast for 6 to 8 minutes, or until browned and blistered on top.

Grill method: Preheat the grill to high. Place the tomato on the grill. Roast, turning with tongs, for 8 to 10 minutes, or until browned and blistered on all sides.

TO PEEL A ROASTED TOMATO

Whichever roasting method you use, once the skin is browned and blistered, transfer the tomato to a plate. When cool enough to handle, pull off as much of the skin as possible using a paring knife or your fingers. Don't worry about a few charred pieces of skin; they'll add a nice smoky flavor.

TO PEEL A FRESH TOMATO

With the tip of a paring knife, core the tomato and cut a shallow X in the other end. Plunge the tomato into rapidly boiling water for 15 to 60 seconds. (The riper the tomato, the shorter the cooking time.) Transfer to a plate. When cool enough to handle, peel off and discard the skin in broad strips using a paring knife or your fingers.

TO SEED A FRESH TOMATO

Cut the tomato in half crosswise. Working over a strainer set over a bowl, hold half of the tomato in your palm, cut side toward the bowl. Gently squeeze and rotate the tomato with your palm, using the fingers on your other hand to work out the seeds, membranes, and liquid. Push the membranes through the strainer with the back of a spoon to extract the juice. Reserve the tomato juice in the bowl for sauces, soups, or drinking. Discard the seeds.

One large peeled and seeded tomato (8 ounces) yields about ¾ cup chopped

HOW TO PEEL AND PIT AN AVOCADO

Nutrition Snapshot	Before	After
Per avocado		
Calories	306	306
Total Fat g.	30	30
Saturated Fat g.	4.5	4.5
Cholesterol mg.	0	0

Avocados are an essential ingredient in Mexican Guacamole (page 75). They're also a popular garnish for numerous other Latino dishes. Here's how to peel and pit an avocado quickly and easily.

1   avocado

TO PIT AN AVOCADO

Using a sharp knife, cut the avocado in half lengthwise to and around the pit. (Move the knife in a circular motion.) Twist the halves in opposite directions. The avocado will separate into 2 halves and the pit will remain lodged in 1 half. Sink the knife into the avocado seed. Twist the seed and pop it out of the avocado. Discard.

TO PEEL AN AVOCADO:

Method 1: To make avocado halves, cubes, or long thin slices of avocado, make 4 or 5 shallow slits in the skin, each running lengthwise from one end of the avocado to the other. Use the tip of the knife to lift 1 corner of the skin at the slit. Gently pull off and discard each strip of skin. Use or cut as needed.

Method 2: To make cubed avocado, cut the avocado in half and remove the pit as described above. Using the tip of a paring knife, cut a crosshatch pattern through the flesh but not through the skin. Use a spoon to scoop the avocado out of the skin. It will break into neat cubes.

Method 3: To make mashed avocado, cut the avocado in half and remove the pit as described above. Use a spoon to scoop the avocado out of the skin.

One peeled and pitted avocado (8 ounces) yields about 1½ cups chopped

Cooking Tips

✦ When buying avocados, be sure that they are ripe. They should be squeezably soft. To ripen an avocado, store it in a paper bag at room temperature for up to 5 days, or until soft to the touch.

✦ Freshly cut avocados discolor quickly. To prevent diced avocados from discoloring, sprinkle them with lime juice.

✦ Florida avocados have half the fat of the more common Haas avocados, but I prefer the flavor and texture of Haas avocados.

HOW TO PEEL A PLANTAIN

Nutrition Snapshot	Before	After
Per plantain		
Calories	218	218
Total Fat g.	0.7	0.7
Saturated Fat g.	0.3	0.3
Cholesterol mg.	0	0

A *plantain may look like a banana, but you'll quickly discover that it's a lot harder to peel. I've bruised more than one thumbnail trying. Here's an easy way to peel a green plantain.*

1   **green plantain**

Cut off the ends. Make 3 or 4 lengthwise slits in the plantain, cutting just through the skin. Place the plantain in a bowl of warm water to cover and let soak for 10 minutes, or until the skin is softened. Run your thumb under the slits to ease the skin off the fruit. The plantain is now ready for slicing and cooking

1 peeled green plantain yields about 1 cup chopped

HOW TO CUT CORN FROM THE COB

Nutrition Snapshot	Before	After
Per 1/2 cup		
Calories	67	67
Total Fat g.	0.1	0.1
Saturated Fat g.	0	0
Cholesterol mg.	0	0

Many *of the recipes in this book call for fresh corn kernels. When buying fresh corn, strip back a few of the outside leaves to examine the kernels, which should be plump and juicy.*

1   **ear corn, shucked**

Lay the ear of corn flat on a work surface. Using a large chef's knife, make lengthwise slices along the cob to cut off the kernels, rotating the cob as you work.

1 ear corn yields about 1/2 cup kernels

Cooking Tip

✦ To cook 1/2 cup fresh corn kernels, place them in a pot containing 1/4 cup lightly salted boiling water. Cook for 5 minutes, or until tender.

HOW TO PREPARE CLAMS AND MUSSELS

Nutrition Snapshot	Before	After
Per serving		
Calories	192	192
Total Fat g.	3.6	3.6
Saturated Fat g.	0.2	0.2
Cholesterol mg.	102	102

Shellfish like clams and mussels are popular throughout Central and South America. When buying clams or mussels, choose the smallest ones that you can find; these are the most tender and flavorful. Most of the shells should be closed. If any are open, they should close when you tap them with your fingertip. If the shellfish has any aroma at all, it should be briny (like the ocean), not fishy. Store clams and mussels in a loosely sealed paper or plastic bag toward the back of the bottom shelf of your refrigerator. It's important that the bag not be tightly sealed, or the shellfish will suffocate. Use shellfish within 24 hours of purchase—preferably, the same day.

8   ounces clams

8   ounces mussels

Sort through the clams and mussels, discarding any with cracked shells or open shells that fail to close when tapped. Scrub the shells under cold running water with a stiff-bristled brush to remove any sand or grit.

Mussels may have a tuft of black threads, called beards, at the hinge (the place where the top and bottom shell are attached). Pull the threads out with a pair of pliers or pinch them between your thumb and the blade of a paring knife and pull. Discard the threads.

The shellfish are now ready for steaming or stewing.

1 pound cleaned clams and mussels yields about 2 servings

Cooking Tip

✦ After cooking, discard any clams or mussels that remain closed.

HOW TO CLEAN AND COOK OCTOPUS

Nutrition Snapshot	Before	After
Per serving		
Calories	156	156
Total Fat g.	1.9	1.9
Saturated Fat g.	0.4	0.4
Cholesterol mg.	82	82

Octopus is popular on both coasts of South America, where it's served in ceviches, soups, stews, and rice dishes. When you buy octopus in the store, chances are it will already be prepared, or "dressed," and probably frozen. The first part of this recipe gives directions for dressing octopus. If you buy pre-dressed octopus, start with the cooking directions.

1   fresh or frozen and thawed octopus (3 pounds)

1   bay leaf

1   onion, quartered

1   whole clove

6   cloves garlic

6   black peppercorns

1   tablespoon salt

12   cups water

Turn the octopus inside out, like a sock. Cut away and discard the beak and mouth, as well as the viscera and ink sac. Rinse the octopus well under cold running water and turn right side out again.

Pin the bay leaf to 1 of the onion quarters with the clove. In a large pot over high heat, combine the onions, garlic, peppercorns, salt, and water. Bring to a boil.

Using tongs, immerse the octopus in the boiling water for 10 seconds. Lift out and let cool for 1 minute. Dip the octopus in the water again for 10 seconds, lift out, and let cool. (The repeated dipping makes the octopus more tender.) Reduce the heat to medium. Place the octopus in the water and simmer for 1 hour, or until tender. Drain and let cool.

Peel off any purplish membrane covering the octopus. (The membrane is perfectly edible, but it's not aesthetically pleasing.)

Makes 1 cooked octopus; about 16 servings

Cooking Tip

✦ If you've never had octopus, try it in Seafood Stew (page 235) or Peruvian Seafood Stew (page 240).

HOW TO CLEAN AND COOK SQUID

Nutrition Snapshot	Before	After
Per serving		
Calories	104	104
Total Fat g.	1.5	1.5
Saturated Fat g.	0.4	0.4
Cholesterol mg.	264	264

Squid is one of Latin America's best-loved foods from the sea. Its popularity is gaining in North America, too. Most of the squid sold in the United States is already cleaned. If you buy it before it's cleaned, here are simple instructions for cleaning and cooking squid yourself.

1   pound squid (about 5 to 6 whole)

To clean squid: Cut off the tentacles just above the eyes. Squeeze the base of the tentacles to remove the beak or mouth. (This looks like a clear plastic chickpea.) Discard the beak. Reserve the tentacles.

Hold the body by the tail and scrape it lengthwise toward the head with the back of a knife. Turn the squid over and scrape again. Pull the head away from the body. (The entrails should come out with the head.) Scrape out any remaining entrails with a small spoon.

Stab the transparent quill, or pen, that protrudes from the head end of the squid body with the knife. Pull the body away, and the quill should slip right out. Discard the quill. Pull off and discard any reddish skin on the body or tentacles with your fingers. Rinse the body inside and out under cold running water. Cut into rings.

To cook squid: Cook for less than 2 minutes or for more than 20 minutes to produce the most tender squid. Use any gentle, brief cooking method such as sautéing when cooking for less than 2 minutes. Or use a long, slow cooking method such as stewing or braising when cooking for more than 20 minutes. Cooking squid for an intermediate amount of time (more than 2 minutes and less than 20 minutes) tends to make it rubbery.

Makes 1 pound cooked squid; about 4 servings

Cooking Tip

✦ If you deep-fried instead of sautéed or stewed the same amount of squid, the fat content would jump to 34 grams for each whole squid.

INDEX

Underscored page references indicate boxed text. **Boldface** references indicate photographs.

Conversion Chart

These equivalents have been slightly rounded to make measuring easier.

VOLUME MEASUREMENTS

U.S.	Imperial	Metric
¼ tsp	–	1.25 ml
½ tsp	–	2.5 ml
1 tsp	–	5 ml
1 Tbsp	–	15 ml
2 Tbsp (1 oz)	1 fl oz	30 ml
¼ cup (2 oz)	2 fl oz	60 ml
⅓ cup (3 oz)	3 fl oz	80 ml
½ cup (4 oz)	4 fl oz	120 ml
⅔ cup (5 oz)	5 fl oz	160 ml
¾ cup (6 oz)	6 fl oz	180 ml
1 cup (8 oz)	8 fl oz	240 ml

WEIGHT MEASUREMENTS

U.S.	Metric
1 oz	30 g
2 oz	60 g
4 oz (¼ lb)	115 g
5 oz (⅓ lb)	145 g
6 oz	170 g
7 oz	200 g
8 oz (½ lb)	230 g
10 oz	285 g
12 oz (¾ lb)	340 g
14 oz	400 g
16 oz (1 lb)	455 g
2.2 lb	1 kg

LENGTH MEASUREMENTS

U.S.	Metric
¼"	0.6 cm
½"	1.25 cm
1"	2.5 cm
2"	5 cm
4"	11 cm
6"	15 cm
8"	20 cm
10"	25 cm
12" (1')	30 cm

PAN SIZES

U.S.	Metric
8" cake pan	20 × 4-cm sandwich or cake tin
9" cake pan	23 × 3.5-cm sandwich or cake tin
11" × 7" baking pan	28 × 18-cm baking pan
13" × 9" baking pan	32.5 × 23-cm baking pan
2-qt rectangular baking dish	30 × 19-cm baking dish
15" × 10" baking pan	38 × 25.5-cm baking pan (Swiss roll tin)
9" pie plate	22 × 4 or 23 × 4-cm pie plate
7" or 8" springform pan	18 or 20-cm springform or loose-bottom cake tin
9" × 5" loaf pan	23 × 13-cm or 2-lb narrow loaf pan or pâté tin
1½-qt casserole	1.5-l casserole
2-qt casserole	2-l casserole

TEMPERATURES

Fahrenheit	Centigrade	Gas
140°	60°	–
160°	70°	–
180°	80°	–
225°	110°	–
250°	120°	½
300°	150°	2
325°	160°	3
350°	180°	4
375°	190°	5
400°	200°	6
450°	230°	8
500°	260°	–